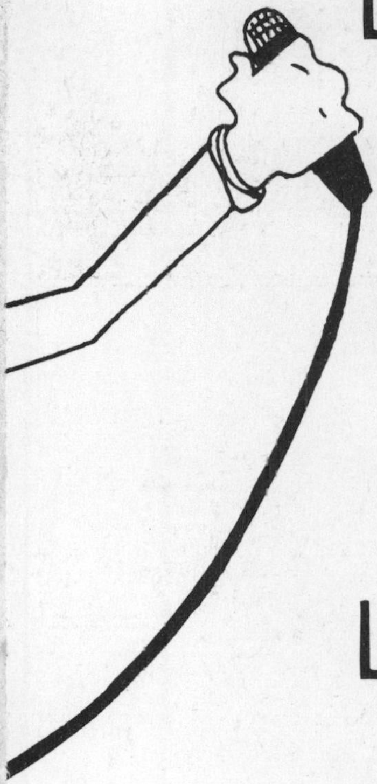

LOVE THE WAY YOU LOVE.

SIDE B:
"Songs of Devotion"

written by
Jamie S. Rich

illustrated by
Marc Ellerby

Designed by Steven Birch
Original Series edited by James Lucas Jones
Collected Edition edited by Jill Beaton

Special thanks to Zack and Sarah Trover,
Adam Cadwell, Steve Rolston, & Chynna Clugston for
pinch-hitting on tones, & Douglas E. Sherwood
for additional lettering.

Published by Oni Press, Inc.
Joe Nozemack, publisher
James Lucas Jones, editor in chief
Randal C. Jarrell, managing editor
Cory Casoni, marketing director
Jill Beaton, assistant editor
Douglas E. Sherwood, editorial assistant

This book contains material originally published as
Love the Way You Love #4-6.

ONI PRESS, INC.
1305 SE Martin Luther King Jr. Blvd.
Suite A
Portland, OR 97214
USA

www.onipress.com
www.confessions123.com
www.marcellerby.com

First edition: August 2008

ISBN-13: 978-1-932664-95-9
ISBN-10: 1-932664-95-5

1 3 5 7 9 10 8 6 4 2
PRINTED IN CANADA.

WHAT GOES ON

Tristan and Isobel fell in love at first sight. Only problem was, Isobel was engaged to Marcus Lee, a record executive that just so happened to be interested in Tristan's band, Like A Dog. Isobel broke the engagement to be with Tristan, and Marcus is angry, naturally. Meanwhile, Like A Dog has agreed to record "Love the Way You Love" as the debut single of a new indie music label.

The Players

Like A Dog

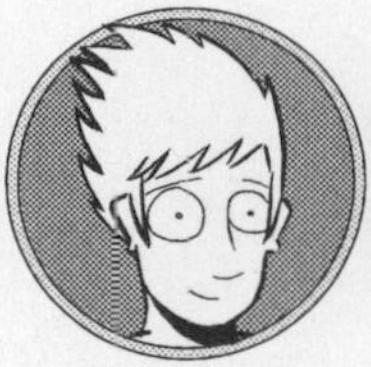

Tristan Scott
singer/heartbreaker

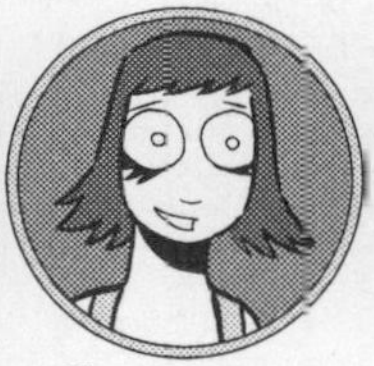

Eleanore James
guitar

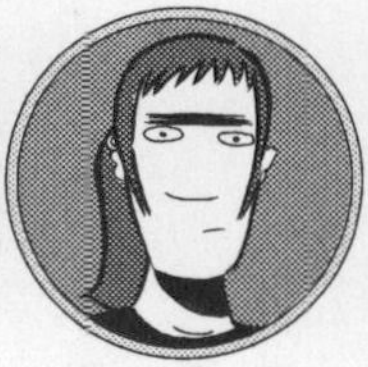

Emery Powell
bass

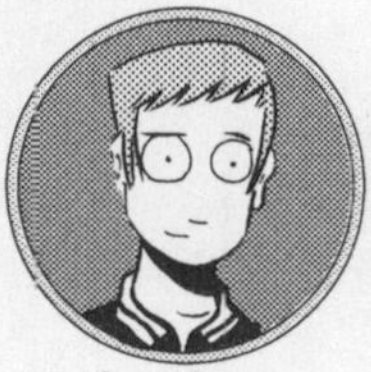

Sean Steen
keyboards

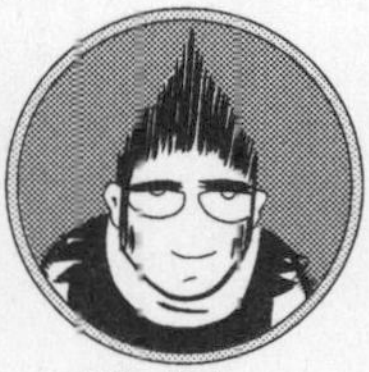

Mike Delano
drums

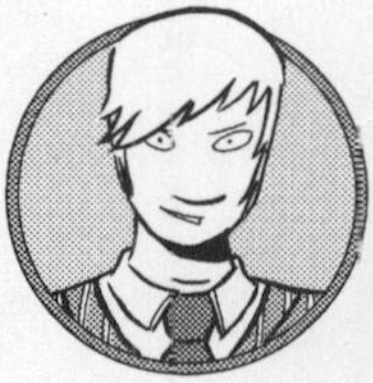

Marcus King
head of Marking Records, engaged to Isobel

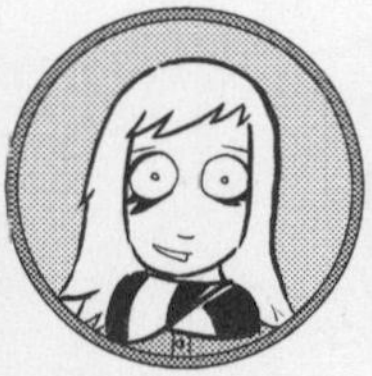

Isobel Anguise
young artist & Marcus' former fiancee

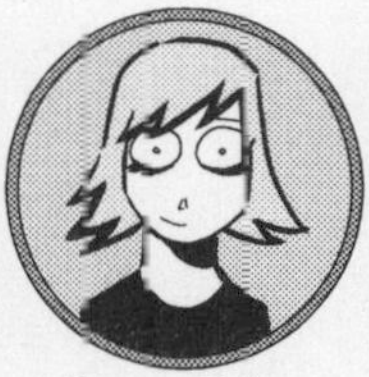

Branden Collins
Isobel's best friend

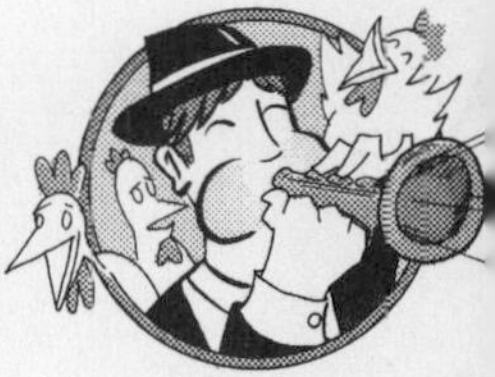

Lance Scott
Tristan's younger brother

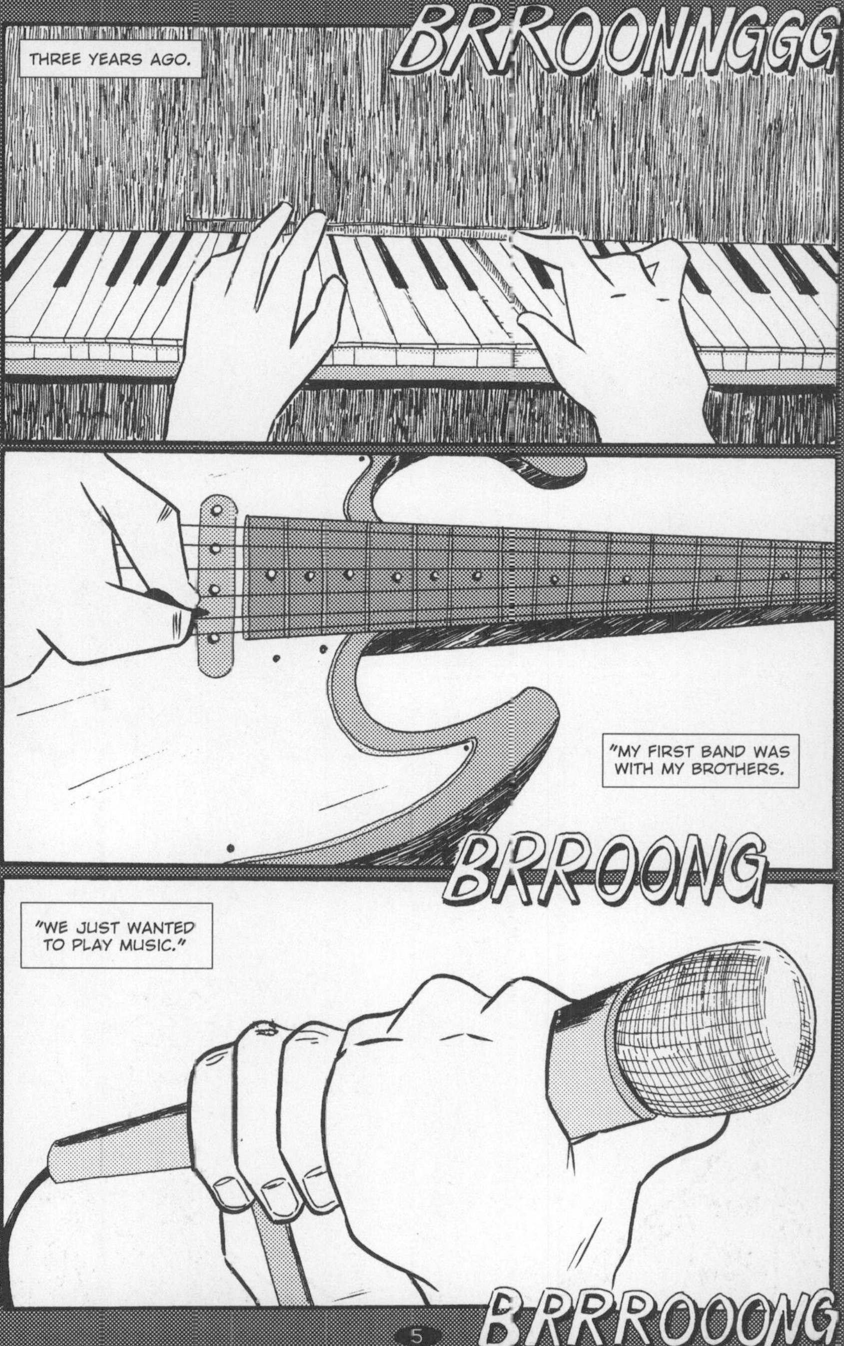
THREE YEARS AGO.
BRROONNGGG
"MY FIRST BAND WAS WITH MY BROTHERS.
BRROONG
"WE JUST WANTED TO PLAY MUSIC."
BRRROOONG

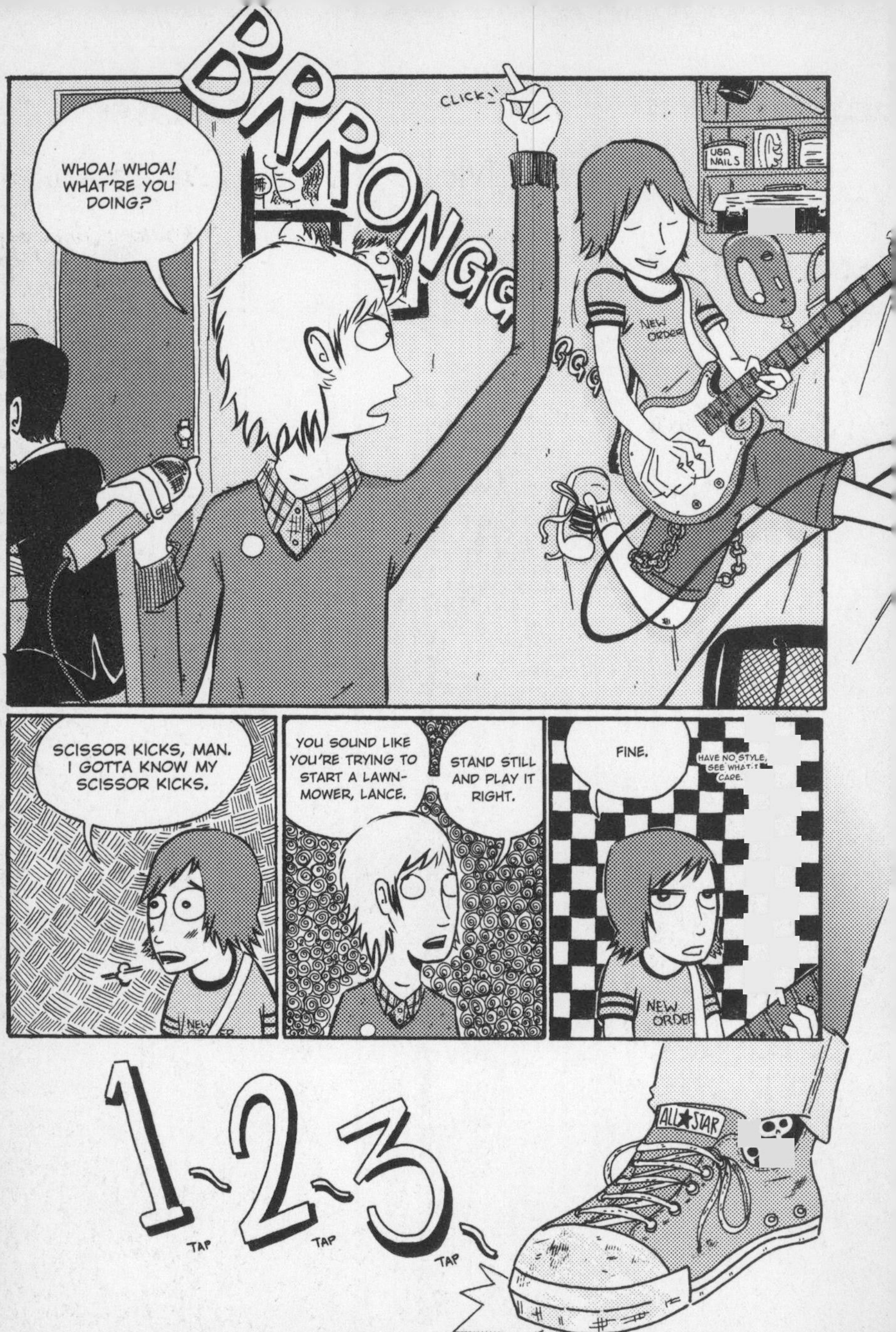
BRRONGG
CLICK
WHOA! WHOA! WHAT'RE YOU DOING?
USA NAILS
NEW ORDER
SCISSOR KICKS, MAN. I GOTTA KNOW MY SCISSOR KICKS.
YOU SOUND LIKE YOU'RE TRYING TO START A LAWN-MOWER, LANCE.
STAND STILL AND PLAY IT RIGHT.
FINE.
HAVE NO STYLE,
NEW ORDER
1-2-3-
TAP
TAP
TAP
ALL STAR

Chapter 9:
Make It Easy On Yourself

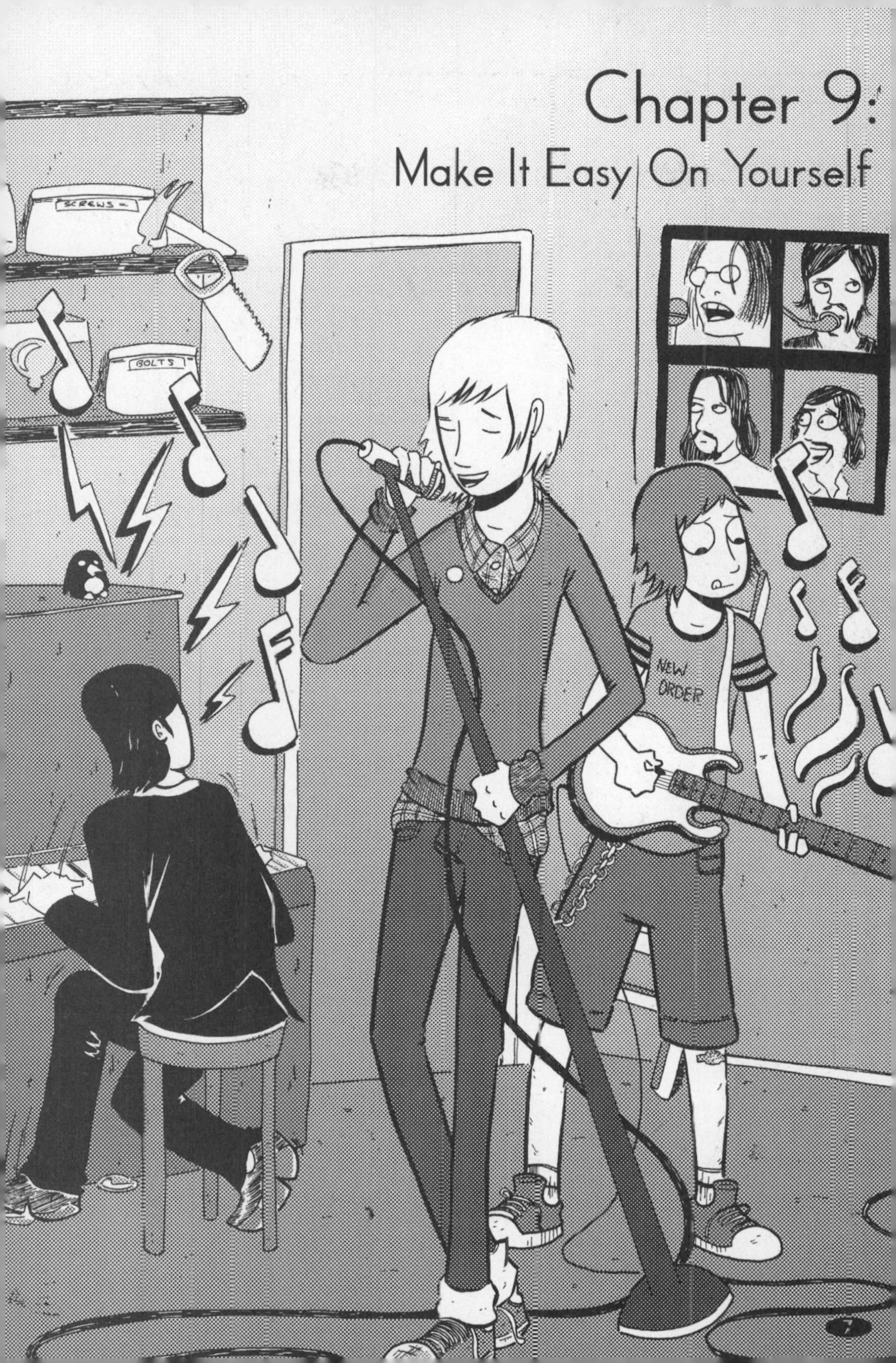
SCREWS
BOLTS
NEW ORDER

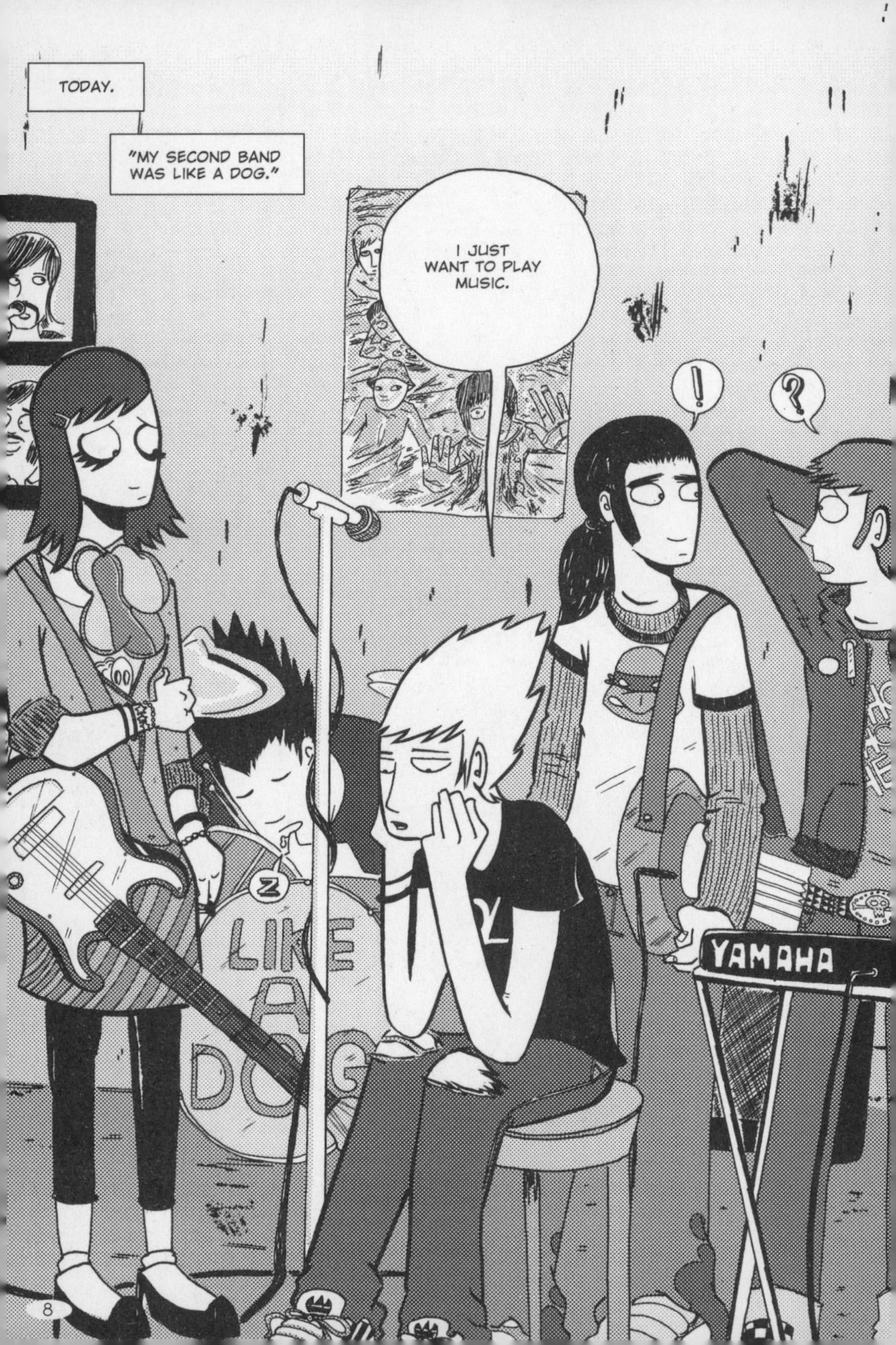
TODAY.
"MY SECOND BAND WAS LIKE A DOG."
I JUST WANT TO PLAY MUSIC.
!
?
Z
LIKE A DOG
YAMAHA

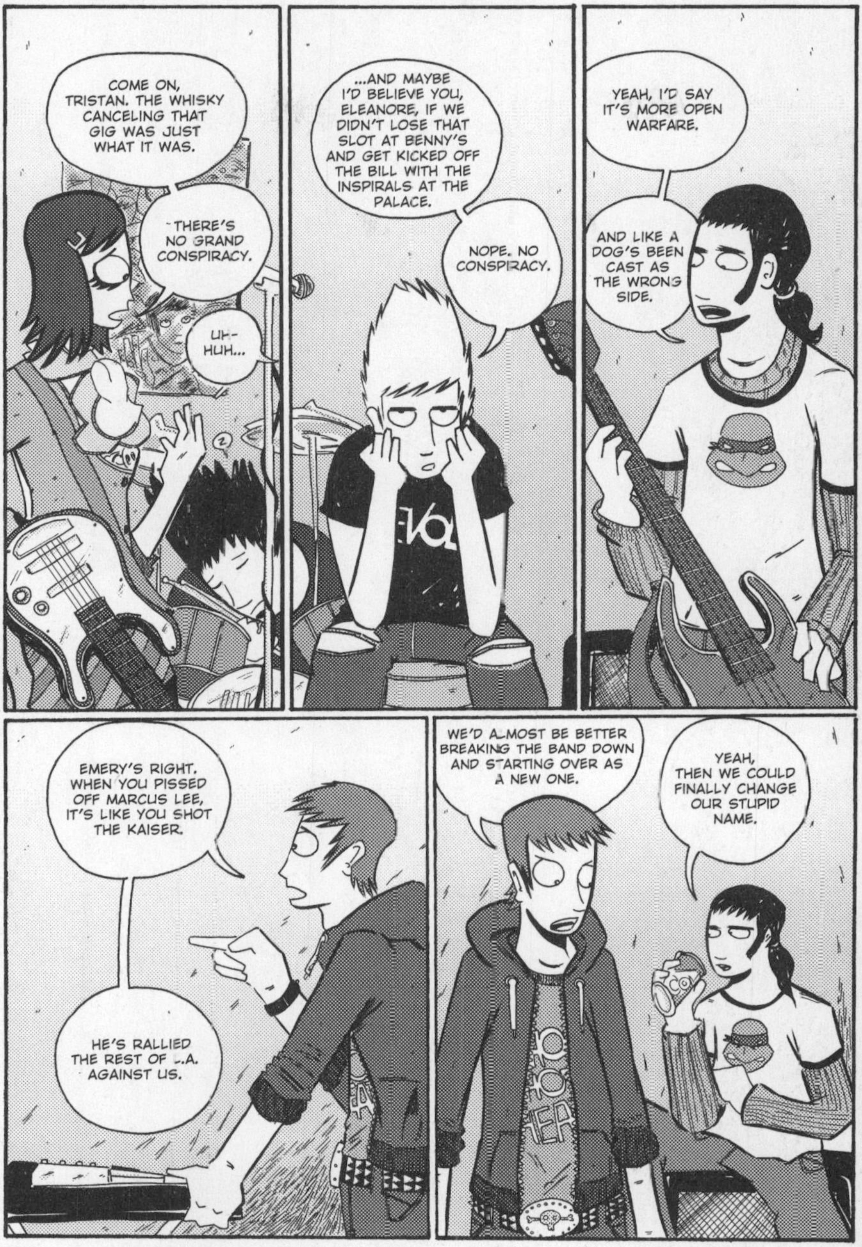
COME ON, TRISTAN. THE WHISKY CANCELING THAT GIG WAS JUST WHAT IT WAS.
THERE'S NO GRAND CONSPIRACY.
UH-HUH...
...AND MAYBE I'D BELIEVE YOU, ELEANORE, IF WE DIDN'T LOSE THAT SLOT AT BENNY'S AND GET KICKED OFF THE BILL WITH THE INSPIRALS AT THE PALACE.
NOPE. NO CONSPIRACY.
YEAH, I'D SAY IT'S MORE OPEN WARFARE.
AND LIKE A DOG'S BEEN CAST AS THE WRONG SIDE.
EMERY'S RIGHT. WHEN YOU PISSED OFF MARCUS LEE, IT'S LIKE YOU SHOT THE KAISER.
HE'S RALLIED THE REST OF L.A. AGAINST US.
WE'D ALMOST BE BETTER BREAKING THE BAND DOWN AND STARTING OVER AS A NEW ONE.
YEAH, THEN WE COULD FINALLY CHANGE OUR STUPID NAME.

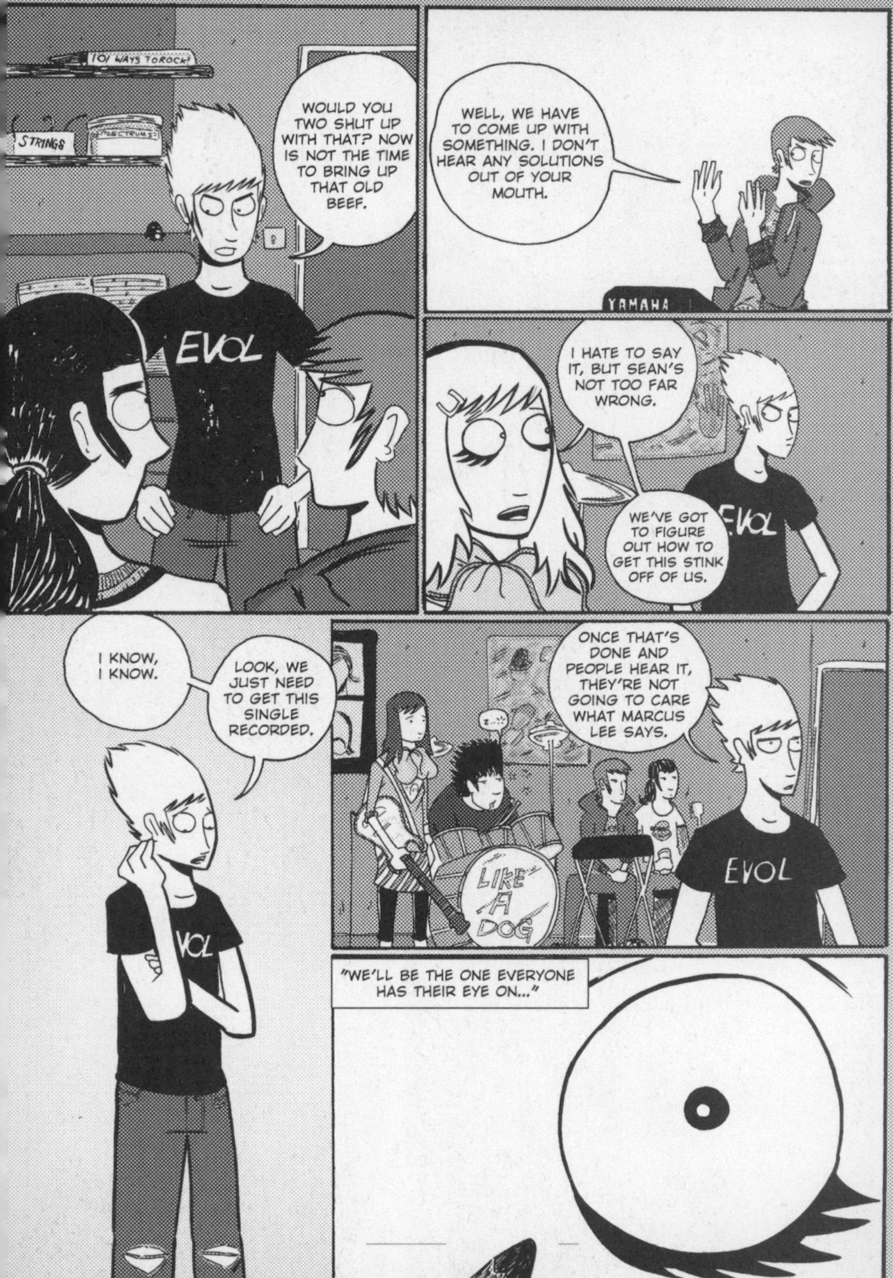

101 WAYS TO ROCK!
STRINGS
PLECTRUMS
WOULD YOU TWO SHUT UP WITH THAT? NOW IS NOT THE TIME TO BRING UP THAT OLD BEEF.
EVOL
WELL, WE HAVE TO COME UP WITH SOMETHING. I DON'T HEAR ANY SOLUTIONS OUT OF YOUR MOUTH.
YAMAHA
I HATE TO SAY IT, BUT SEAN'S NOT TOO FAR WRONG.
WE'VE GOT TO FIGURE OUT HOW TO GET THIS STINK OFF OF US.
EVOL
I KNOW, I KNOW.
LOOK, WE JUST NEED TO GET THIS SINGLE RECORDED.
EVOL
ONCE THAT'S DONE AND PEOPLE HEAR IT, THEY'RE NOT GOING TO CARE WHAT MARCUS LEE SAYS.
LIKE A DOG
EVOL
"WE'LL BE THE ONE EVERYONE HAS THEIR EYE ON..."

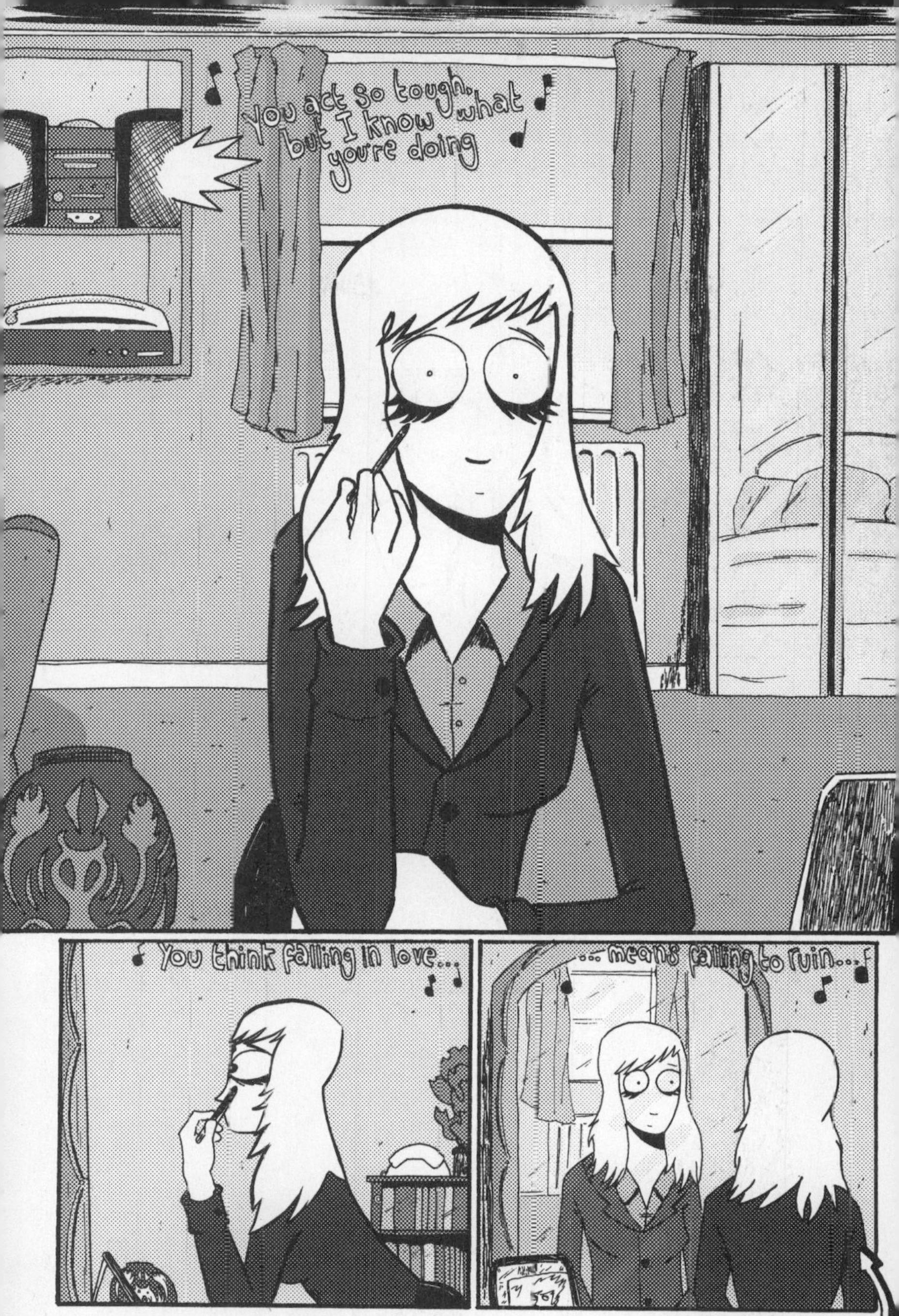
You act so tough, but I know what you're doing
You think falling in love...
...means falling to ruin...

Listening to the Go Go's turned down low.

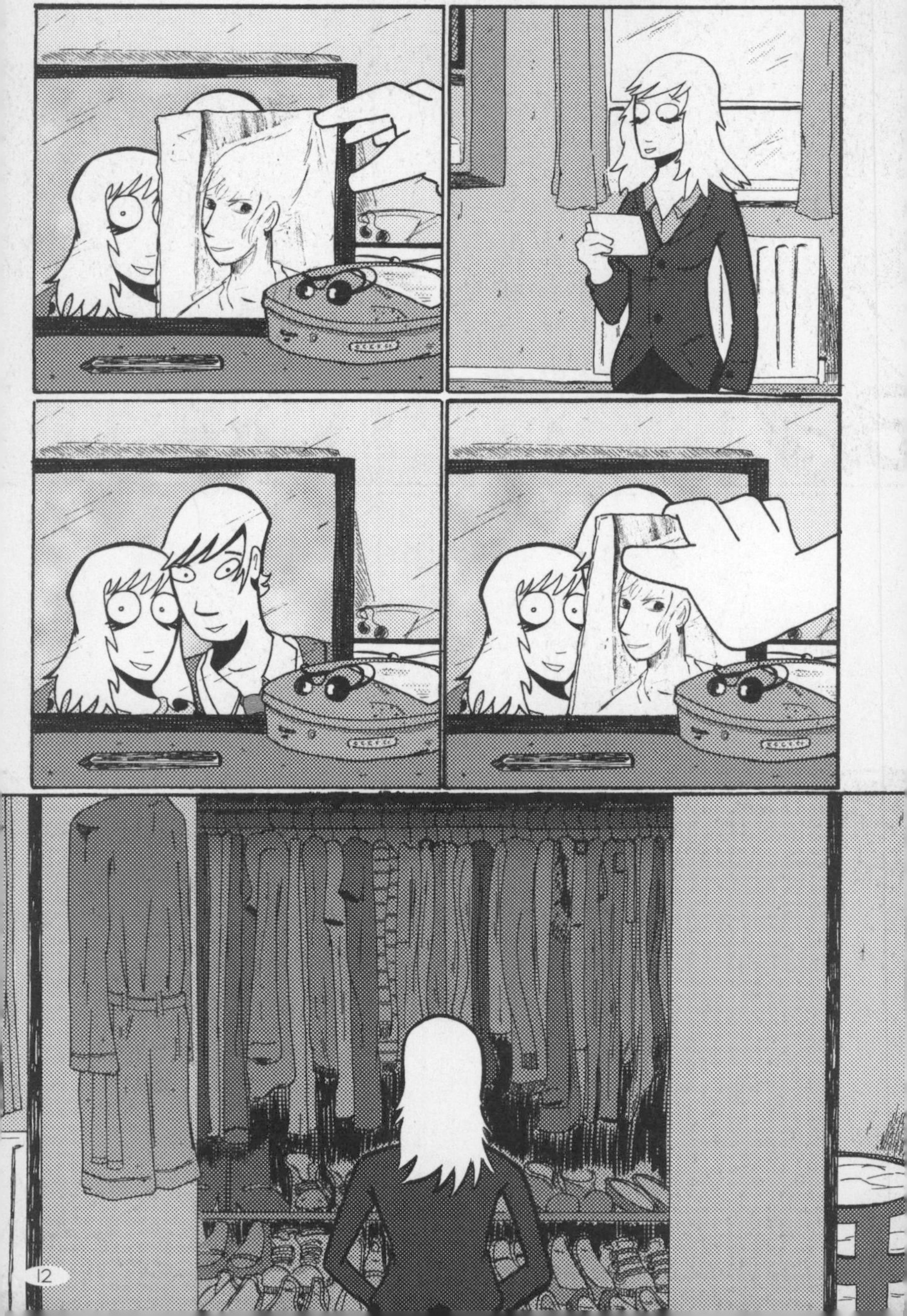

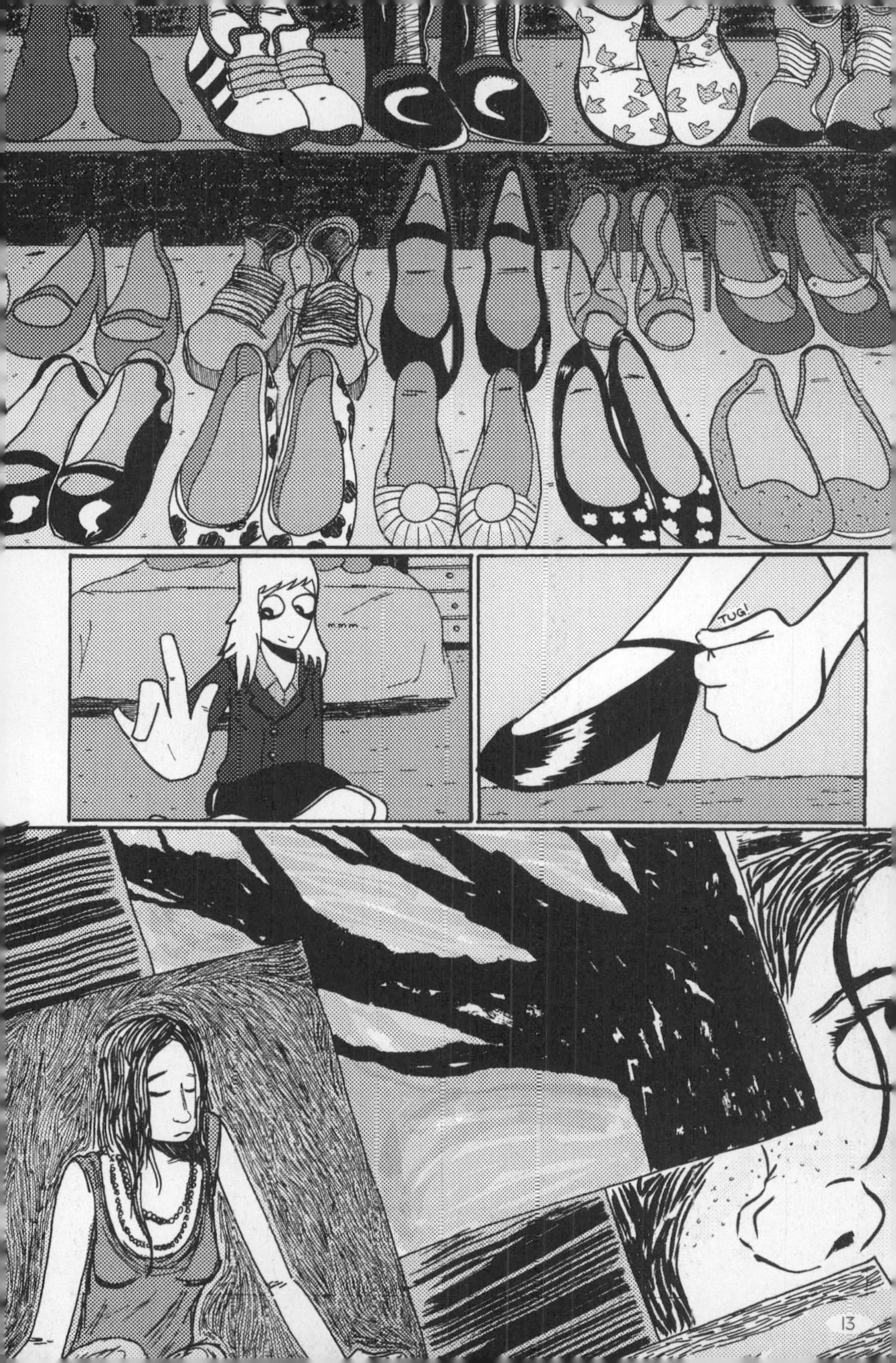
TUG!

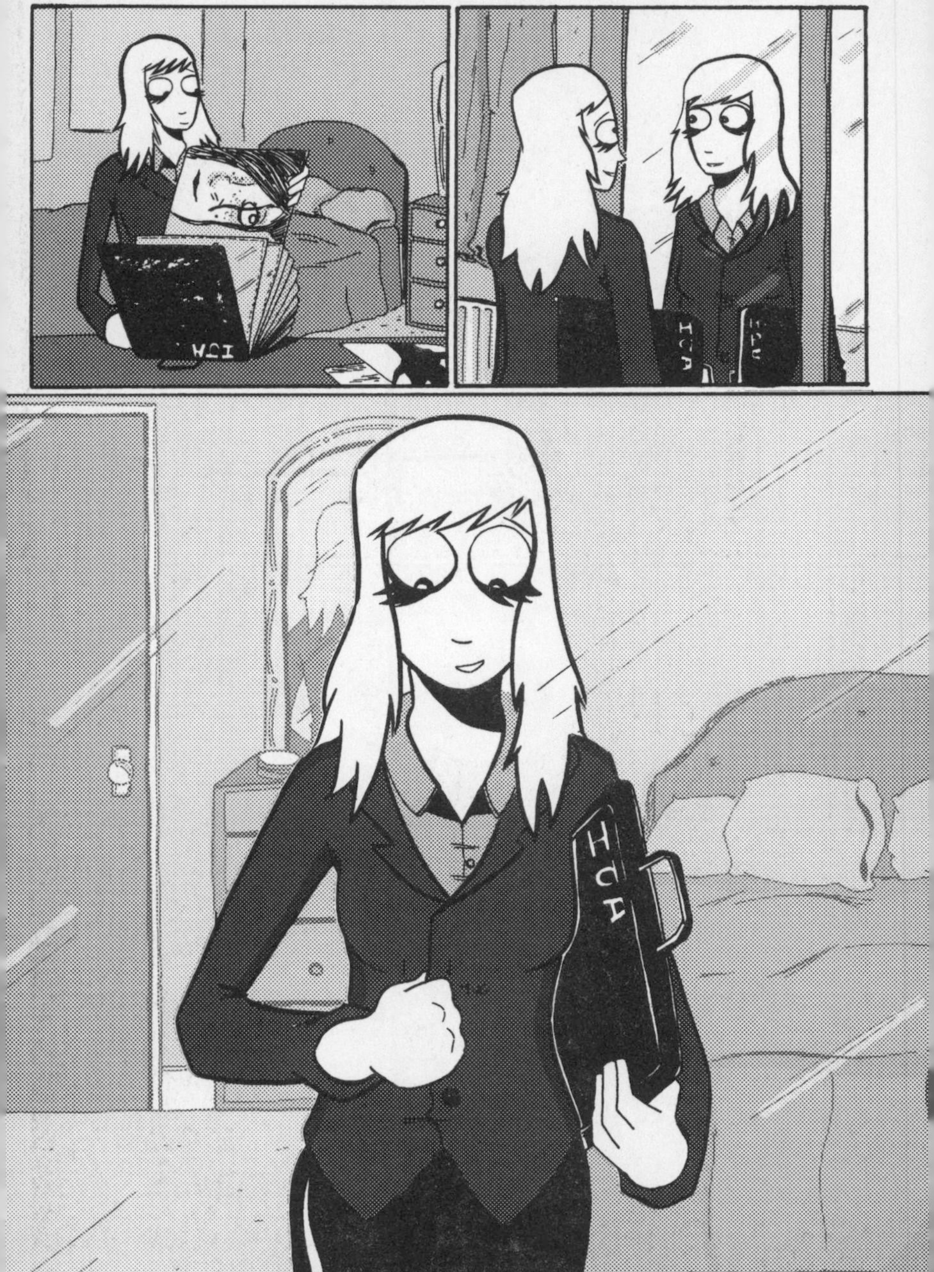
HCA

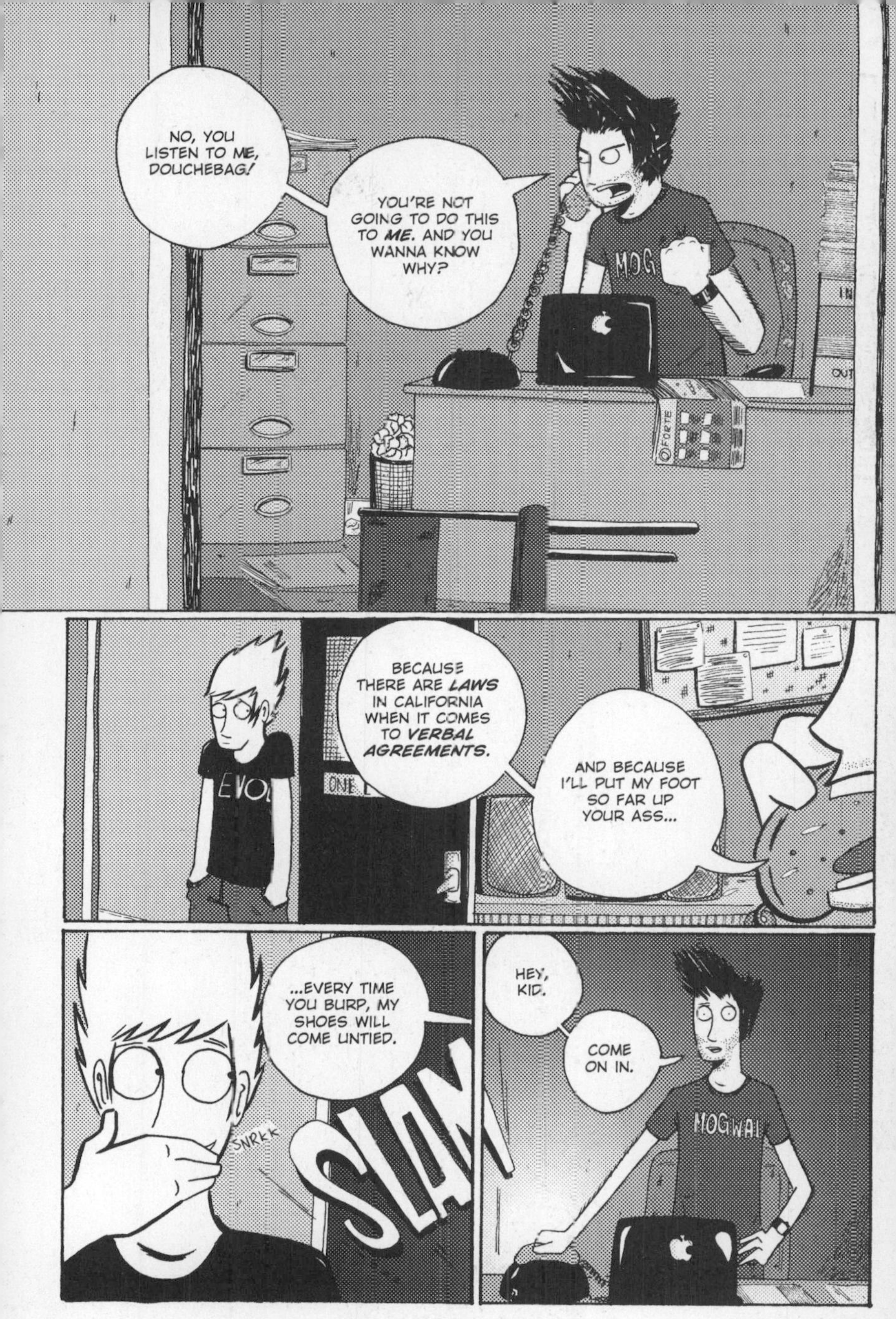
NO, YOU LISTEN TO ME, DOUCHEBAG!
YOU'RE NOT GOING TO DO THIS TO ***ME.*** AND YOU WANNA KNOW WHY?
MOG
IN
OUT
FORTE
EVOL
ONE
BECAUSE THERE ARE ***LAWS*** IN CALIFORNIA WHEN IT COMES TO ***VERBAL AGREEMENTS.***
AND BECAUSE I'LL PUT MY FOOT SO FAR UP YOUR ASS...
...EVERY TIME YOU BURP, MY SHOES WILL COME UNTIED.
SNRKK
SLAM
HEY, KID.
COME ON IN.
MOGWAI

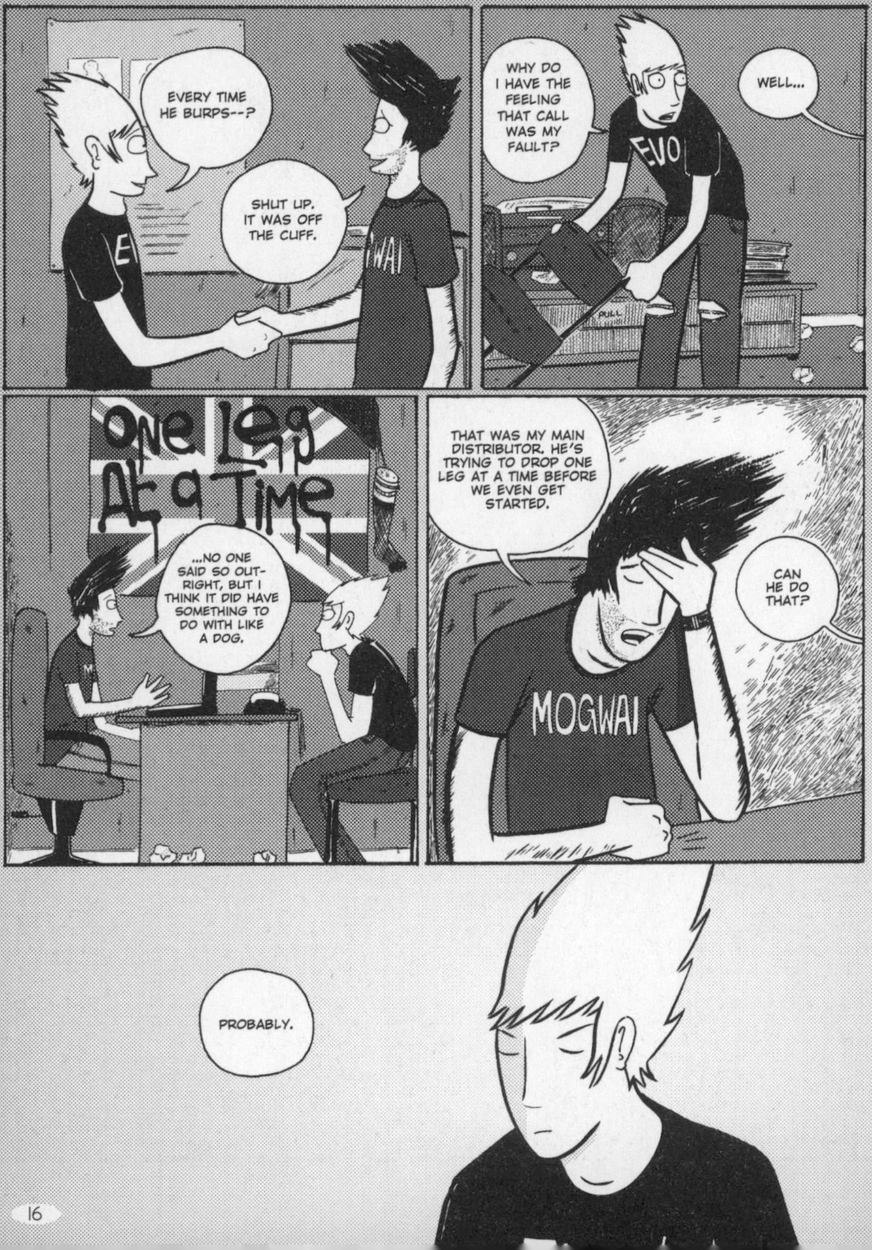
EVERY TIME HE BURPS--?
SHUT UP. IT WAS OFF THE CUFF.
WHY DO I HAVE THE FEELING THAT CALL WAS MY FAULT?
WELL...
One Leg At a Time
...NO ONE SAID SO OUT-RIGHT, BUT I THINK IT DID HAVE SOMETHING TO DO WITH LIKE A DOG.
THAT WAS MY MAIN DISTRIBUTOR. HE'S TRYING TO DROP ONE LEG AT A TIME BEFORE WE EVEN GET STARTED.
CAN HE DO THAT?
MOGWAI
PROBABLY.

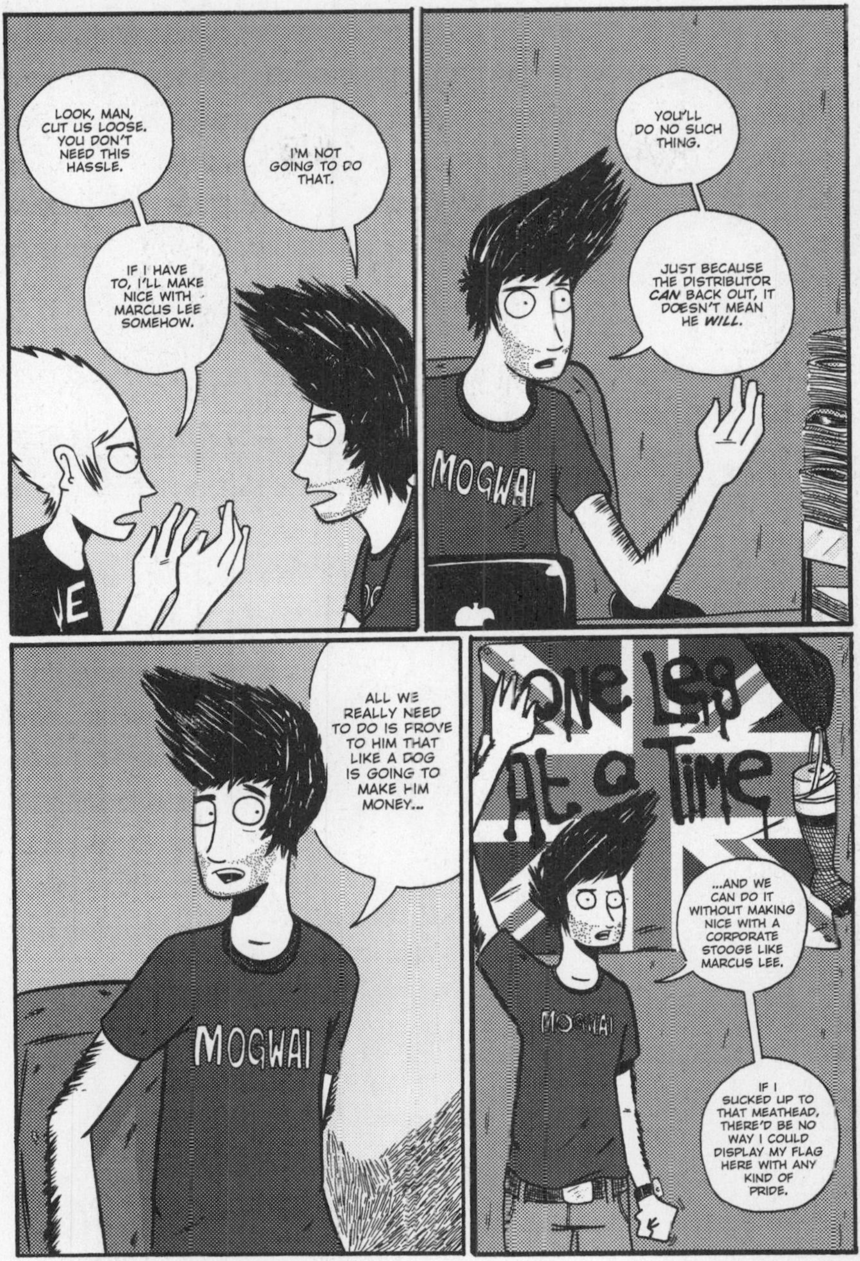
LOOK, MAN, CUT US LOOSE. YOU DON'T NEED THIS HASSLE.
I'M NOT GOING TO DO THAT.
IF I HAVE TO, I'LL MAKE NICE WITH MARCUS LEE SOMEHOW.
YOU'LL DO NO SUCH THING.
JUST BECAUSE THE DISTRIBUTOR *CAN* BACK OUT, IT DOESN'T MEAN HE *WILL*.
MOGWAI
ALL WE REALLY NEED TO DO IS PROVE TO HIM THAT LIKE A DOG IS GOING TO MAKE HIM MONEY...
MOGWAI
One Leg At a Time
...AND WE CAN DO IT WITHOUT MAKING NICE WITH A CORPORATE STOOGE LIKE MARCUS LEE.
MOGWAI
IF I SUCKED UP TO THAT MEATHEAD, THERE'D BE NO WAY I COULD DISPLAY MY FLAG HERE WITH ANY KIND OF PRIDE.

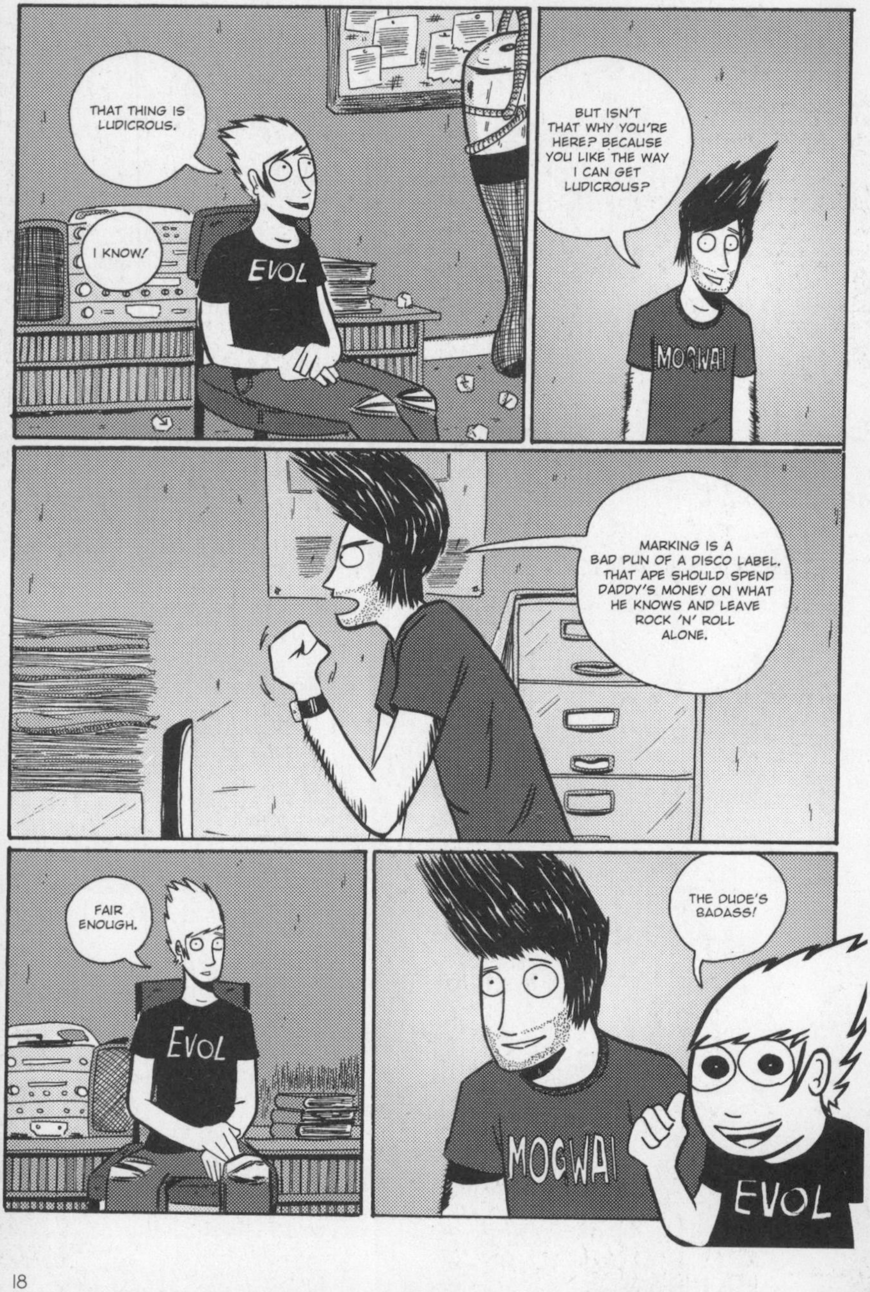
THAT THING IS LUDICROUS.
I KNOW!
EVOL
BUT ISN'T THAT WHY YOU'RE HERE? BECAUSE YOU LIKE THE WAY I CAN GET LUDICROUS?
MOGWAI
MARKING IS A BAD PUN OF A DISCO LABEL. THAT APE SHOULD SPEND DADDY'S MONEY ON WHAT HE KNOWS AND LEAVE ROCK 'N' ROLL ALONE.
FAIR ENOUGH.
EVOL
THE DUDE'S BADASS!
MOGWAI
EVOL

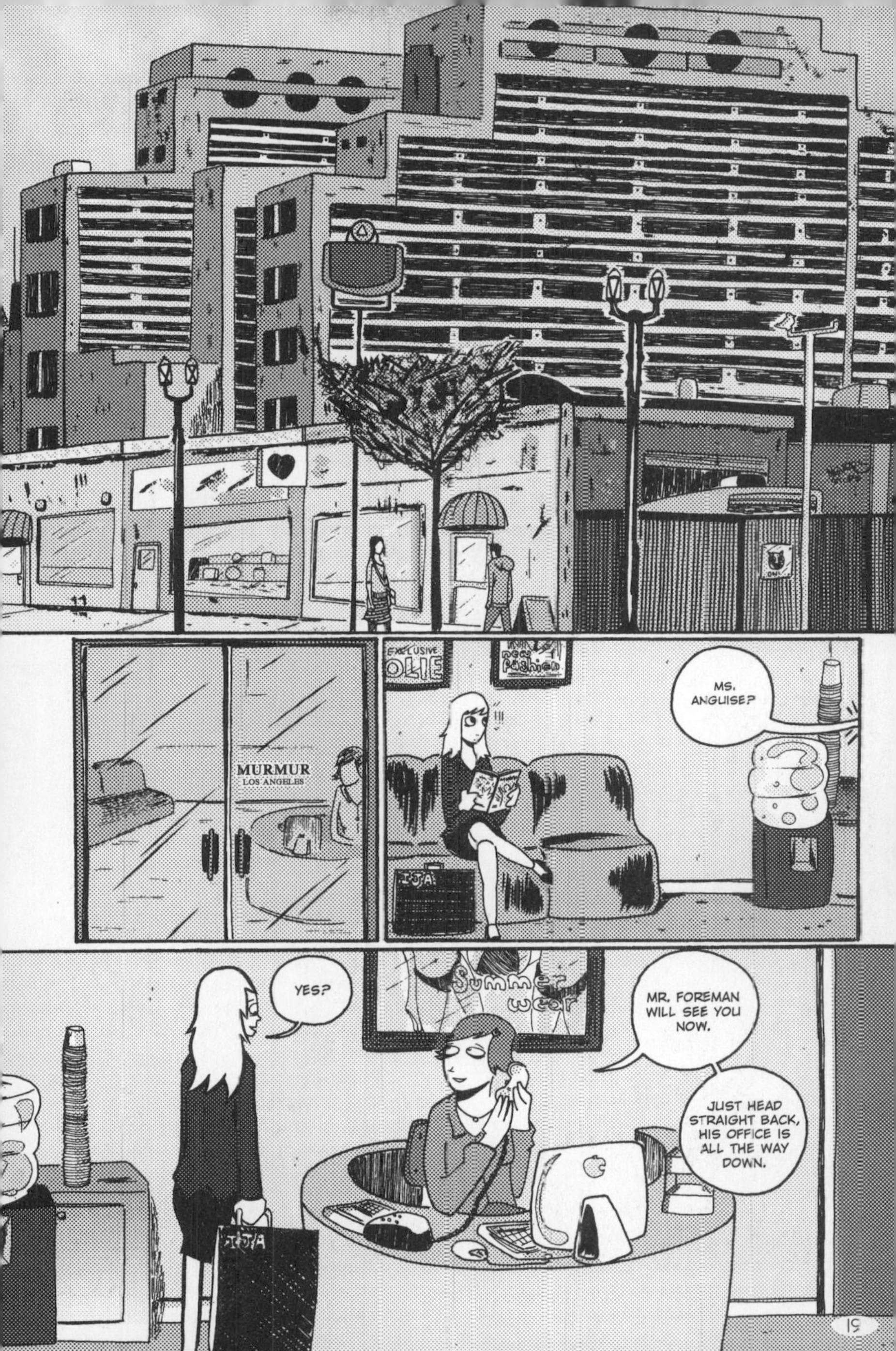
MURMUR
LOS ANGELES
EXCLUSIVE OLIE
new fashion
MS. ANGUISE?
Summer wear
YES?
MR. FOREMAN WILL SEE YOU NOW.
JUST HEAD STRAIGHT BACK, HIS OFFICE IS ALL THE WAY DOWN.

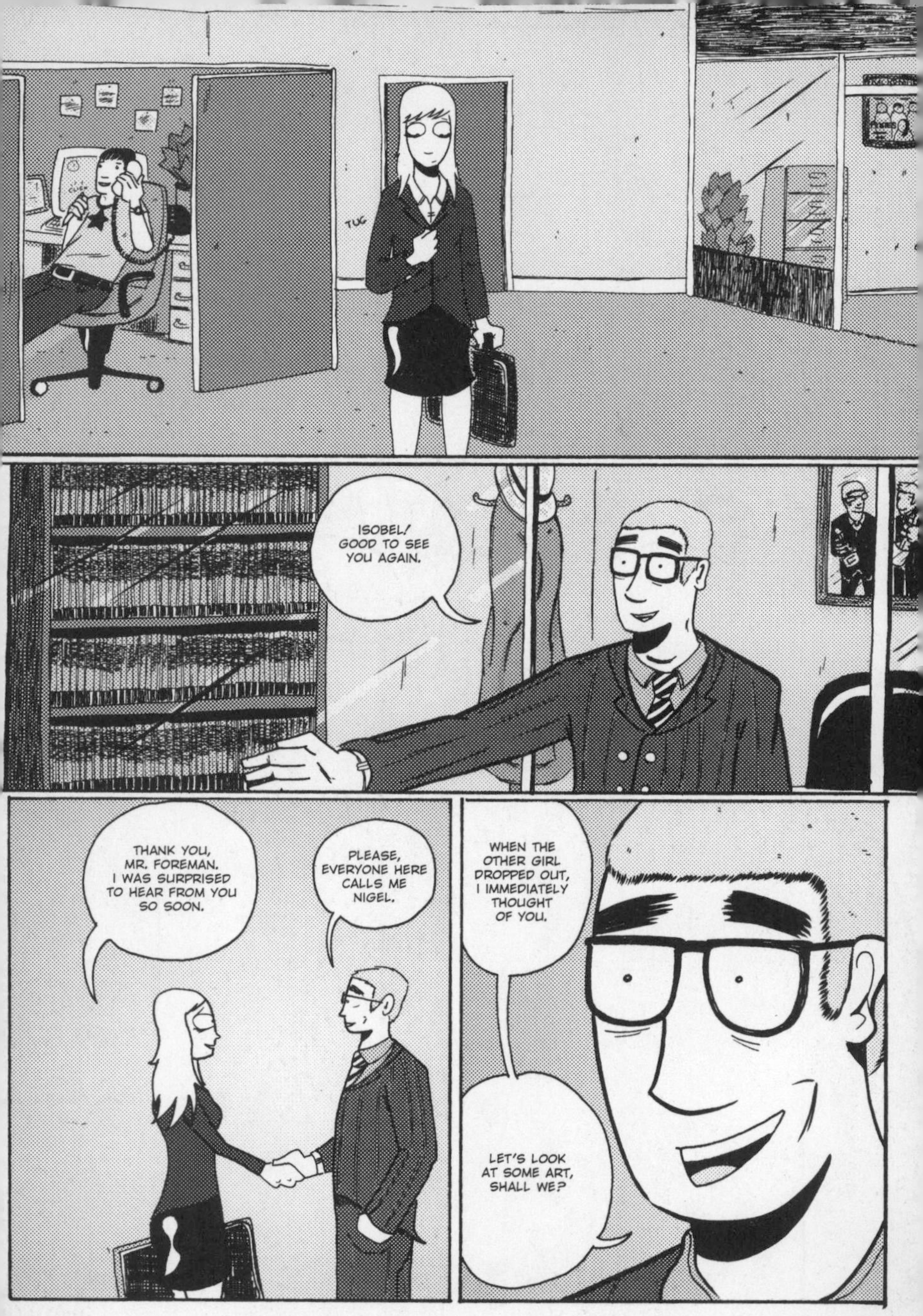
TUG
ISOBEL! GOOD TO SEE YOU AGAIN.
THANK YOU, MR. FOREMAN. I WAS SURPRISED TO HEAR FROM YOU SO SOON.
PLEASE, EVERYONE HERE CALLS ME NIGEL.
WHEN THE OTHER GIRL DROPPED OUT, I IMMEDIATELY THOUGHT OF YOU.
LET'S LOOK AT SOME ART, SHALL WE?

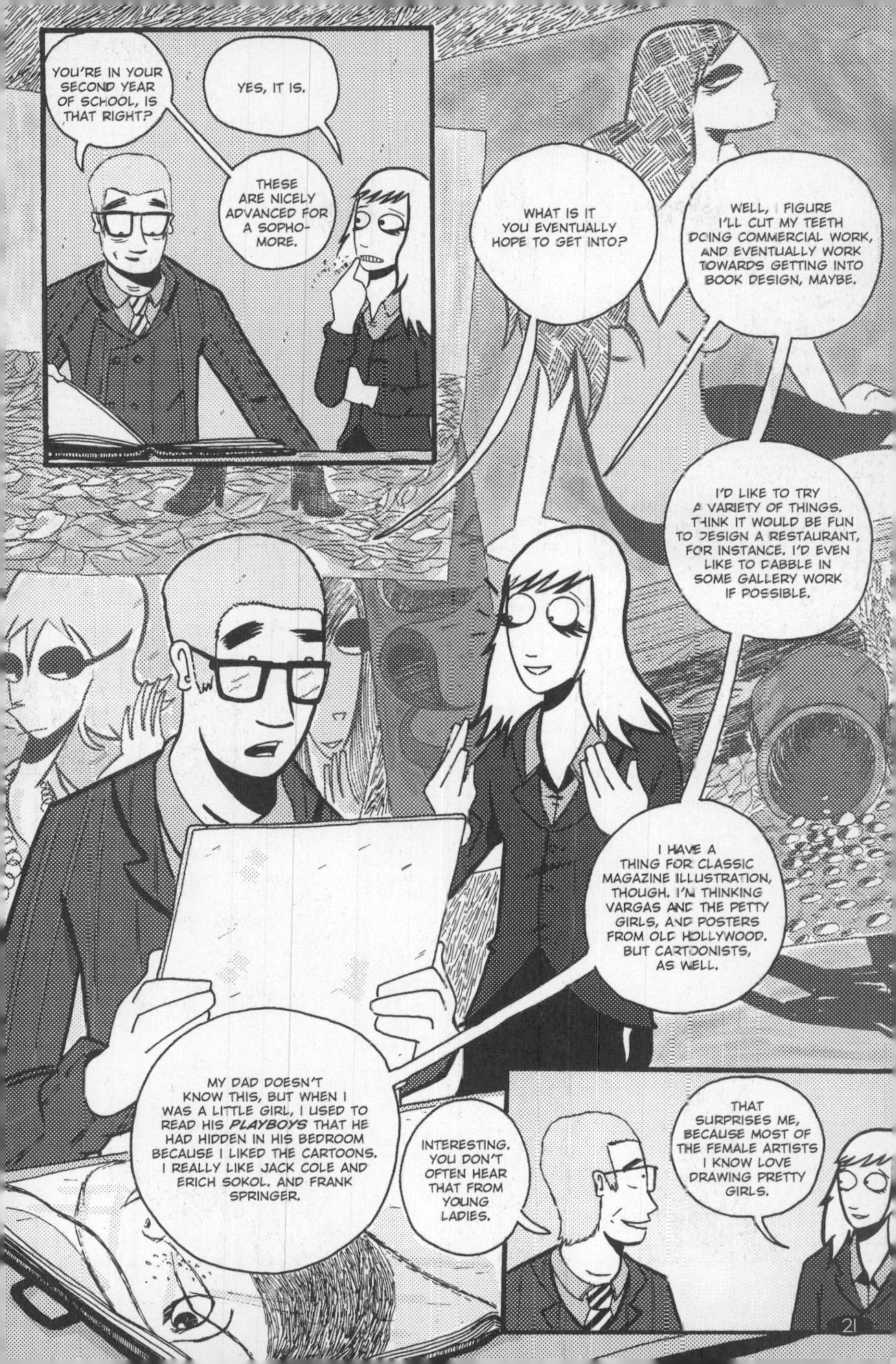
YOU'RE IN YOUR SECOND YEAR OF SCHOOL, IS THAT RIGHT?
YES, IT IS.
THESE ARE NICELY ADVANCED FOR A SOPHO-MORE.
WHAT IS IT YOU EVENTUALLY HOPE TO GET INTO?
WELL, I FIGURE I'LL CUT MY TEETH DOING COMMERCIAL WORK, AND EVENTUALLY WORK TOWARDS GETTING INTO BOOK DESIGN, MAYBE.
I'D LIKE TO TRY A VARIETY OF THINGS. THINK IT WOULD BE FUN TO DESIGN A RESTAURANT, FOR INSTANCE. I'D EVEN LIKE TO DABBLE IN SOME GALLERY WORK IF POSSIBLE.
I HAVE A THING FOR CLASSIC MAGAZINE ILLUSTRATION, THOUGH. I'M THINKING VARGAS AND THE PETTY GIRLS, AND POSTERS FROM OLD HOLLYWOOD. BUT CARTOONISTS, AS WELL.
MY DAD DOESN'T KNOW THIS, BUT WHEN I WAS A LITTLE GIRL, I USED TO READ HIS *PLAYBOYS* THAT HE HAD HIDDEN IN HIS BEDROOM BECAUSE I LIKED THE CARTOONS. I REALLY LIKE JACK COLE AND ERICH SOKOL. AND FRANK SPRINGER.
INTERESTING. YOU DON'T OFTEN HEAR THAT FROM YOUNG LADIES.
THAT SURPRISES ME, BECAUSE MOST OF THE FEMALE ARTISTS I KNOW LOVE DRAWING PRETTY GIRLS.

YOU REALIZE THIS INTERNSHIP WON'T ACTUALLY CALL FOR YOU TO DRAW, THOUGH?

OH, SURE. I FIGURE I'M A COUPLE OF YEARS AWAY FROM EVEN THINKING ABOUT GETTING PUBLISHED.

RIGHT NOW I WANT TO LEARN THE MECHANICS OF THE BUSINESS.

WELL, DON'T SELL YOURSELF SHORT, BUT THAT'S A GOOD ATTITUDE TO HAVE.

"KNOW THE TRACK BEFORE YOU GET OUT AND RUN THE RACE."

IF YOU CAN GUARANTEE ME THE COVER, I'LL MAKE SURE SHE'S AT THE SHOOT.

I CAN GUARANTEE THE COVER.

BIGGEST ACT IN THE WORLD

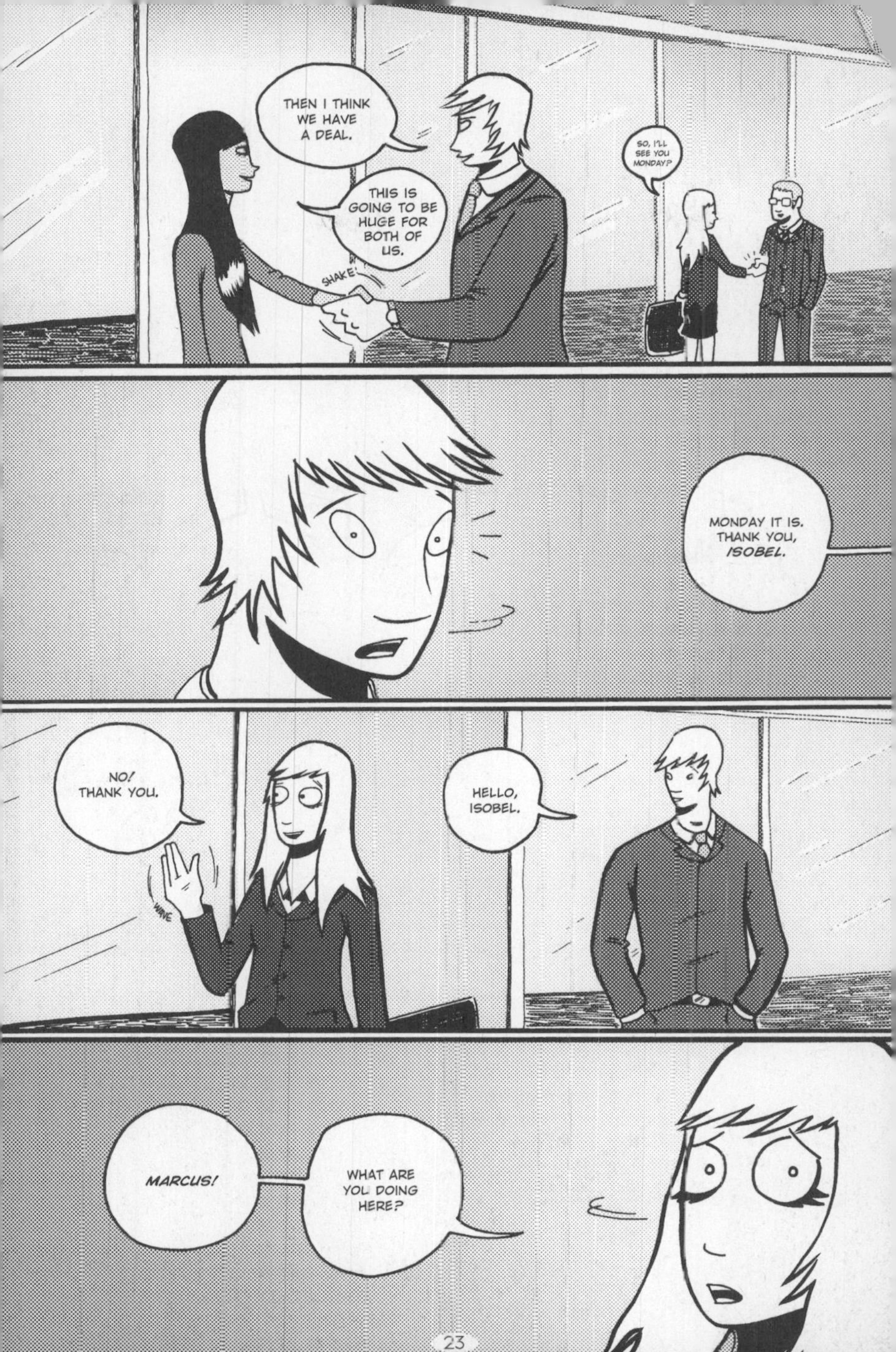

THEN I THINK WE HAVE A DEAL.
THIS IS GOING TO BE HUGE FOR BOTH OF US.
SHAKE!
SO, I'LL SEE YOU MONDAY?
MONDAY IT IS. THANK YOU, *ISOBEL.*
NO! THANK YOU.
WAVE
HELLO, ISOBEL.
MARCUS!
WHAT ARE YOU DOING HERE?

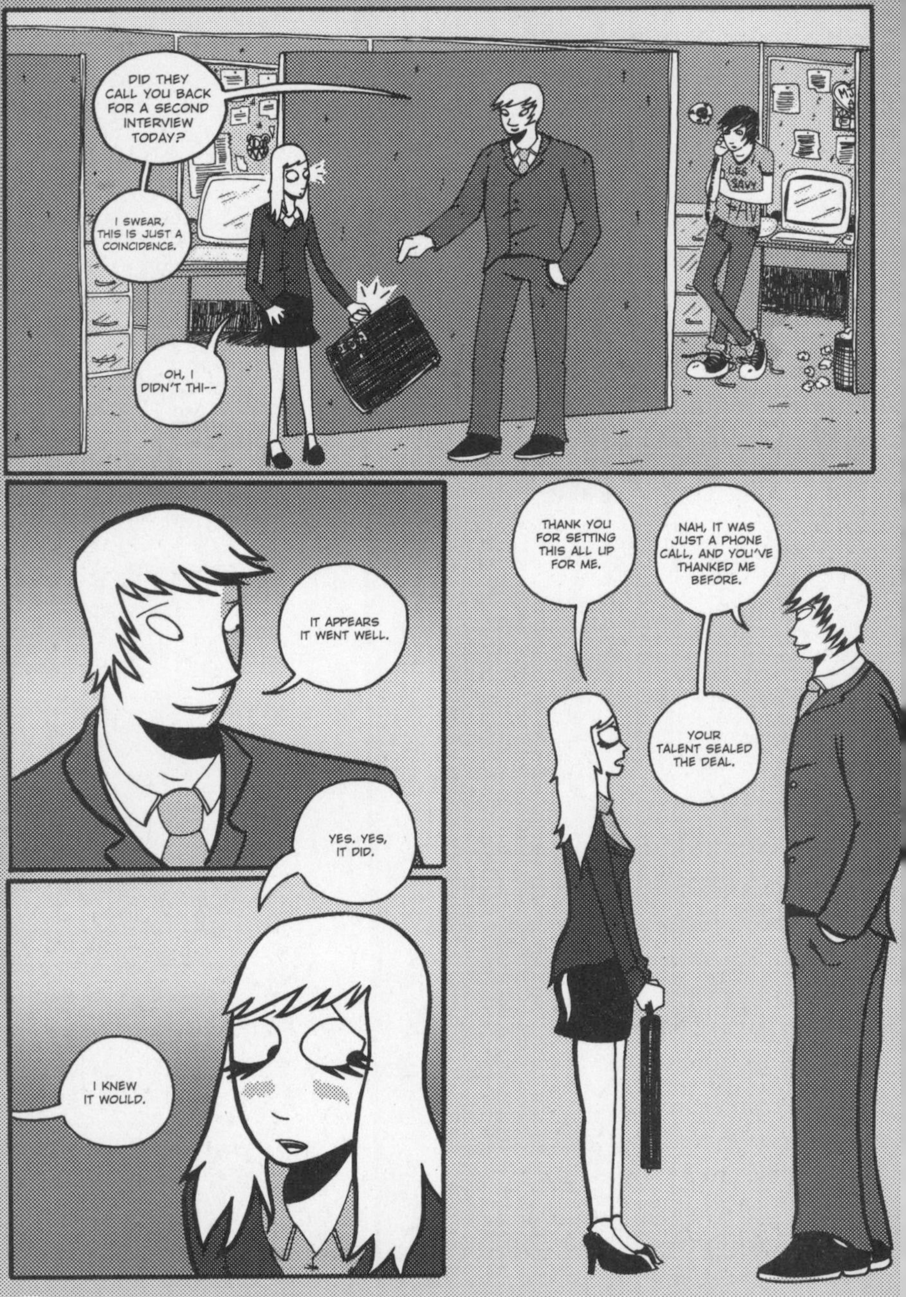
DID THEY CALL YOU BACK FOR A SECOND INTERVIEW TODAY?
I SWEAR, THIS IS JUST A COINCIDENCE.
OH, I DIDN'T THI--
IT APPEARS IT WENT WELL.
YES. YES, IT DID.
I KNEW IT WOULD.
THANK YOU FOR SETTING THIS ALL UP FOR ME.
NAH, IT WAS JUST A PHONE CALL, AND YOU'VE THANKED ME BEFORE.
YOUR TALENT SEALED THE DEAL.

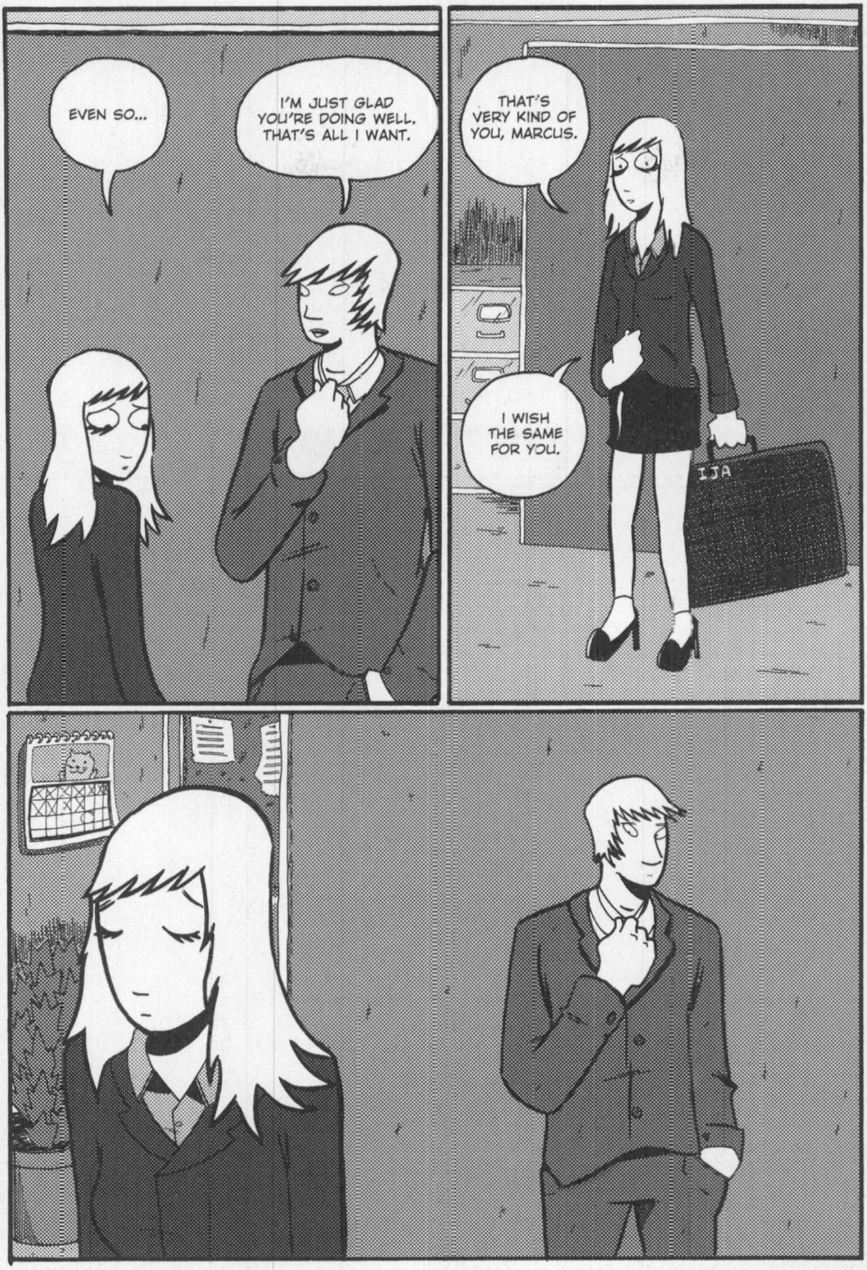
EVEN SO...
I'M JUST GLAD YOU'RE DOING WELL. THAT'S ALL I WANT.
THAT'S VERY KIND OF YOU, MARCUS.
I WISH THE SAME FOR YOU.
IJA

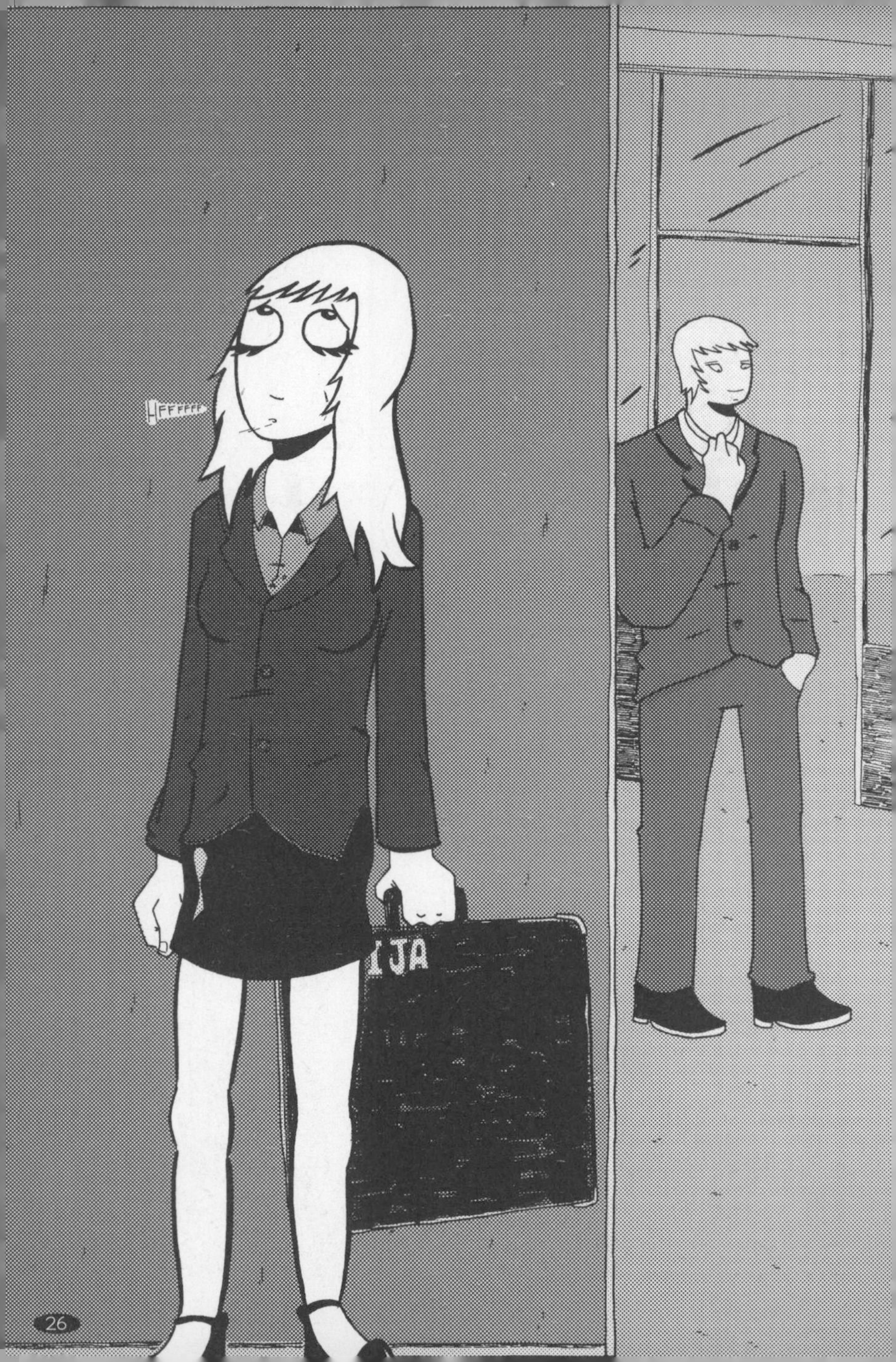
HFFFFFFF
IJA

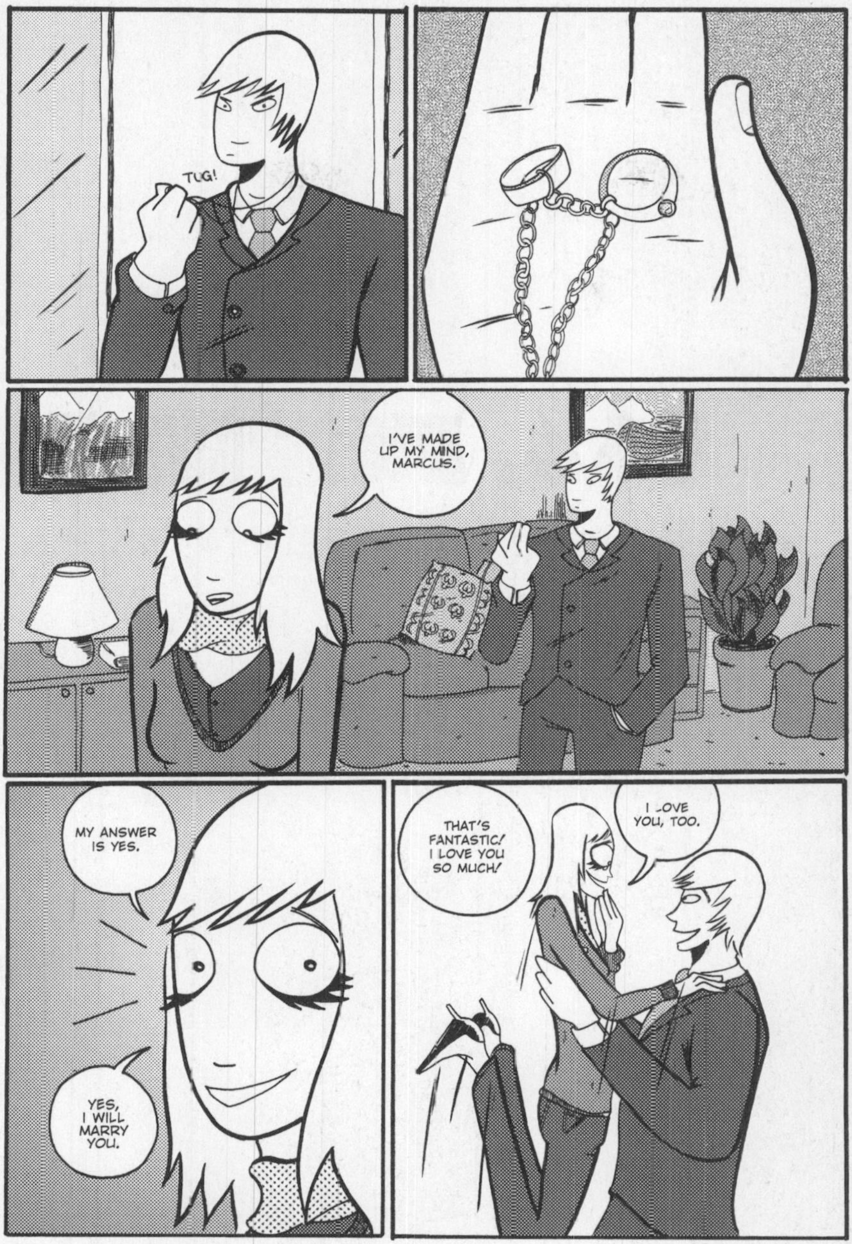
TUG!
I'VE MADE UP MY MIND, MARCUS.
MY ANSWER IS YES.
YES, I WILL MARRY YOU.
THAT'S FANTASTIC! I LOVE YOU SO MUCH!
I LOVE YOU, TOO.

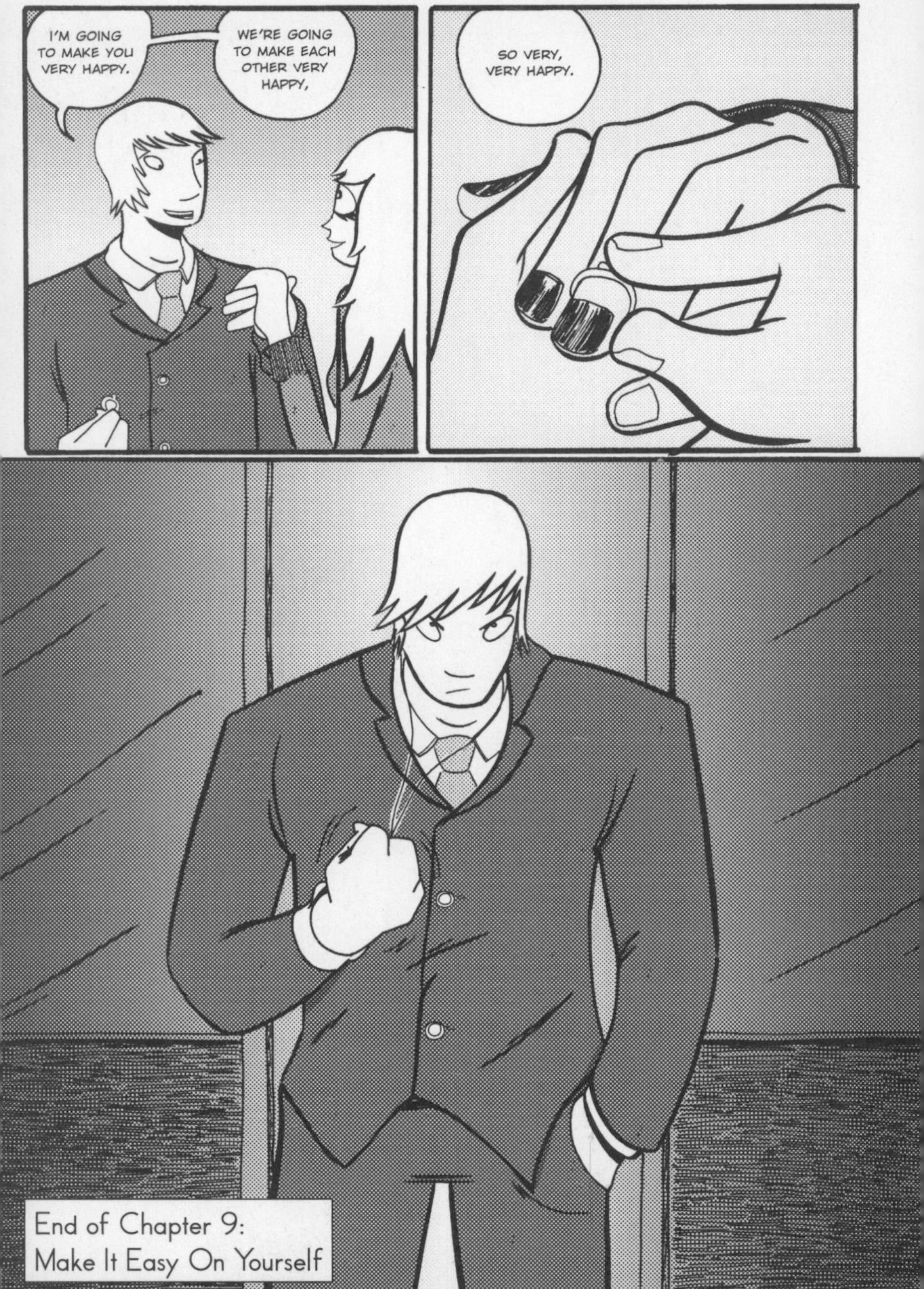
I'M GOING TO MAKE YOU VERY HAPPY.
WE'RE GOING TO MAKE EACH OTHER VERY HAPPY,
SO VERY, VERY HAPPY.
End of Chapter 9: Make It Easy On Yourself

Chapter 10:
The Drift

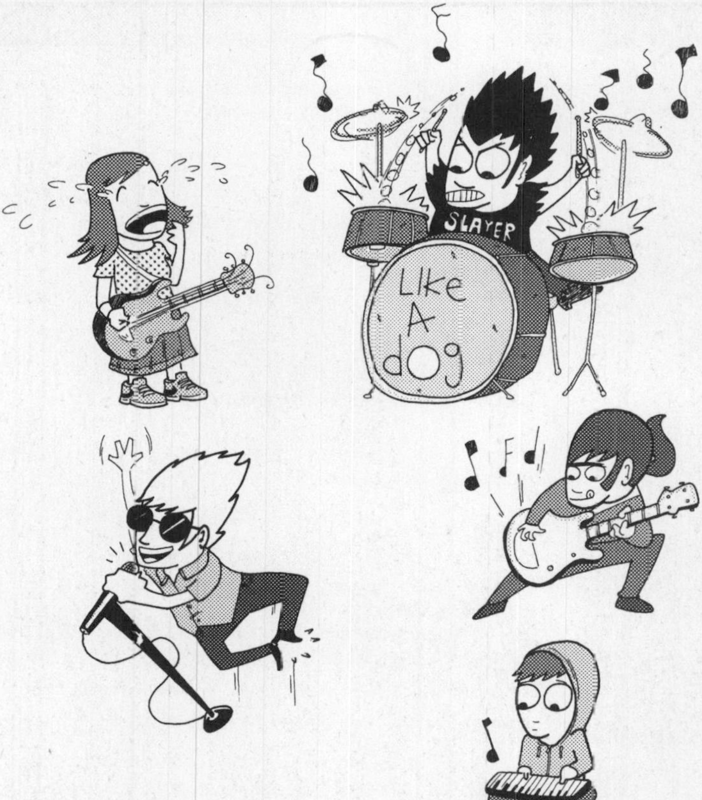
SLAYER
Like
A
dog

KITTEN STOMP FUTURE DREAM
ELEGANTLY ELEANORE!

Full Name:
Eleanore Eileen James

Band Affiliation:
Guitarist, Like A Dog

Birthdate:
July 29 (Leo)

Hometown:
Boise, ID

Artistic Heroes:
Johnny Marr
George Harrison
Lindsey Buckingham
Kristin Hersh

Prior Experience:
Camp counselor four summers in a row in Southern Oregon

Hobbies:
"I like to garden. For a city girl, I'm cool with the outdoors."

Essential Supply:
Barrettes, champagne pop

Group Nickname:
"Give 'em Hellinore"

Favorite Candy:
White chocolate with raspberry filling.

Hates to Admit:
She has an unhealthy attraction to the Justine Bateman movie *Satisfaction*. "One week, I watched it once a day, seven days in a row."

Worst Thing Ever:
"Guys who think that girls can't play guitar. They also think every girl in the world wants them, but guess what?"

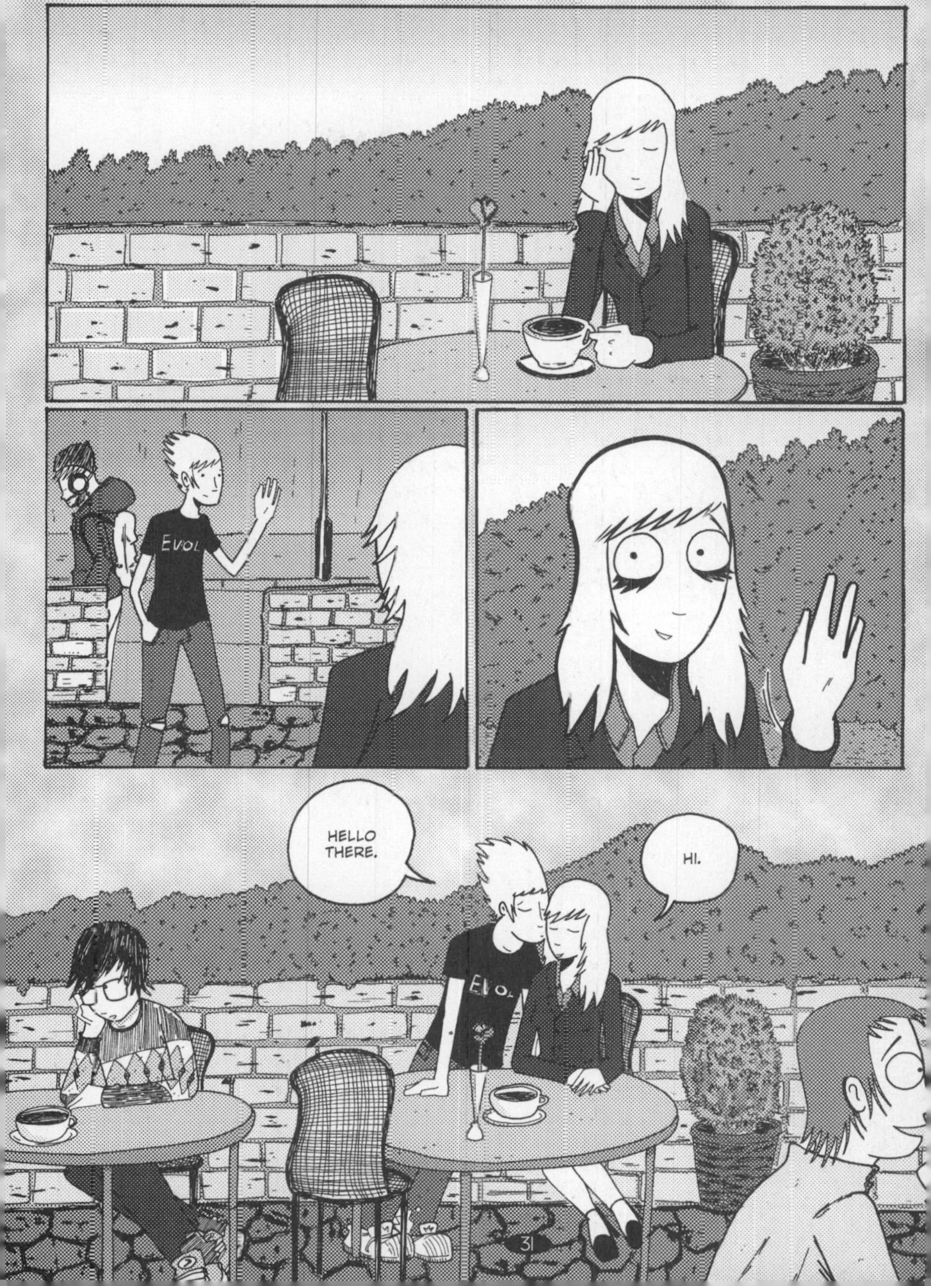
EVOL
EVOL
HELLO THERE.
HI.

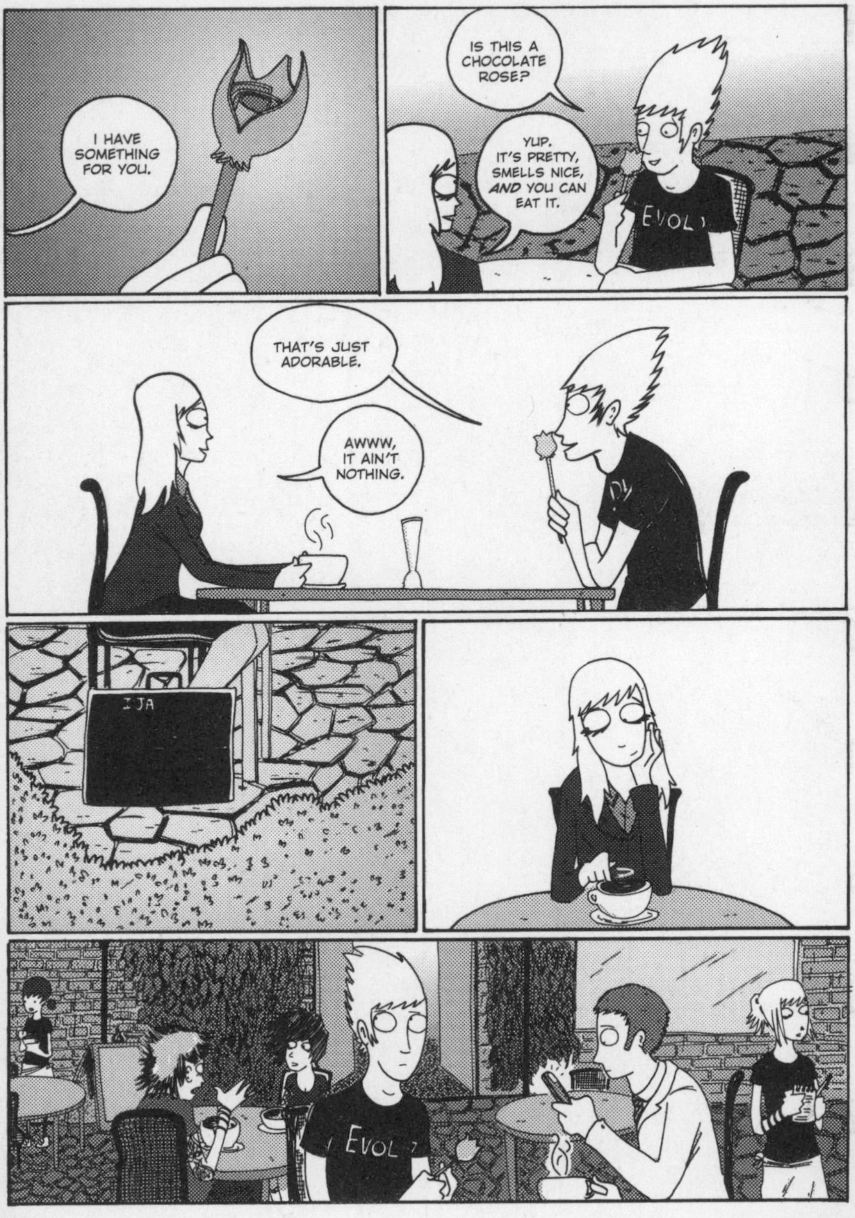
I HAVE SOMETHING FOR YOU.
IS THIS A CHOCOLATE ROSE?
YUP. IT'S PRETTY, SMELLS NICE, *AND* YOU CAN EAT IT.
EVOL
THAT'S JUST ADORABLE.
AWWW, IT AIN'T NOTHING.
EVOL

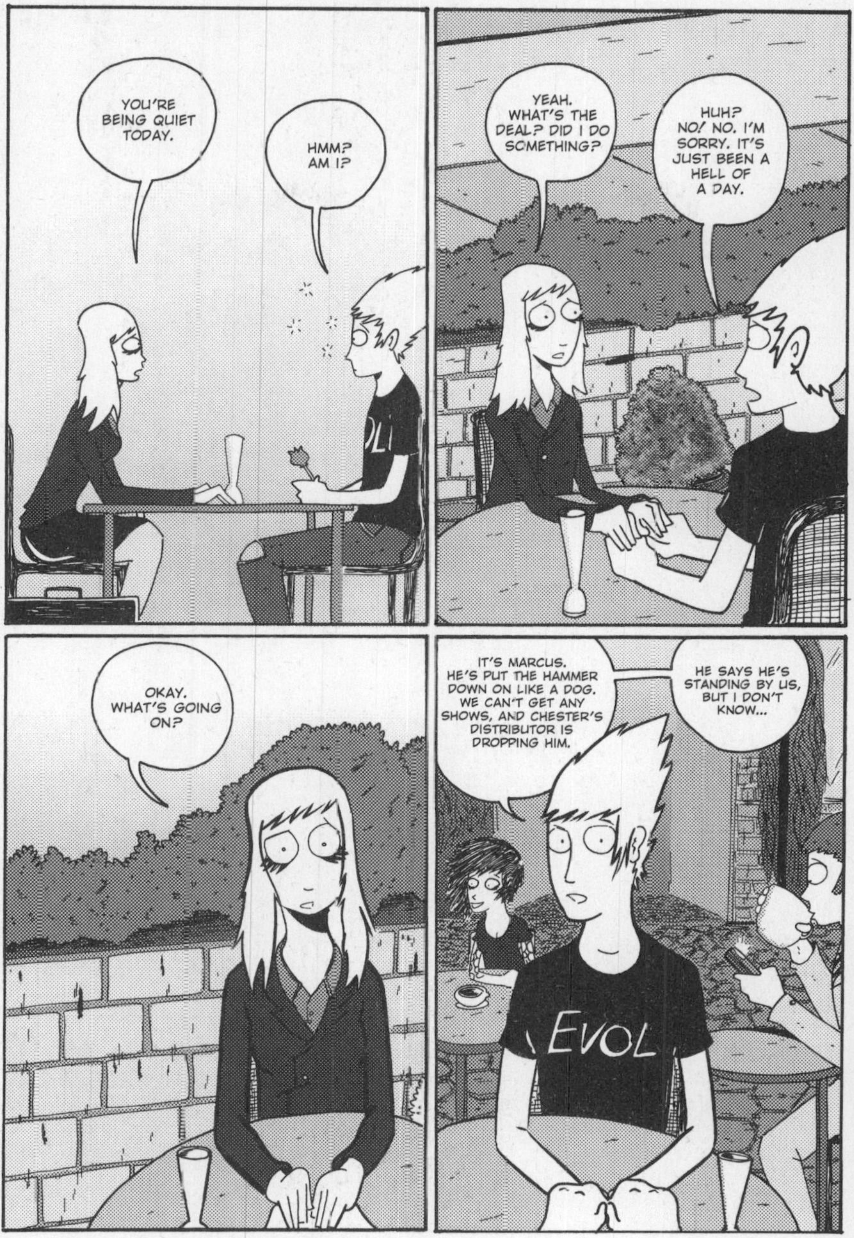
YOU'RE BEING QUIET TODAY.
HMM? AM I?
YEAH. WHAT'S THE DEAL? DID I DO SOMETHING?
HUH? NO! NO. I'M SORRY. IT'S JUST BEEN A HELL OF A DAY.
OKAY. WHAT'S GOING ON?
IT'S MARCUS. HE'S PUT THE HAMMER DOWN ON LIKE A DOG. WE CAN'T GET ANY SHOWS, AND CHESTER'S DISTRIBUTOR IS DROPPING HIM.
EVOL
HE SAYS HE'S STANDING BY US, BUT I DON'T KNOW...

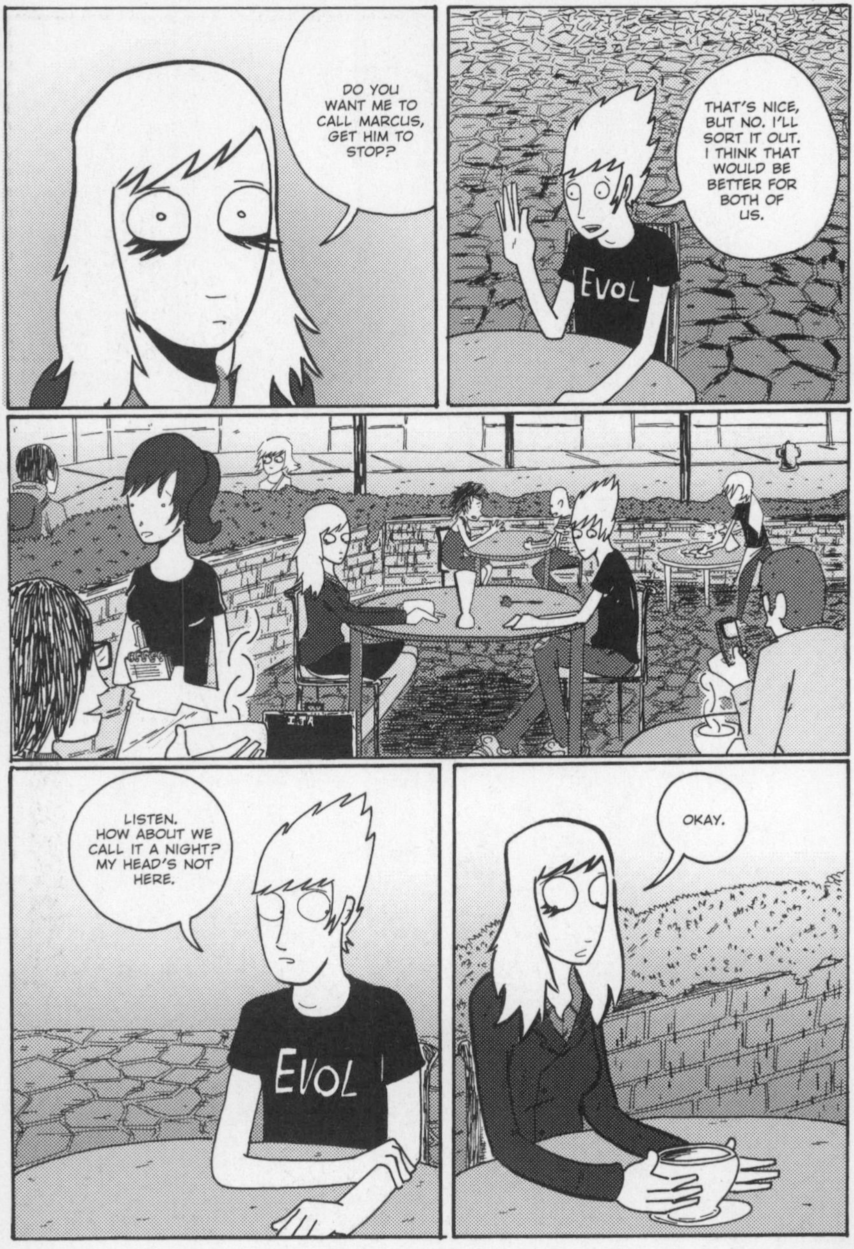
DO YOU WANT ME TO CALL MARCUS, GET HIM TO STOP?
THAT'S NICE, BUT NO. I'LL SORT IT OUT. I THINK THAT WOULD BE BETTER FOR BOTH OF US.
EVOL
I.T.A
LISTEN. HOW ABOUT WE CALL IT A NIGHT? MY HEAD'S NOT HERE.
EVOL
OKAY.

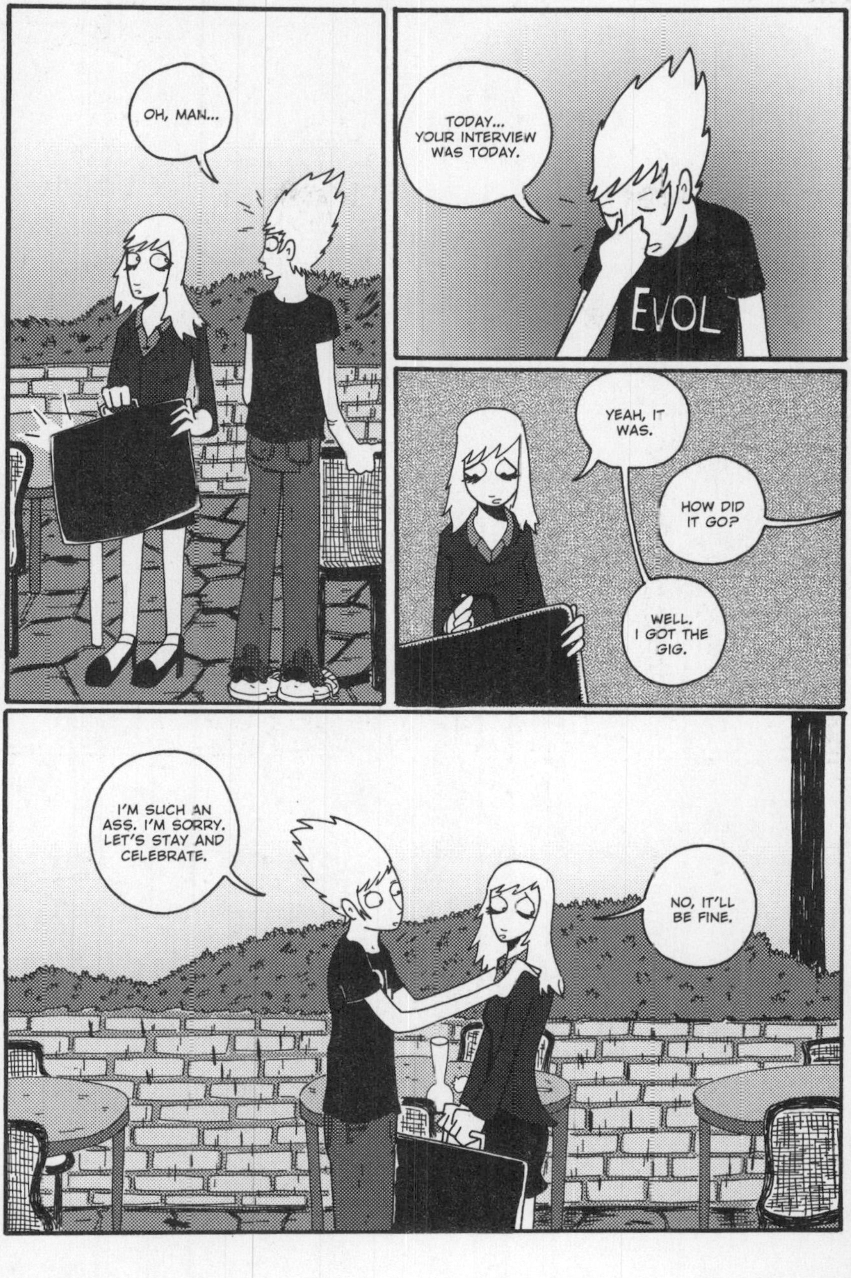

OH, MAN...
TODAY... YOUR INTERVIEW WAS TODAY.
EVOL
YEAH, IT WAS.
HOW DID IT GO?
WELL. I GOT THE GIG.
I'M SUCH AN ASS. I'M SORRY. LET'S STAY AND CELEBRATE.
NO, IT'LL BE FINE.

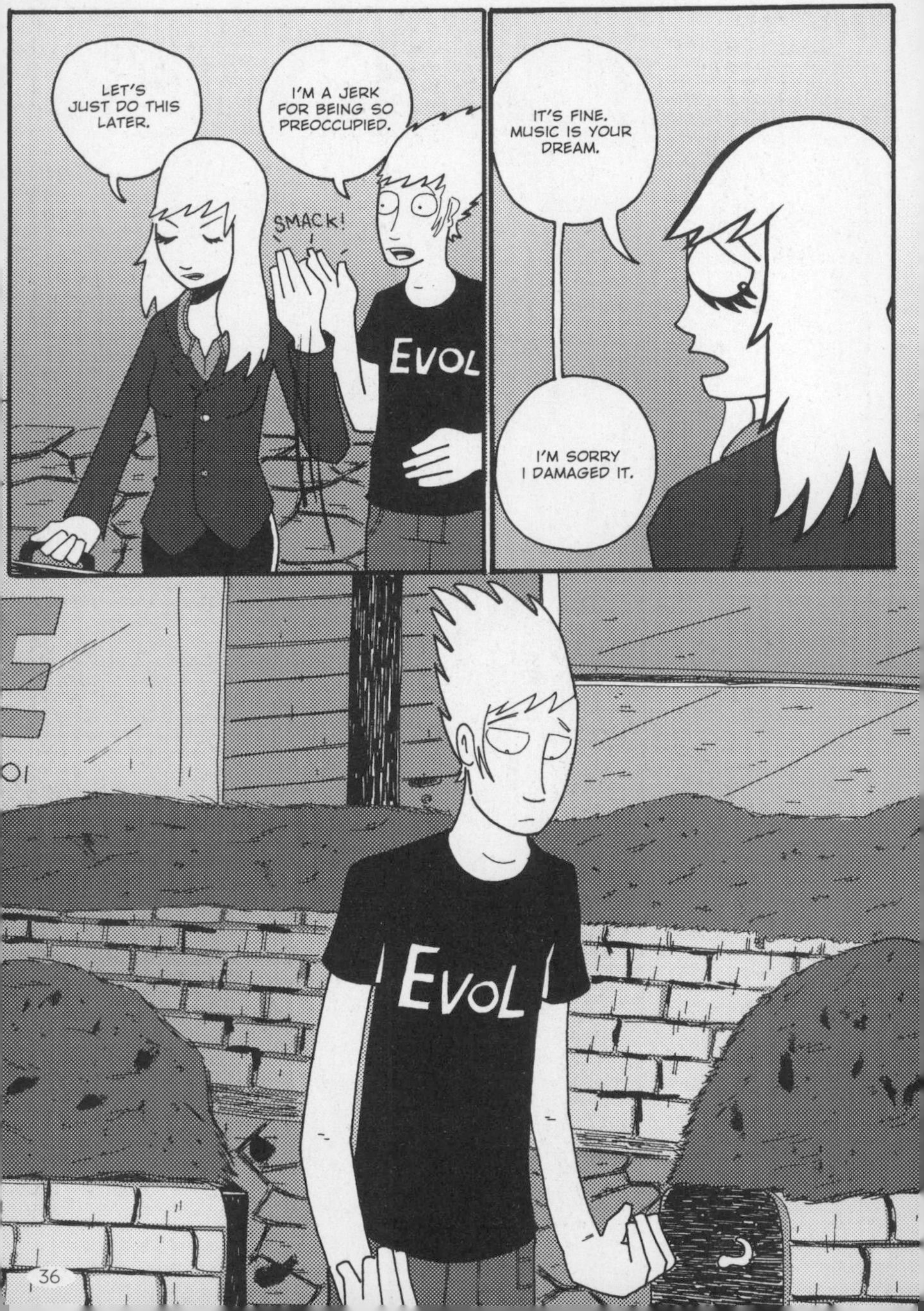
LET'S JUST DO THIS LATER.
I'M A JERK FOR BEING SO PREOCCUPIED.
SMACK!
EVOL
IT'S FINE. MUSIC IS YOUR DREAM.
I'M SORRY I DAMAGED IT.
EVOL

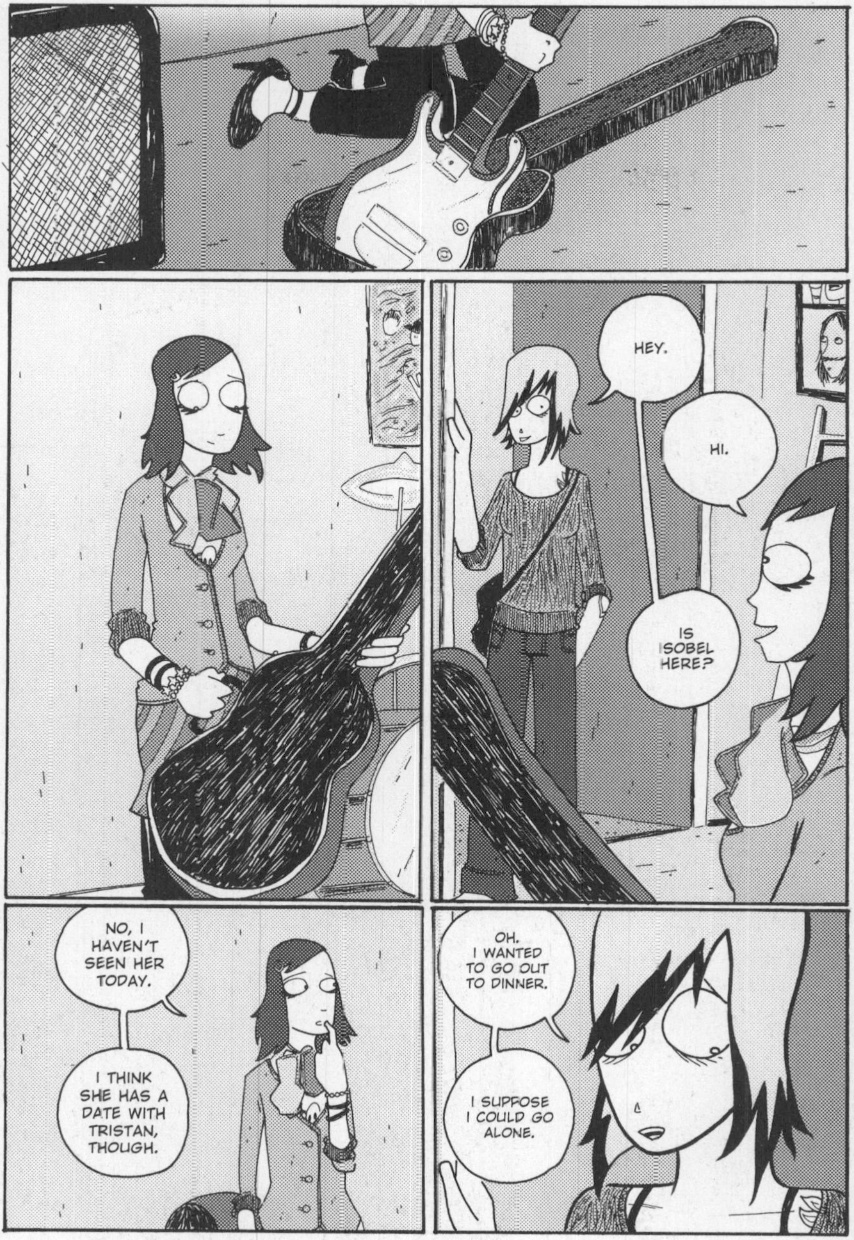
HEY.
HI.
IS ISOBEL HERE?
NO, I HAVEN'T SEEN HER TODAY.
I THINK SHE HAS A DATE WITH TRISTAN, THOUGH.
OH. I WANTED TO GO OUT TO DINNER.
I SUPPOSE I COULD GO ALONE.

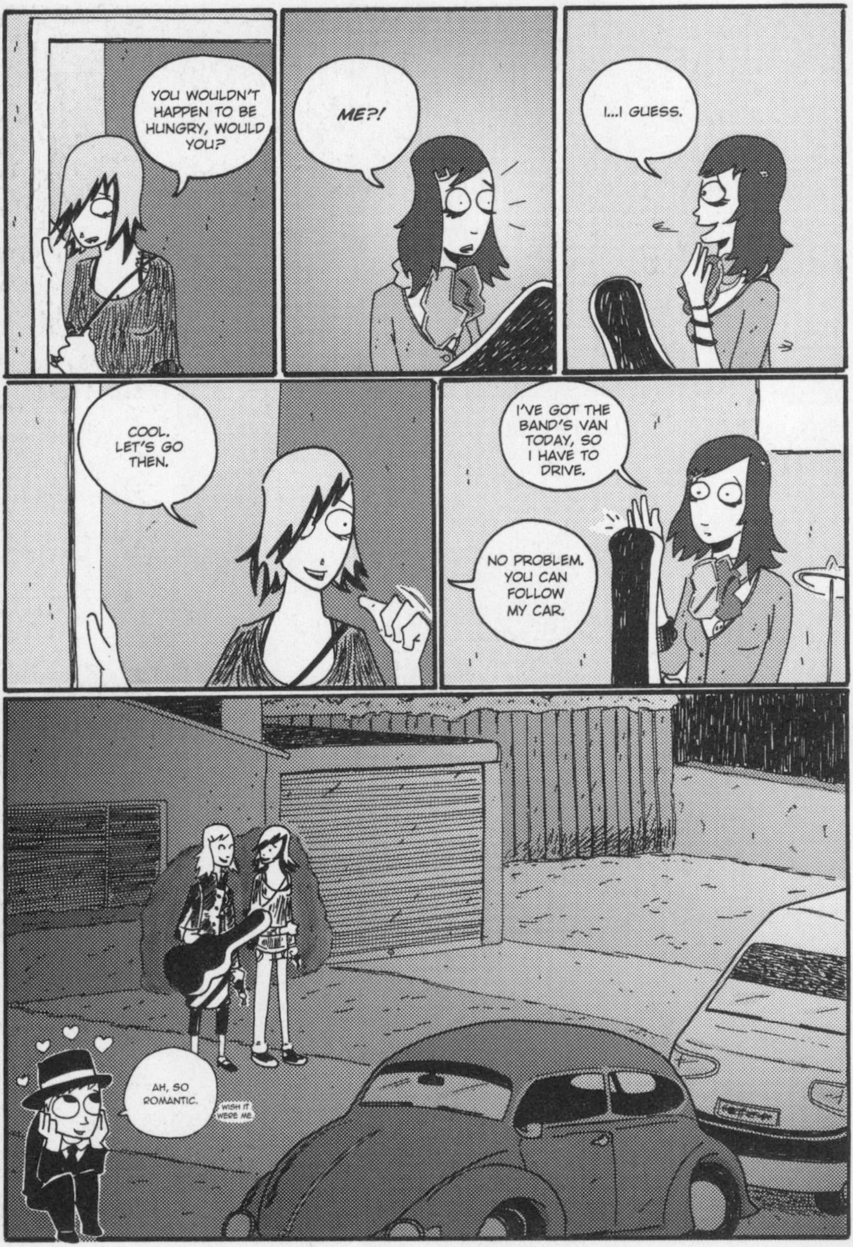

YOU WOULDN'T HAPPEN TO BE HUNGRY, WOULD YOU?
ME?!
I...I GUESS.
COOL. LET'S GO THEN.
I'VE GOT THE BAND'S VAN TODAY, SO I HAVE TO DRIVE.
NO PROBLEM. YOU CAN FOLLOW MY CAR.
AH, SO ROMANTIC.
WISH IT WERE ME.

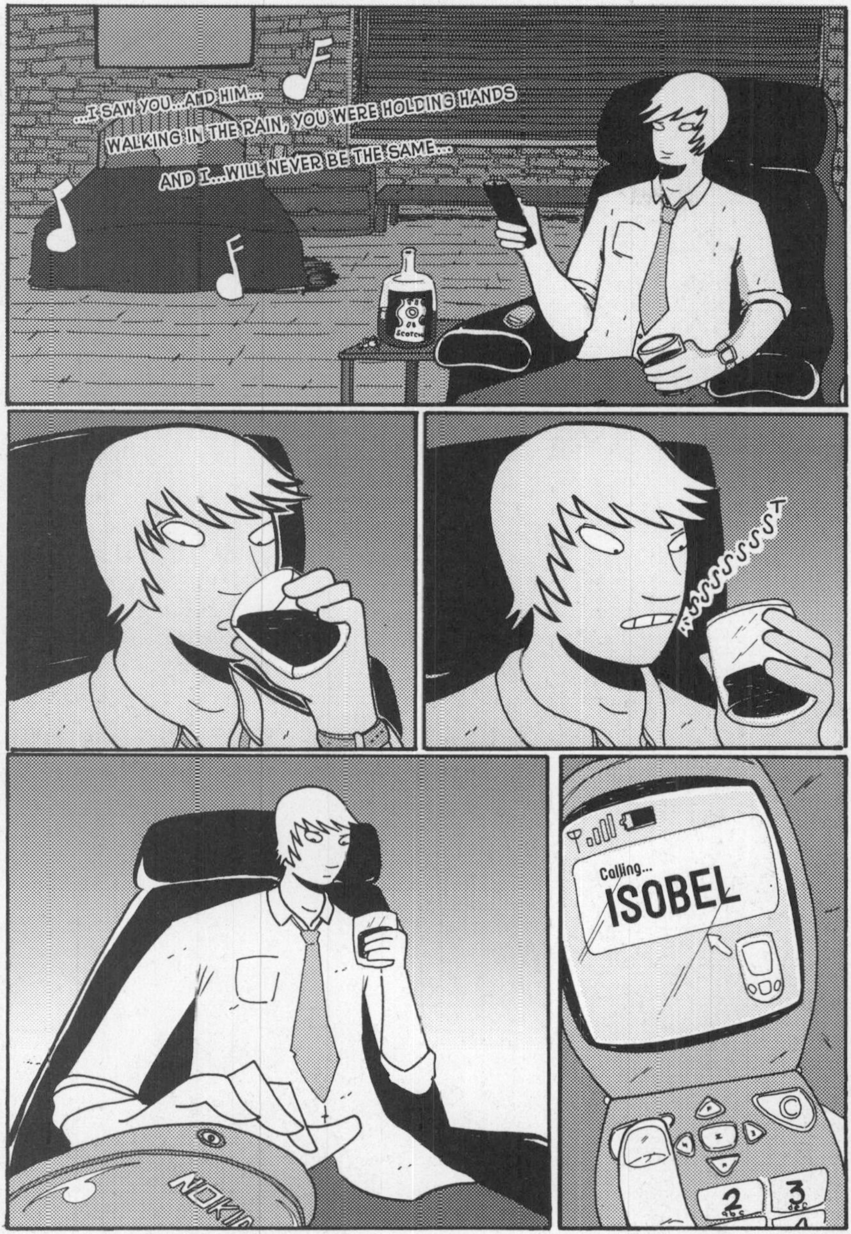
...I SAW YOU...AND HIM...
WALKING IN THE RAIN, YOU WERE HOLDING HANDS
AND I...WILL NEVER BE THE SAME...
Scotch
WSSSSSSSST
Calling...
ISOBEL
NOKI

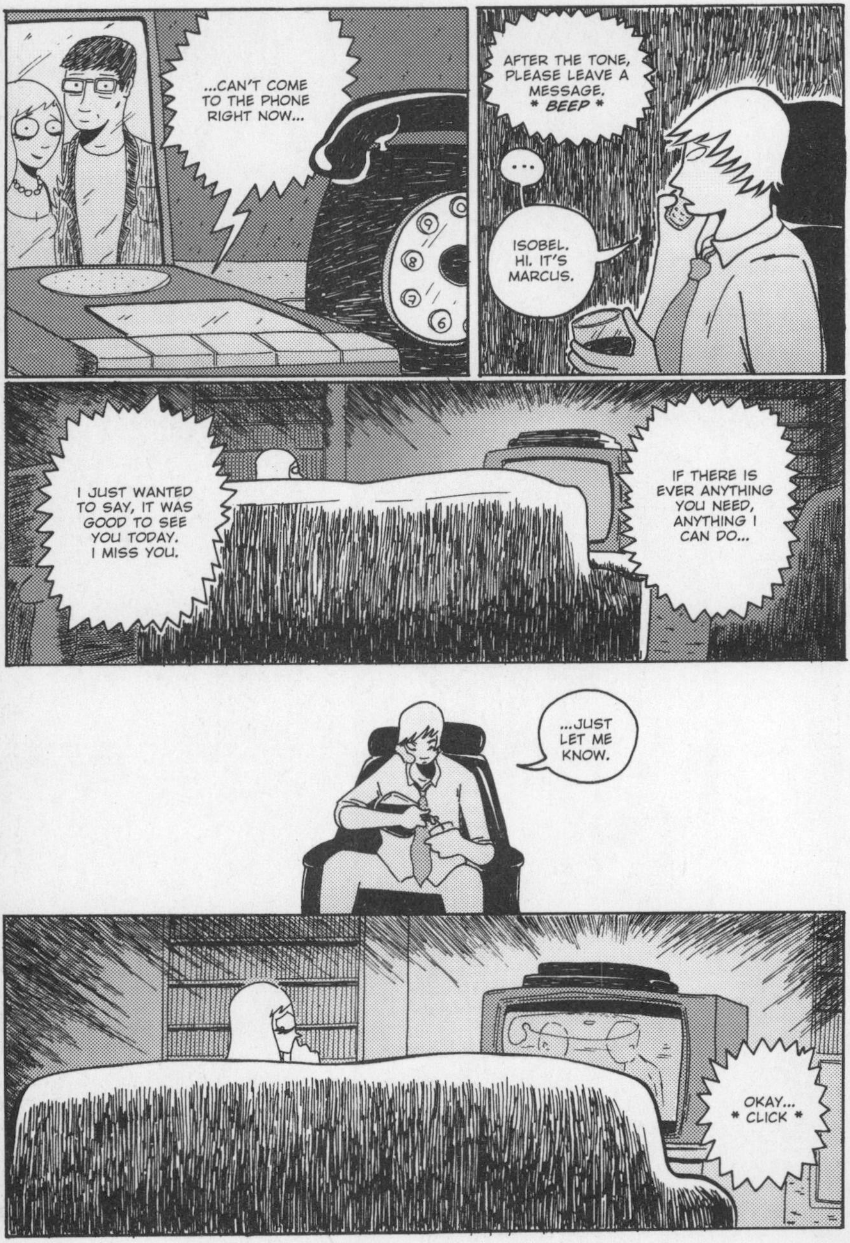
...CAN'T COME TO THE PHONE RIGHT NOW...
AFTER THE TONE, PLEASE LEAVE A MESSAGE. * BEEP *
...
ISOBEL. HI. IT'S MARCUS.
I JUST WANTED TO SAY, IT WAS GOOD TO SEE YOU TODAY. I MISS YOU.
IF THERE IS EVER ANYTHING YOU NEED, ANYTHING I CAN DO...
...JUST LET ME KNOW.
OKAY... * CLICK *

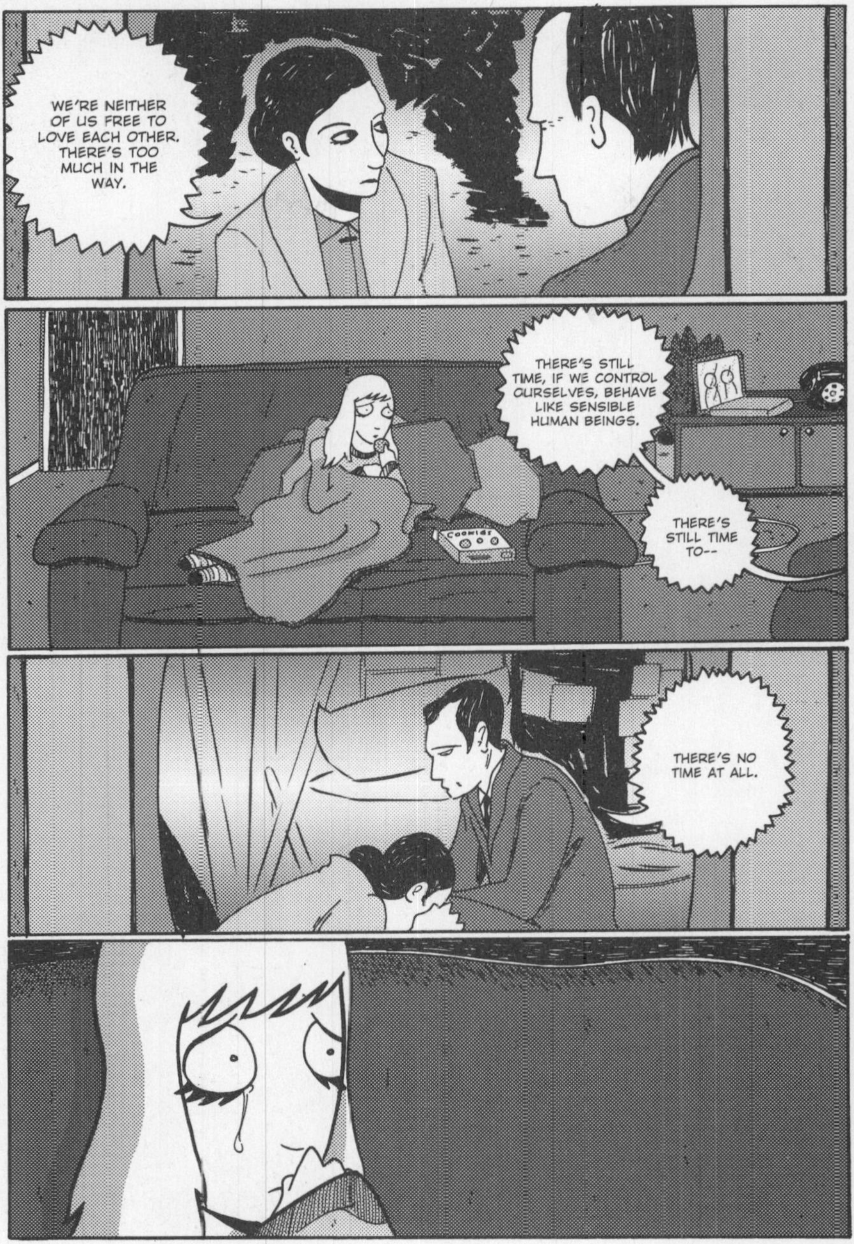
WE'RE NEITHER OF US FREE TO LOVE EACH OTHER. THERE'S TOO MUCH IN THE WAY.
THERE'S STILL TIME, IF WE CONTROL OURSELVES, BEHAVE LIKE SENSIBLE HUMAN BEINGS.
COOKIES
THERE'S STILL TIME TO--
THERE'S NO TIME AT ALL.

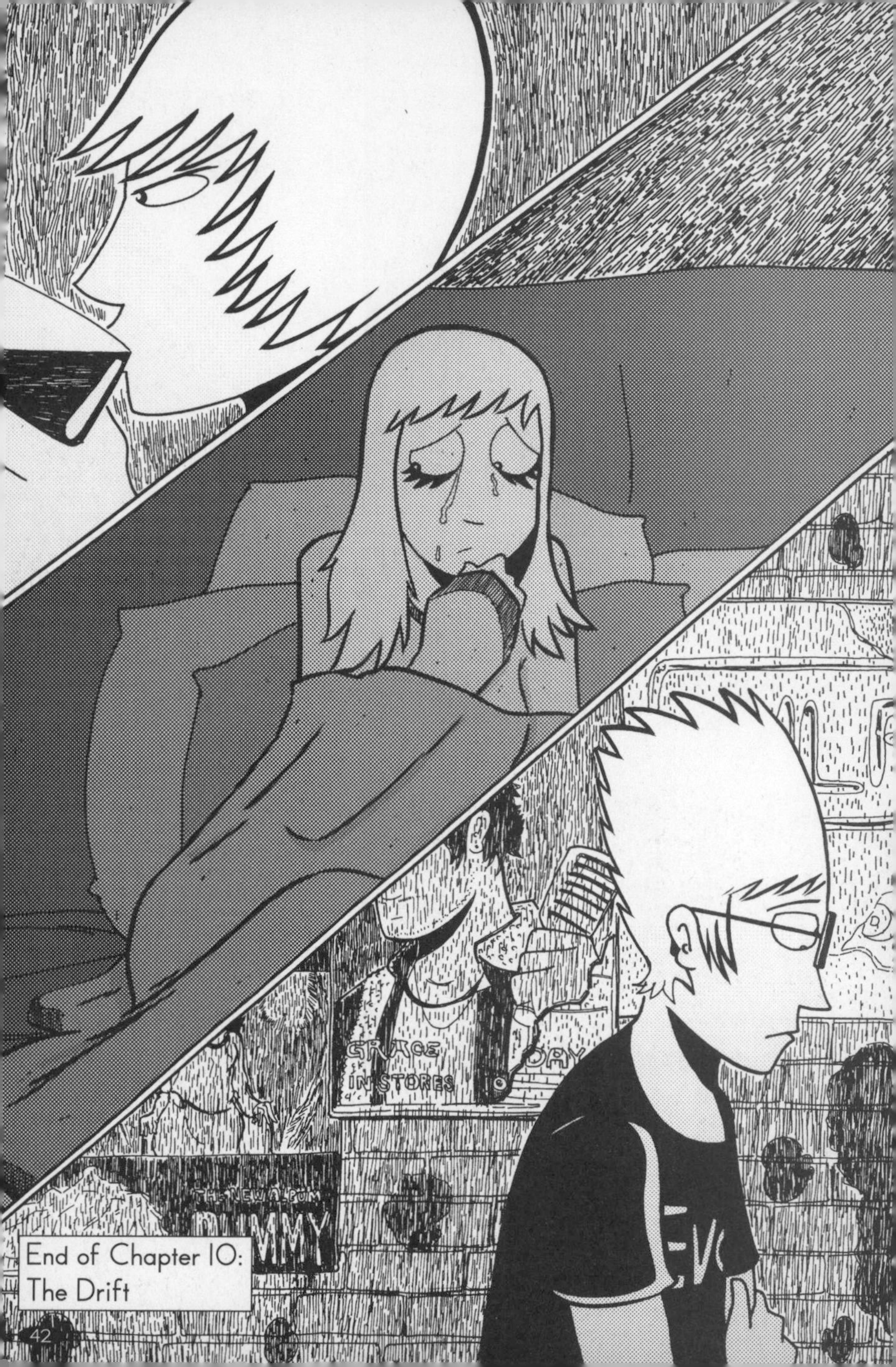
End of Chapter 10:
The Drift

Chapter II:
First Love Never Dies...?

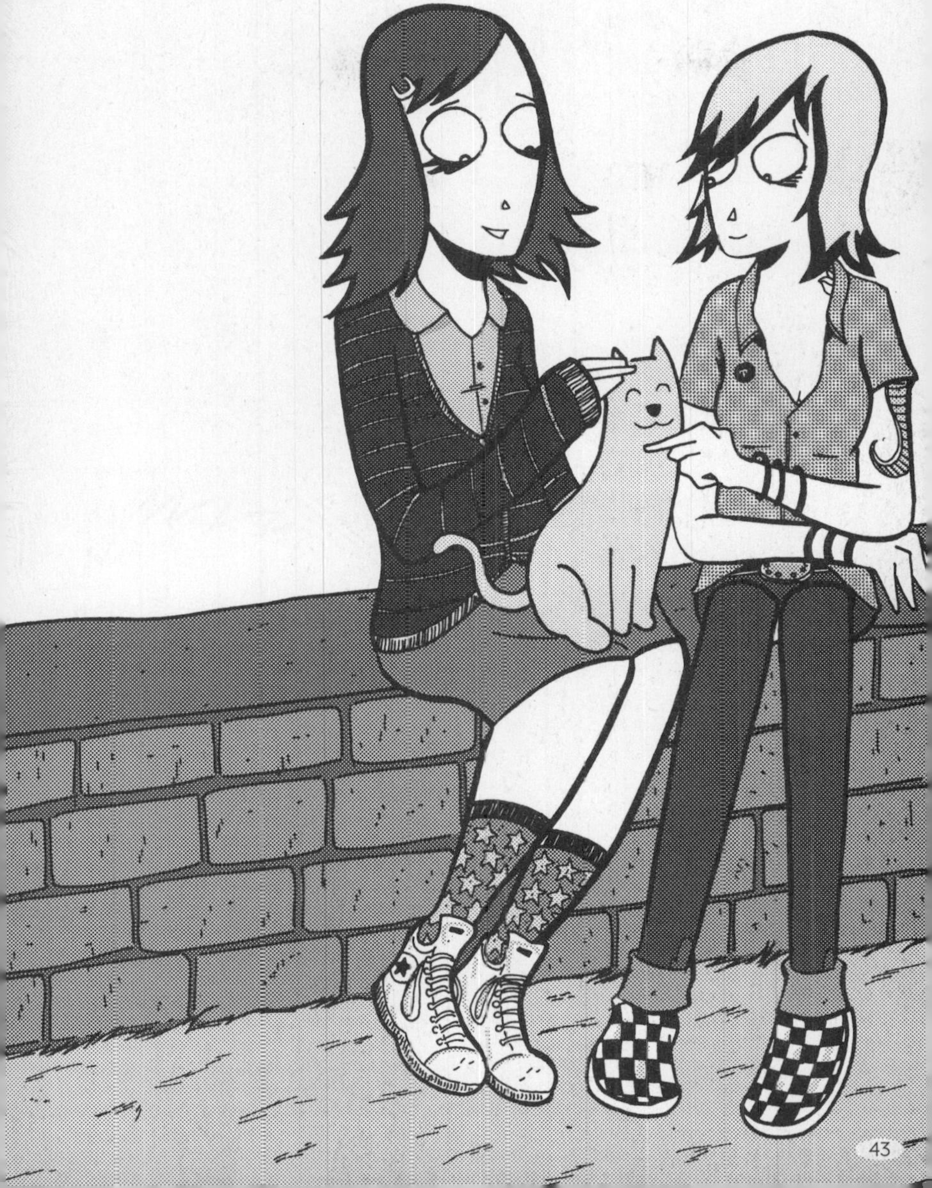

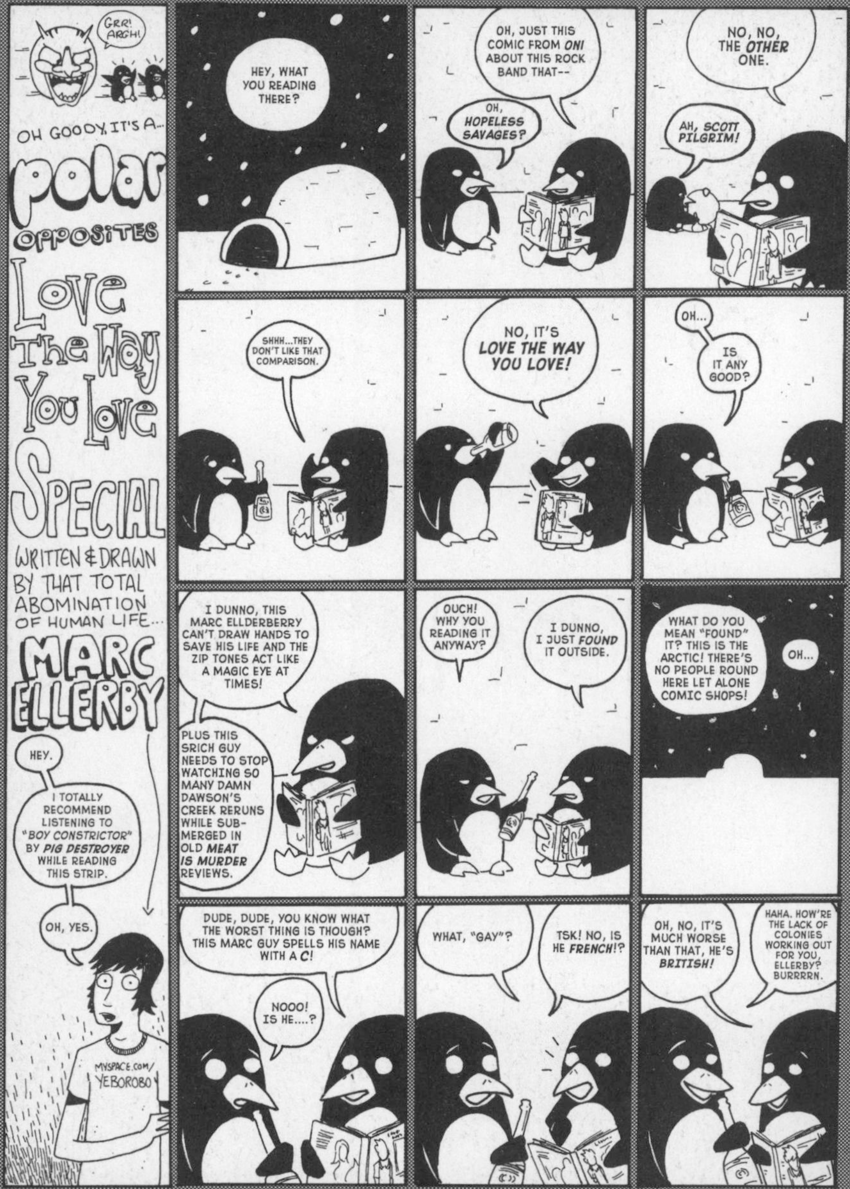
GRR! ARGH!
OH GOODY, IT'S A...
polar opposites
Love The Way You Love
SPECIAL
WRITTEN & DRAWN BY THAT TOTAL ABOMINATION OF HUMAN LIFE...
MARC ELLERBY
HEY.
I TOTALLY RECOMMEND LISTENING TO "BOY CONSTRICTOR" BY PIG DESTROYER WHILE READING THIS STRIP.
OH, YES.
MYSPACE.COM/ YEBOROBO
HEY, WHAT YOU READING THERE?
OH, JUST THIS COMIC FROM ONI ABOUT THIS ROCK BAND THAT--
OH, HOPELESS SAVAGES?
NO, NO, THE OTHER ONE.
AH, SCOTT PILGRIM!
SHHH...THEY DON'T LIKE THAT COMPARISON.
NO, IT'S LOVE THE WAY YOU LOVE!
OH...
IS IT ANY GOOD?
I DUNNO, THIS MARC ELLDERBERRY CAN'T DRAW HANDS TO SAVE HIS LIFE AND THE ZIP TONES ACT LIKE A MAGIC EYE AT TIMES!
PLUS THIS SRICH GUY NEEDS TO STOP WATCHING SO MANY DAMN DAWSON'S CREEK RERUNS WHILE SUBMERGED IN OLD MEAT IS MURDER REVIEWS.
OUCH! WHY YOU READING IT ANYWAY?
I DUNNO, I JUST FOUND IT OUTSIDE.
WHAT DO YOU MEAN "FOUND" IT? THIS IS THE ARCTIC! THERE'S NO PEOPLE ROUND HERE LET ALONE COMIC SHOPS!
OH...
DUDE, DUDE, YOU KNOW WHAT THE WORST THING IS THOUGH? THIS MARC GUY SPELLS HIS NAME WITH A C!
NOOO! IS HE....?
WHAT, "GAY"?
TSK! NO, IS HE FRENCH!?
OH, NO, IT'S MUCH WORSE THAN THAT, HE'S BRITISH!
HAHA. HOW'RE THE LACK OF COLONIES WORKING OUT FOR YOU, ELLERBY? BURRRRN.

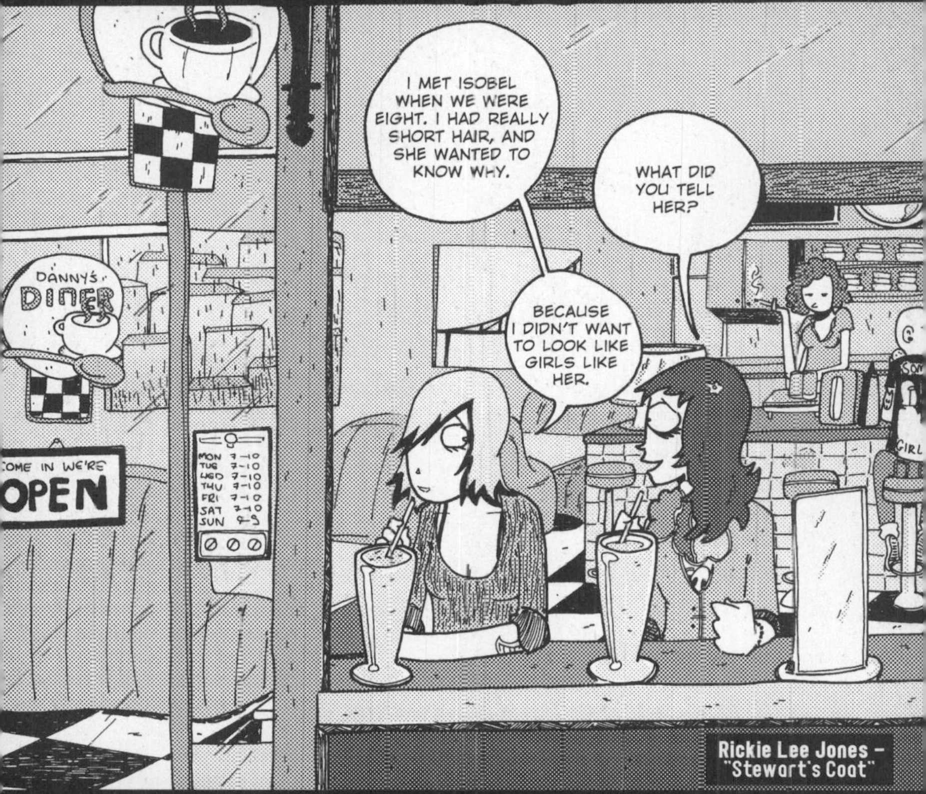
DANNY'S DINER
COME IN WE'RE OPEN
MON 7-10
TUE 7-10
WED 7-10
THU 7-10
FRI 7-10
SAT 7-10
SUN 9-5
I MET ISOBEL WHEN WE WERE EIGHT. I HAD REALLY SHORT HAIR, AND SHE WANTED TO KNOW WHY.
WHAT DID YOU TELL HER?
BECAUSE I DIDN'T WANT TO LOOK LIKE GIRLS LIKE HER.
Rickie Lee Jones - "Stewart's Coat"

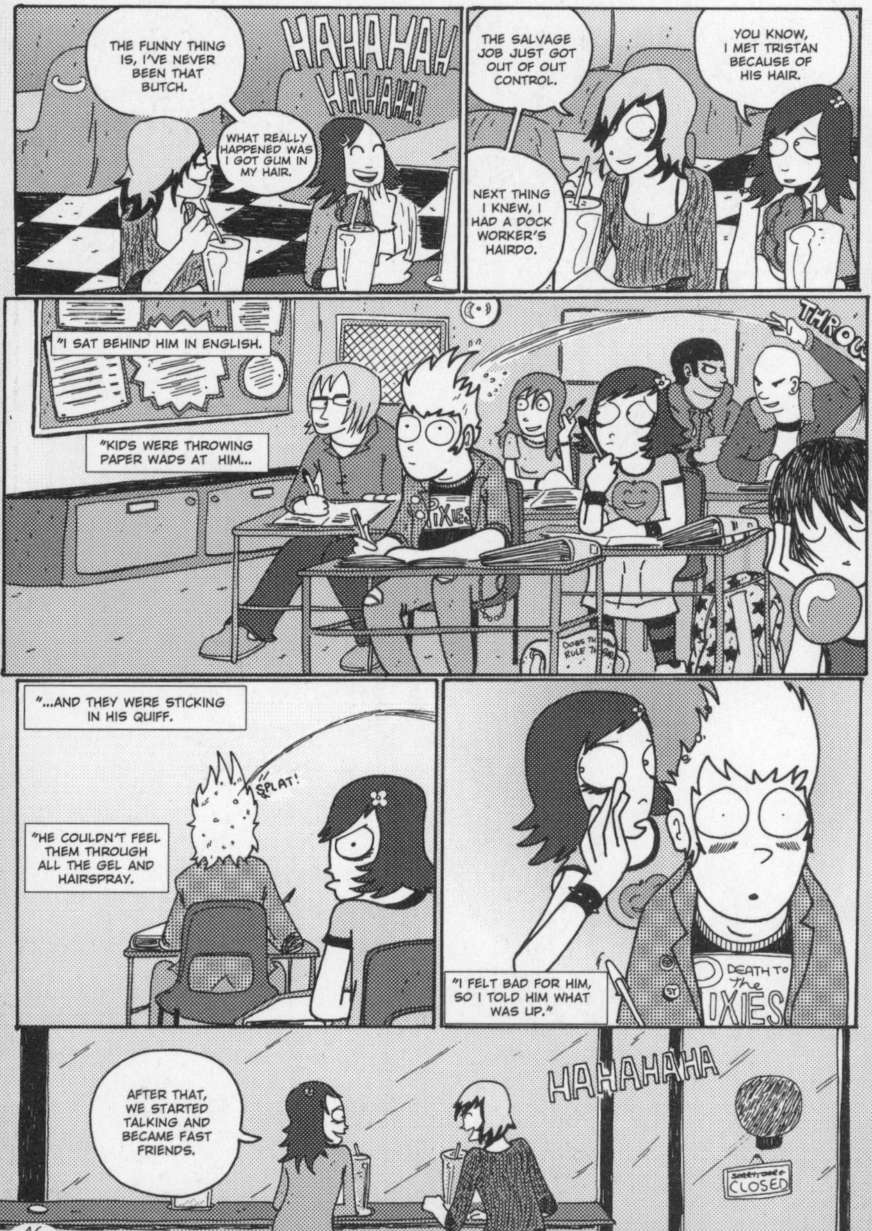

THE FUNNY THING IS, I'VE NEVER BEEN THAT BUTCH.
HAHAHAH! HAHAHAHA!
WHAT REALLY HAPPENED WAS I GOT GUM IN MY HAIR.
THE SALVAGE JOB JUST GOT OUT OF OUT CONTROL.
NEXT THING I KNEW, I HAD A DOCK WORKER'S HAIRDO.
YOU KNOW, I MET TRISTAN BECAUSE OF HIS HAIR.
"I SAT BEHIND HIM IN ENGLISH.
"KIDS WERE THROWING PAPER WADS AT HIM...
THROW
PIXIES
"...AND THEY WERE STICKING IN HIS QUIFF.
SPLAT!
"HE COULDN'T FEEL THEM THROUGH ALL THE GEL AND HAIRSPRAY.
"I FELT BAD FOR HIM, SO I TOLD HIM WHAT WAS UP."
DEATH TO the PIXIES
AFTER THAT, WE STARTED TALKING AND BECAME FAST FRIENDS.
HAHAHAHA
CLOSED

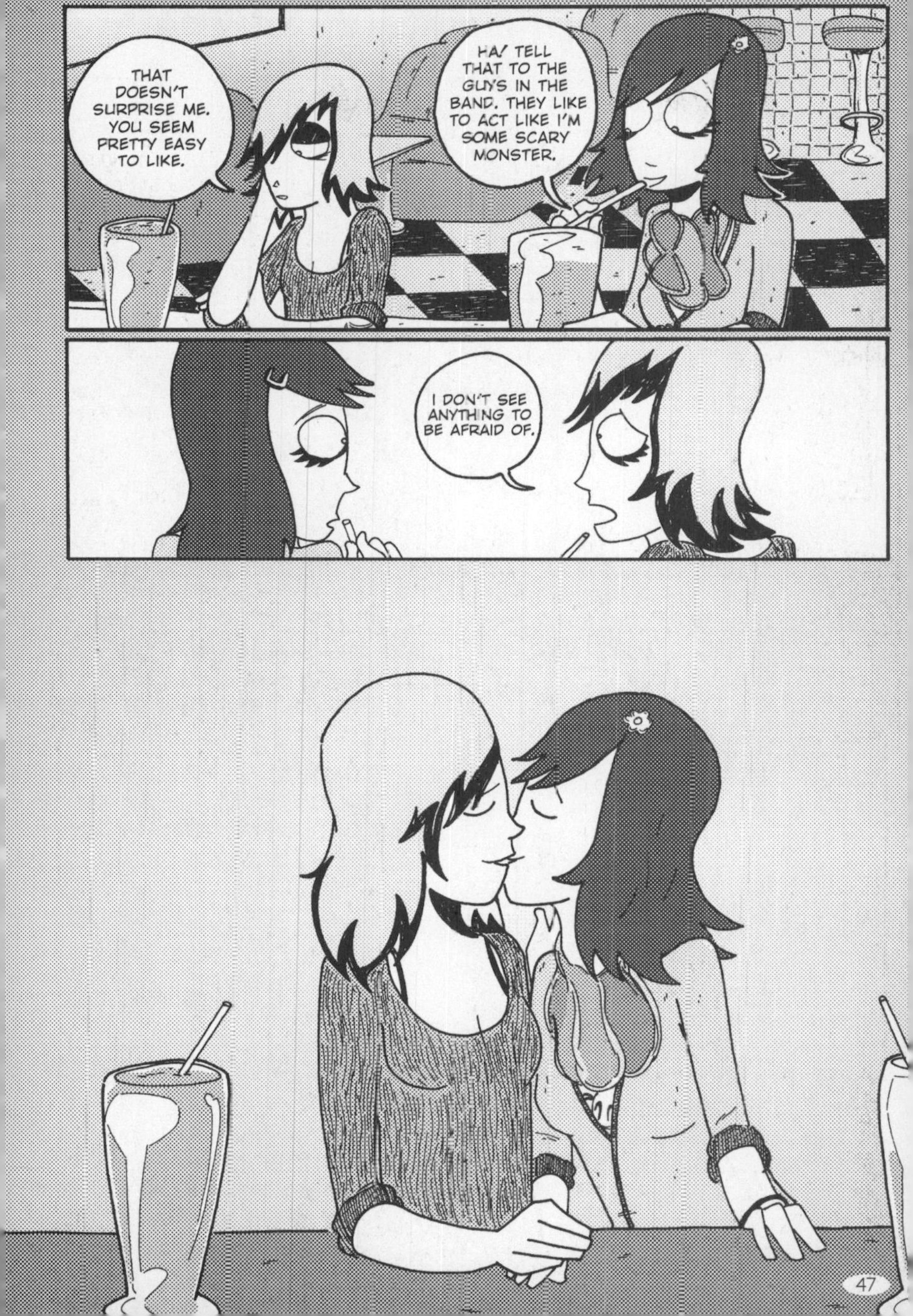
THAT DOESN'T SURPRISE ME. YOU SEEM PRETTY EASY TO LIKE.
HA! TELL THAT TO THE GUYS IN THE BAND. THEY LIKE TO ACT LIKE I'M SOME SCARY MONSTER.
I DON'T SEE ANYTHING TO BE AFRAID OF.

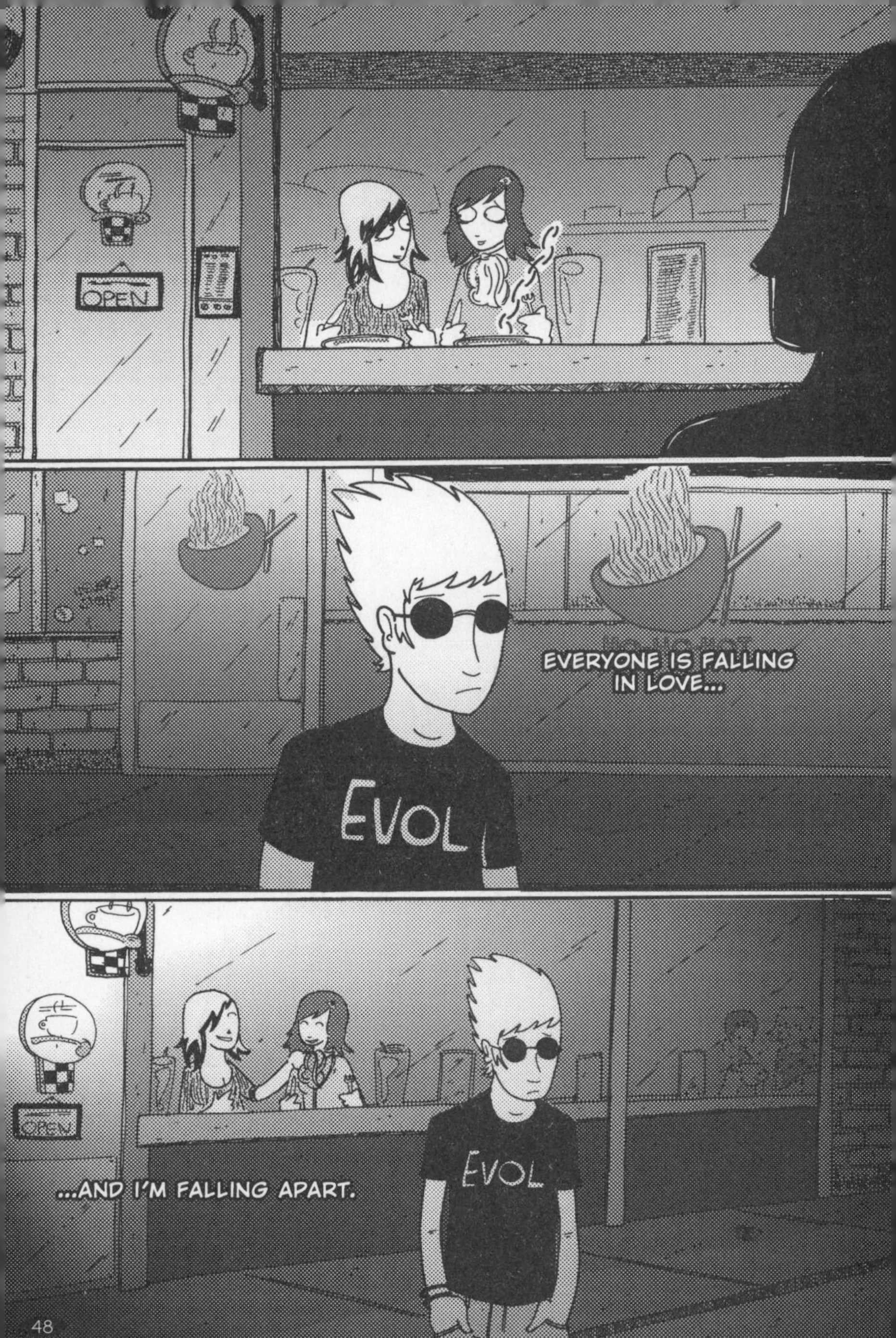
OPEN
EVOL
EVERYONE IS FALLING IN LOVE...
OPEN
...AND I'M FALLING APART.
EVOL

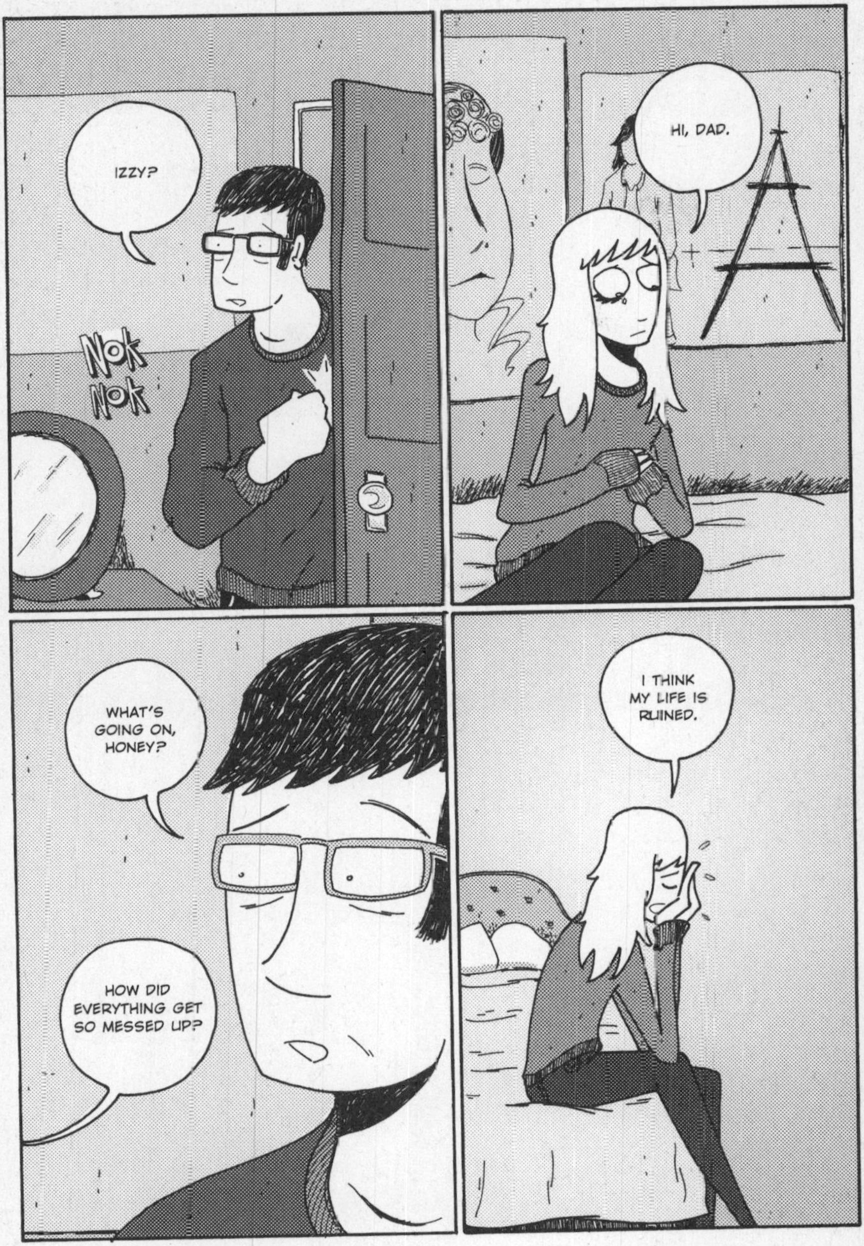
IZZY?
NOK NOK
HI, DAD.
WHAT'S GOING ON, HONEY?
HOW DID EVERYTHING GET SO MESSED UP?
I THINK MY LIFE IS RUINED.

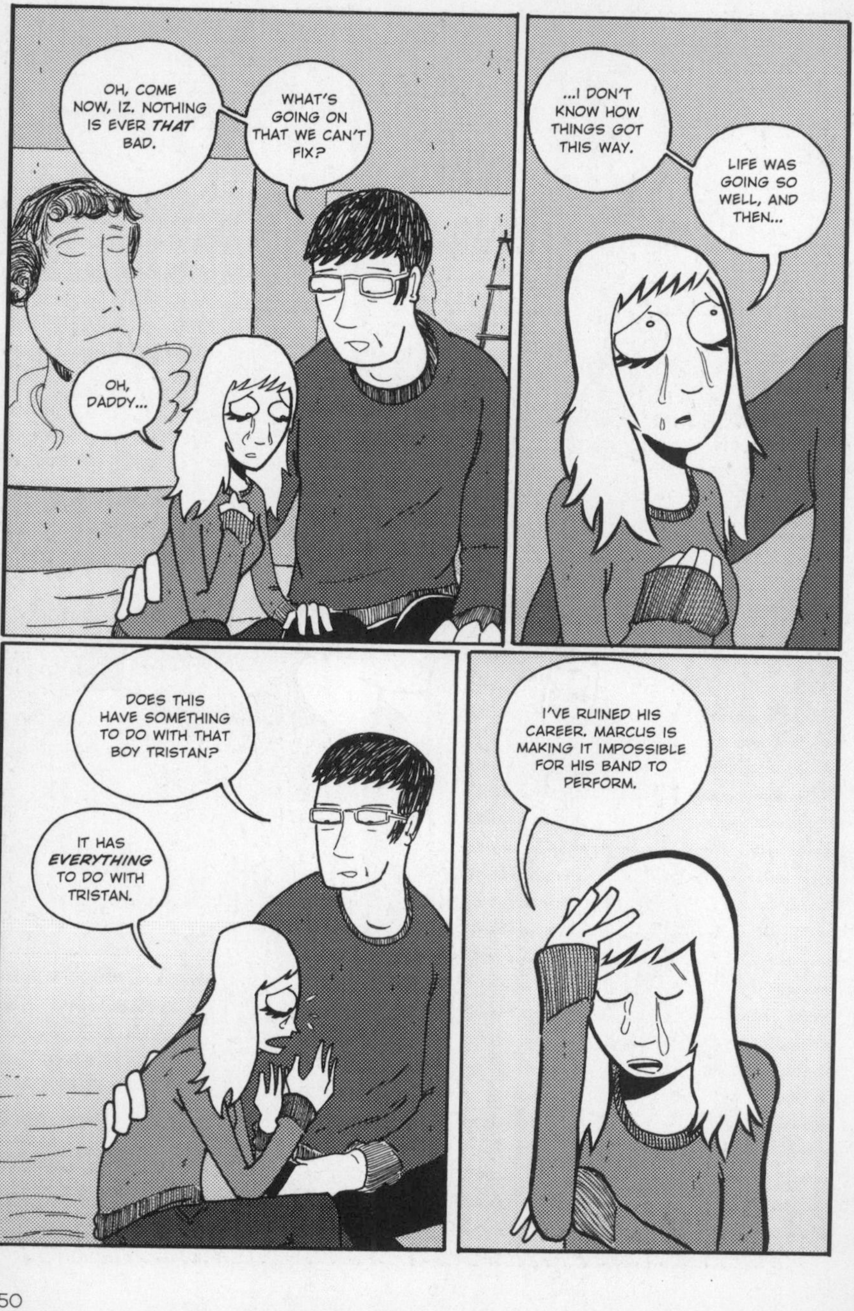
OH, COME NOW, IZ. NOTHING IS EVER *THAT* BAD.
WHAT'S GOING ON THAT WE CAN'T FIX?
OH, DADDY...
...I DON'T KNOW HOW THINGS GOT THIS WAY.
LIFE WAS GOING SO WELL, AND THEN...
DOES THIS HAVE SOMETHING TO DO WITH THAT BOY TRISTAN?
IT HAS *EVERYTHING* TO DO WITH TRISTAN.
I'VE RUINED HIS CAREER. MARCUS IS MAKING IT IMPOSSIBLE FOR HIS BAND TO PERFORM.

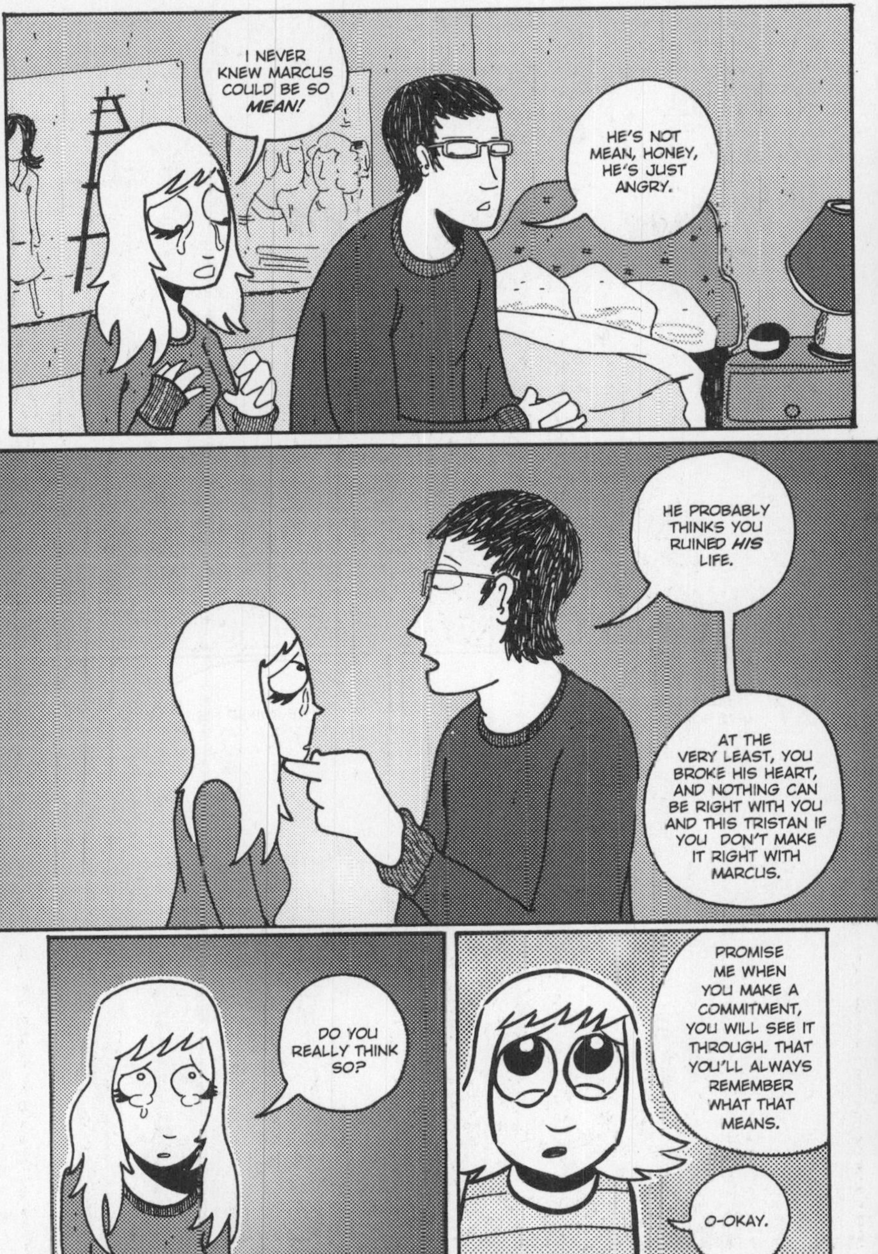
I NEVER KNEW MARCUS COULD BE SO *MEAN!*
HE'S NOT MEAN, HONEY, HE'S JUST ANGRY.
HE PROBABLY THINKS YOU RUINED *HIS* LIFE.
AT THE VERY LEAST, YOU BROKE HIS HEART, AND NOTHING CAN BE RIGHT WITH YOU AND THIS TRISTAN IF YOU DON'T MAKE IT RIGHT WITH MARCUS.
DO YOU REALLY THINK SO?
PROMISE ME WHEN YOU MAKE A COMMITMENT, YOU WILL SEE IT THROUGH. THAT YOU'LL ALWAYS REMEMBER WHAT THAT MEANS.
O-OKAY.

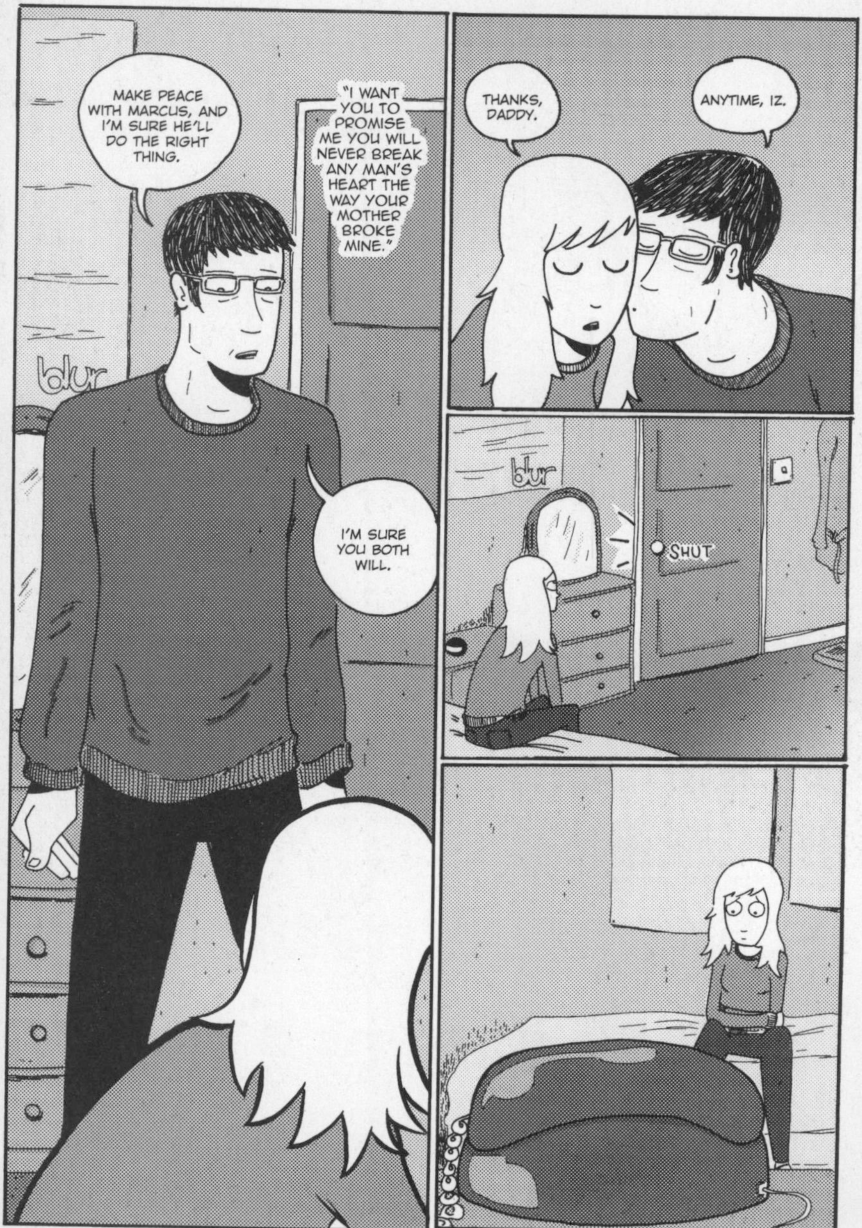
MAKE PEACE WITH MARCUS, AND I'M SURE HE'LL DO THE RIGHT THING.
"I WANT YOU TO PROMISE ME YOU WILL NEVER BREAK ANY MAN'S HEART THE WAY YOUR MOTHER BROKE MINE."
I'M SURE YOU BOTH WILL.
blur
THANKS, DADDY.
ANYTIME, IZ.
blur
SHUT

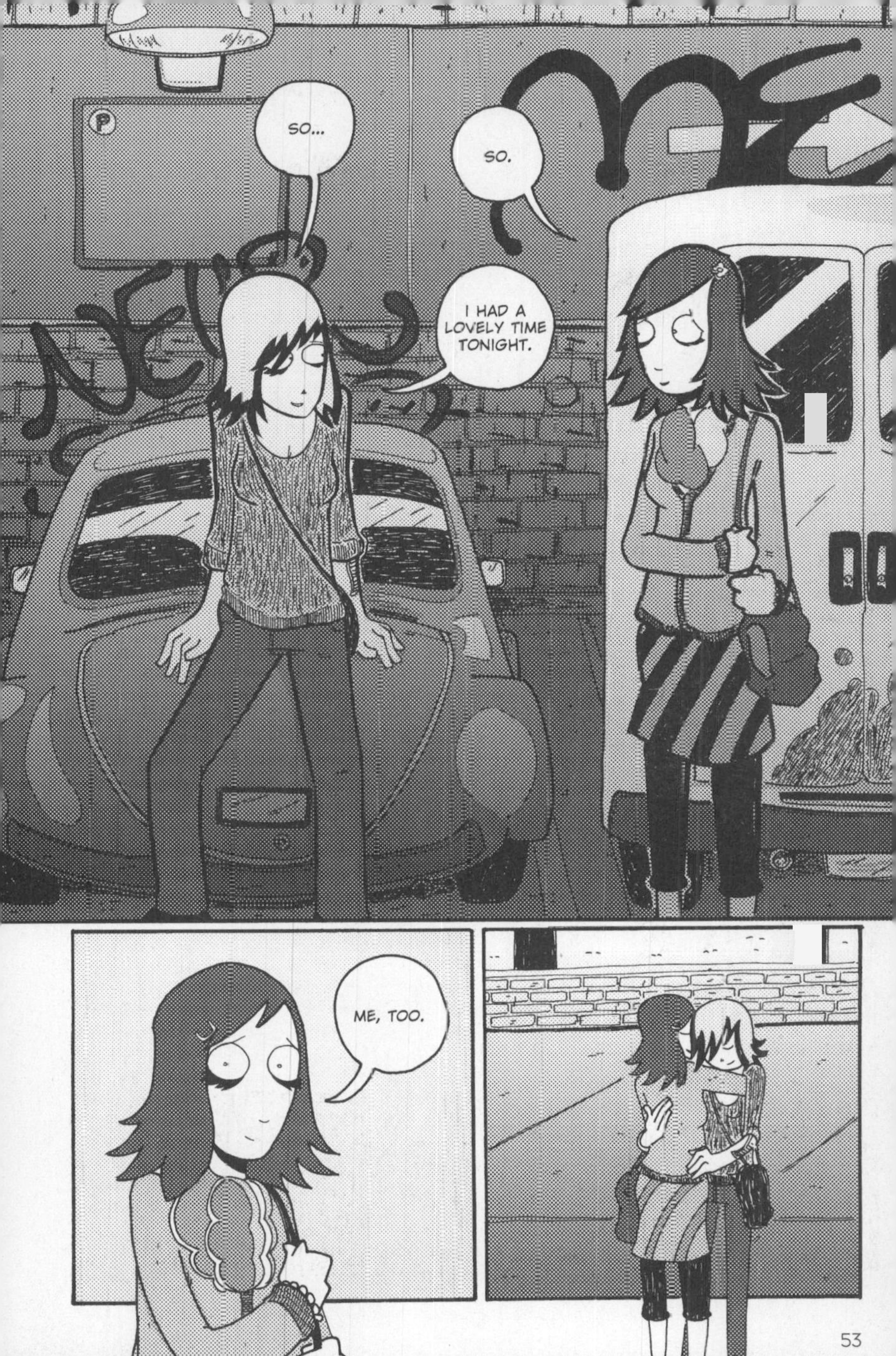
SO...
SO.
I HAD A LOVELY TIME TONIGHT.
ME, TOO.

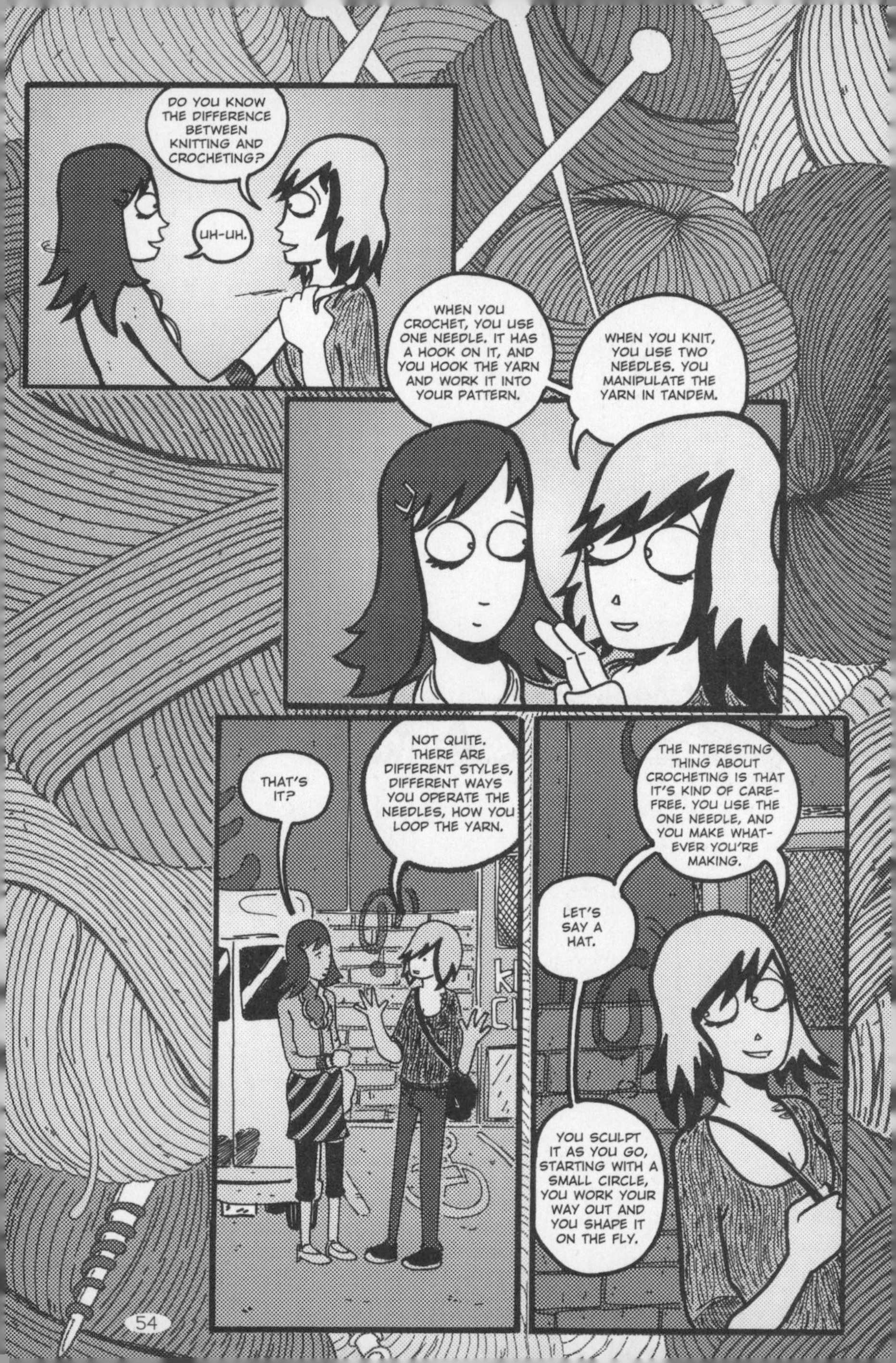

DO YOU KNOW THE DIFFERENCE BETWEEN KNITTING AND CROCHETING?
UH-UH.
WHEN YOU CROCHET, YOU USE ONE NEEDLE. IT HAS A HOOK ON IT, AND YOU HOOK THE YARN AND WORK IT INTO YOUR PATTERN.
WHEN YOU KNIT, YOU USE TWO NEEDLES. YOU MANIPULATE THE YARN IN TANDEM.
THAT'S IT?
NOT QUITE. THERE ARE DIFFERENT STYLES, DIFFERENT WAYS YOU OPERATE THE NEEDLES, HOW YOU LOOP THE YARN.
THE INTERESTING THING ABOUT CROCHETING IS THAT IT'S KIND OF CARE-FREE. YOU USE THE ONE NEEDLE, AND YOU MAKE WHAT-EVER YOU'RE MAKING.
LET'S SAY A HAT.
YOU SCULPT IT AS YOU GO, STARTING WITH A SMALL CIRCLE, YOU WORK YOUR WAY OUT AND YOU SHAPE IT ON THE FLY.

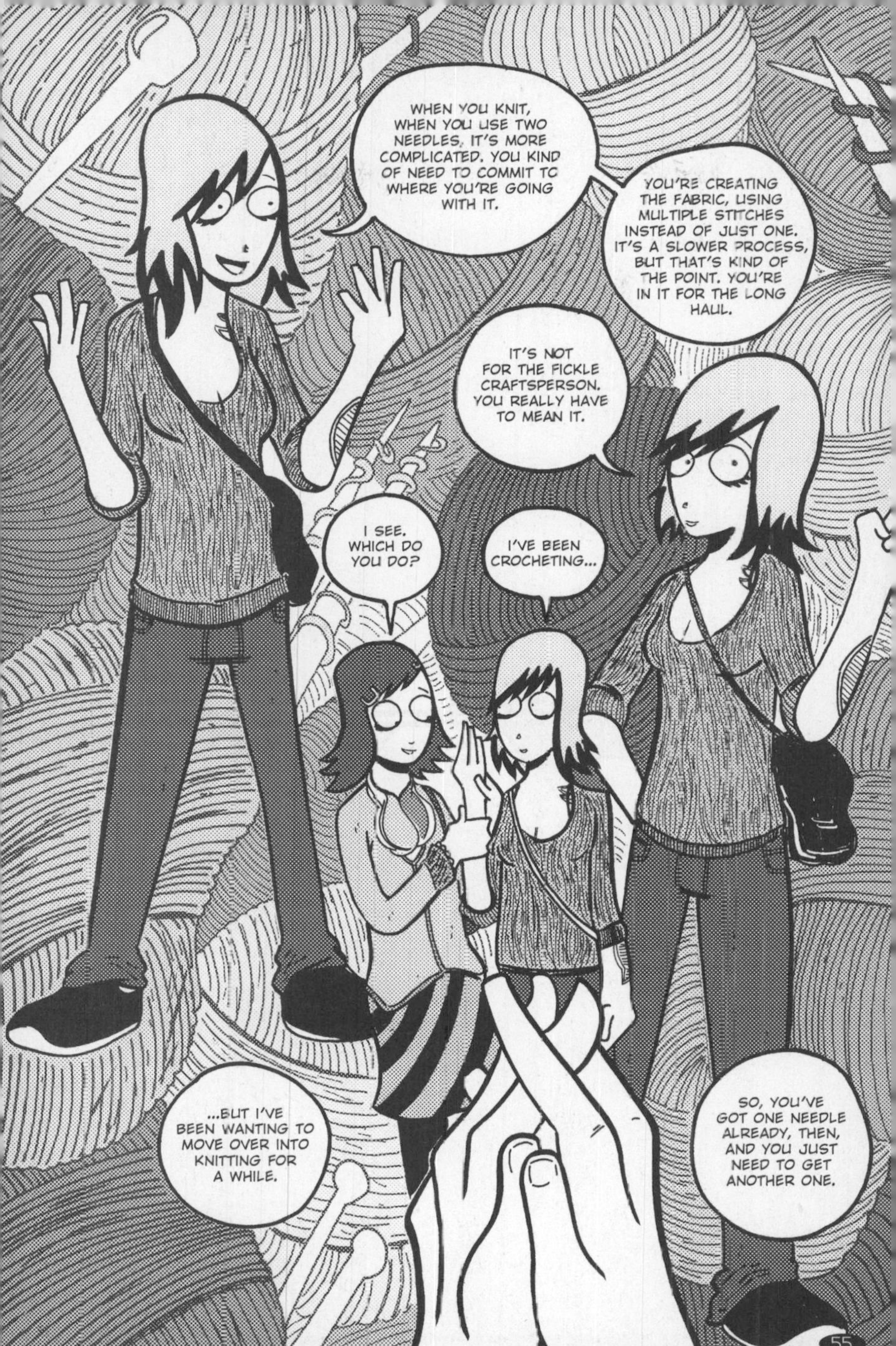
WHEN YOU KNIT, WHEN YOU USE TWO NEEDLES, IT'S MORE COMPLICATED. YOU KIND OF NEED TO COMMIT TO WHERE YOU'RE GOING WITH IT.
YOU'RE CREATING THE FABRIC, USING MULTIPLE STITCHES INSTEAD OF JUST ONE. IT'S A SLOWER PROCESS, BUT THAT'S KIND OF THE POINT. YOU'RE IN IT FOR THE LONG HAUL.
IT'S NOT FOR THE FICKLE CRAFTSPERSON. YOU REALLY HAVE TO MEAN IT.
I SEE. WHICH DO YOU DO?
I'VE BEEN CROCHETING...
...BUT I'VE BEEN WANTING TO MOVE OVER INTO KNITTING FOR A WHILE.
SO, YOU'VE GOT ONE NEEDLE ALREADY, THEN, AND YOU JUST NEED TO GET ANOTHER ONE.

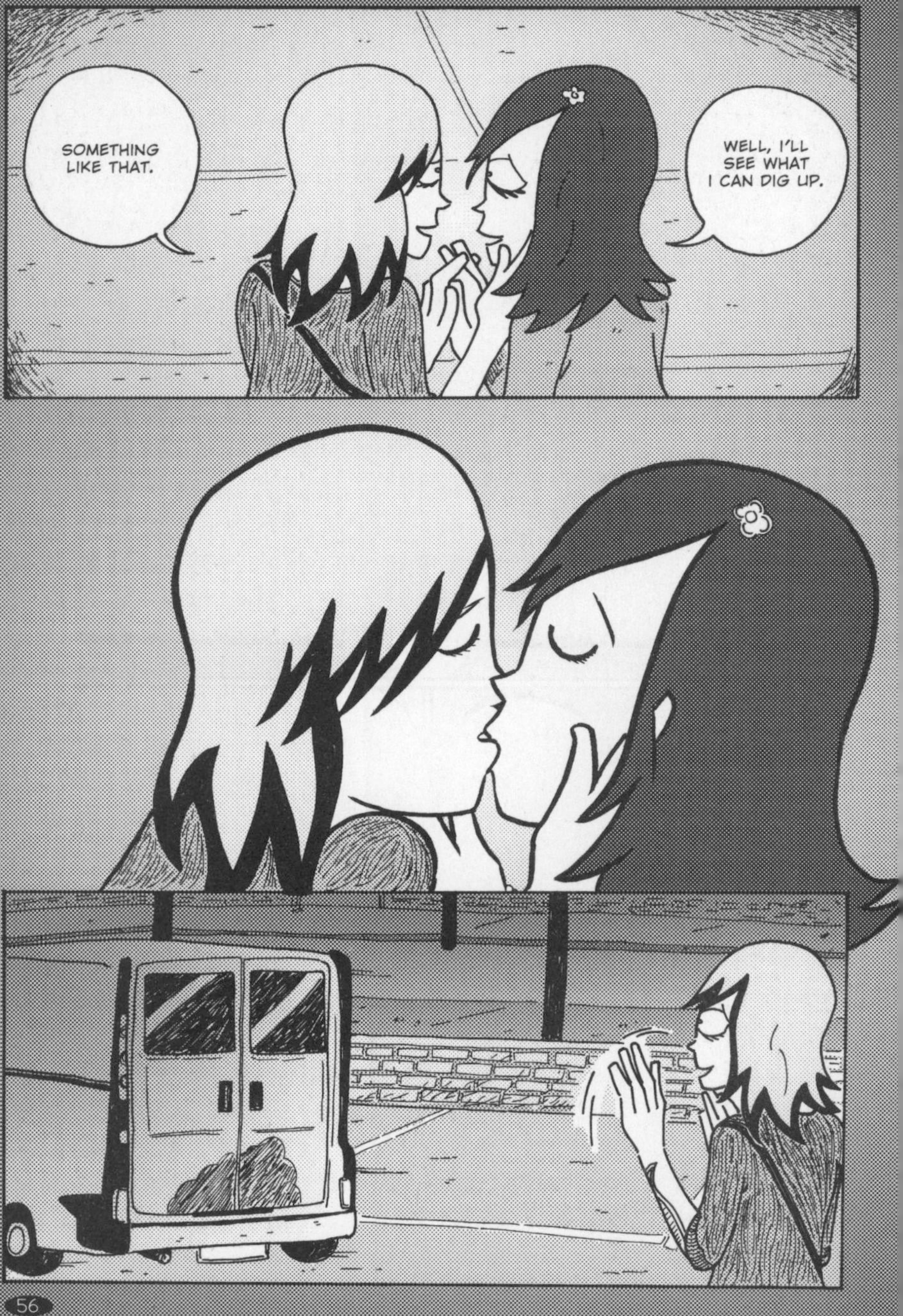
SOMETHING LIKE THAT.
WELL, I'LL SEE WHAT I CAN DIG UP.

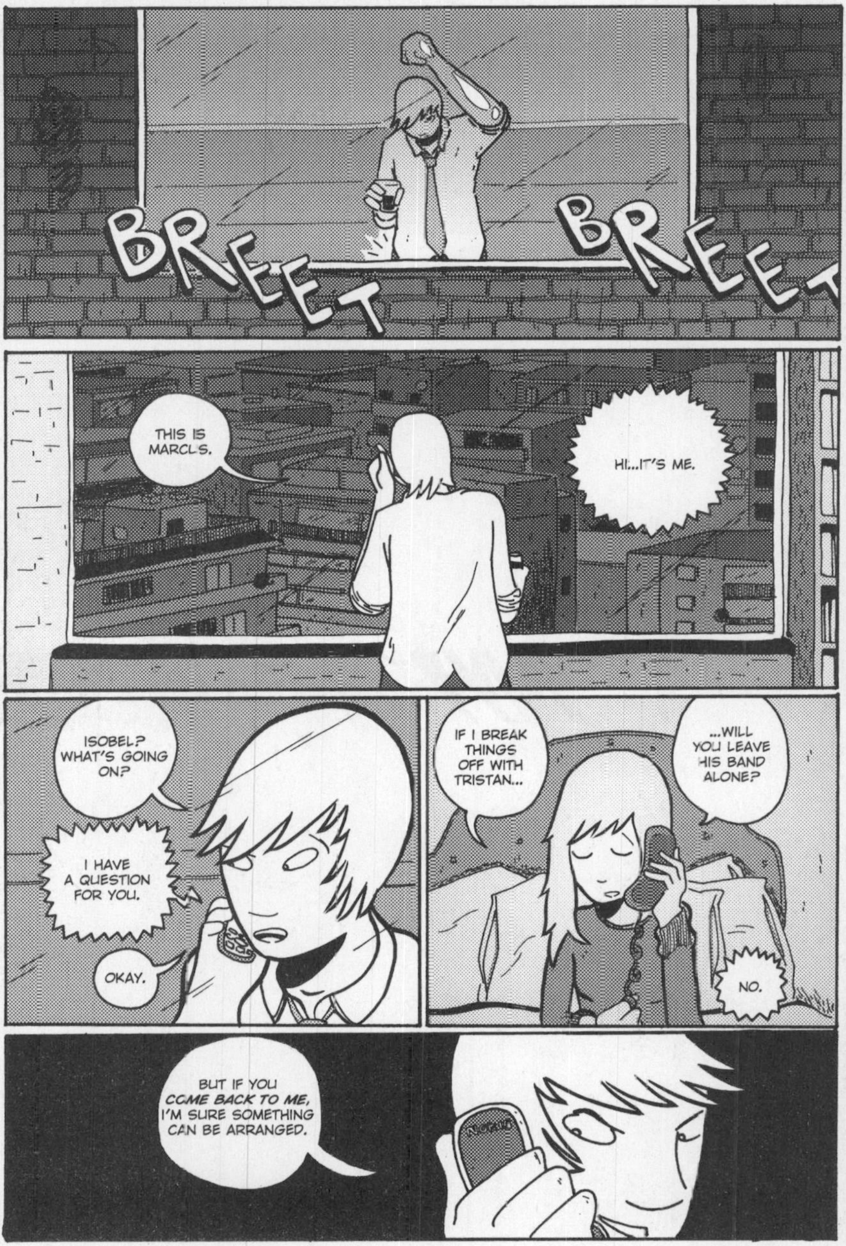
BREEET
BREEET
THIS IS MARCUS.
HI...IT'S ME.
ISOBEL? WHAT'S GOING ON?
I HAVE A QUESTION FOR YOU.
OKAY.
IF I BREAK THINGS OFF WITH TRISTAN...
...WILL YOU LEAVE HIS BAND ALONE?
NO.
BUT IF YOU *COME BACK TO ME,* I'M SURE SOMETHING CAN BE ARRANGED.

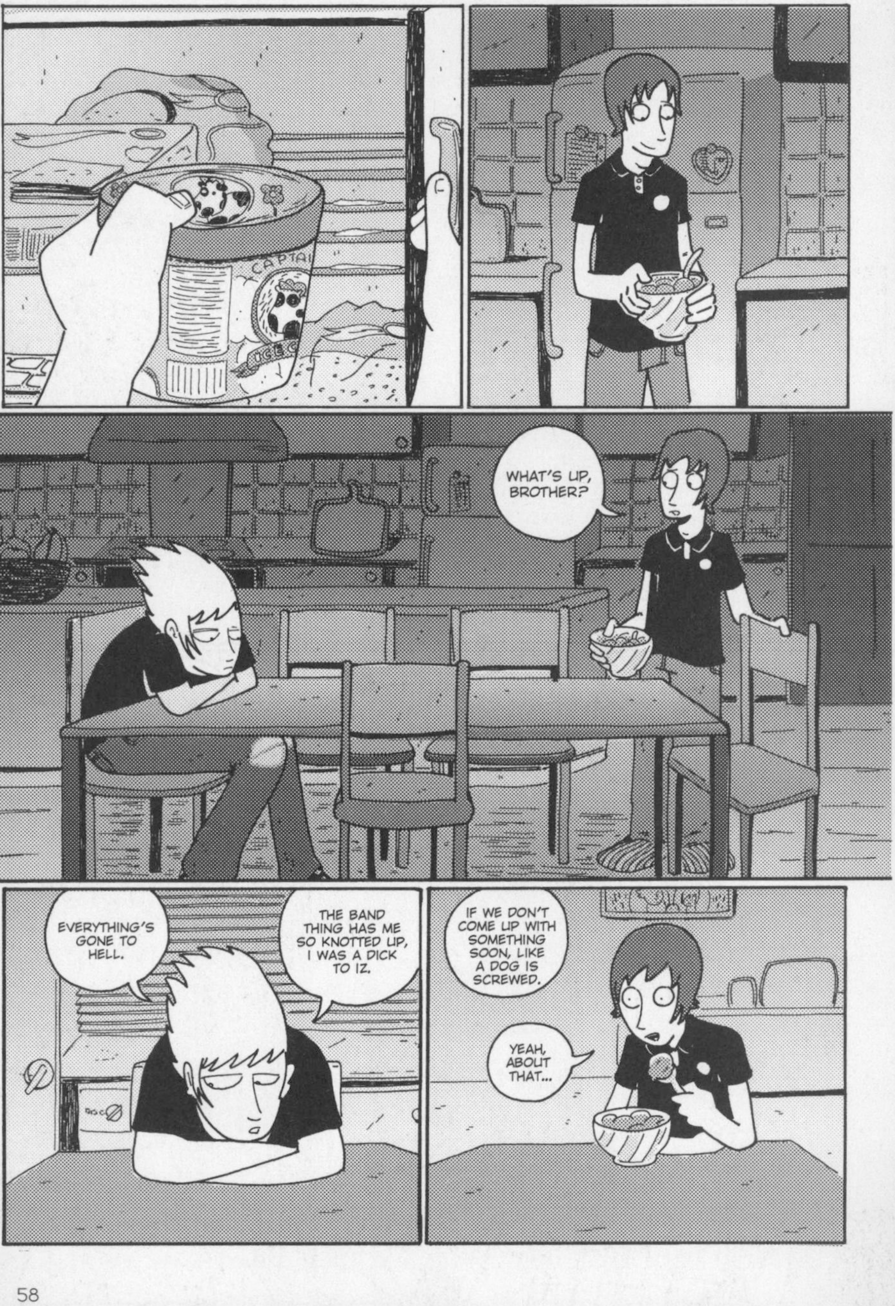
WHAT'S UP, BROTHER?
EVERYTHING'S GONE TO HELL.
THE BAND THING HAS ME SO KNOTTED UP, I WAS A DICK TO IZ.
IF WE DON'T COME UP WITH SOMETHING SOON, LIKE A DOG IS SCREWED.
YEAH, ABOUT THAT...

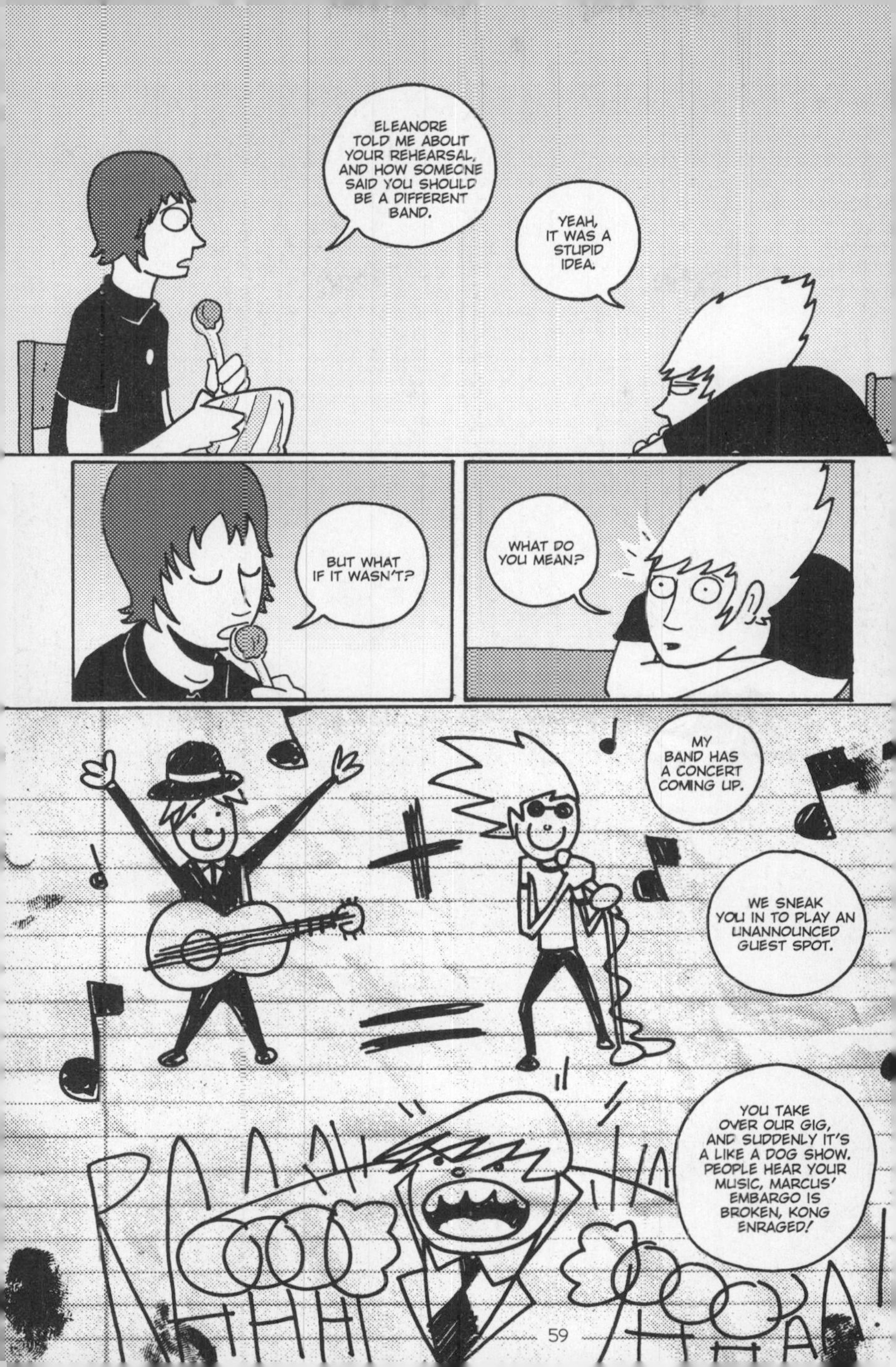
ELEANORE TOLD ME ABOUT YOUR REHEARSAL, AND HOW SOMEONE SAID YOU SHOULD BE A DIFFERENT BAND.
YEAH, IT WAS A STUPID IDEA.
BUT WHAT IF IT WASN'T?
WHAT DO YOU MEAN?
MY BAND HAS A CONCERT COMING UP.
WE SNEAK YOU IN TO PLAY AN UNANNOUNCED GUEST SPOT.
YOU TAKE OVER OUR GIG, AND SUDDENLY IT'S A LIKE A DOG SHOW. PEOPLE HEAR YOUR MUSIC, MARCUS' EMBARGO IS BROKEN, KONG ENRAGED!

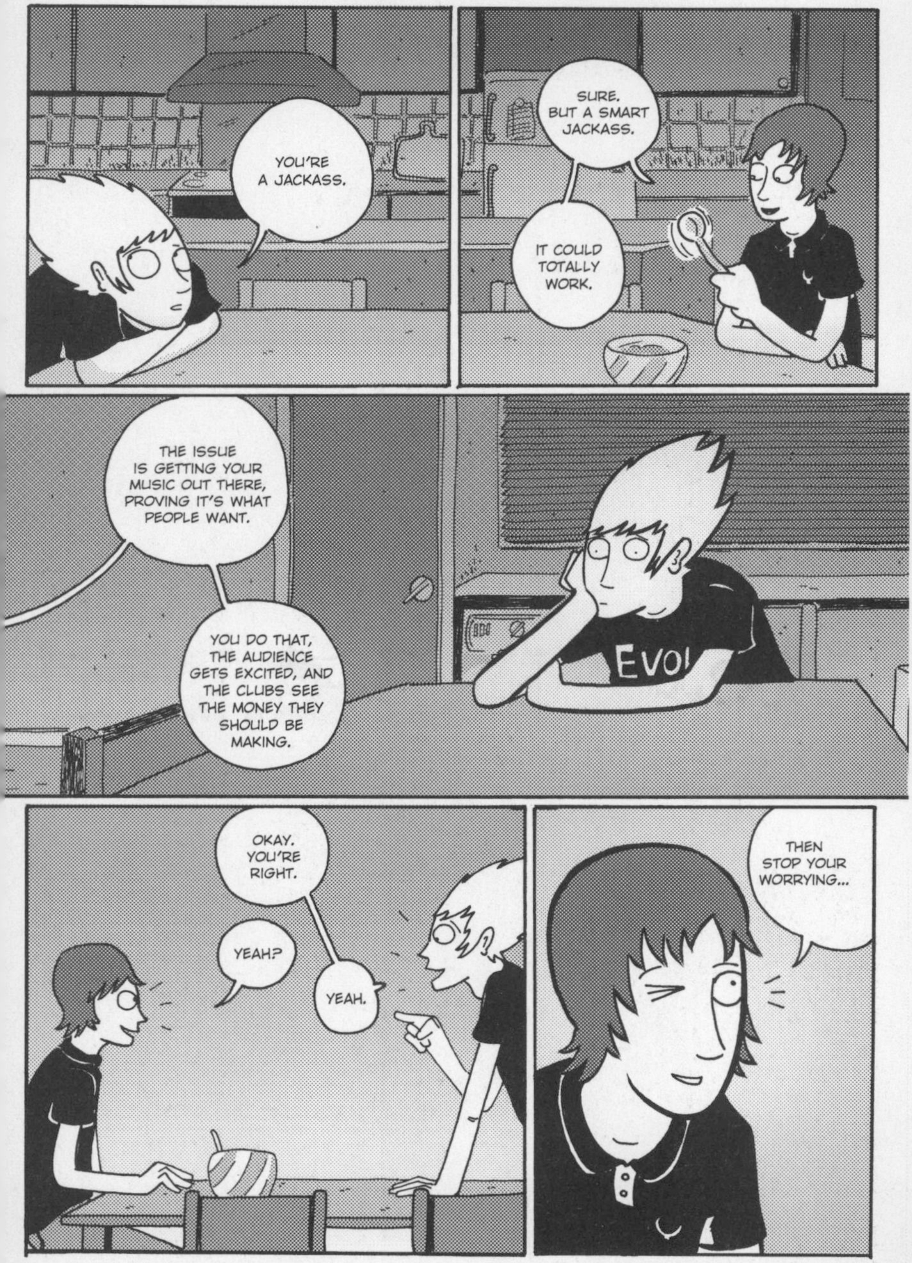
YOU'RE A JACKASS.
SURE. BUT A SMART JACKASS.
IT COULD TOTALLY WORK.
THE ISSUE IS GETTING YOUR MUSIC OUT THERE, PROVING IT'S WHAT PEOPLE WANT.
YOU DO THAT, THE AUDIENCE GETS EXCITED, AND THE CLUBS SEE THE MONEY THEY SHOULD BE MAKING.
EVOl
OKAY. YOU'RE RIGHT.
YEAH?
YEAH.
THEN STOP YOUR WORRYING...

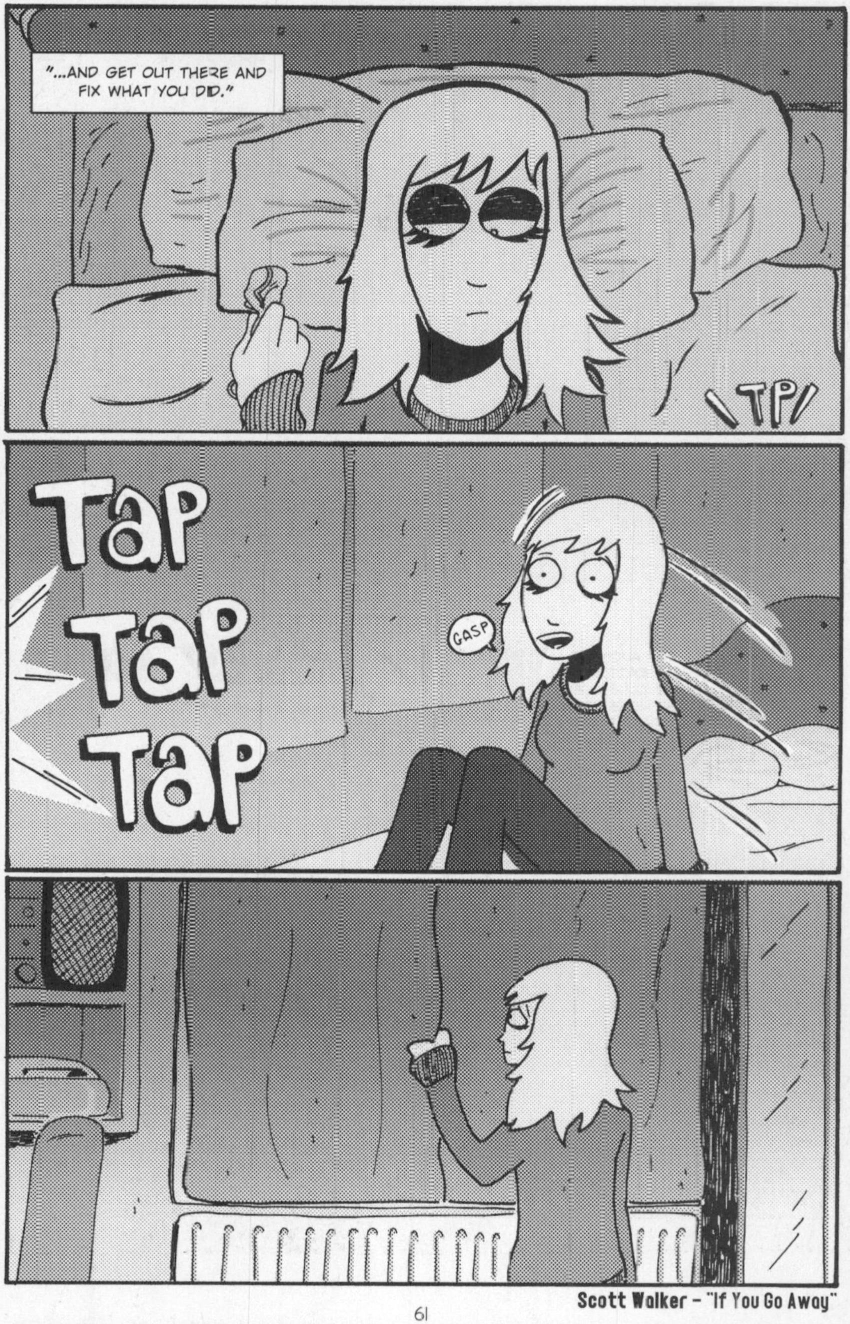
"...AND GET OUT THERE AND FIX WHAT YOU DID."
TP
Tap Tap Tap
GASP

Scott Walker - "If You Go Away"

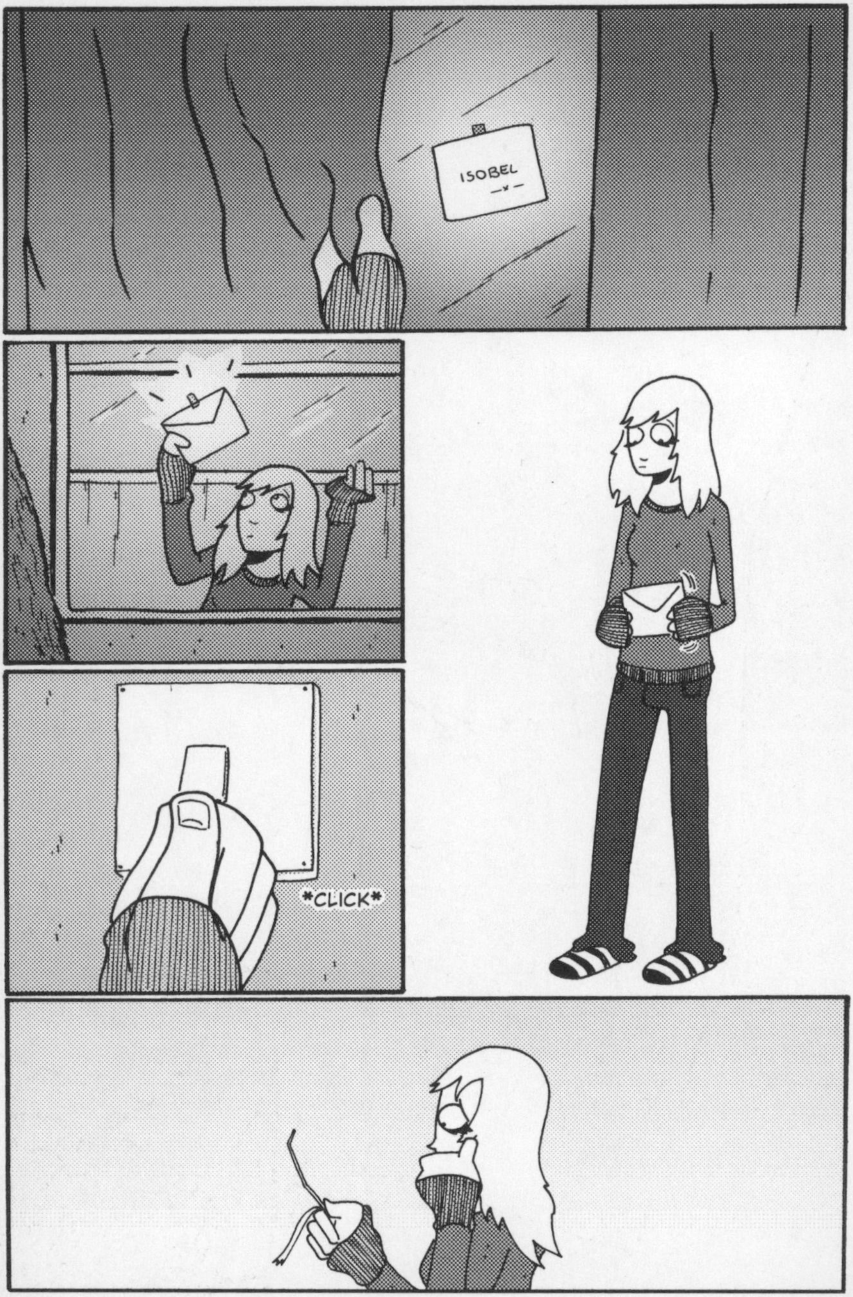
ISOBEL
—x—
CLICK

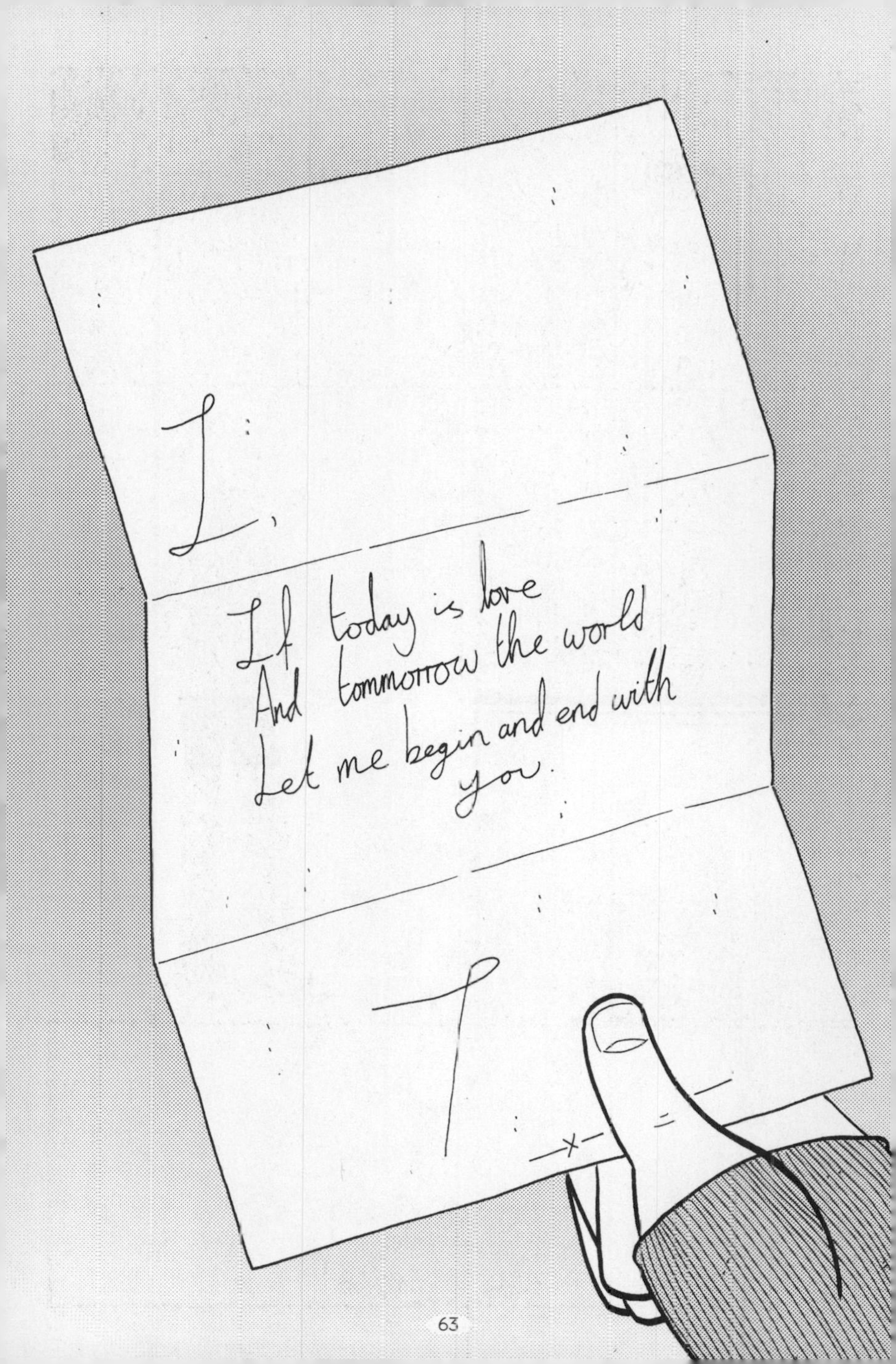
L,
If today is love
And tommorrow the world
Let me begin and end with
you.
T

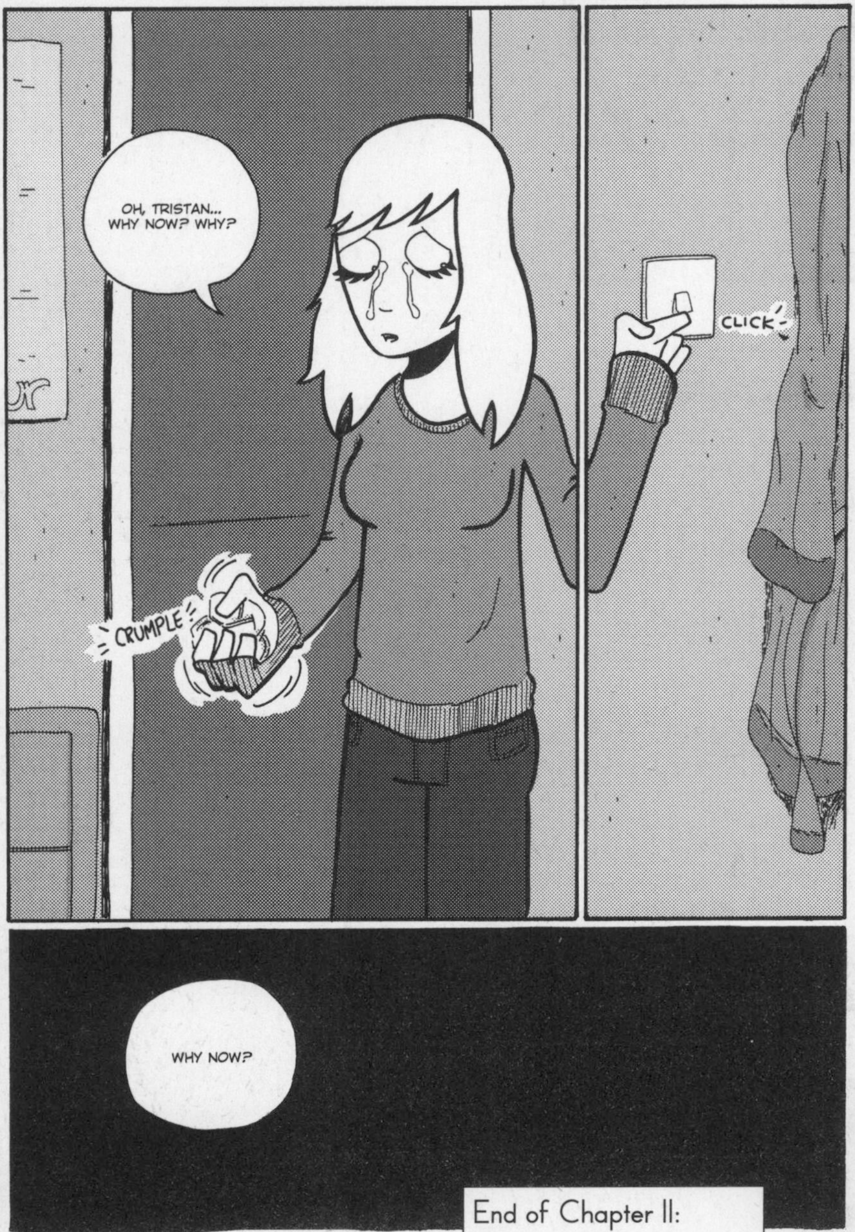
OH, TRISTAN... WHY NOW? WHY?
CRUMPLE
CLICK
WHY NOW?

End of Chapter II:
First Love Never Dies...?

Chapter 12:
They Say That Every Man Goes Blind In His Heart

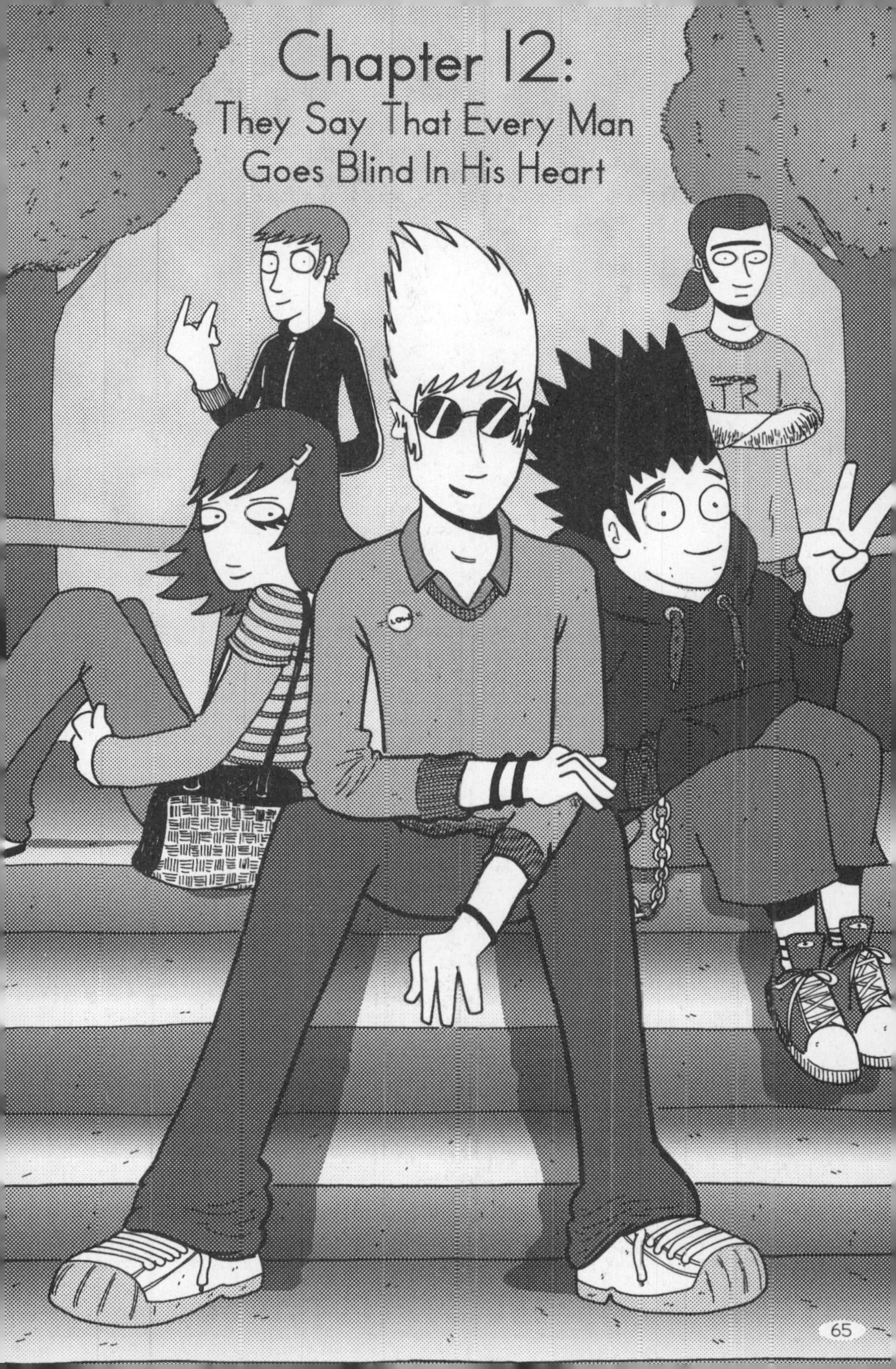
LOW

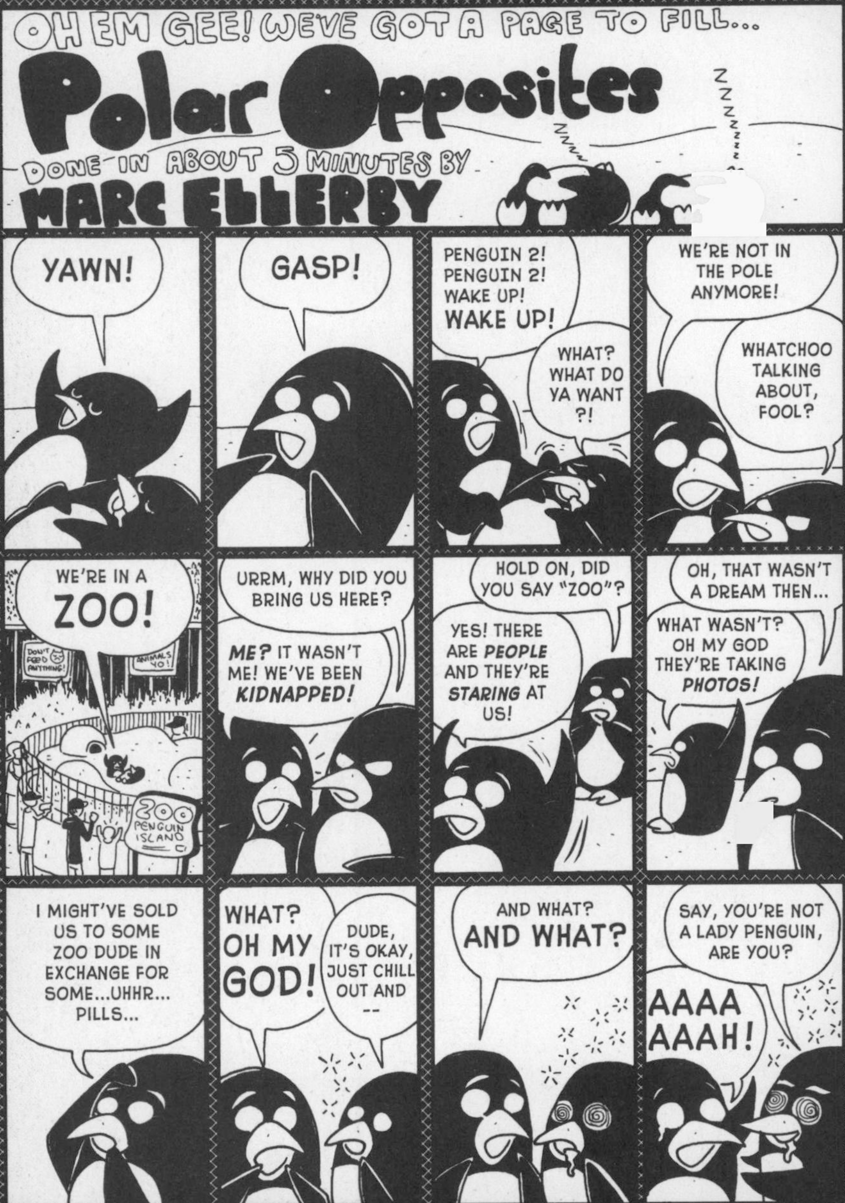
OH EM GEE! WE'VE GOT A PAGE TO FILL...
Polar Opposites
DONE IN ABOUT 5 MINUTES BY
MARC ELLERBY
ZZZZ
ZZZZZZZ
YAWN!
GASP!
PENGUIN 2! PENGUIN 2! WAKE UP! WAKE UP!
WHAT? WHAT DO YA WANT ?!
WE'RE NOT IN THE POLE ANYMORE!
WHATCHOO TALKING ABOUT, FOOL?
WE'RE IN A ZOO!
DON'T FEED ANYTHING!
ANIMALS YO!
ZOO PENGUIN ISLAND
URRM, WHY DID YOU BRING US HERE?
ME? IT WASN'T ME! WE'VE BEEN KIDNAPPED!
HOLD ON, DID YOU SAY "ZOO"?
YES! THERE ARE PEOPLE AND THEY'RE STARING AT US!
OH, THAT WASN'T A DREAM THEN...
WHAT WASN'T? OH MY GOD THEY'RE TAKING PHOTOS!
I MIGHT'VE SOLD US TO SOME ZOO DUDE IN EXCHANGE FOR SOME...UHHR... PILLS...
WHAT? OH MY GOD!
DUDE, IT'S OKAY, JUST CHILL OUT AND --
AND WHAT? AND WHAT?
SAY, YOU'RE NOT A LADY PENGUIN, ARE YOU?
AAAA AAAH!

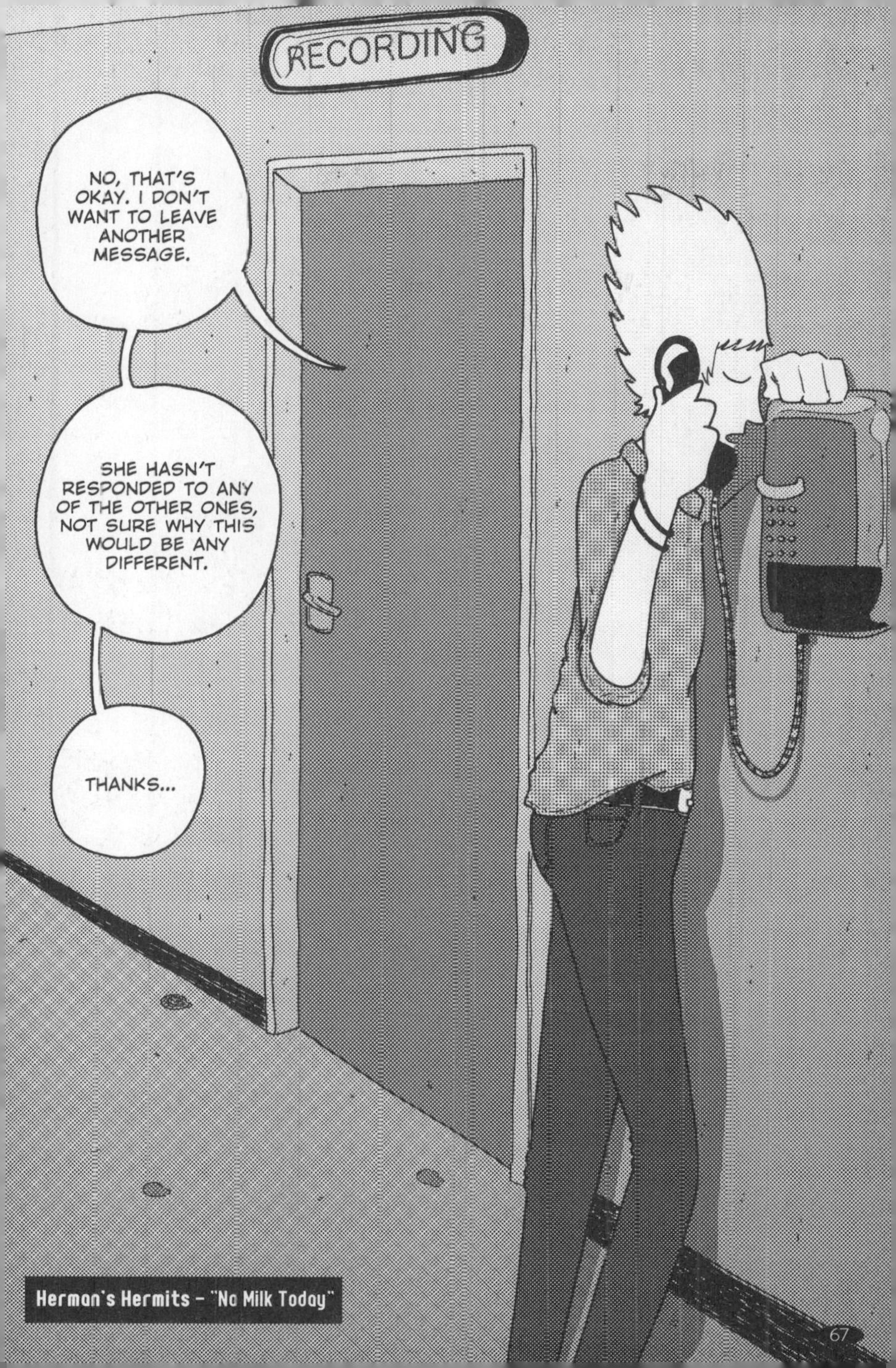

RECORDING
NO, THAT'S OKAY. I DON'T WANT TO LEAVE ANOTHER MESSAGE.
SHE HASN'T RESPONDED TO ANY OF THE OTHER ONES, NOT SURE WHY THIS WOULD BE ANY DIFFERENT.
THANKS...
Herman's Hermits - "No Milk Today"

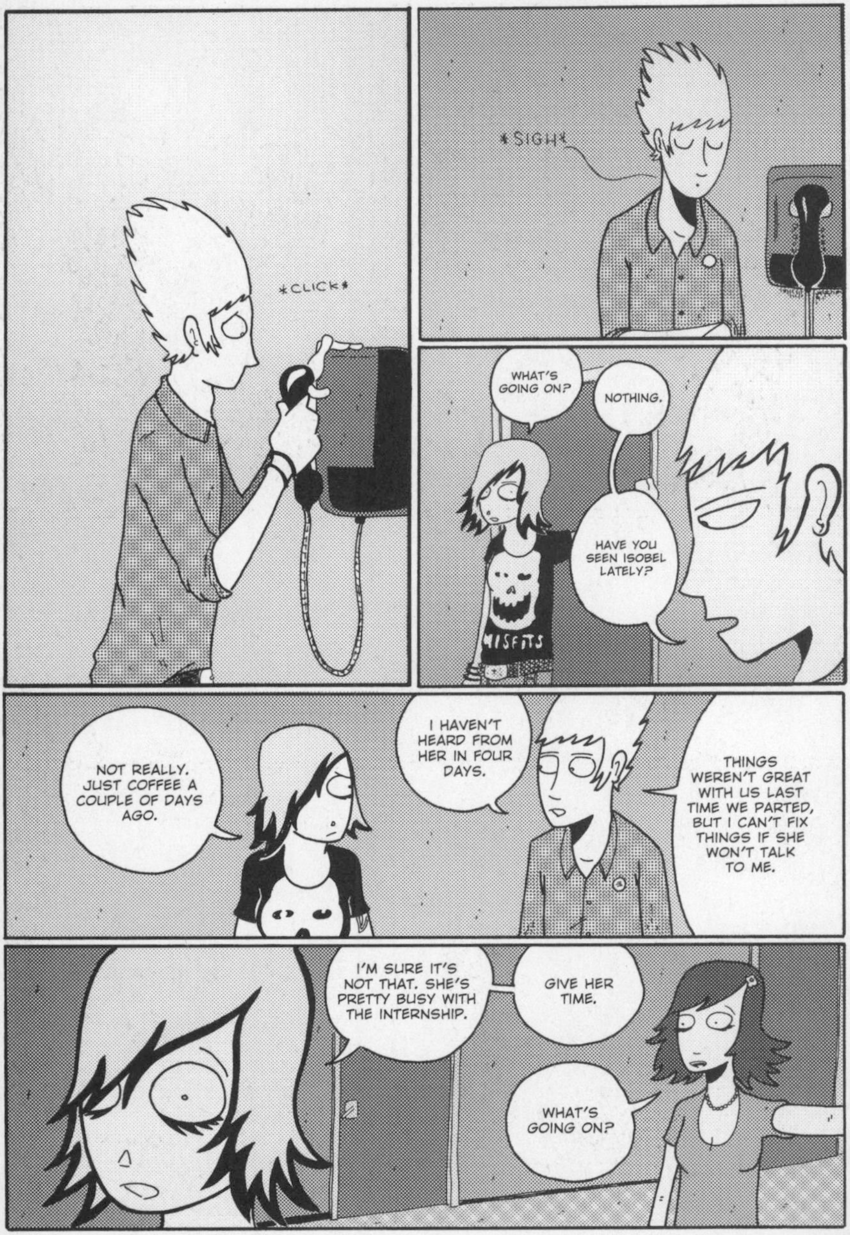
CLICK
SIGH
WHAT'S GOING ON?
NOTHING.
HAVE YOU SEEN ISOBEL LATELY?
MISFITS
NOT REALLY. JUST COFFEE A COUPLE OF DAYS AGO.
I HAVEN'T HEARD FROM HER IN FOUR DAYS.
THINGS WEREN'T GREAT WITH US LAST TIME WE PARTED, BUT I CAN'T FIX THINGS IF SHE WON'T TALK TO ME.
I'M SURE IT'S NOT THAT. SHE'S PRETTY BUSY WITH THE INTERNSHIP.
GIVE HER TIME.
WHAT'S GOING ON?

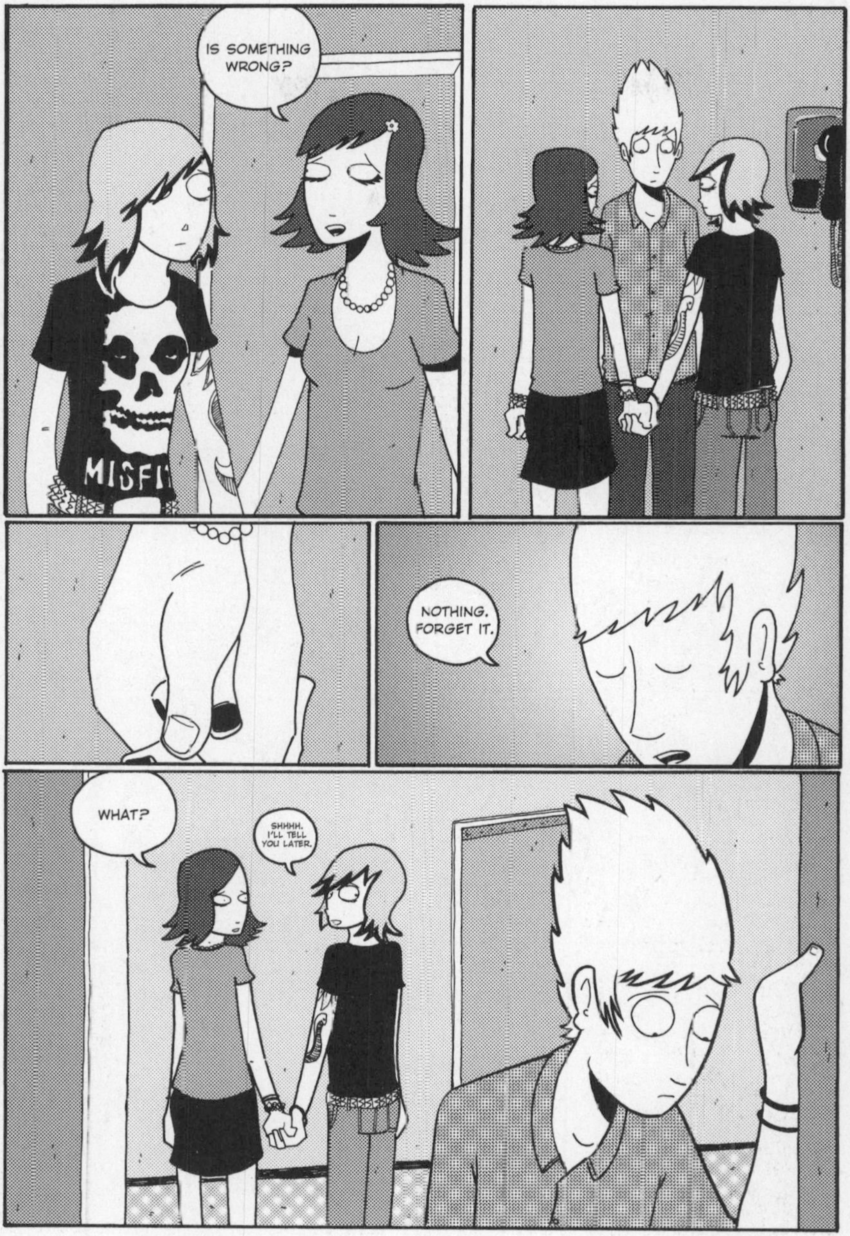
IS SOMETHING WRONG?
NOTHING. FORGET IT.
WHAT?
SHHHH. I'LL TELL YOU LATER.

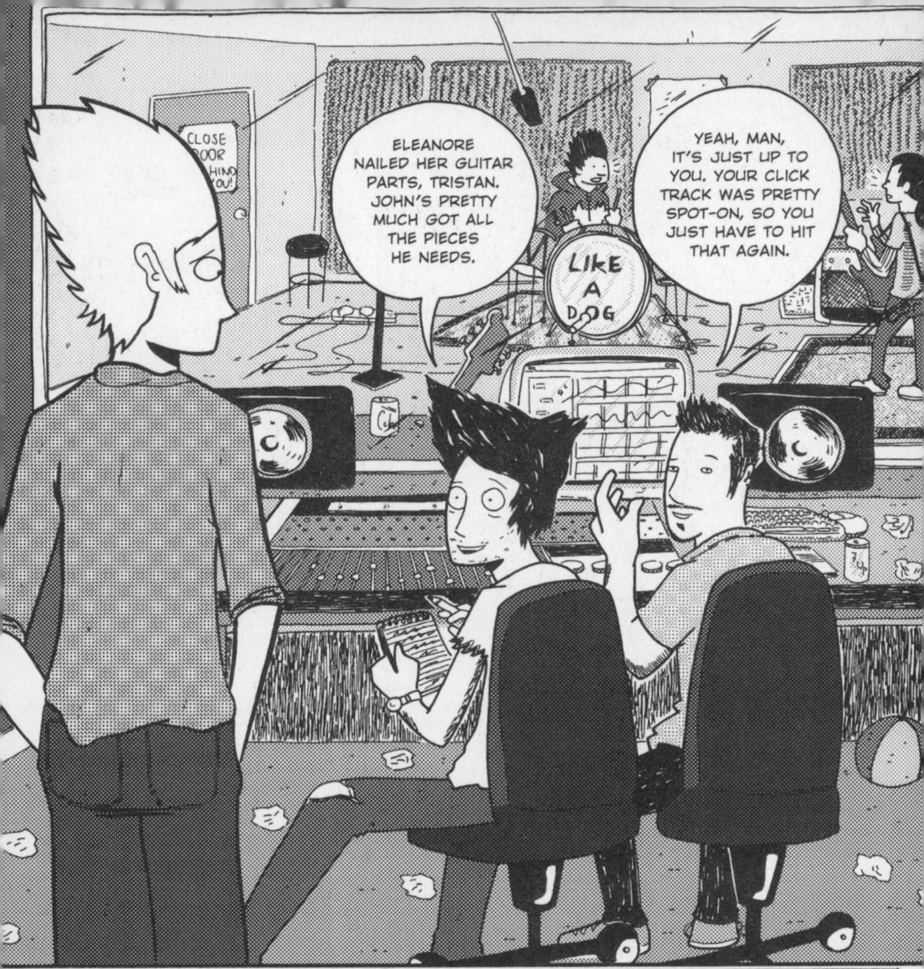
CLOSE
LIKE A DOG
ELEANORE NAILED HER GUITAR PARTS, TRISTAN. JOHN'S PRETTY MUCH GOT ALL THE PIECES HE NEEDS.
YEAH, MAN, IT'S JUST UP TO YOU. YOUR CLICK TRACK WAS PRETTY SPOT-ON, SO YOU JUST HAVE TO HIT THAT AGAIN.

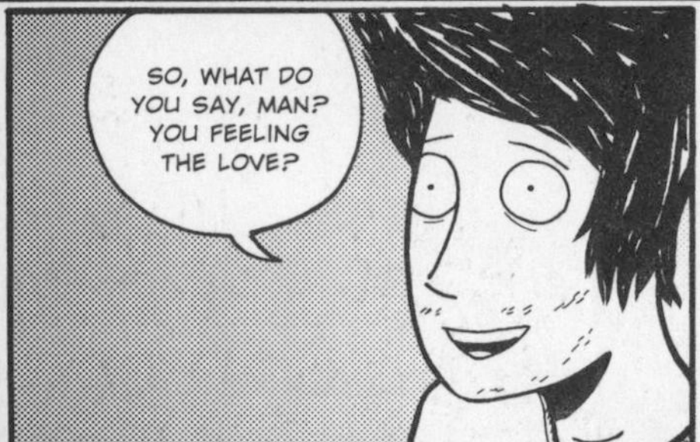
SO, WHAT DO YOU SAY, MAN? YOU FEELING THE LOVE?

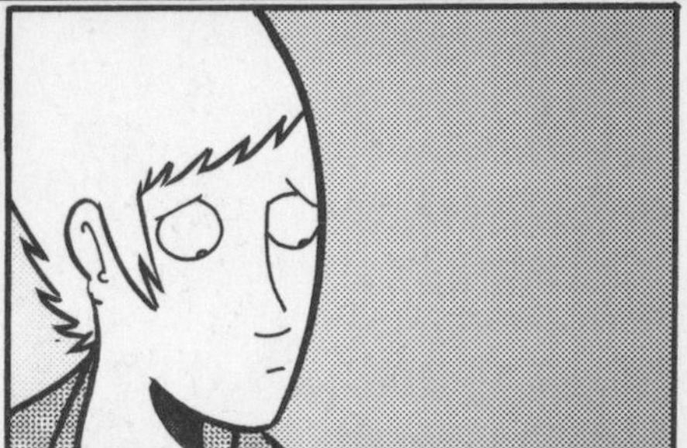
"ISOBEL!"

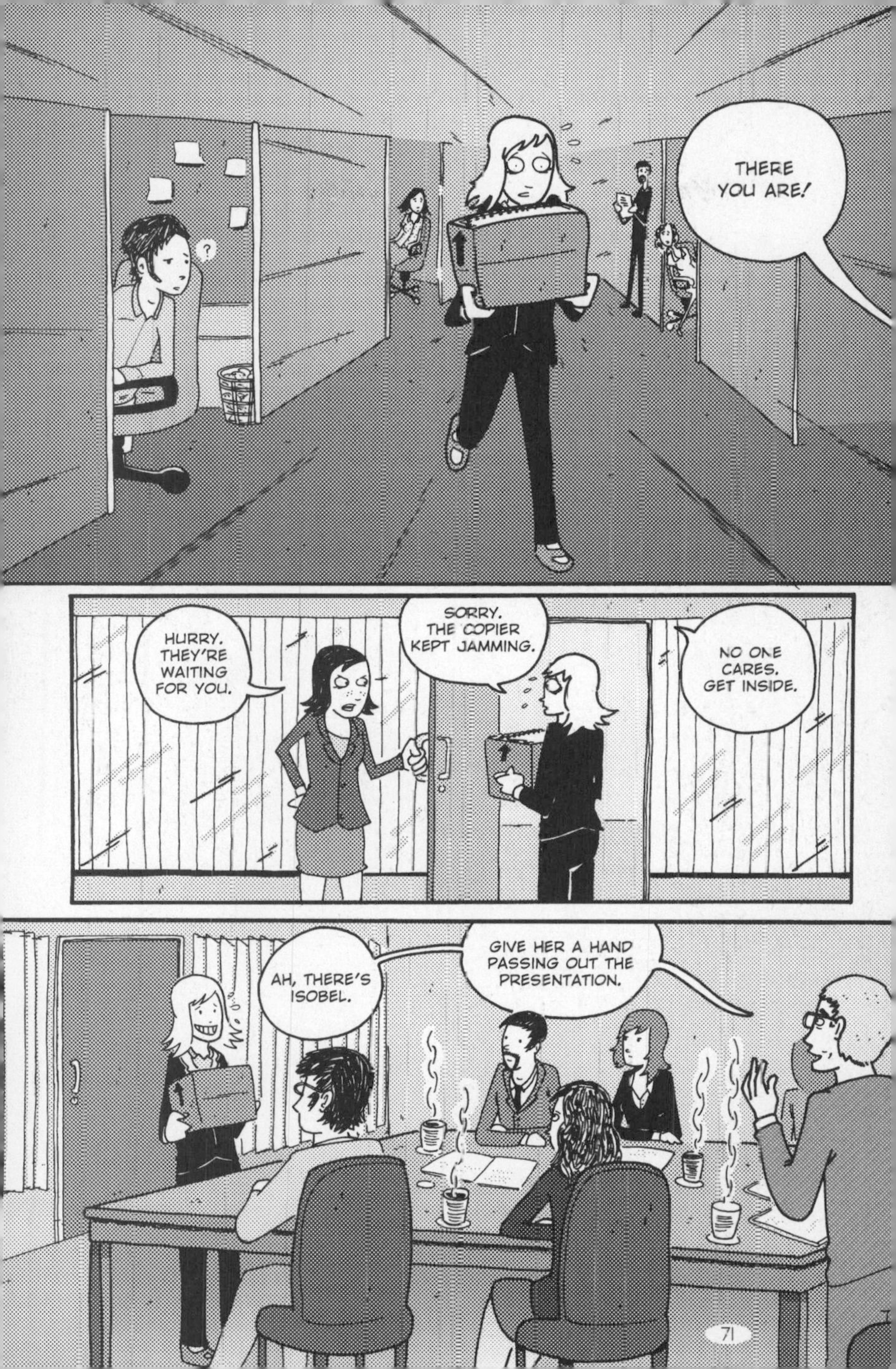
THERE YOU ARE!
HURRY. THEY'RE WAITING FOR YOU.
SORRY. THE COPIER KEPT JAMMING.
NO ONE CARES. GET INSIDE.
AH, THERE'S ISOBEL.
GIVE HER A HAND PASSING OUT THE PRESENTATION.

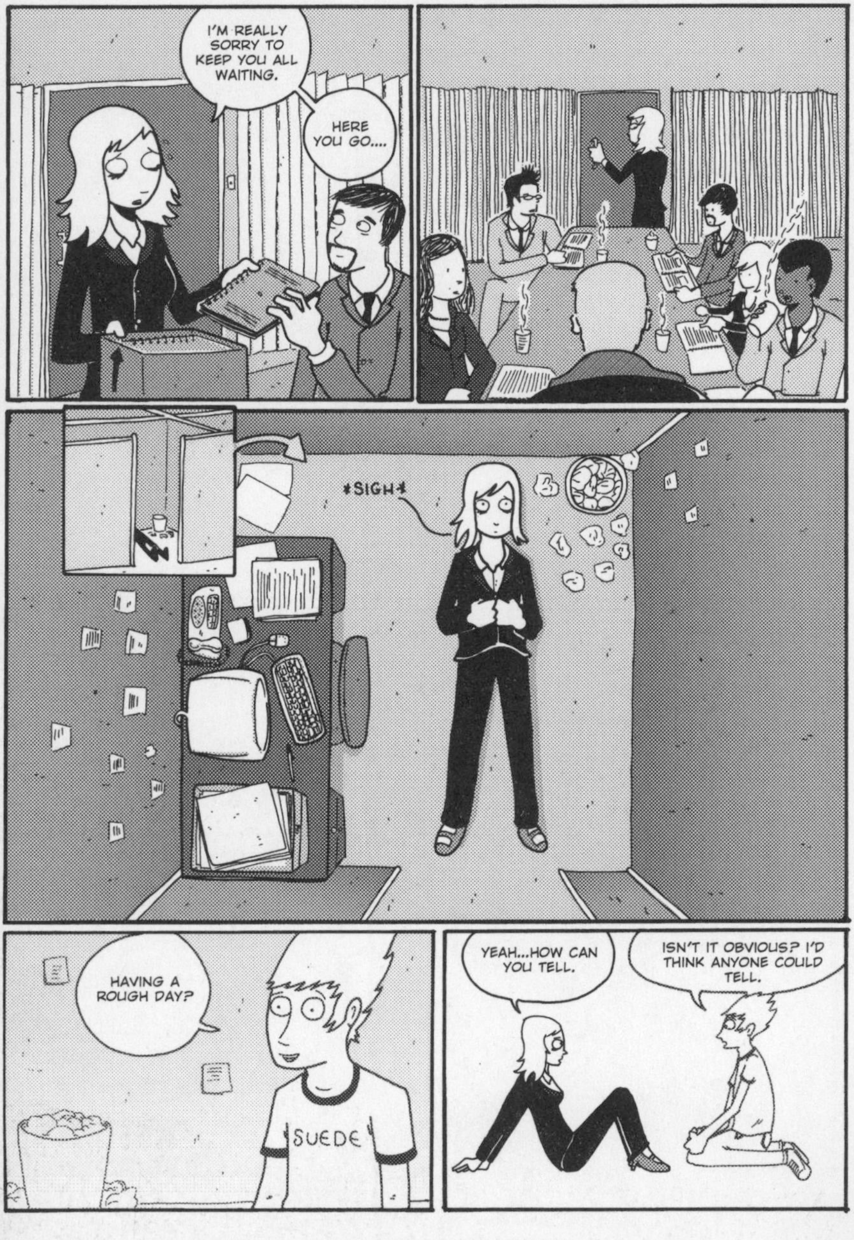
I'M REALLY SORRY TO KEEP YOU ALL WAITING.
HERE YOU GO....
SIGH
HAVING A ROUGH DAY?
SUEDE
YEAH...HOW CAN YOU TELL.
ISN'T IT OBVIOUS? I'D THINK ANYONE COULD TELL.

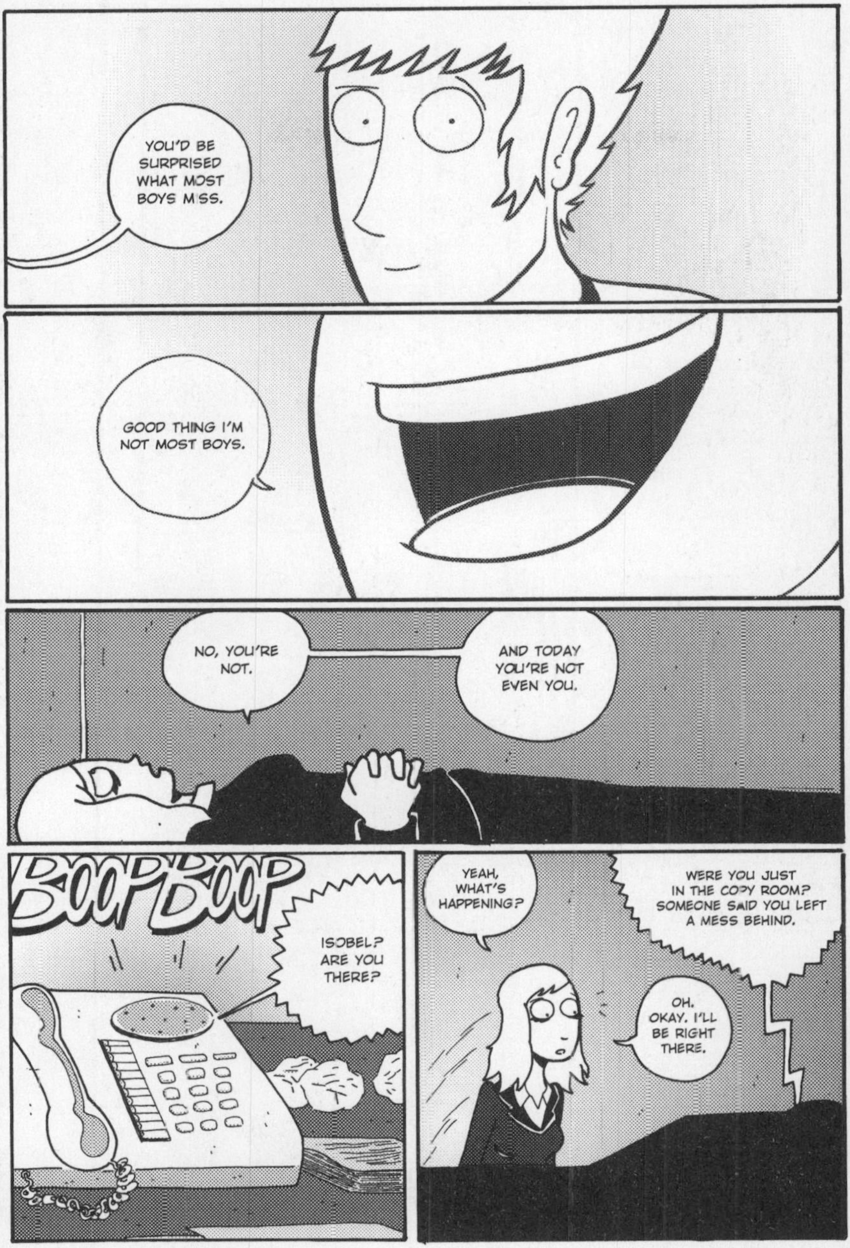

YOU'D BE SURPRISED WHAT MOST BOYS MISS.
GOOD THING I'M NOT MOST BOYS.
NO, YOU'RE NOT.
AND TODAY YOU'RE NOT EVEN YOU.
BOOP BOOP
ISOBEL? ARE YOU THERE?
YEAH, WHAT'S HAPPENING?
WERE YOU JUST IN THE COPY ROOM? SOMEONE SAID YOU LEFT A MESS BEHIND.
OH. OKAY. I'LL BE RIGHT THERE.

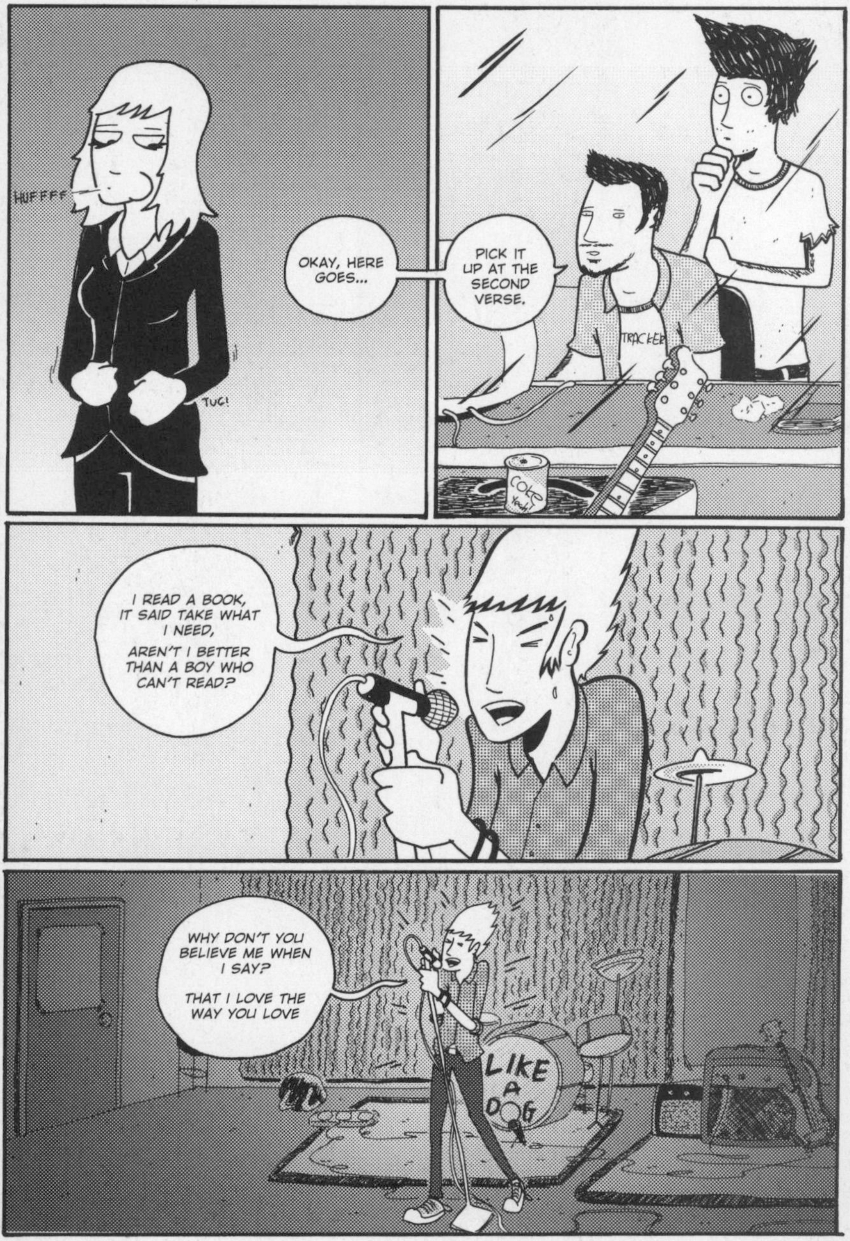
HUFFFF
TUG!
OKAY, HERE GOES...
PICK IT UP AT THE SECOND VERSE.
TRACKER
COKE
I READ A BOOK, IT SAID TAKE WHAT I NEED, ARE'N'T I BETTER THAN A BOY WHO CAN'T READ?
WHY DON'T YOU BELIEVE ME WHEN I SAY? THAT I LOVE THE WAY YOU LOVE
LIKE A DOG

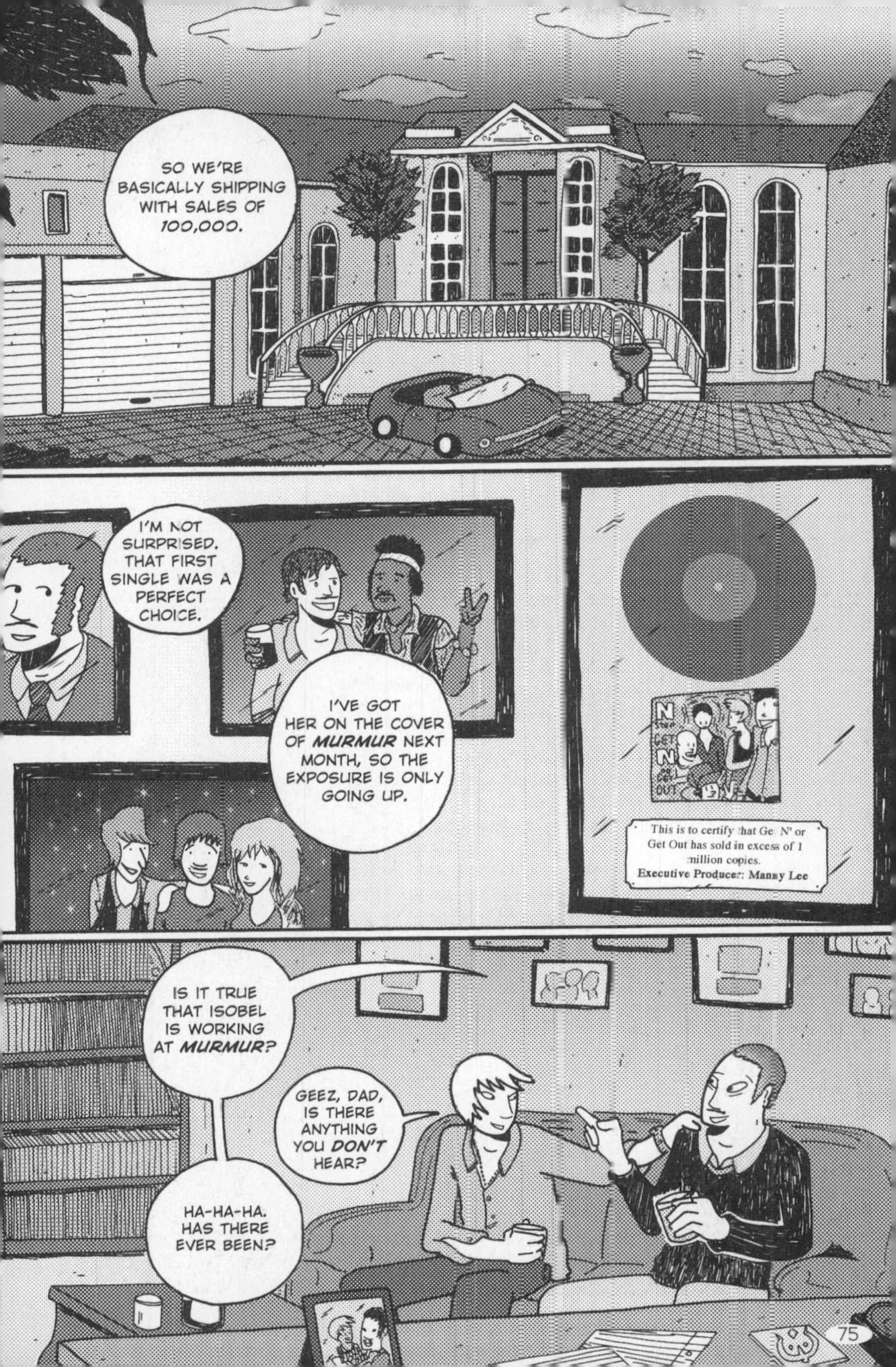
SO WE'RE BASICALLY SHIPPING WITH SALES OF *100,000.*
I'M NOT SURPRISED. THAT FIRST SINGLE WAS A PERFECT CHOICE.
I'VE GOT HER ON THE COVER OF ***MURMUR*** NEXT MONTH, SO THE EXPOSURE IS ONLY GOING UP.
This is to certify that Get N' or Get Out has sold in excess of 1 million copies.
Executive Producer: Manny Lee
IS IT TRUE THAT ISOBEL IS WORKING AT ***MURMUR?***
GEEZ, DAD, IS THERE ANYTHING YOU ***DON'T*** HEAR?
HA-HA-HA. HAS THERE EVER BEEN?

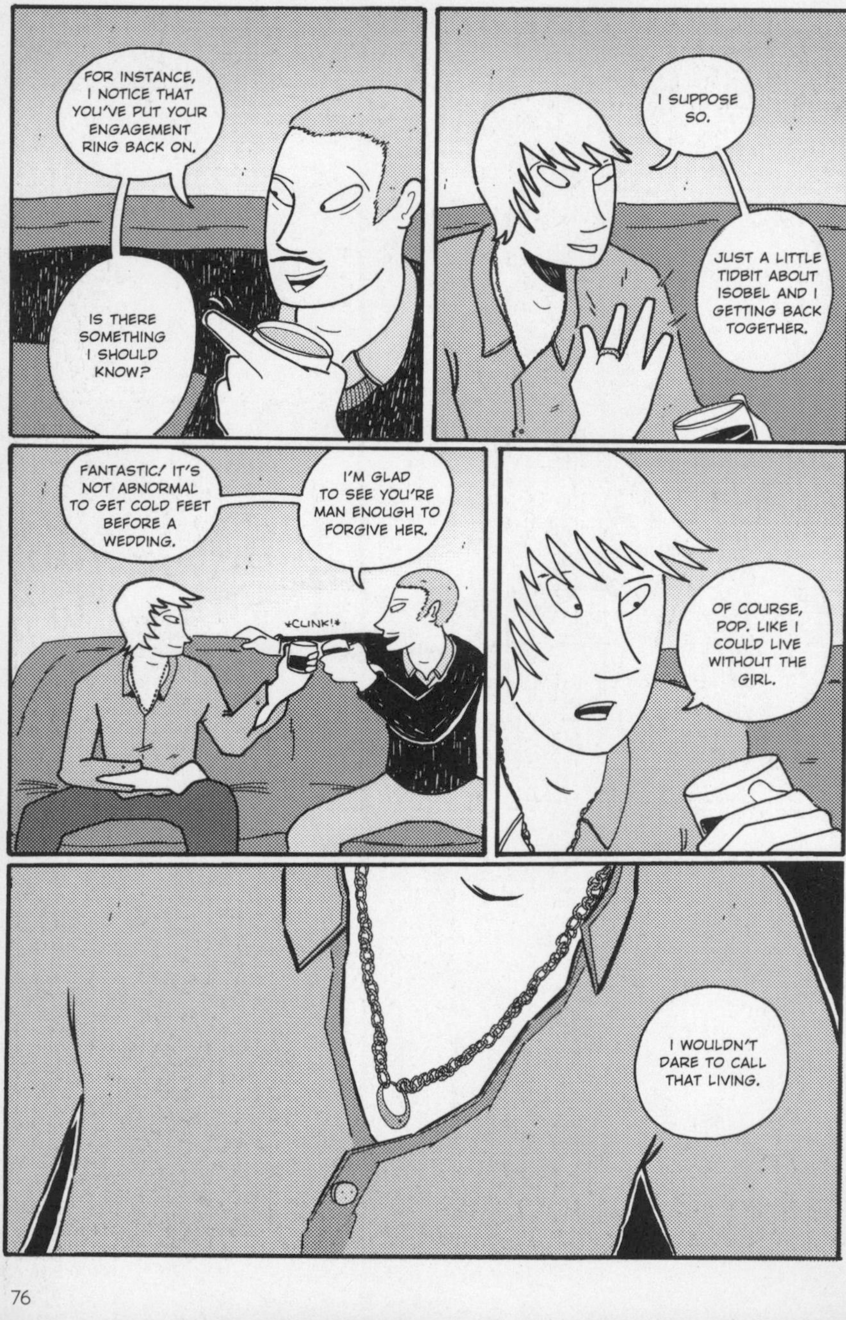
FOR INSTANCE, I NOTICE THAT YOU'VE PUT YOUR ENGAGEMENT RING BACK ON.
IS THERE SOMETHING I SHOULD KNOW?
I SUPPOSE SO.
JUST A LITTLE TIDBIT ABOUT ISOBEL AND I GETTING BACK TOGETHER.
FANTASTIC! IT'S NOT ABNORMAL TO GET COLD FEET BEFORE A WEDDING.
I'M GLAD TO SEE YOU'RE MAN ENOUGH TO FORGIVE HER.
CLINK!
OF COURSE, POP. LIKE I COULD LIVE WITHOUT THE GIRL.
I WOULDN'T DARE TO CALL THAT LIVING.

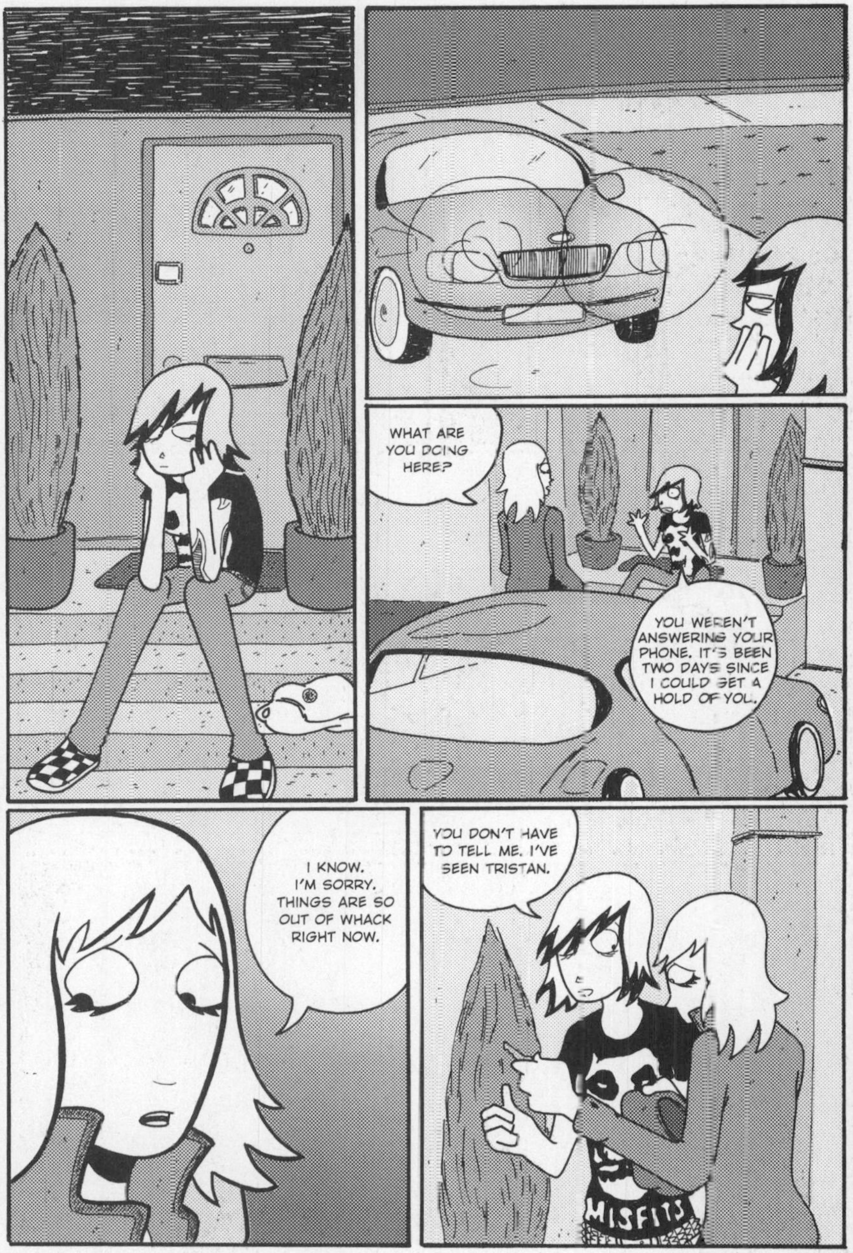
WHAT ARE YOU DOING HERE?
YOU WEREN'T ANSWERING YOUR PHONE. IT'S BEEN TWO DAYS SINCE I COULD GET A HOLD OF YOU.
I KNOW. I'M SORRY. THINGS ARE SO OUT OF WHACK RIGHT NOW.
YOU DON'T HAVE TO TELL ME. I'VE SEEN TRISTAN.
MISFITS

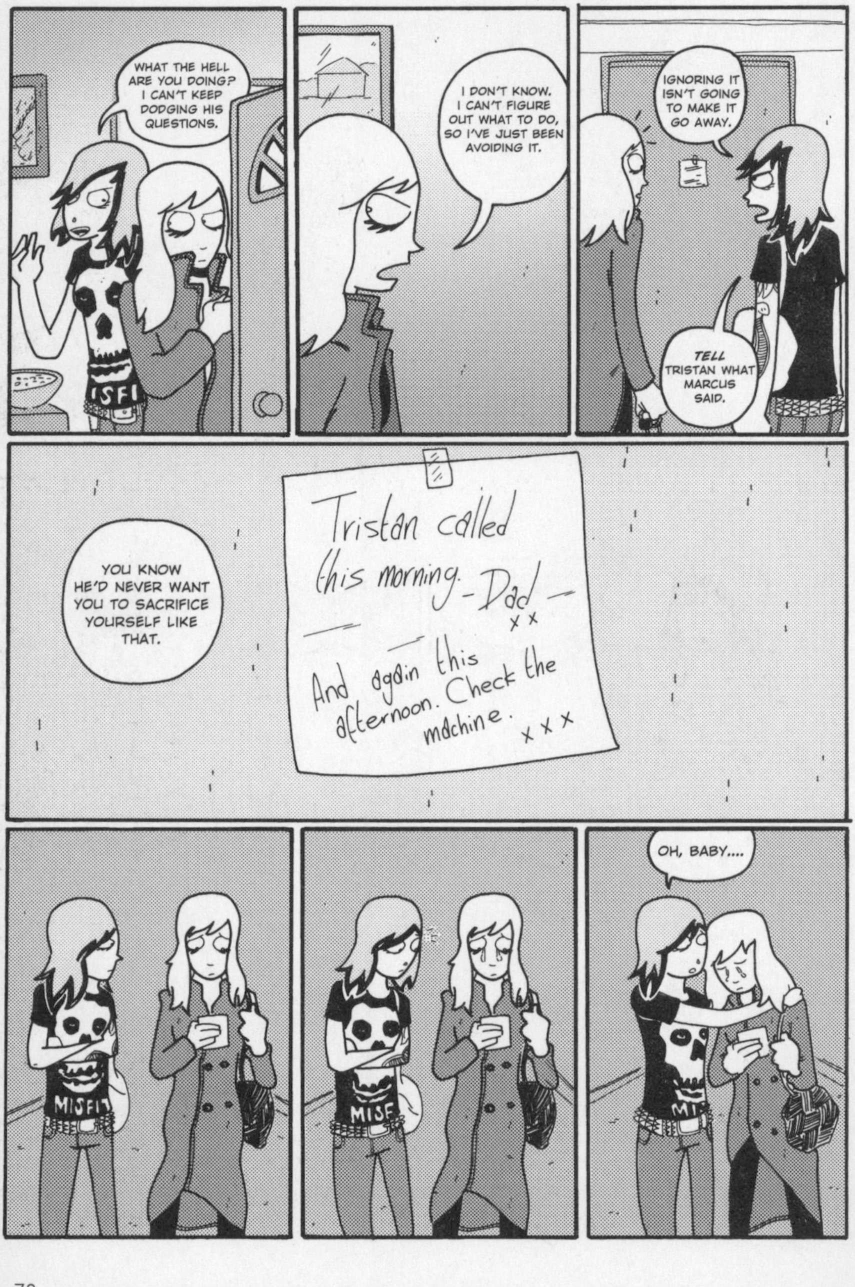
WHAT THE HELL ARE YOU DOING? I CAN'T KEEP DODGING HIS QUESTIONS.
I DON'T KNOW. I CAN'T FIGURE OUT WHAT TO DO, SO I'VE JUST BEEN AVOIDING IT.
IGNORING IT ISN'T GOING TO MAKE IT GO AWAY.
TELL TRISTAN WHAT MARCUS SAID.
YOU KNOW HE'D NEVER WANT YOU TO SACRIFICE YOURSELF LIKE THAT.
Tristan called this morning. -Dad xx
And again this afternoon. Check the machine. xxx
OH, BABY....

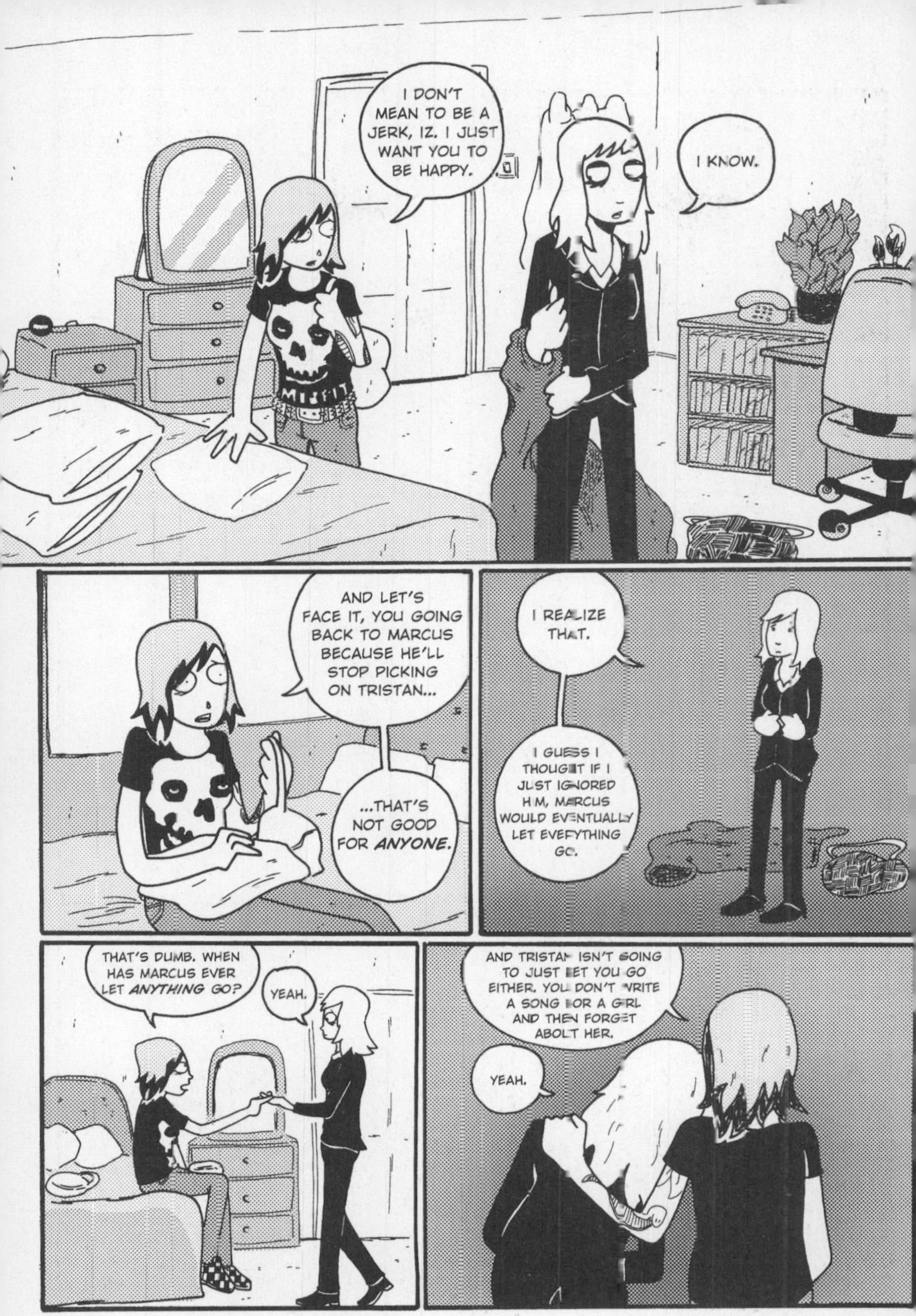
I DON'T MEAN TO BE A JERK, IZ. I JUST WANT YOU TO BE HAPPY.
I KNOW.
AND LET'S FACE IT, YOU GOING BACK TO MARCUS BECAUSE HE'LL STOP PICKING ON TRISTAN...
...THAT'S NOT GOOD FOR *ANYONE*.
I REALIZE THAT.
I GUESS I THOUGHT IF I JUST IGNORED HIM, MARCUS WOULD EVENTUALLY LET EVERYTHING GO.
THAT'S DUMB. WHEN HAS MARCUS EVER LET *ANYTHING* GO?
YEAH.
AND TRISTAN ISN'T GOING TO JUST LET YOU GO EITHER. YOU DON'T WRITE A SONG FOR A GIRL AND THEN FORGET ABOUT HER.
YEAH.

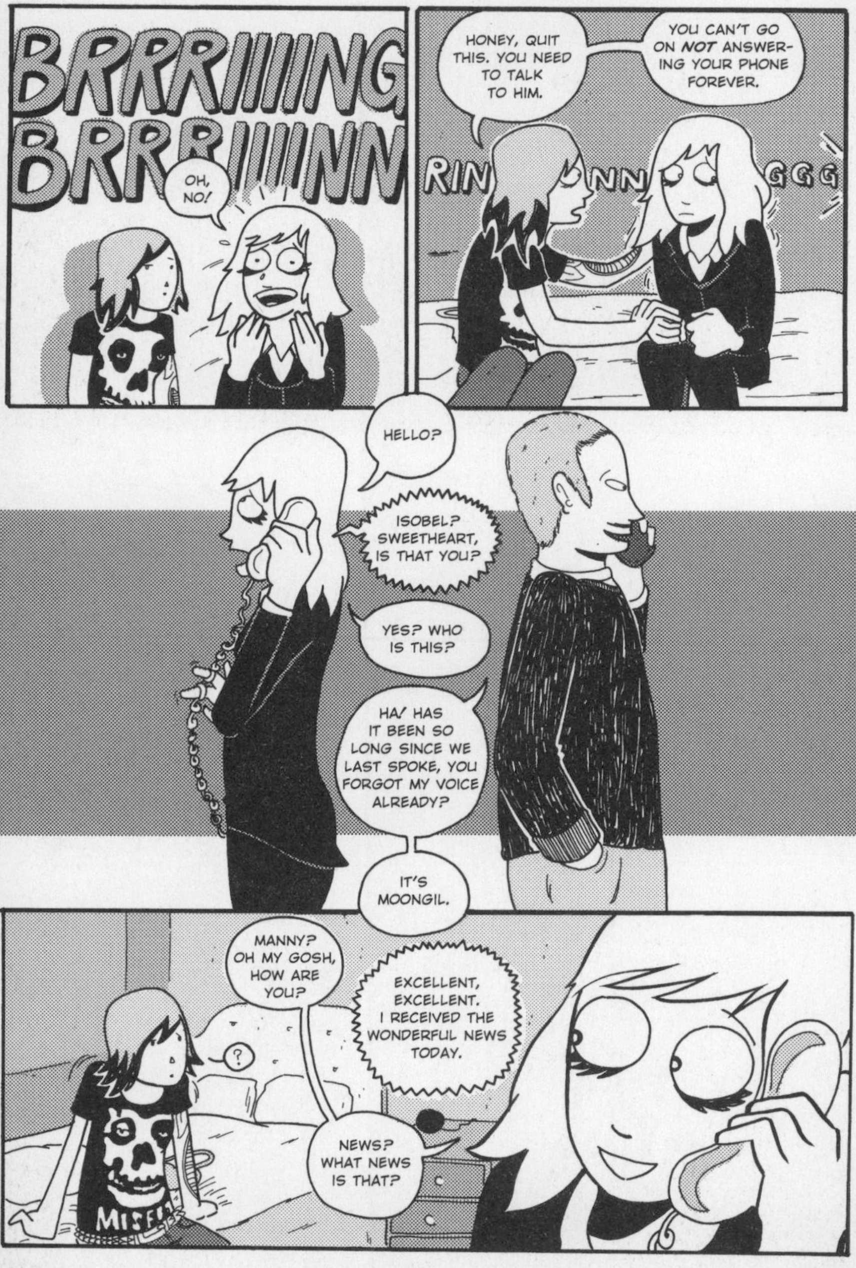
BRRRIIIING
BRRRIIIINN
OH, NO!
HONEY, QUIT THIS. YOU NEED TO TALK TO HIM.
YOU CAN'T GO ON *NOT* ANSWERING YOUR PHONE FOREVER.
RINNNNGGG
HELLO?
ISOBEL? SWEETHEART, IS THAT YOU?
YES? WHO IS THIS?
HA! HAS IT BEEN SO LONG SINCE WE LAST SPOKE, YOU FORGOT MY VOICE ALREADY?
IT'S MOONGIL.
MANNY? OH MY GOSH, HOW ARE YOU?
EXCELLENT, EXCELLENT. I RECEIVED THE WONDERFUL NEWS TODAY.
?
NEWS? WHAT NEWS IS THAT?

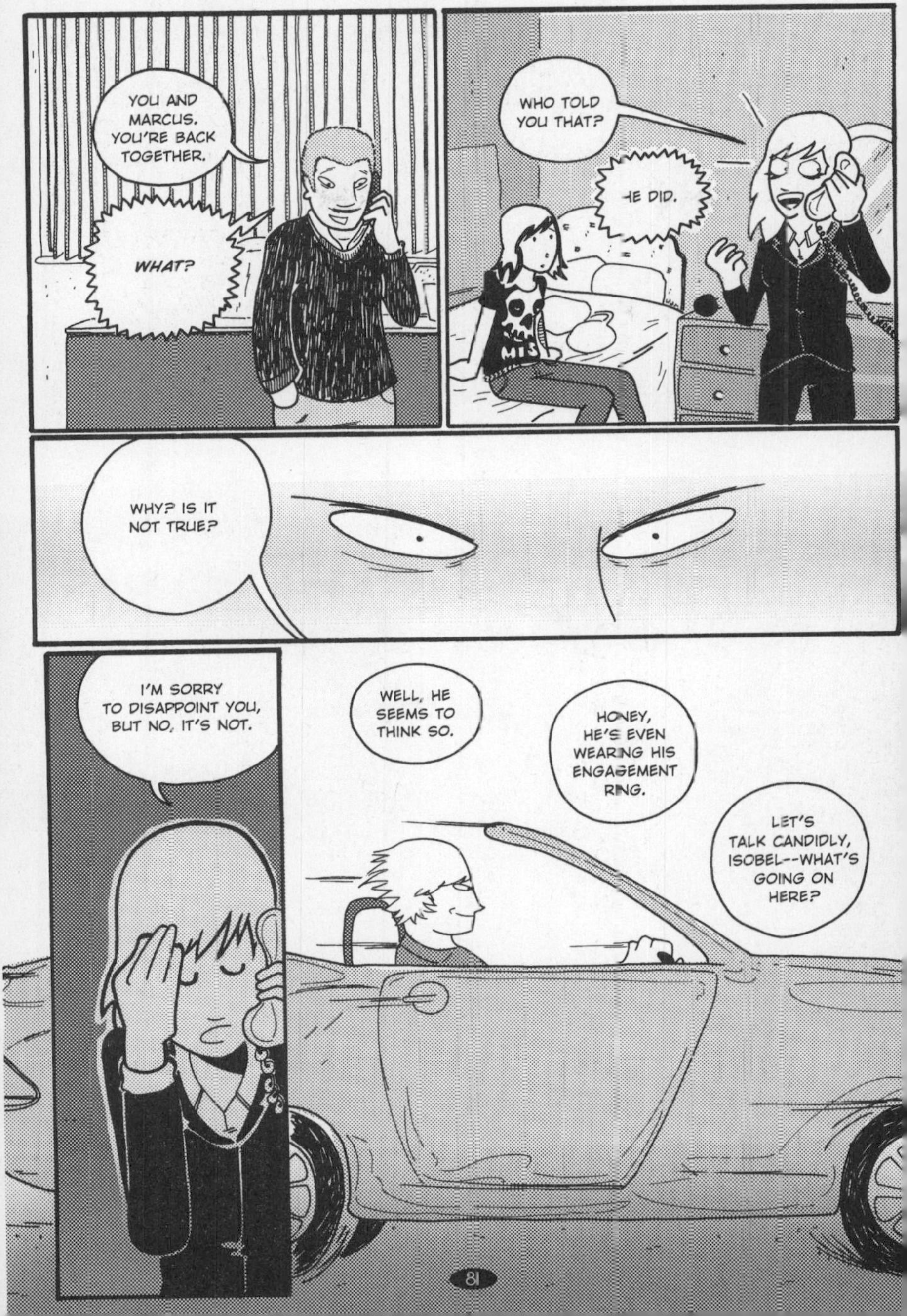
YOU AND MARCUS. YOU'RE BACK TOGETHER.
WHAT?
WHO TOLD YOU THAT?
HE DID.
WHY? IS IT NOT TRUE?
I'M SORRY TO DISAPPOINT YOU, BUT NO, IT'S NOT.
WELL, HE SEEMS TO THINK SO.
HONEY, HE'S EVEN WEARING HIS ENGAGEMENT RING.
LET'S TALK CANDIDLY, ISOBEL--WHAT'S GOING ON HERE?

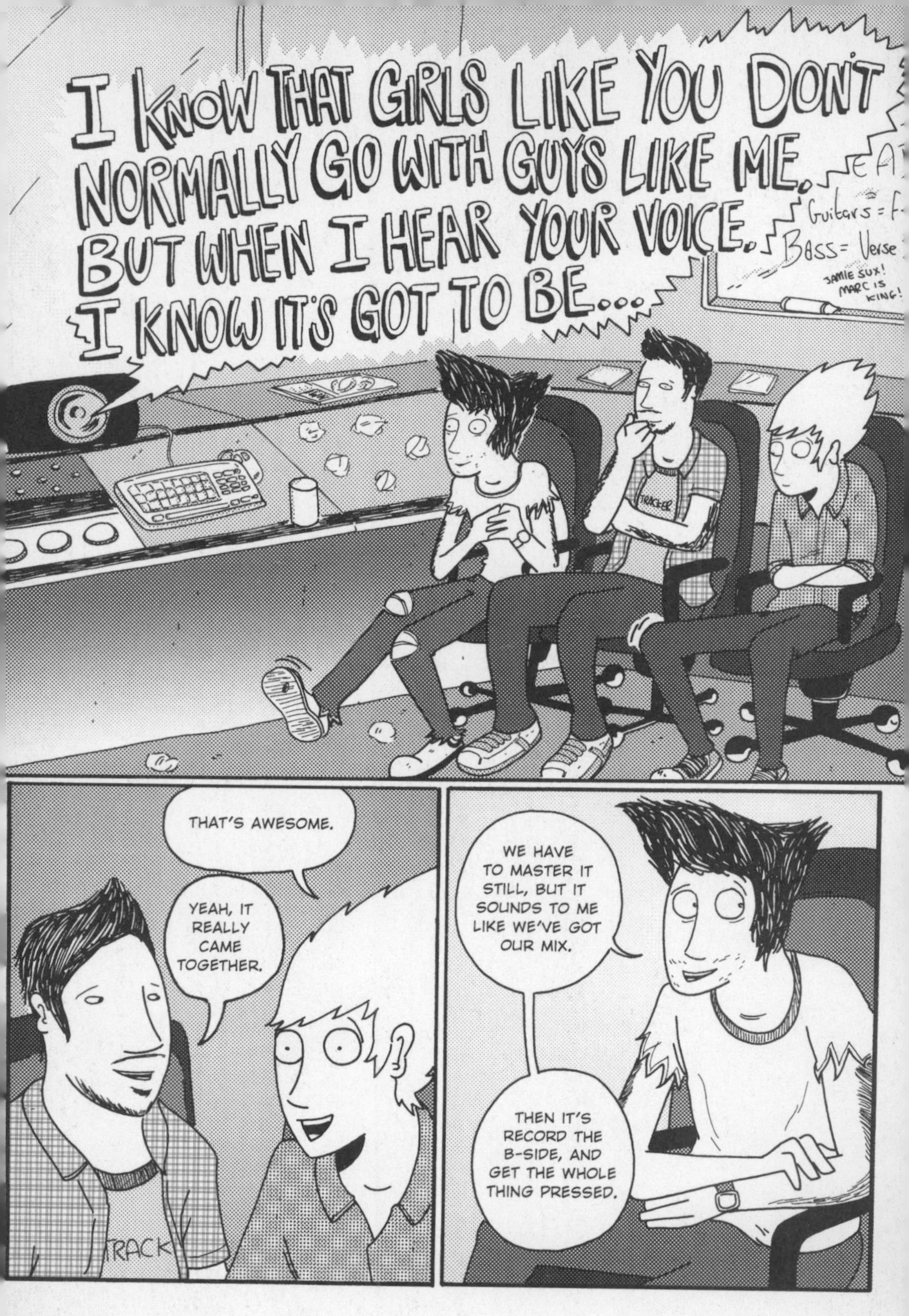
I KNOW THAT GIRLS LIKE YOU DON'T NORMALLY GO WITH GUYS LIKE ME. BUT WHEN I HEAR YOUR VOICE. I KNOW IT'S GOT TO BE...
Bass= Verse
JAMIE SUX! MARC IS KING!
THAT'S AWESOME.
YEAH, IT REALLY CAME TOGETHER.
WE HAVE TO MASTER IT STILL, BUT IT SOUNDS TO ME LIKE WE'VE GOT OUR MIX.
THEN IT'S RECORD THE B-SIDE, AND GET THE WHOLE THING PRESSED.

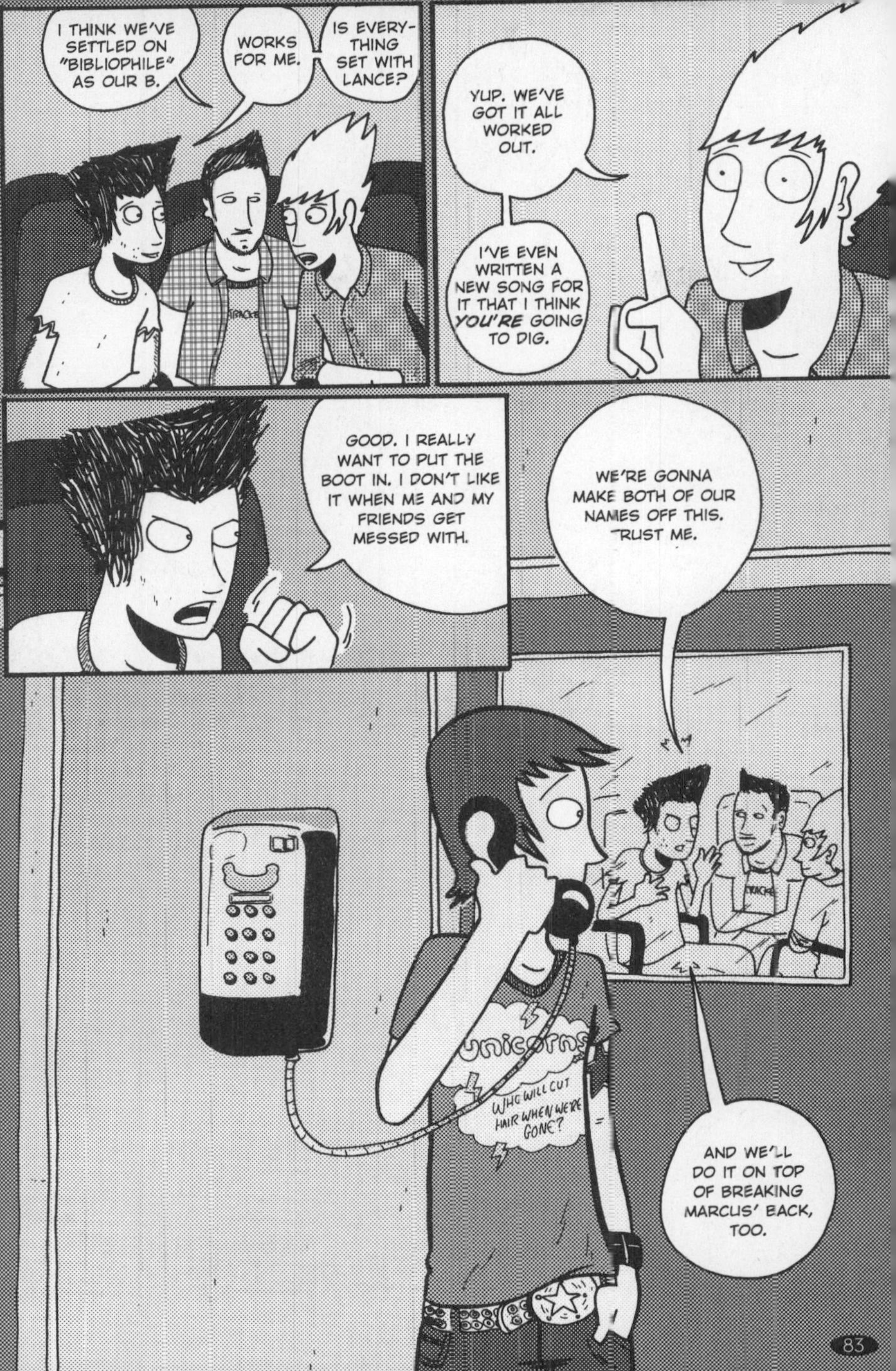
I THINK WE'VE SETTLED ON "BIBLIOPHILE" AS OUR B.
WORKS FOR ME.
IS EVERY-THING SET WITH LANCE?
YUP. WE'VE GOT IT ALL WORKED OUT.
I'VE EVEN WRITTEN A NEW SONG FOR IT THAT I THINK *YOU'RE* GOING TO DIG.
GOOD. I REALLY WANT TO PUT THE BOOT IN. I DON'T LIKE IT WHEN ME AND MY FRIENDS GET MESSED WITH.
WE'RE GONNA MAKE BOTH OF OUR NAMES OFF THIS. TRUST ME.
AND WE'LL DO IT ON TOP OF BREAKING MARCUS' BACK, TOO.
unicorns
WHO WILL CUT HAIR WHEN WE'RE GONE?

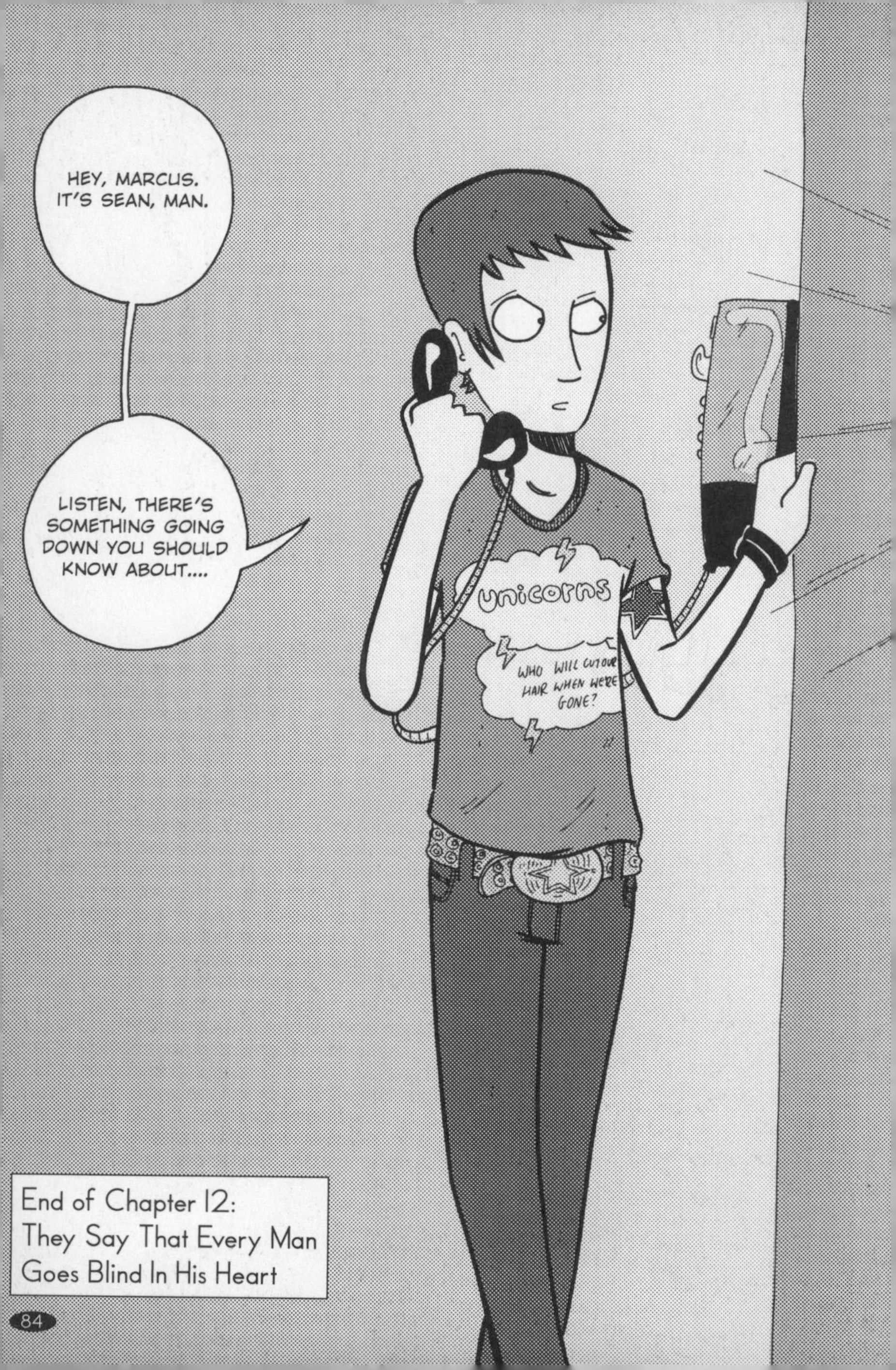
HEY, MARCUS. IT'S SEAN, MAN.
LISTEN, THERE'S SOMETHING GOING DOWN YOU SHOULD KNOW ABOUT....
unicorns
WHO WILL CUT OUR HAIR WHEN WE'RE GONE?
End of Chapter 12: They Say That Every Man Goes Blind In His Heart

Chapter 13: Boys Keep Swinging

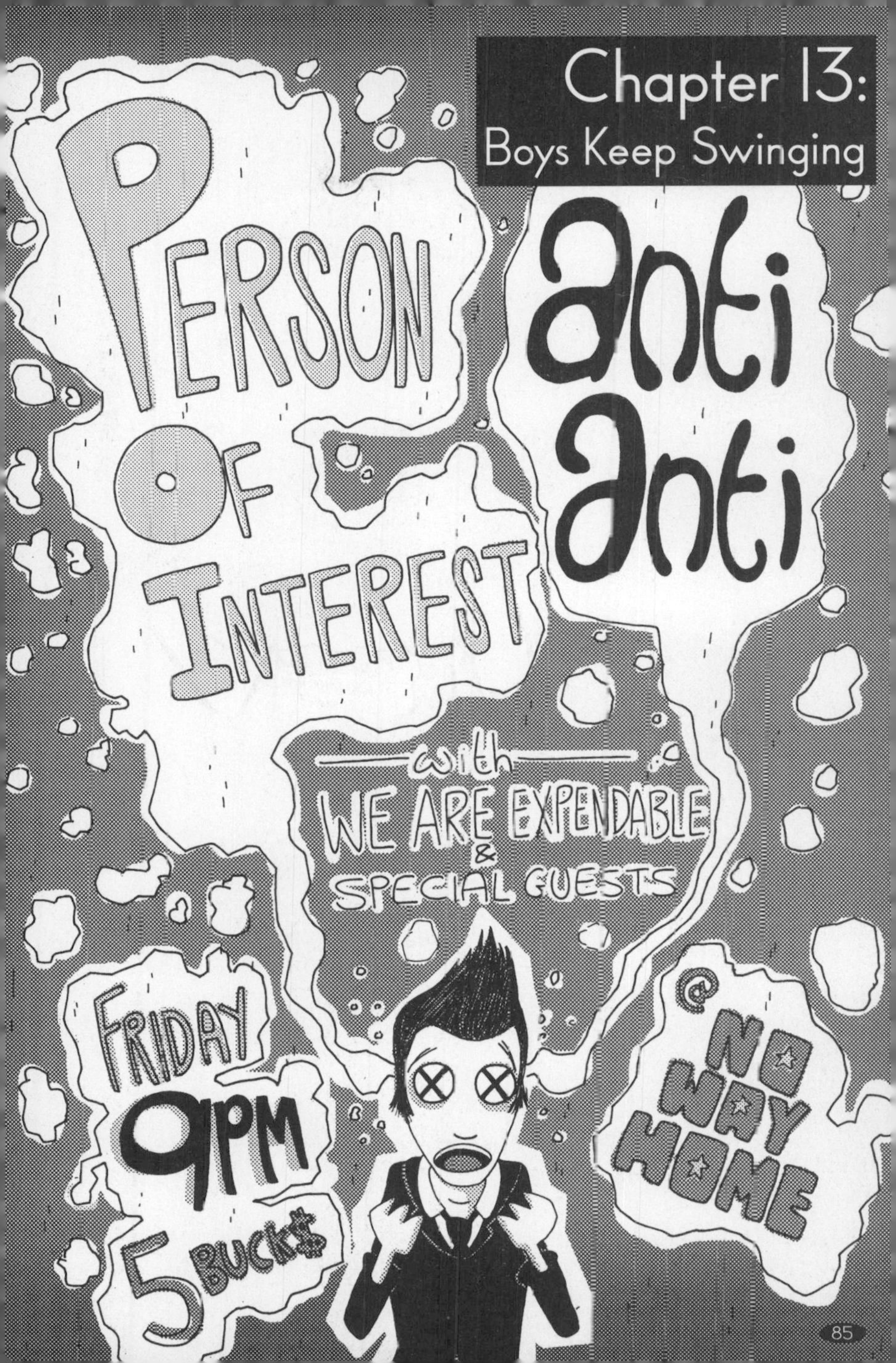

PERSON OF INTEREST
anti anti
with
WE ARE EXPENDABLE
&
SPECIAL GUESTS
FRIDAY
9PM
5 BUCK$
@
NO WAY HOME

KITTEN STOMP FUTURE DREAM
ENDING UP EMERY!

Full Name:
Emery Richard Powell

Band Affiliation:
Bass player, Like A Dog

Birthdate:
March 26 (Aries)

Hometown:
Brentwood, CA

Musical Heroes:
John Entwistle
Manny
Roger Waters

Prior Experience:
Played in a Dixieland jazz band at Knott's Berry Farm.

Essential Supply:
Rubber bands, caramel

Worst Lie the Band Tells About Me:
According to Eleanore, "His ponytail is filthy. Whenever he's been laying down, it leaves a grease stain on the pillow." Emery denies this "flat out."

Family:
Emery's father was once the Mayor of Brentwood.

Best Thing Ever:
"Meeting models. Or so I'm told. I'm waiting to get more famous so they'll start coming to our shows. Ladies, look at a bass player's fingers. Trust me."

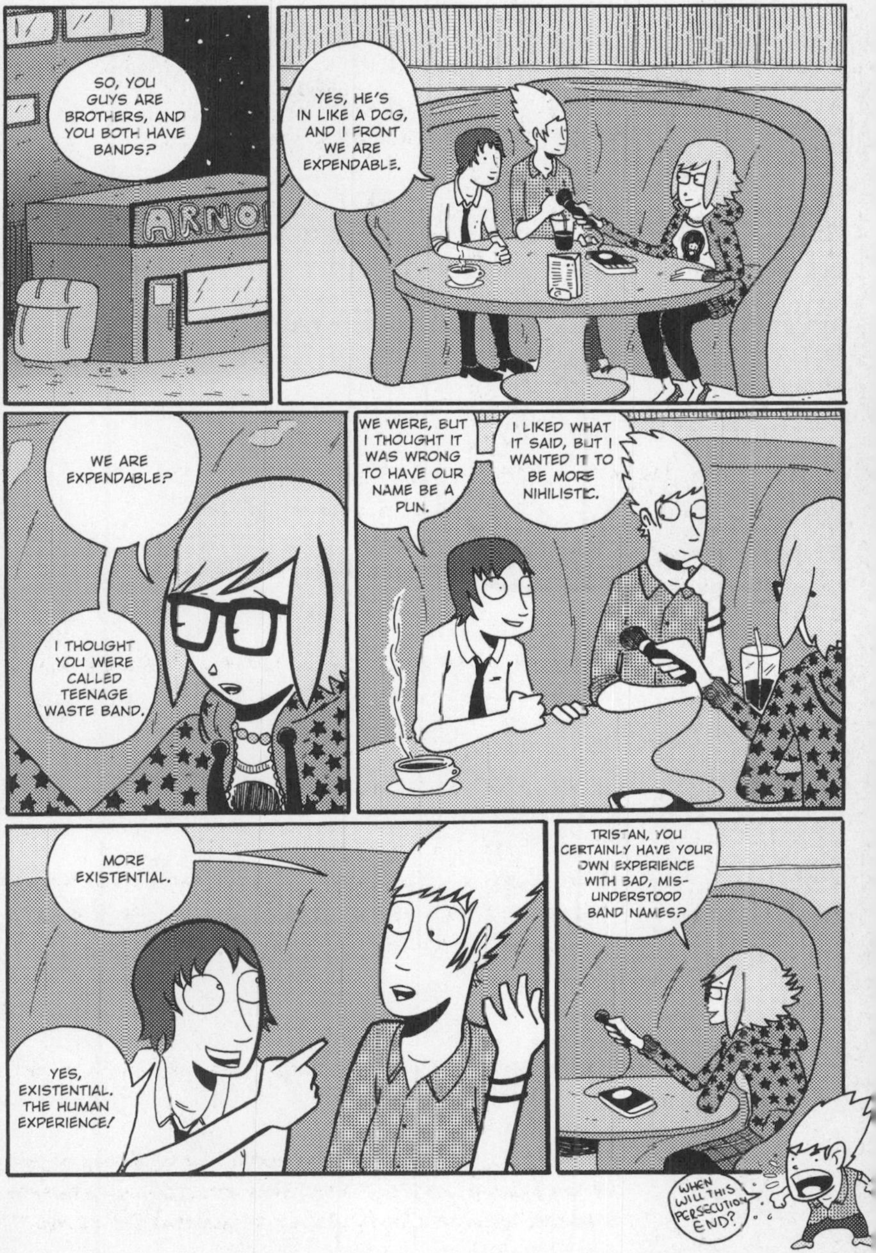

SO, YOU GUYS ARE BROTHERS, AND YOU BOTH HAVE BANDS?
ARNO
YES, HE'S IN LIKE A DCG, AND I FRONT WE ARE EXPENDABLE.
WE ARE EXPENDABLE?
I THOUGHT YOU WERE CALLED TEENAGE WASTE BAND.
WE WERE, BUT I THOUGHT IT WAS WRONG TO HAVE OUR NAME BE A PUN.
I LIKED WHAT IT SAID, BUT I WANTED IT TO BE MORE NIHILISTIC.
MORE EXISTENTIAL.
YES, EXISTENTIAL. THE HUMAN EXPERIENCE!
TRISTAN, YOU CERTAINLY HAVE YOUR OWN EXPERIENCE WITH BAD, MIS-UNDERSTOOD BAND NAMES?
WHEN WILL THIS PERSECUTION END?

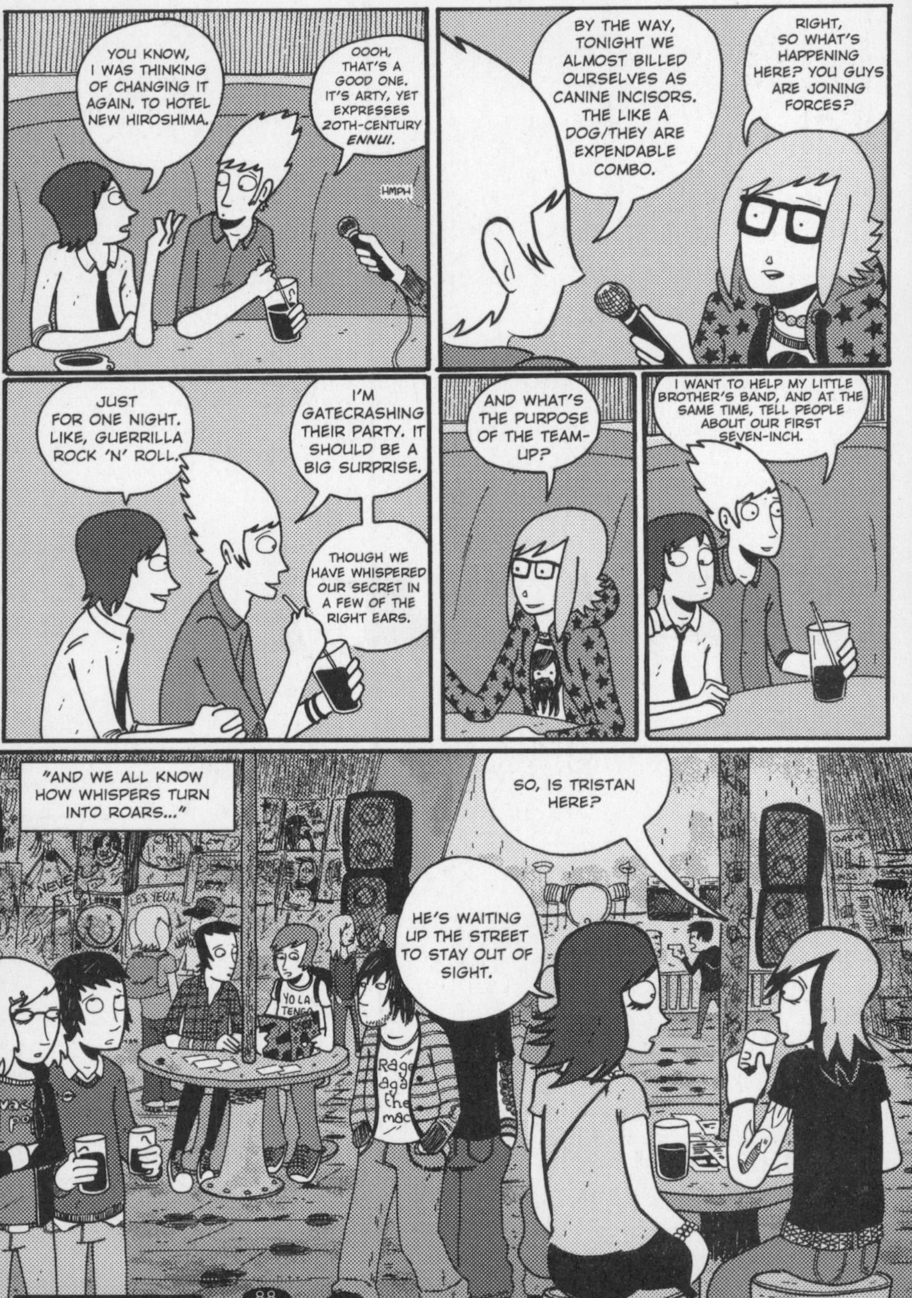
YOU KNOW, I WAS THINKING OF CHANGING IT AGAIN. TO HOTEL NEW HIROSHIMA.
OOOH, THAT'S A GOOD ONE. IT'S ARTY, YET EXPRESSES 20TH-CENTURY *ENNUI*.
HMPH
BY THE WAY, TONIGHT WE ALMOST BILLED OURSELVES AS CANINE INCISORS. THE LIKE A DOG/THEY ARE EXPENDABLE COMBO.
RIGHT, SO WHAT'S HAPPENING HERE? YOU GUYS ARE JOINING FORCES?
JUST FOR ONE NIGHT. LIKE, GUERRILLA ROCK 'N' ROLL.
I'M GATECRASHING THEIR PARTY. IT SHOULD BE A BIG SURPRISE.
THOUGH WE HAVE WHISPERED OUR SECRET IN A FEW OF THE RIGHT EARS.
AND WHAT'S THE PURPOSE OF THE TEAM-UP?
I WANT TO HELP MY LITTLE BROTHER'S BAND, AND AT THE SAME TIME, TELL PEOPLE ABOUT OUR FIRST SEVEN-INCH.
"AND WE ALL KNOW HOW WHISPERS TURN INTO ROARS..."
SO, IS TRISTAN HERE?
HE'S WAITING UP THE STREET TO STAY OUT OF SIGHT.

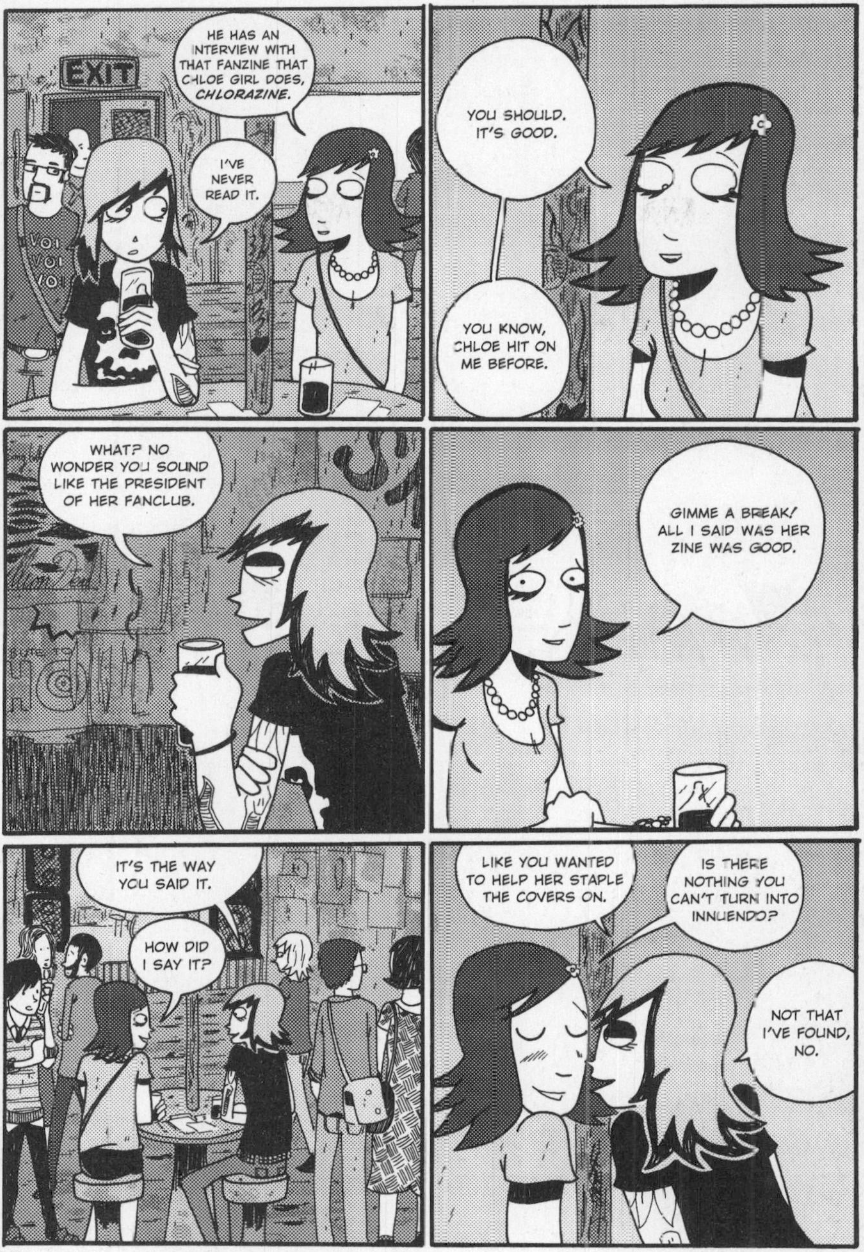
EXIT
HE HAS AN INTERVIEW WITH THAT FANZINE THAT CHLOE GIRL DOES, ***CHLORAZINE.***
I'VE NEVER READ IT.
VOI VOI VOI
YOU SHOULD. IT'S GOOD.
YOU KNOW, CHLOE HIT ON ME BEFORE.
WHAT? NO WONDER YOU SOUND LIKE THE PRESIDENT OF HER FANCLUB.
GIMME A BREAK! ALL I SAID WAS HER ZINE WAS GOOD.
IT'S THE WAY YOU SAID IT.
HOW DID I SAY IT?
LIKE YOU WANTED TO HELP HER STAPLE THE COVERS ON.
IS THERE NOTHING YOU CAN'T TURN INTO INNUENDO?
NOT THAT I'VE FOUND, NO.

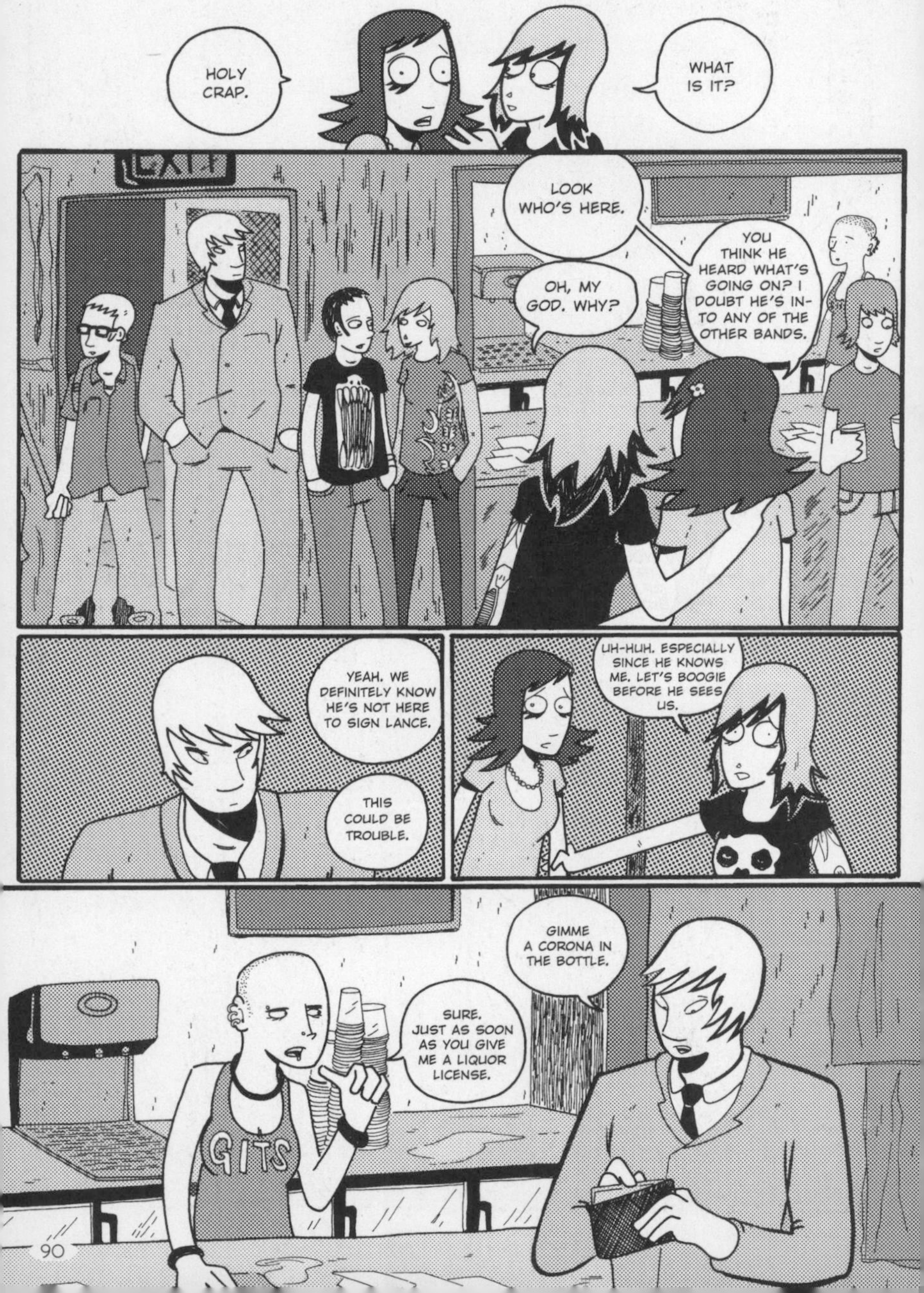
HOLY CRAP.
WHAT IS IT?
EXIT
LOOK WHO'S HERE.
OH, MY GOD. WHY?
YOU THINK HE HEARD WHAT'S GOING ON? I DOUBT HE'S IN-TO ANY OF THE OTHER BANDS.
YEAH. WE DEFINITELY KNOW HE'S NOT HERE TO SIGN LANCE.
THIS COULD BE TROUBLE.
UH-HUH. ESPECIALLY SINCE HE KNOWS ME. LET'S BOOGIE BEFORE HE SEES US.
GIMME A CORONA IN THE BOTTLE.
SURE. JUST AS SOON AS YOU GIVE ME A LIQUOR LICENSE.
GITS

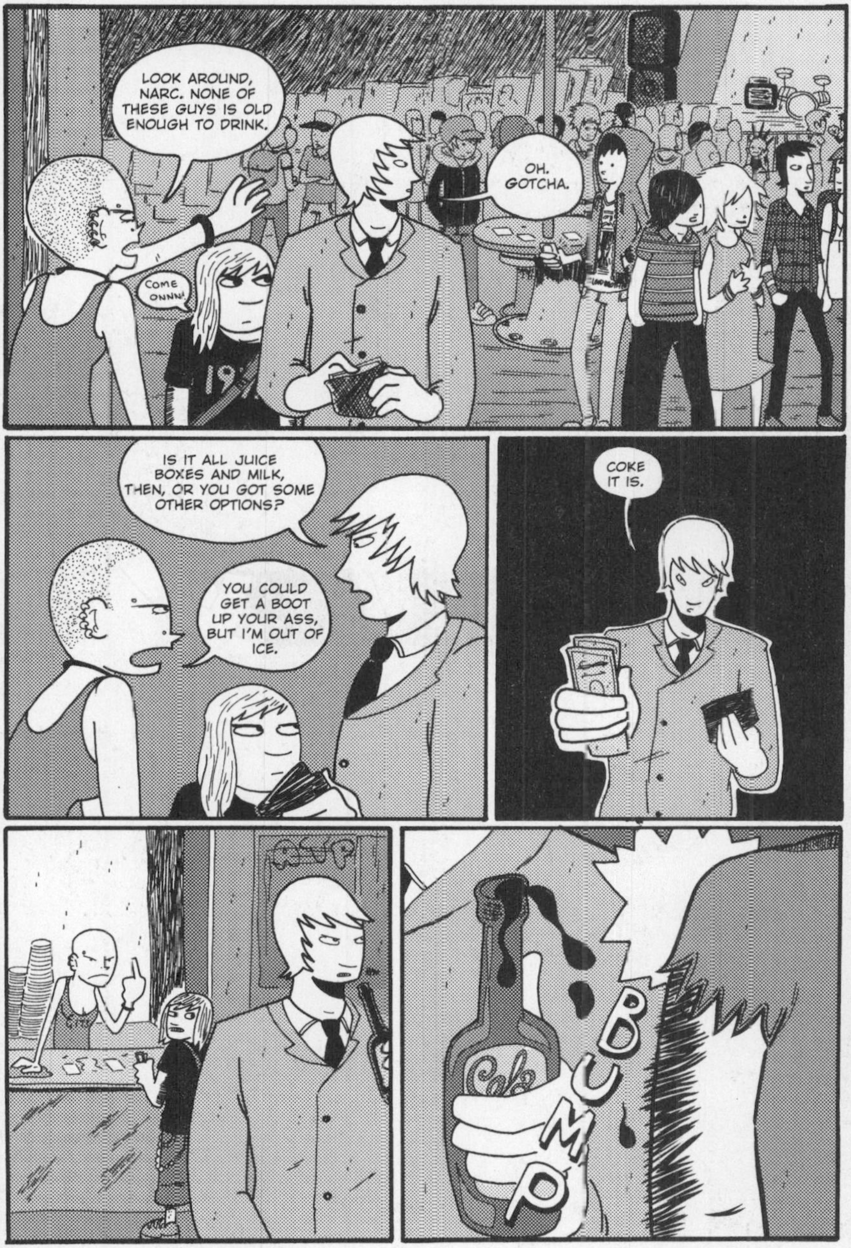
LOOK AROUND, NARC. NONE OF THESE GUYS IS OLD ENOUGH TO DRINK.
OH. GOTCHA.
COME ONNN!
IS IT ALL JUICE BOXES AND MILK, THEN, OR YOU GOT SOME OTHER OPTIONS?
YOU COULD GET A BOOT UP YOUR ASS, BUT I'M OUT OF ICE.
COKE IT IS.
BUMP

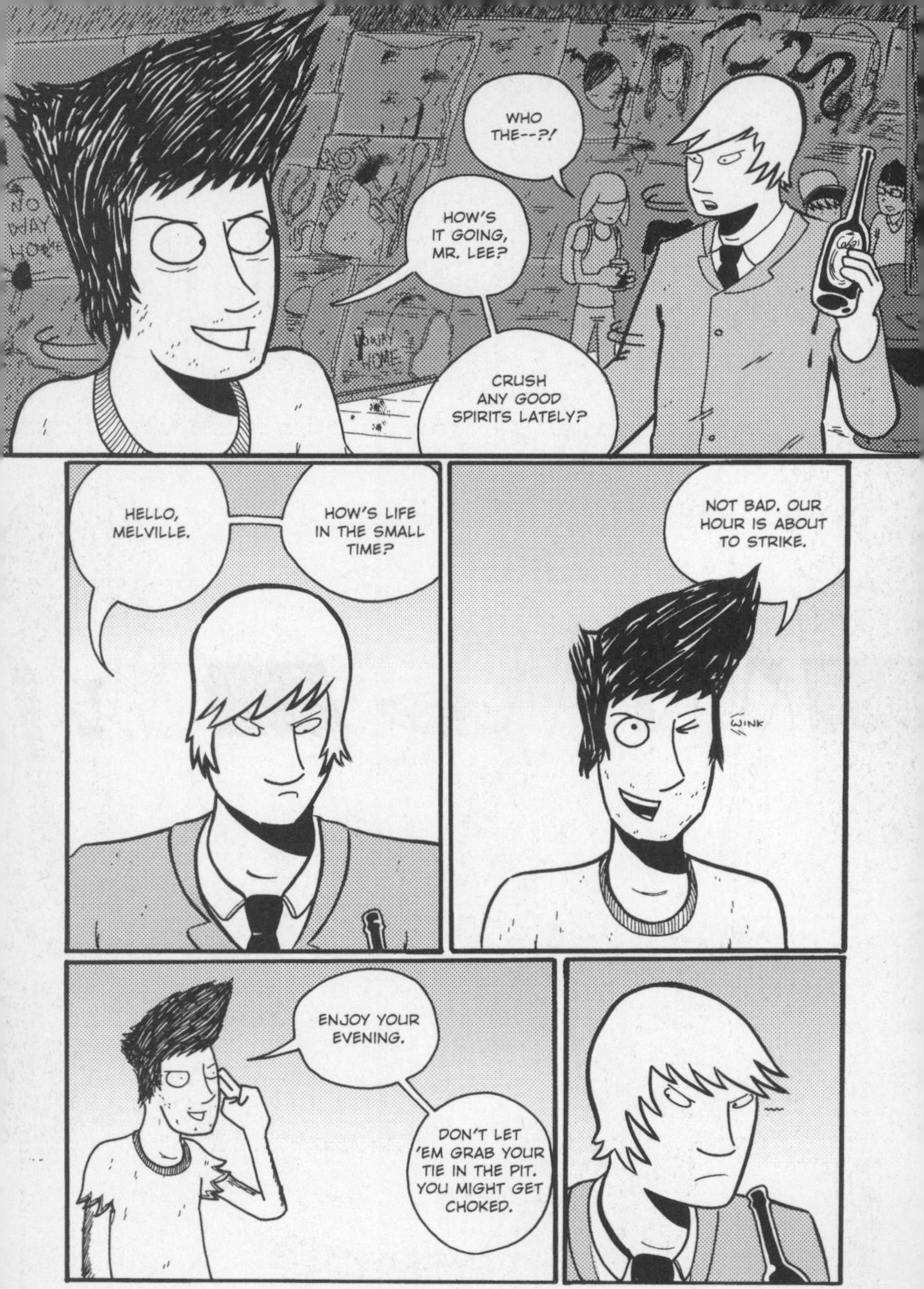
WHO THE--?!
HOW'S IT GOING, MR. LEE?
CRUSH ANY GOOD SPIRITS LATELY?
HELLO, MELVILLE.
HOW'S LIFE IN THE SMALL TIME?
NOT BAD. OUR HOUR IS ABOUT TO STRIKE.
WINK
ENJOY YOUR EVENING.
DON'T LET 'EM GRAB YOUR TIE IN THE PIT. YOU MIGHT GET CHOKED.

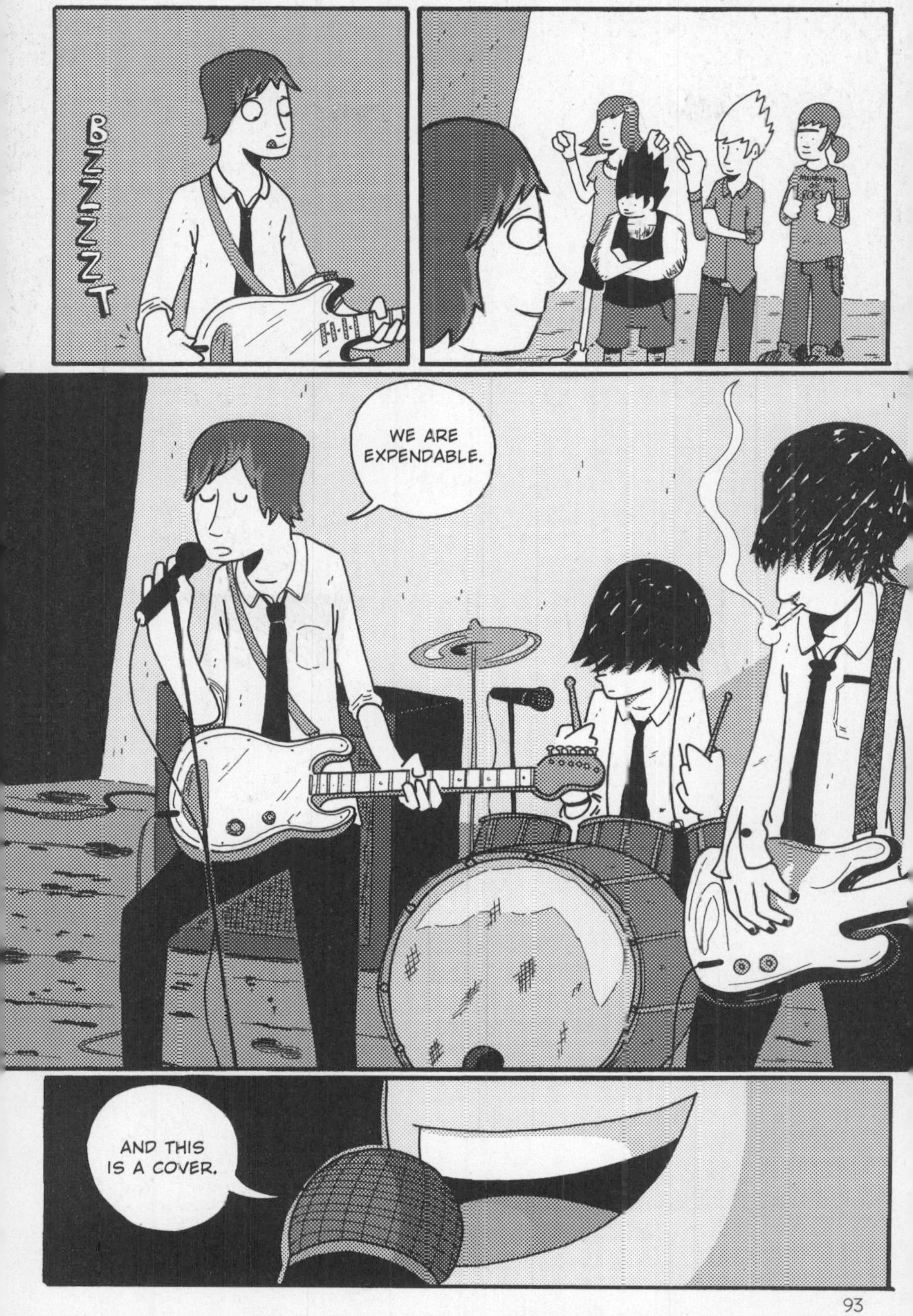
BZZZZT
WE ARE EXPENDABLE.
AND THIS IS A COVER.

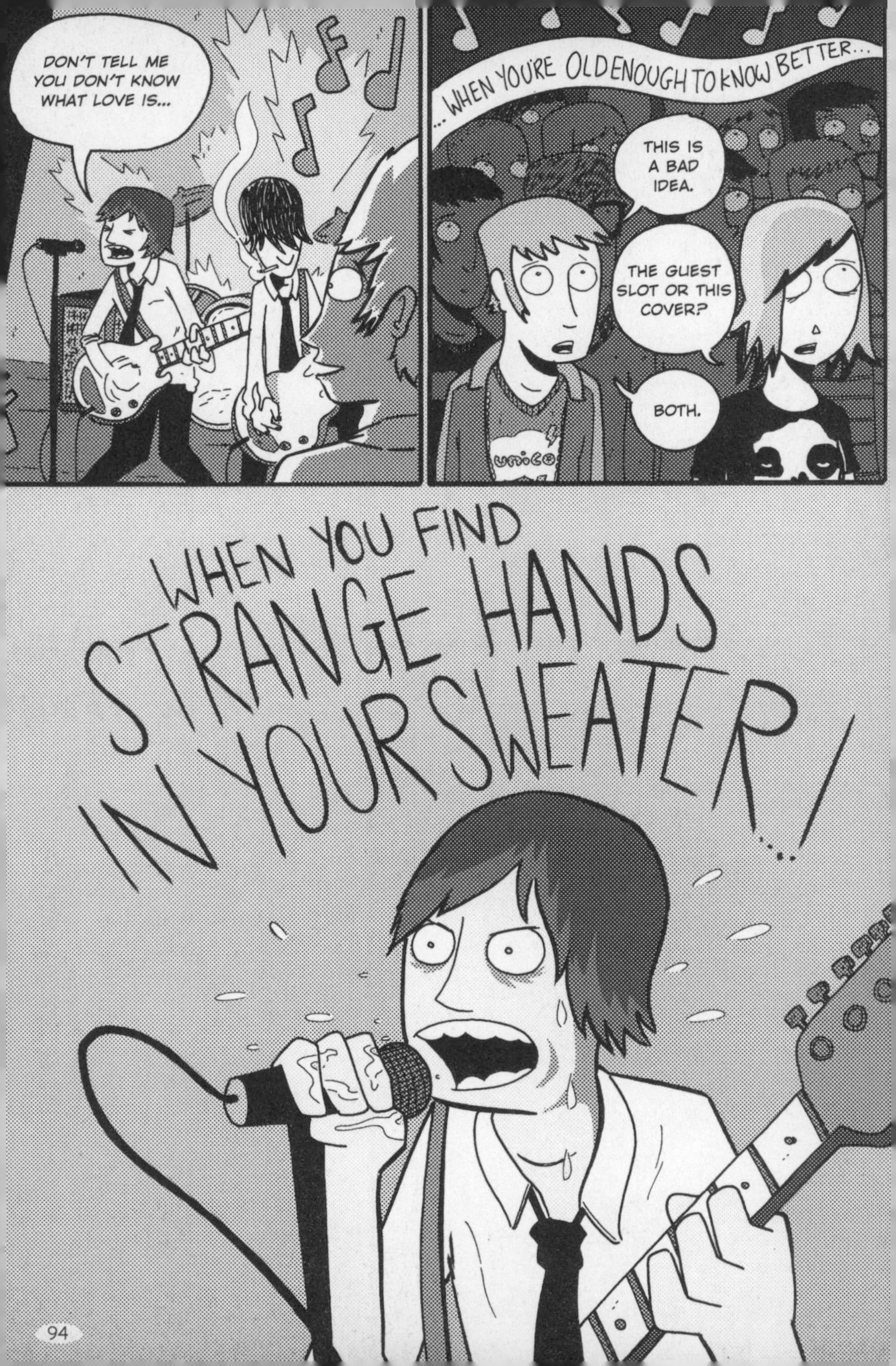
DON'T TELL ME YOU DON'T KNOW WHAT LOVE IS...
...WHEN YOU'RE OLD ENOUGH TO KNOW BETTER...
THIS IS A BAD IDEA.
THE GUEST SLOT OR THIS COVER?
BOTH.
WHEN YOU FIND STRANGE HANDS IN YOUR SWEATER!!...

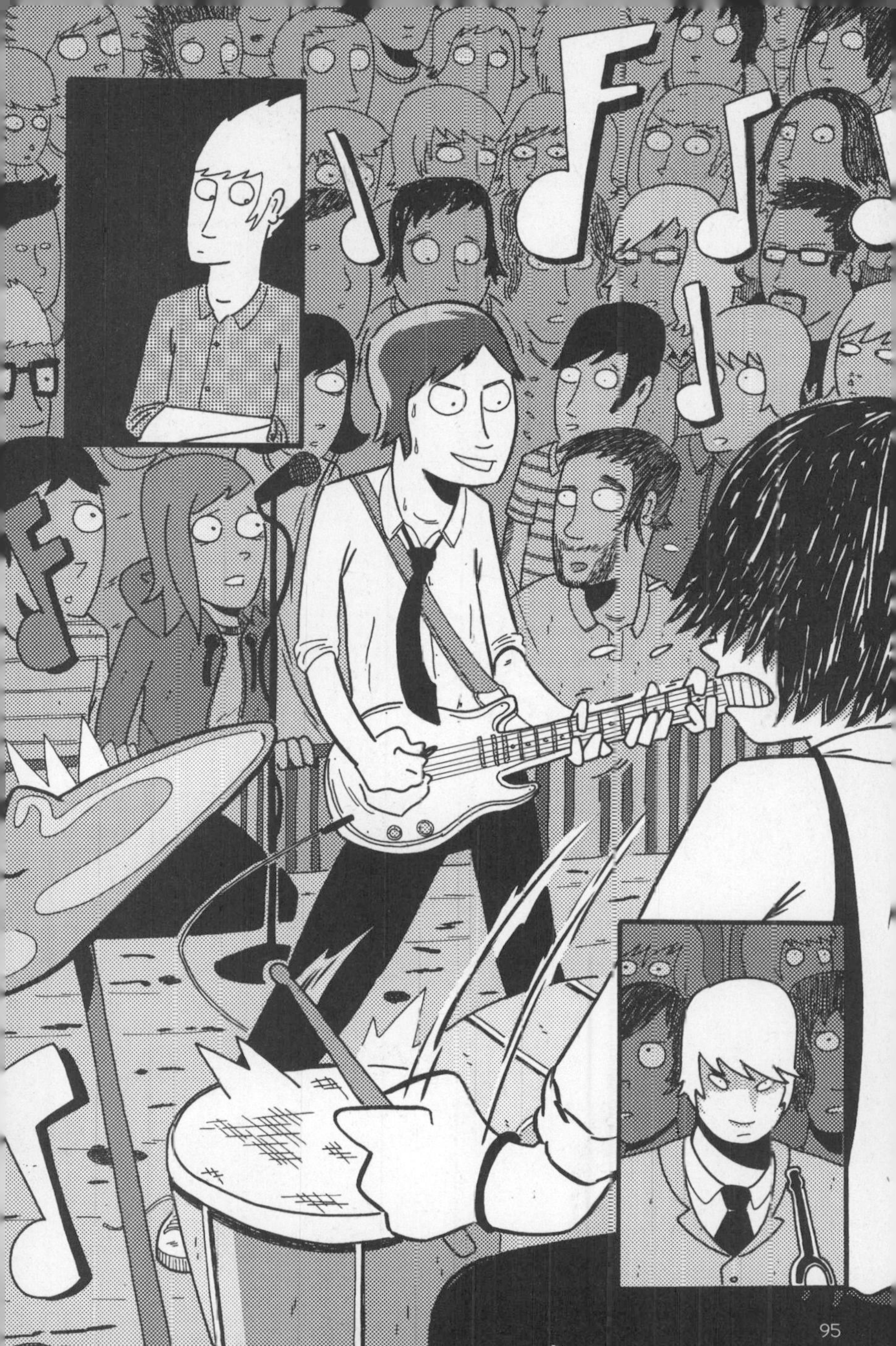

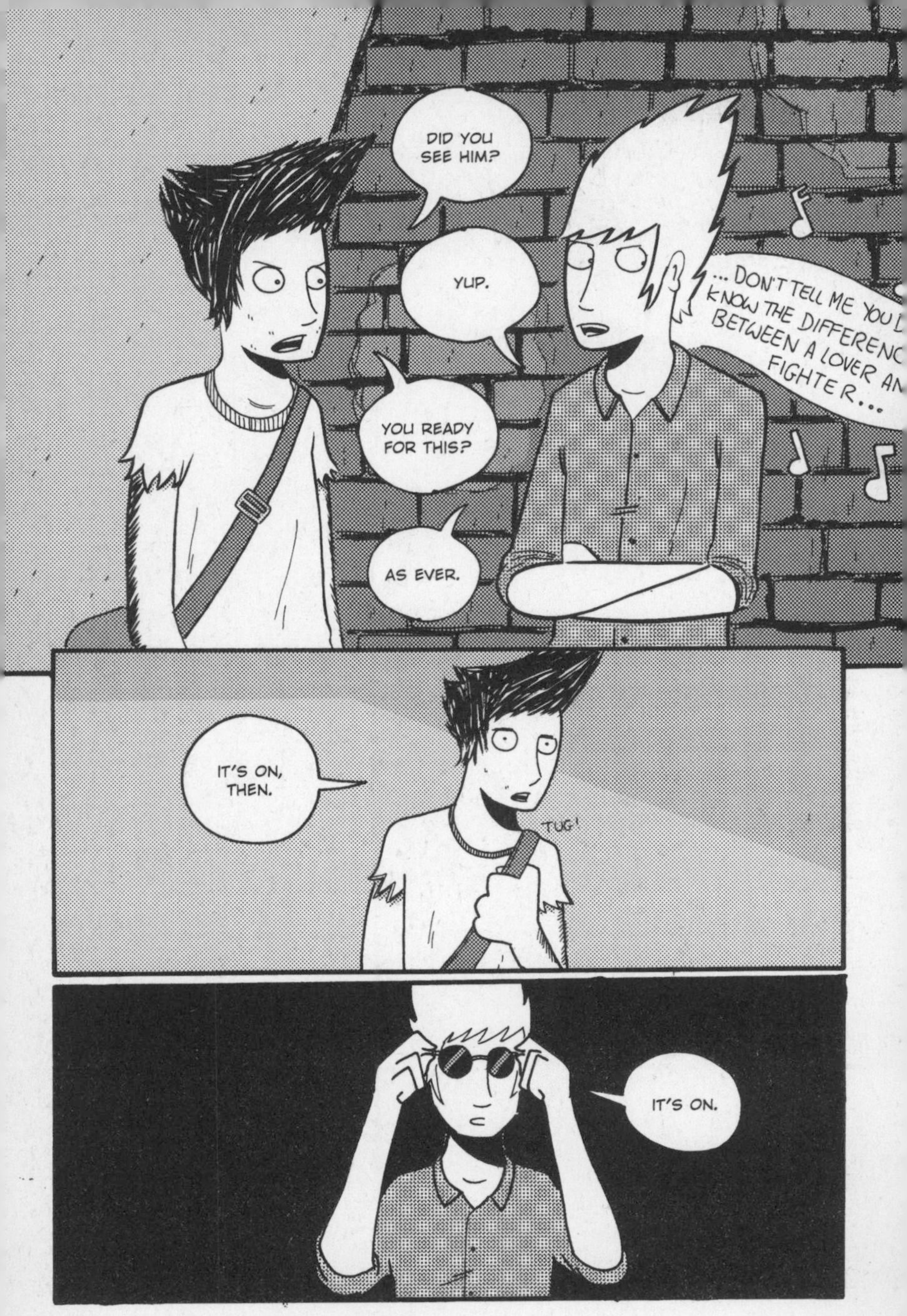
DID YOU SEE HIM?
YUP.
... DON'T TELL ME YOU D
KNOW THE DIFFERENC
BETWEEN A LOVER AN
FIGHTER...
YOU READY FOR THIS?
AS EVER.
IT'S ON, THEN.
TUG!
IT'S ON.

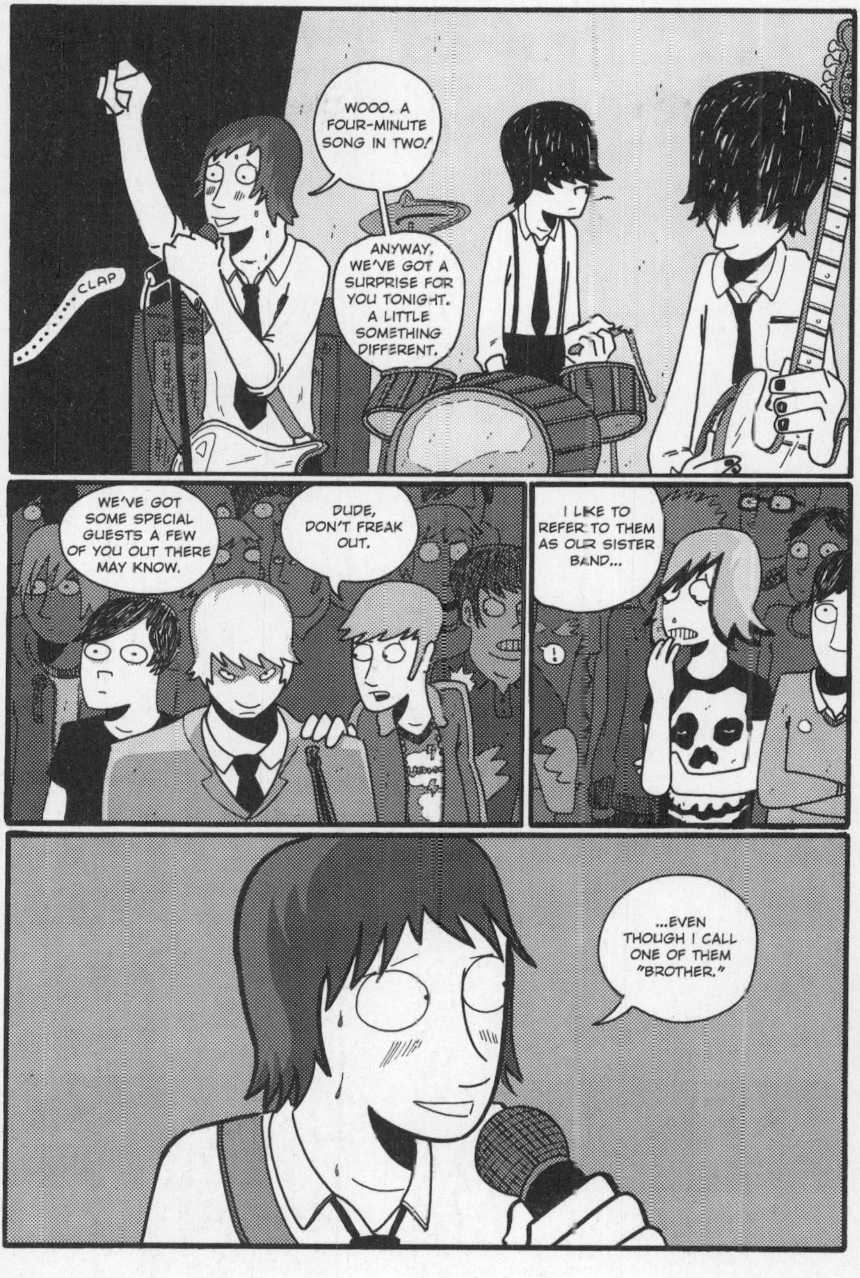
WOOO. A FOUR-MINUTE SONG IN TWO!
CLAP
ANYWAY, WE'VE GOT A SURPRISE FOR YOU TONIGHT. A LITTLE SOMETHING DIFFERENT.
WE'VE GOT SOME SPECIAL GUESTS A FEW OF YOU OUT THERE MAY KNOW.
DUDE, DON'T FREAK OUT.
I LIKE TO REFER TO THEM AS OUR SISTER BAND...
!
...EVEN THOUGH I CALL ONE OF THEM "BROTHER."

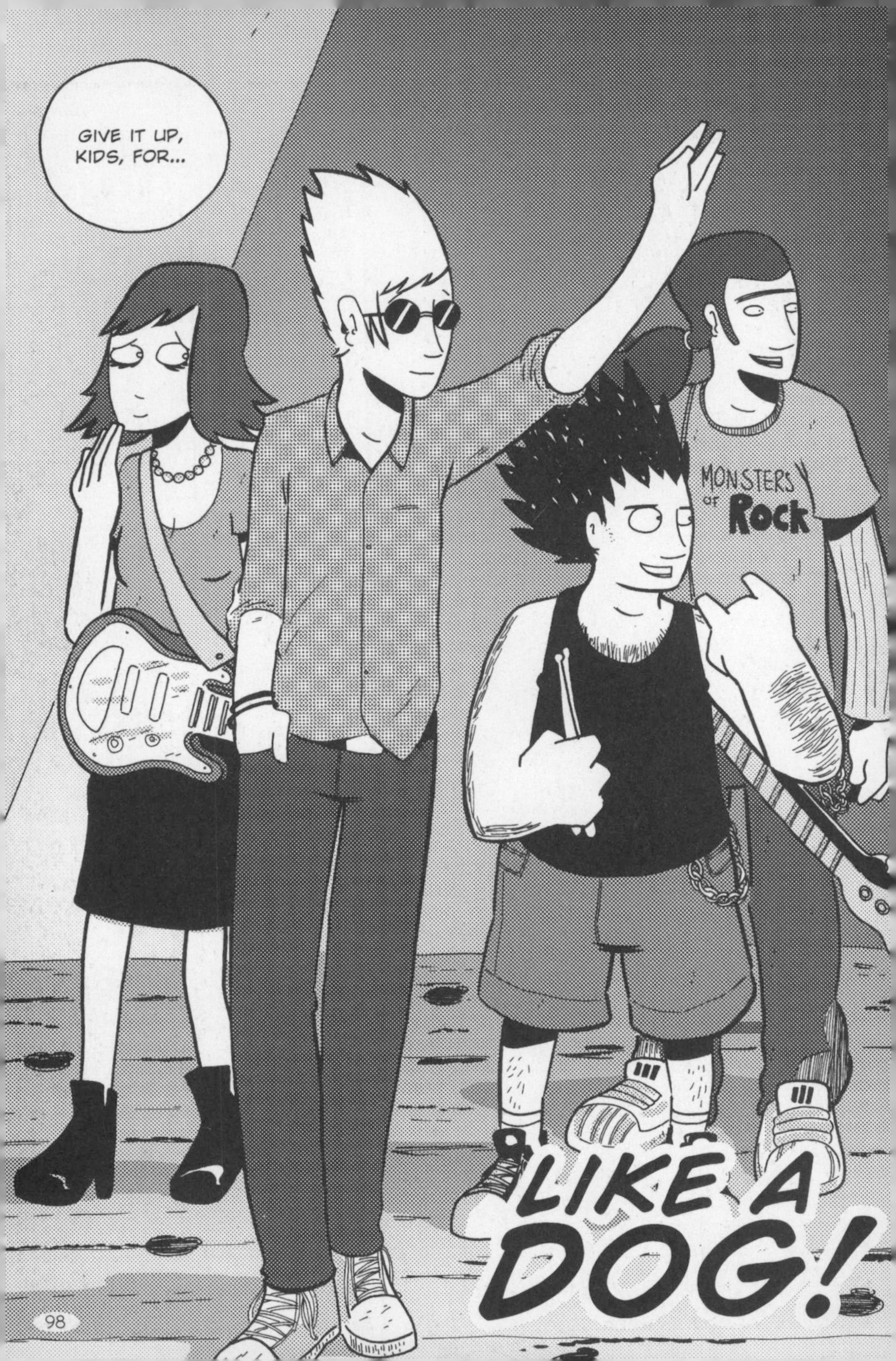
GIVE IT UP, KIDS, FOR...
MONSTERS of Rock
LIKE A DOG!

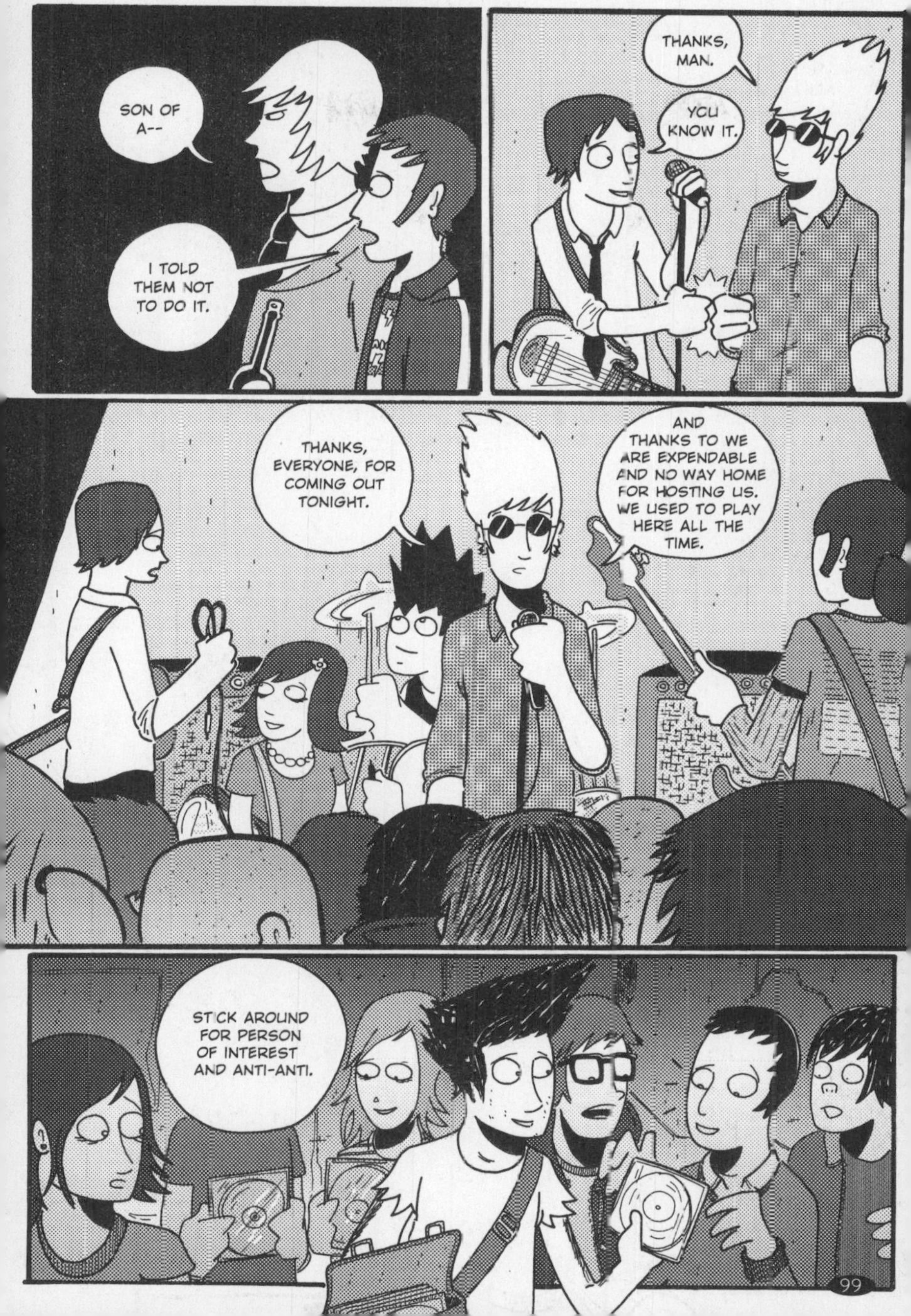
SON OF A--
I TOLD THEM NOT TO DO IT.
THANKS, MAN.
YOU KNOW IT.
THANKS, EVERYONE, FOR COMING OUT TONIGHT.
AND THANKS TO WE ARE EXPENDABLE AND NO WAY HOME FOR HOSTING US. WE USED TO PLAY HERE ALL THE TIME.
STICK AROUND FOR PERSON OF INTEREST AND ANTI-ANTI.

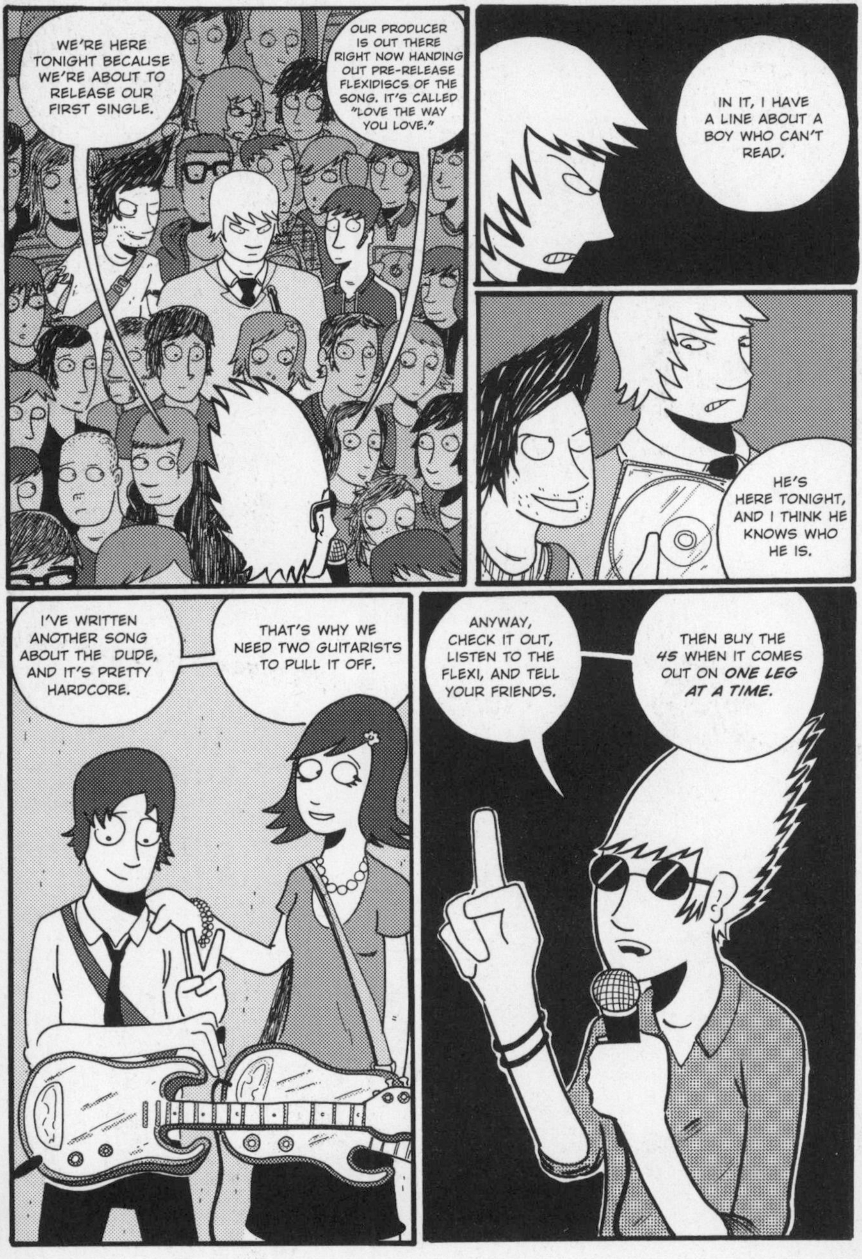
WE'RE HERE TONIGHT BECAUSE WE'RE ABOUT TO RELEASE OUR FIRST SINGLE.
OUR PRODUCER IS OUT THERE RIGHT NOW HANDING OUT PRE-RELEASE FLEXIDISCS OF THE SONG. IT'S CALLED "LOVE THE WAY YOU LOVE."
IN IT, I HAVE A LINE ABOUT A BOY WHO CAN'T READ.
HE'S HERE TONIGHT, AND I THINK HE KNOWS WHO HE IS.
I'VE WRITTEN ANOTHER SONG ABOUT THE DUDE, AND IT'S PRETTY HARDCORE.
THAT'S WHY WE NEED TWO GUITARISTS TO PULL IT OFF.
ANYWAY, CHECK IT OUT, LISTEN TO THE FLEXI, AND TELL YOUR FRIENDS.
THEN BUY THE *45* WHEN IT COMES OUT ON ***ONE LEG AT A TIME.***

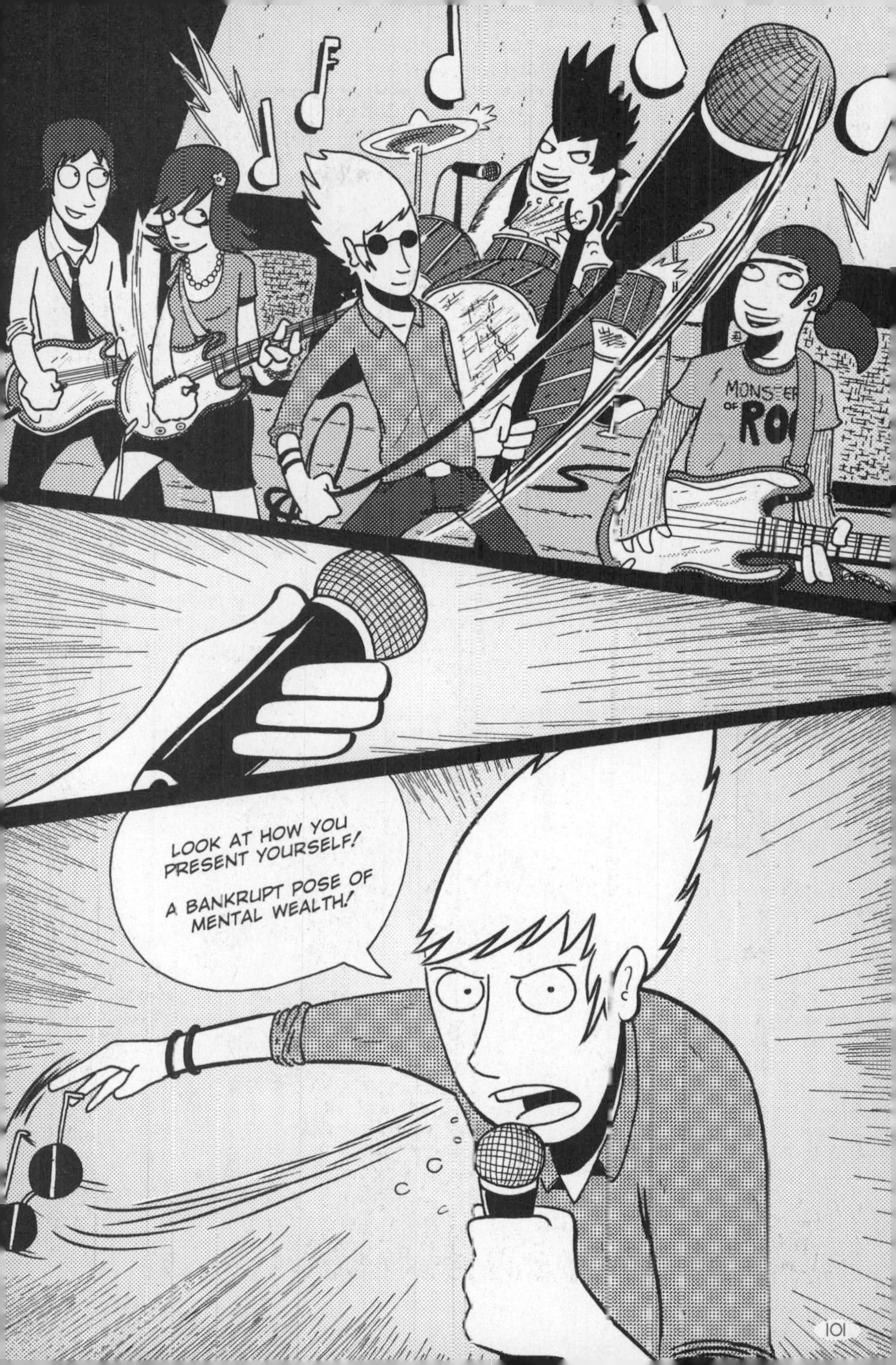
MONSTERS OF ROC
LOOK AT HOW YOU PRESENT YOURSELF!
A BANKRUPT POSE OF MENTAL WEALTH!

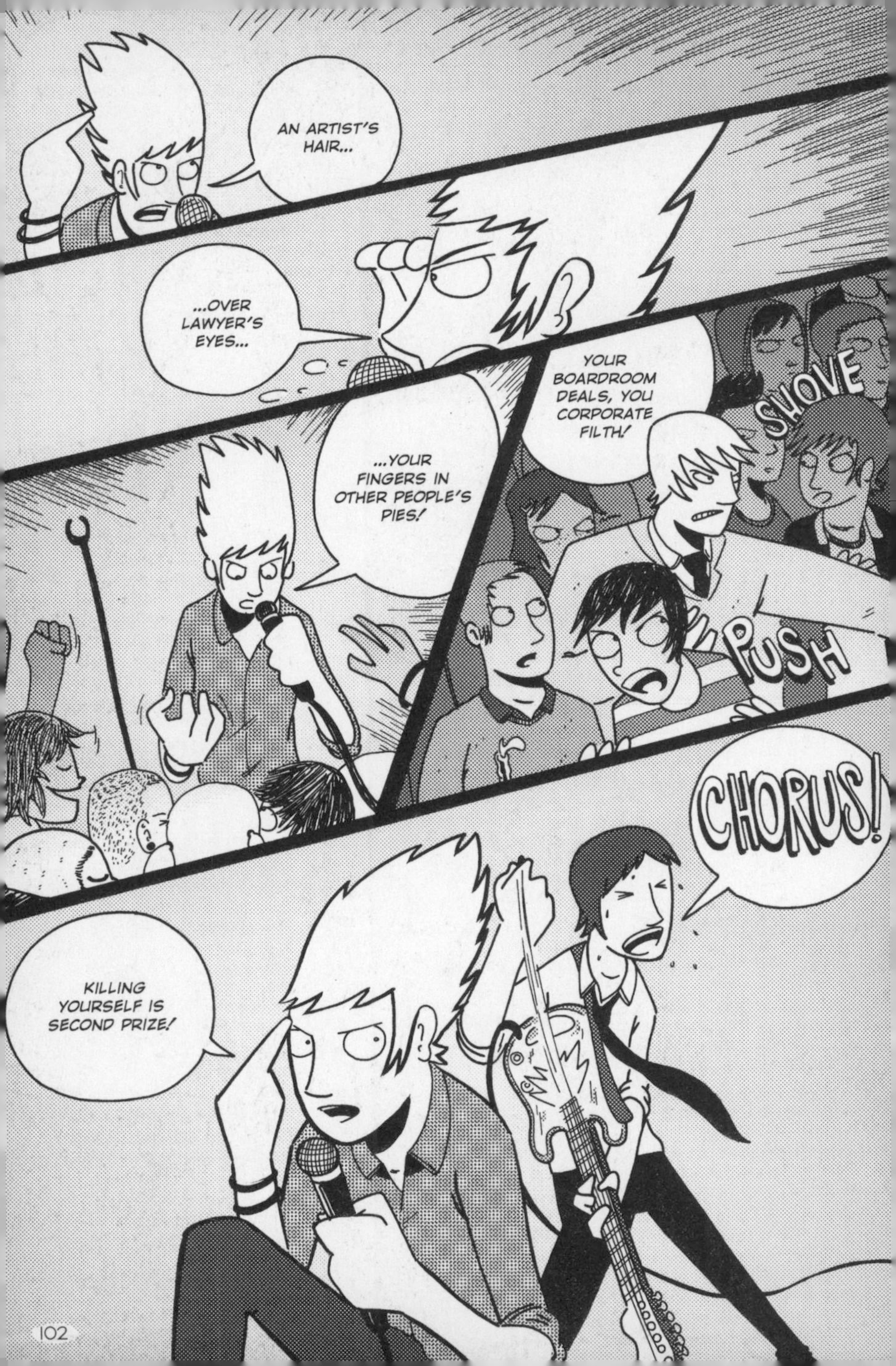
AN ARTIST'S HAIR...
...OVER LAWYER'S EYES...
...YOUR FINGERS IN OTHER PEOPLE'S PIES!
YOUR BOARDROOM DEALS, YOU CORPORATE FILTH!
SHOVE
PUSH
KILLING YOURSELF IS SECOND PRIZE!
CHORUS!

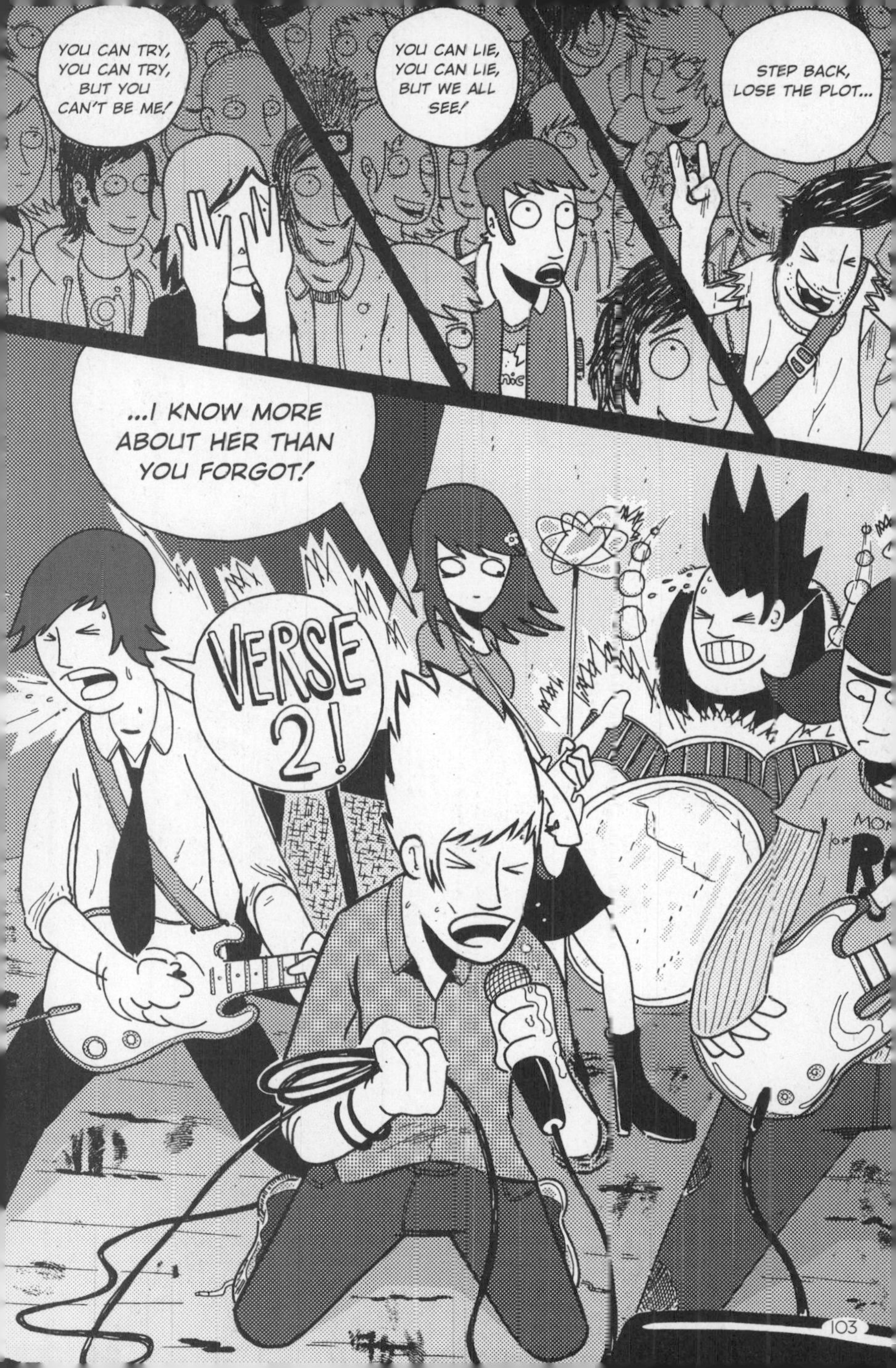

YOU CAN TRY, YOU CAN TRY, BUT YOU CAN'T BE ME!
YOU CAN LIE, YOU CAN LIE, BUT WE ALL SEE!
STEP BACK, LOSE THE PLOT...
...I KNOW MORE ABOUT HER THAN YOU FORGOT!
VERSE 2!

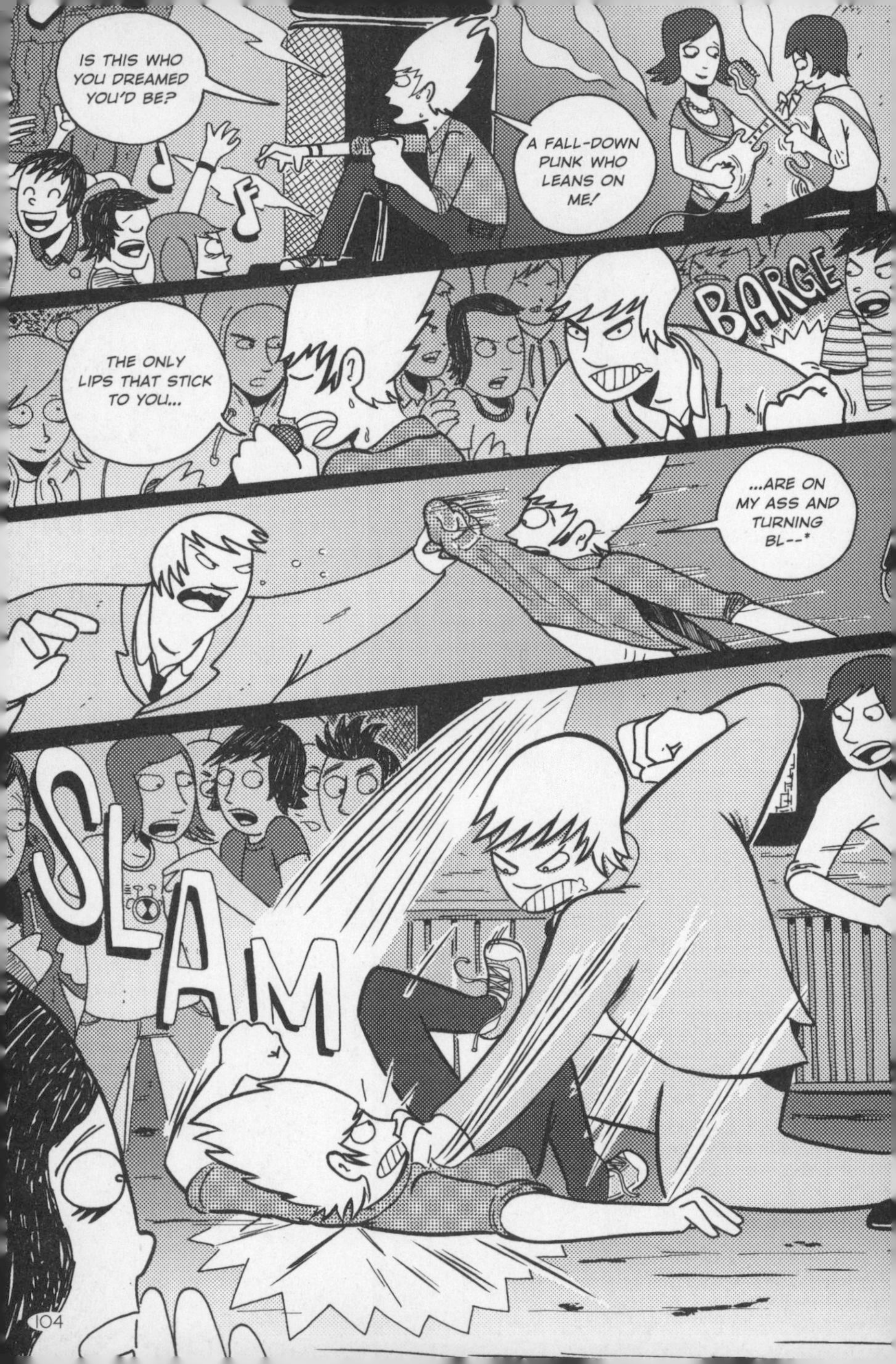
IS THIS WHO YOU DREAMED YOU'D BE?
A FALL-DOWN PUNK WHO LEANS ON ME!
THE ONLY LIPS THAT STICK TO YOU...
BARGE
...ARE ON MY ASS AND TURNING BL--*
SLAM

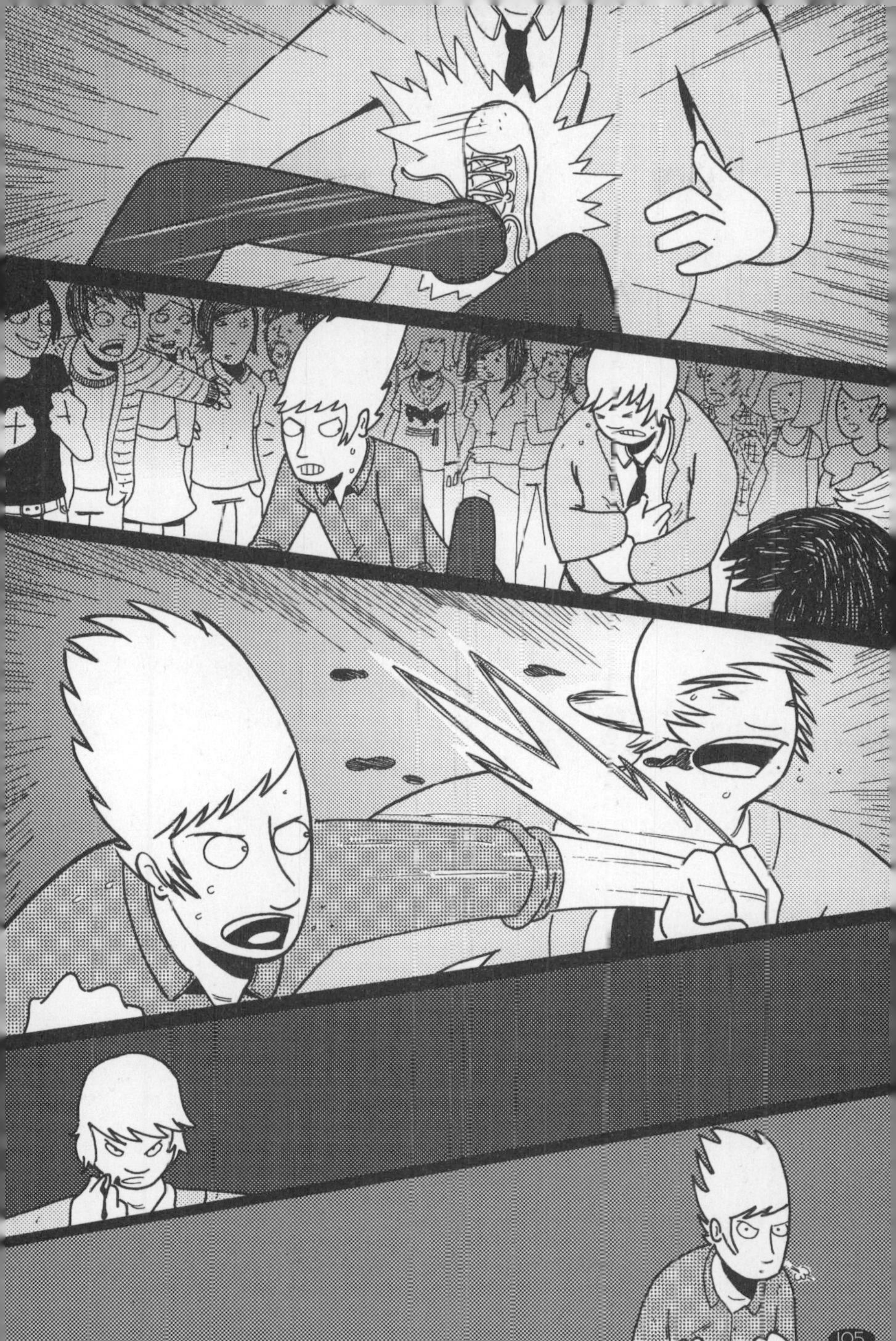

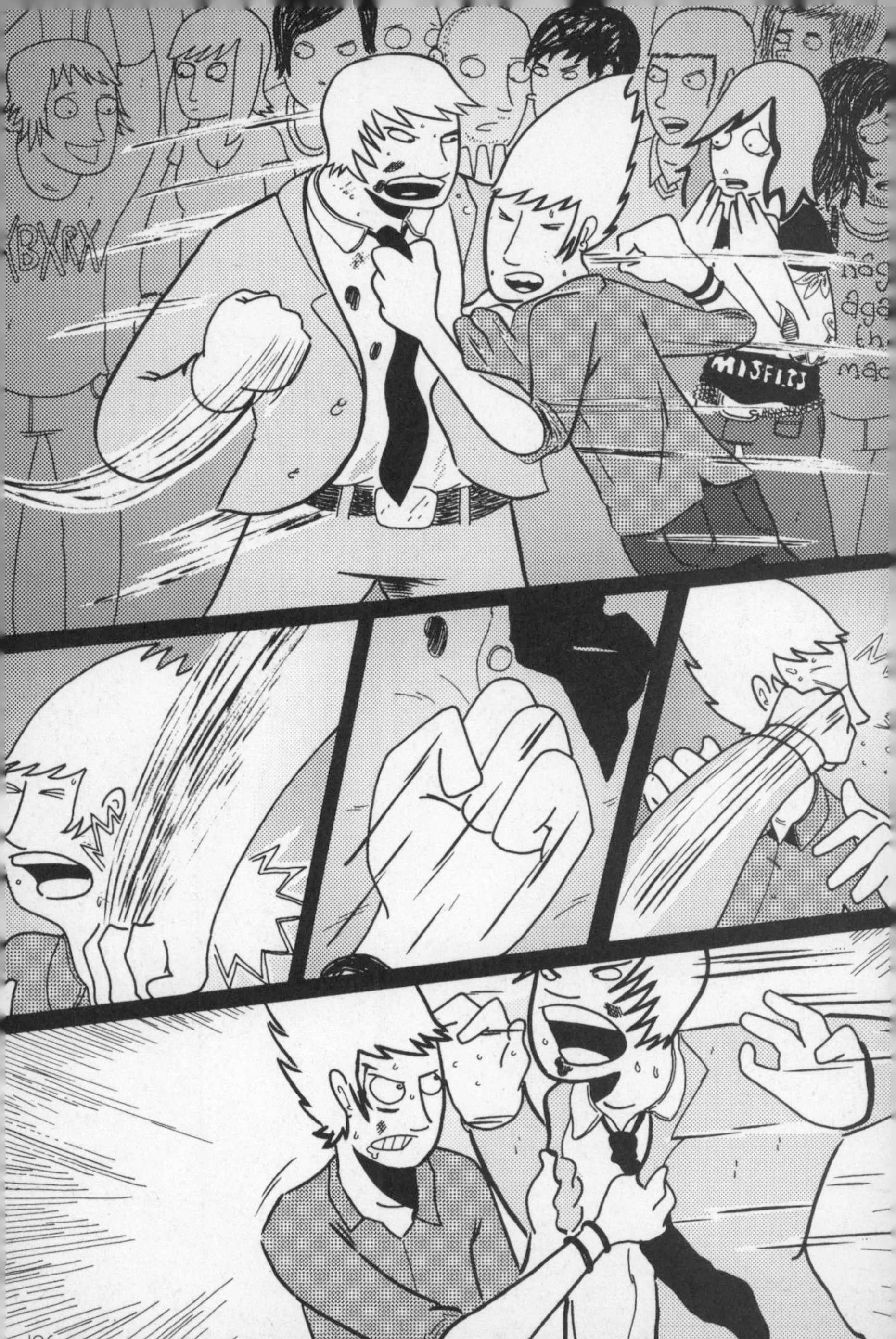
BXRX
MISFITS

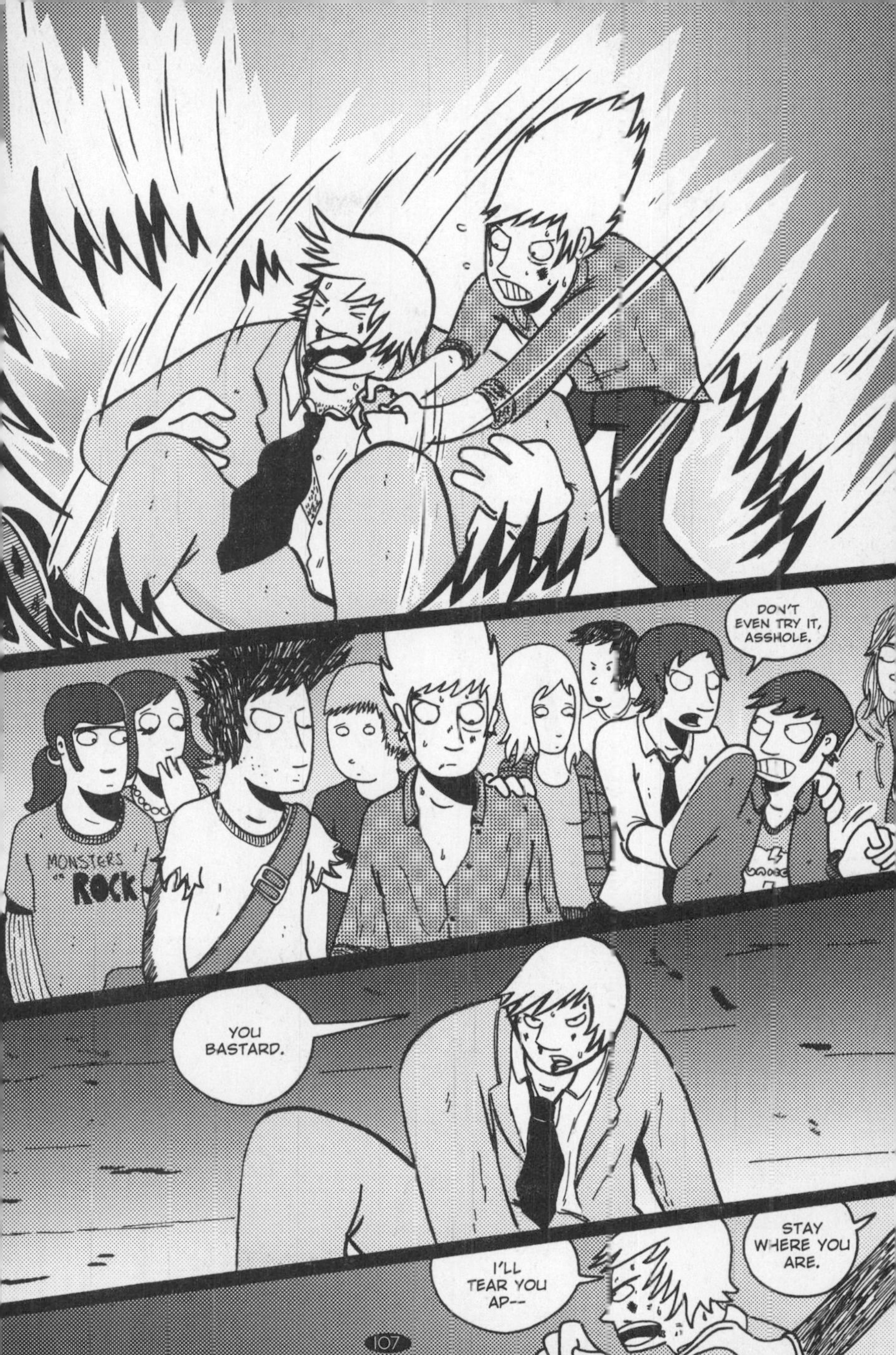
DON'T EVEN TRY IT, ASSHOLE.
MONSTERS OF ROCK
YOU BASTARD.
STAY WHERE YOU ARE.
I'LL TEAR YOU AP--

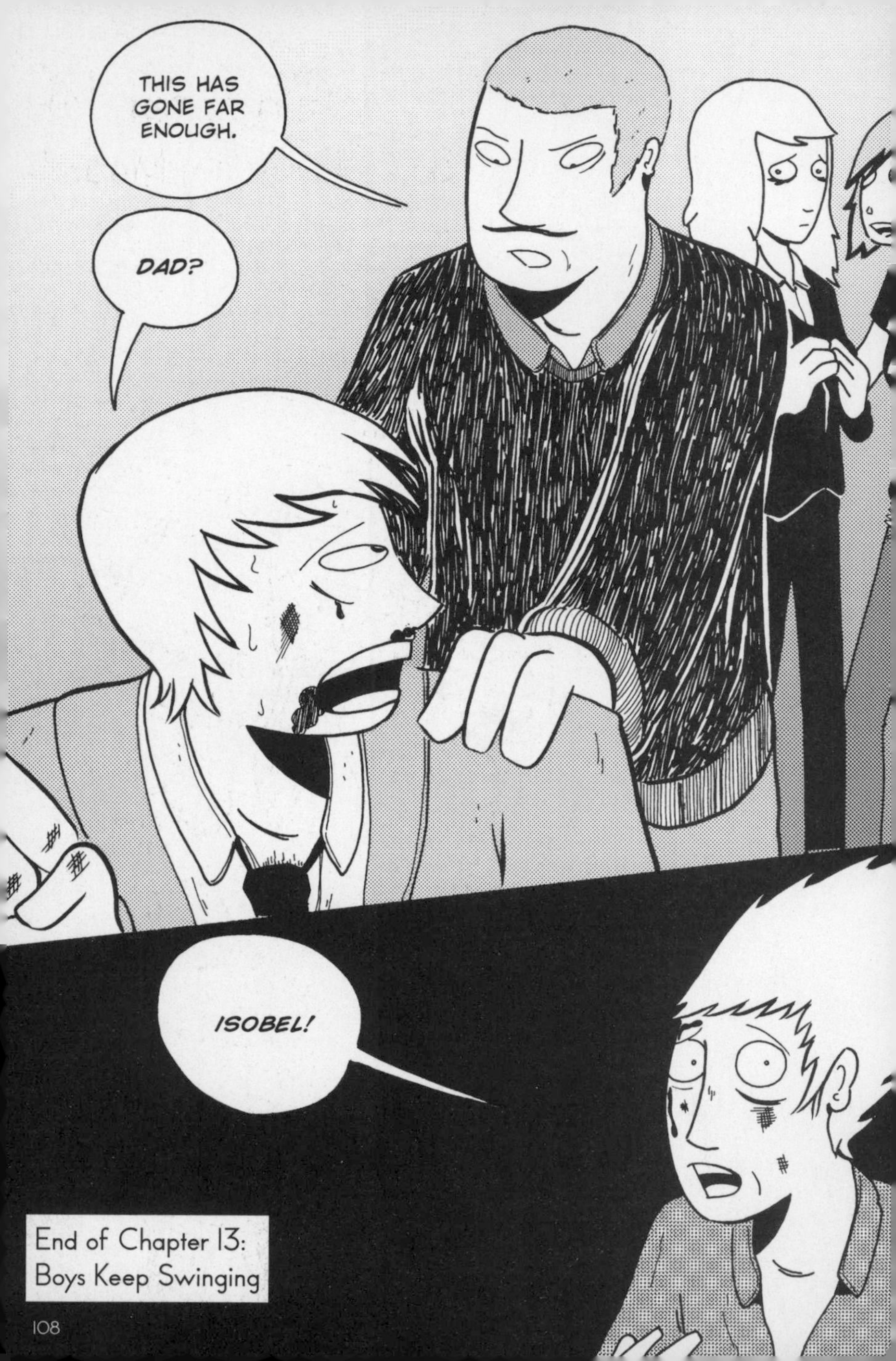
THIS HAS GONE FAR ENOUGH.
DAD?
ISOBEL!
End of Chapter 13: Boys Keep Swinging

Chapter 14:
Smile Like You Mean It

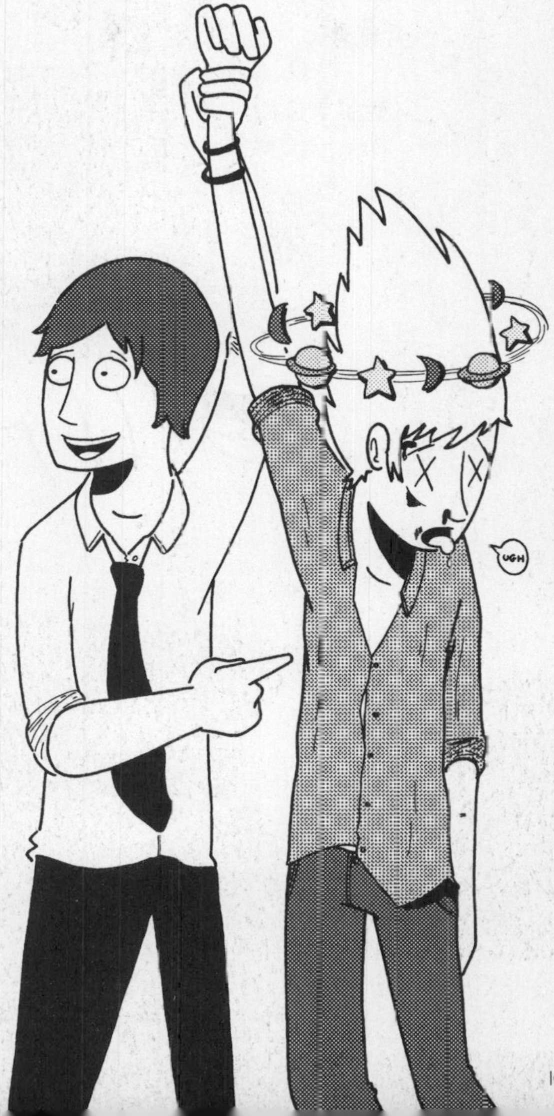
UGH

KITTEN STOMP FUTURE DREAM
LANCELOT LINK!

Full Name:
Lancelot James Scott

Band Affiliation:
Singer and guitarist for We Are Expendable, formerly know by the names Teenage Waste Band, Winston, and the Hundred Faces

Birthdate:
June 16 (Gemini)

Heroes:
Paul Weller
Arthur Lee from Love
Cary Grant
Parker Posey ("Really, I just want to meet her and have her fall in love with me.")

Prior Experience:
"Hanging around backstage watching my brother play."

Essential Supply:
Suit, tie, hat. "Everything the classic film noir gentleman might employ. I wear a fedora because that's what private dicks wear. Plus, I like the sound of the word."

Nickname:
Mary

Family:
His older brother is Tristan Scott, the leader of Like A Dog. His younger half-brother is Percival Mendelssohn, the up-and-coming philosopher.

Worst Thing Ever:
"It would be easier to figure out when things actually went right than to pick amongst the worst. Earlier today I bought a cappuccino and dropped it as soon as I got out the door of the coffee shop. That was pretty bad."

Quote:
"I sometimes wish I was dead. And by sometimes, I mean all the time."

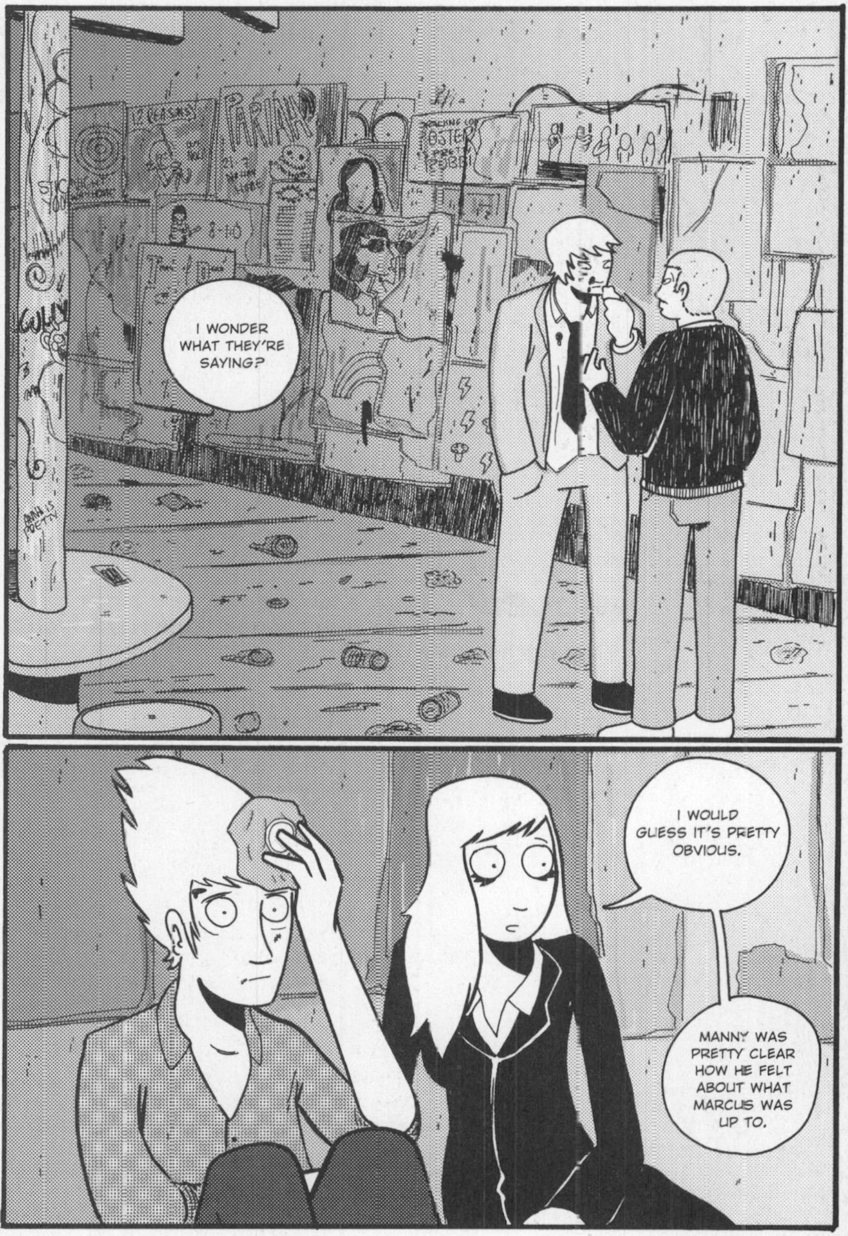
I WONDER WHAT THEY'RE SAYING?
I WOULD GUESS IT'S PRETTY OBVIOUS.
MANNY WAS PRETTY CLEAR HOW HE FELT ABOUT WHAT MARCUS WAS UP TO.

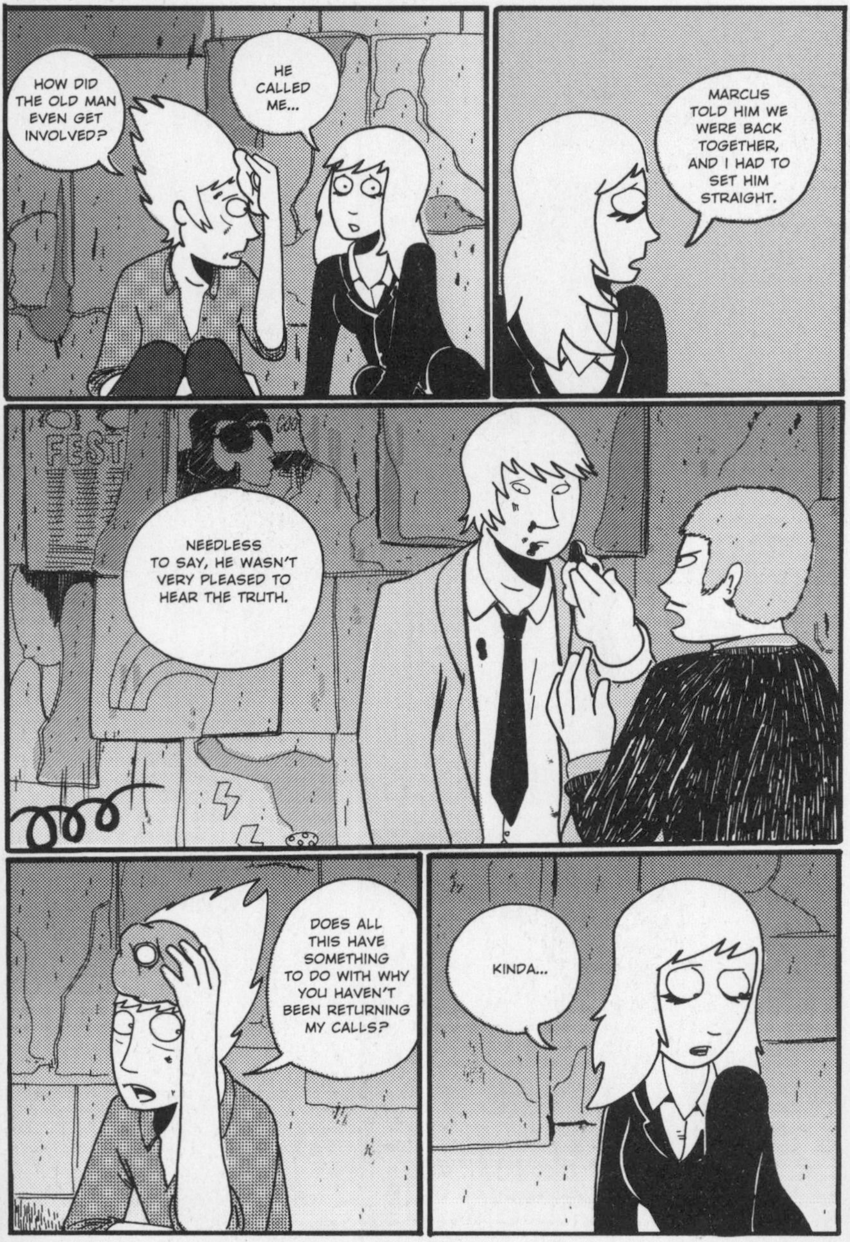
HOW DID THE OLD MAN EVEN GET INVOLVED?
HE CALLED ME...
MARCUS TOLD HIM WE WERE BACK TOGETHER, AND I HAD TO SET HIM STRAIGHT.
FEST
NEEDLESS TO SAY, HE WASN'T VERY PLEASED TO HEAR THE TRUTH.
DOES ALL THIS HAVE SOMETHING TO DO WITH WHY YOU HAVEN'T BEEN RETURNING MY CALLS?
KINDA...

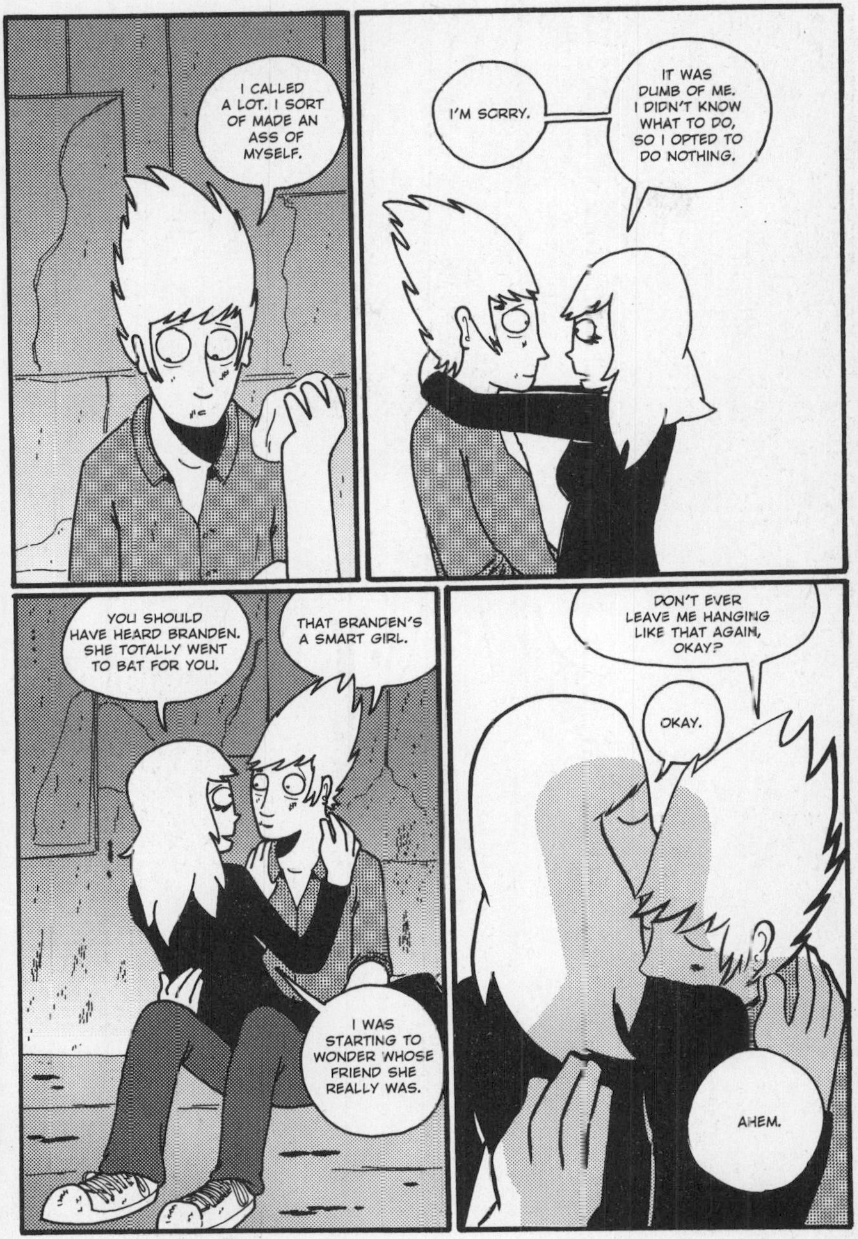
I CALLED A LOT. I SORT OF MADE AN ASS OF MYSELF.
I'M SORRY.
IT WAS DUMB OF ME. I DIDN'T KNOW WHAT TO DO, SO I OPTED TO DO NOTHING.
YOU SHOULD HAVE HEARD BRANDEN. SHE TOTALLY WENT TO BAT FOR YOU.
THAT BRANDEN'S A SMART GIRL.
I WAS STARTING TO WONDER WHOSE FRIEND SHE REALLY WAS.
DON'T EVER LEAVE ME HANGING LIKE THAT AGAIN, OKAY?
OKAY.
AHEM.

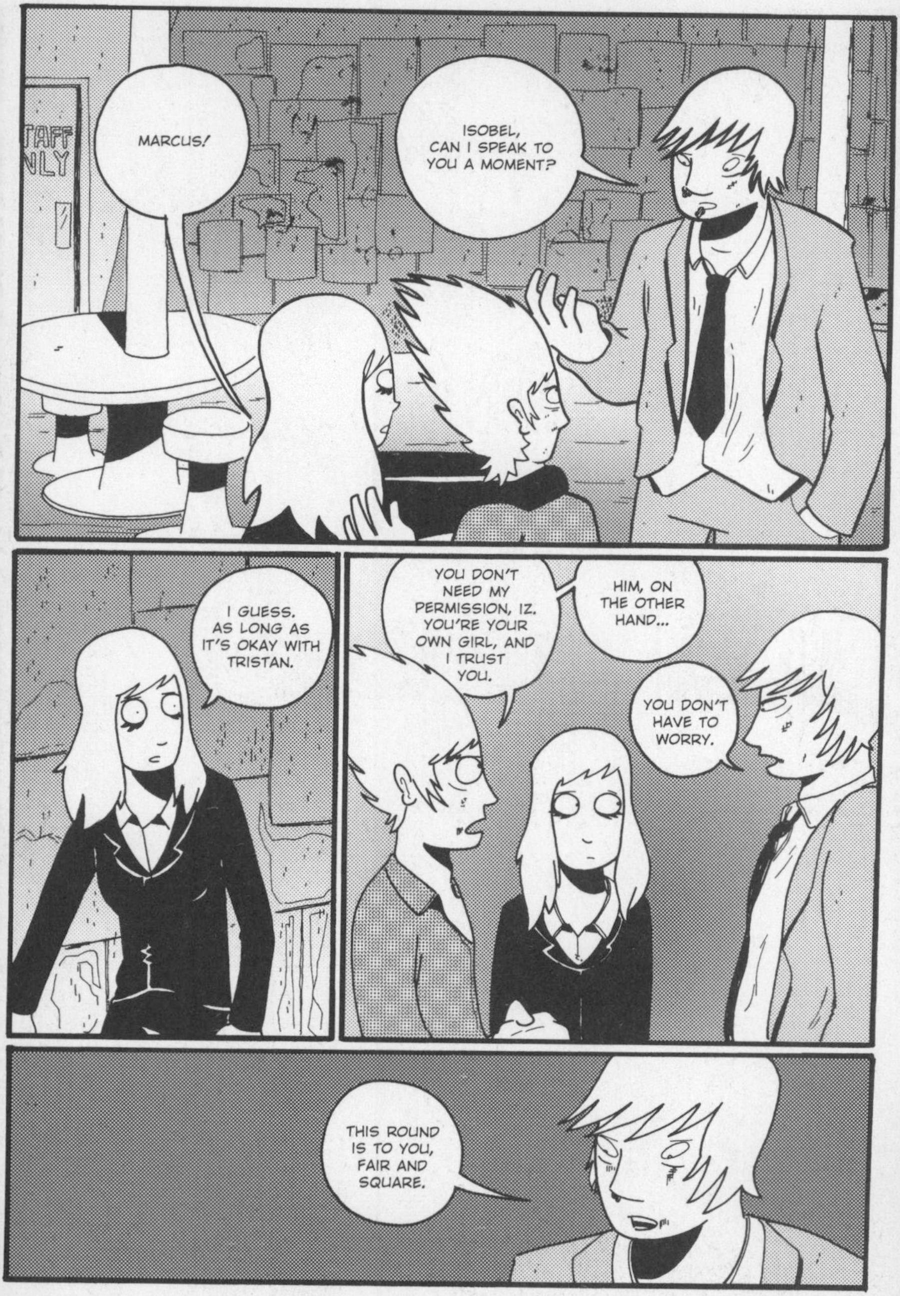
MARCUS!
ISOBEL, CAN I SPEAK TO YOU A MOMENT?
I GUESS. AS LONG AS IT'S OKAY WITH TRISTAN.
YOU DON'T NEED MY PERMISSION, IZ. YOU'RE YOUR OWN GIRL, AND I TRUST YOU.
HIM, ON THE OTHER HAND...
YOU DON'T HAVE TO WORRY.
THIS ROUND IS TO YOU, FAIR AND SQUARE.

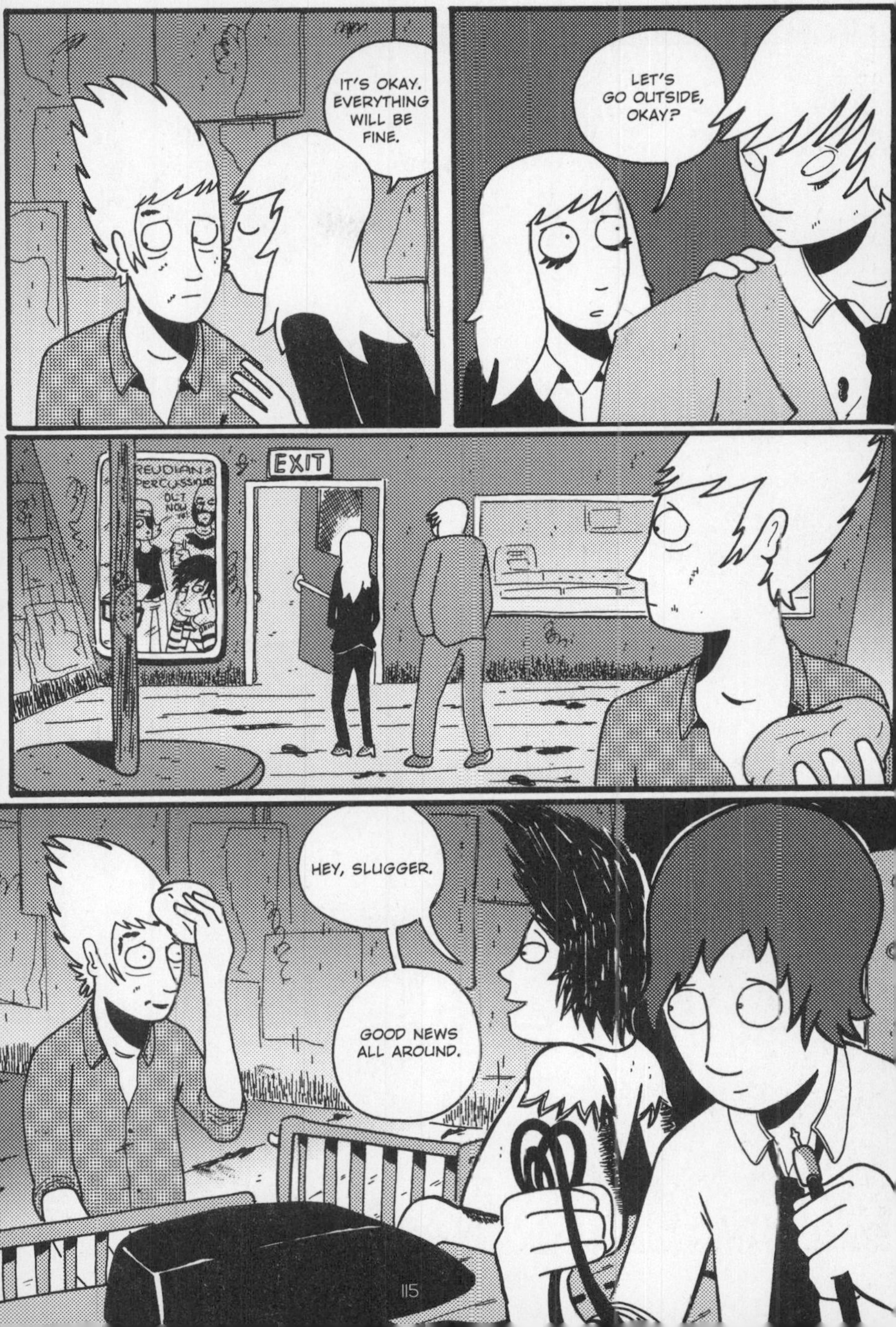
IT'S OKAY. EVERYTHING WILL BE FINE.
LET'S GO OUTSIDE, OKAY?
EXIT
HEY, SLUGGER.
GOOD NEWS ALL AROUND.

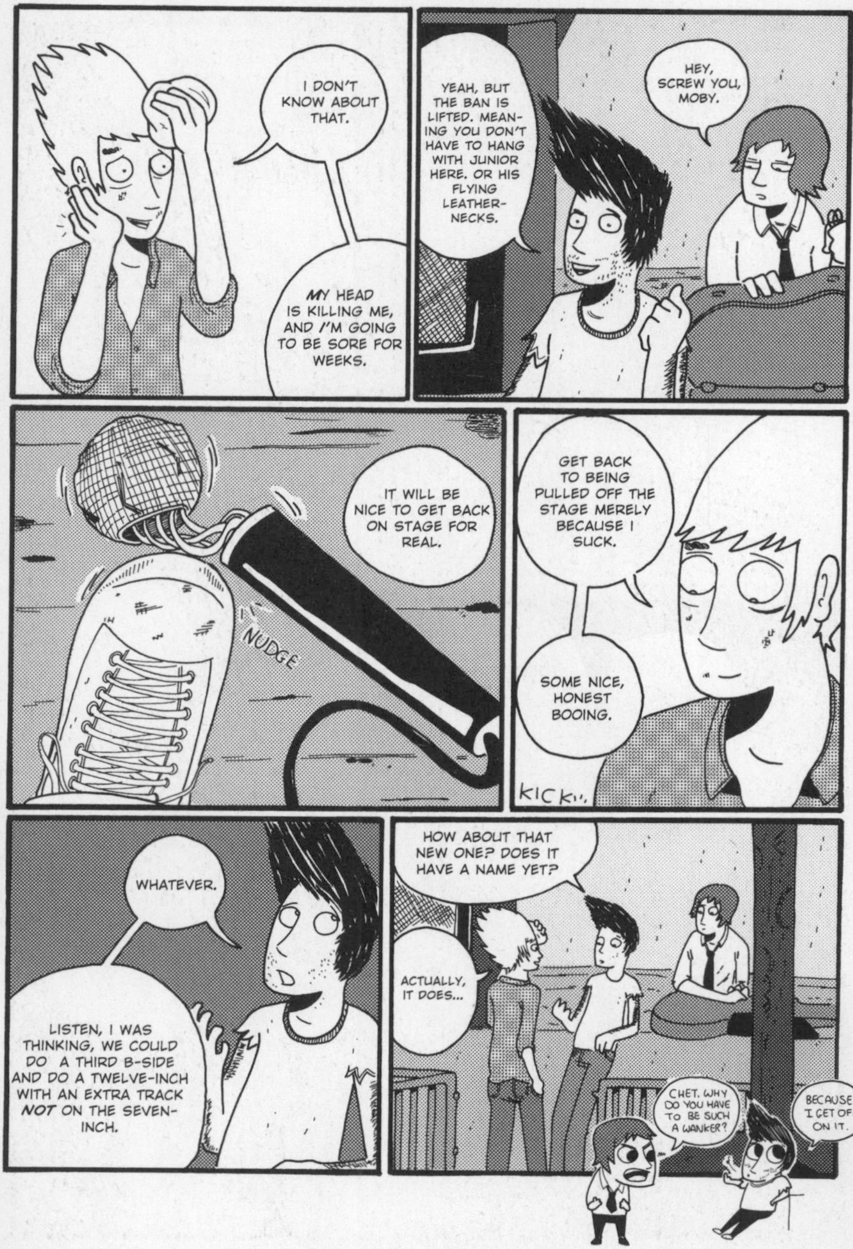
I DON'T KNOW ABOUT THAT.
MY HEAD IS KILLING ME, AND I'M GOING TO BE SORE FOR WEEKS.
YEAH, BUT THE BAN IS LIFTED. MEANING YOU DON'T HAVE TO HANG WITH JUNIOR HERE. OR HIS FLYING LEATHERNECKS.
HEY, SCREW YOU, MOBY.
IT WILL BE NICE TO GET BACK ON STAGE FOR REAL.
NUDGE
GET BACK TO BEING PULLED OFF THE STAGE MERELY BECAUSE I SUCK.
SOME NICE, HONEST BOOING.
KICK
WHATEVER.
LISTEN, I WAS THINKING, WE COULD DO A THIRD B-SIDE AND DO A TWELVE-INCH WITH AN EXTRA TRACK NOT ON THE SEVEN-INCH.
HOW ABOUT THAT NEW ONE? DOES IT HAVE A NAME YET?
ACTUALLY, IT DOES...
CHET, WHY DO YOU HAVE TO BE SUCH A WANKER?
BECAUSE I GET OFF ON IT.

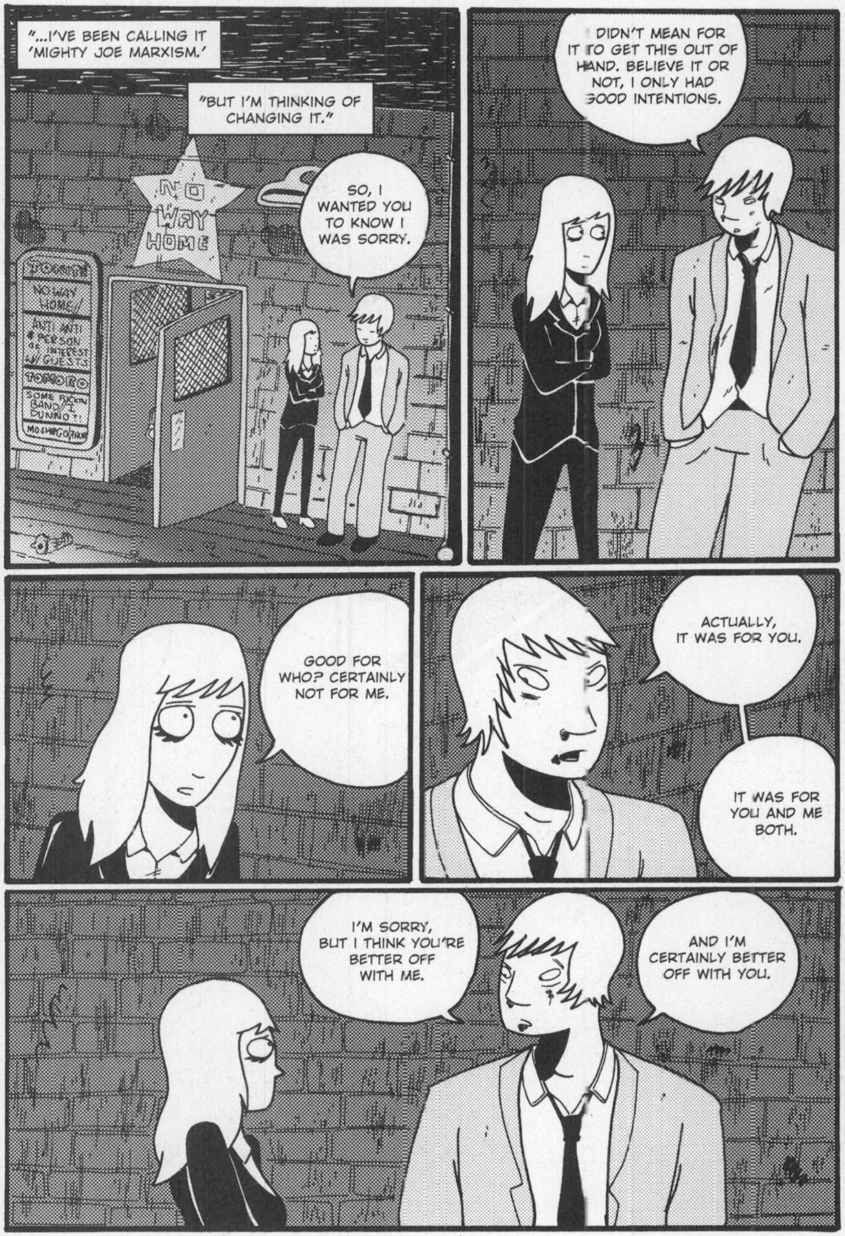
"...I'VE BEEN CALLING IT 'MIGHTY JOE MARXISM.'
"BUT I'M THINKING OF CHANGING IT."
NO WAY HOME
NO WAY HOME/ ANTI ANTI PERSON OF INTEREST W/ GUESTS
TOMORO
SOME FUCKIN BAND/ I DUNNO
SO, I WANTED YOU TO KNOW I WAS SORRY.
I DIDN'T MEAN FOR IT TO GET THIS OUT OF HAND. BELIEVE IT OR NOT, I ONLY HAD GOOD INTENTIONS.
GOOD FOR WHO? CERTAINLY NOT FOR ME.
ACTUALLY, IT WAS FOR YOU.
IT WAS FOR YOU AND ME BOTH.
I'M SORRY, BUT I THINK YOU'RE BETTER OFF WITH ME.
AND I'M CERTAINLY BETTER OFF WITH YOU.

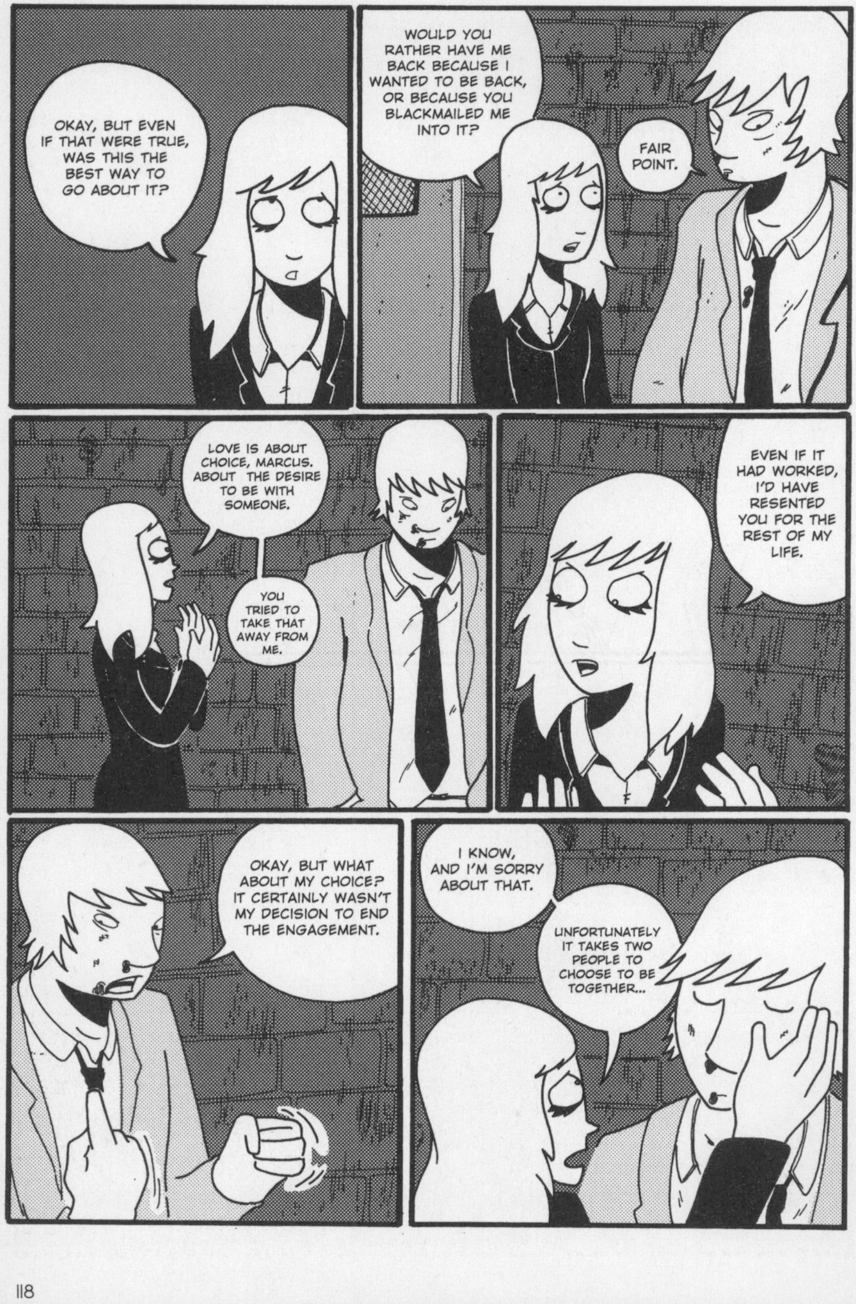
OKAY, BUT EVEN IF THAT WERE TRUE, WAS THIS THE BEST WAY TO GO ABOUT IT?
WOULD YOU RATHER HAVE ME BACK BECAUSE I WANTED TO BE BACK, OR BECAUSE YOU BLACKMAILED ME INTO IT?
FAIR POINT.
LOVE IS ABOUT CHOICE, MARCUS. ABOUT THE DESIRE TO BE WITH SOMEONE.
YOU TRIED TO TAKE THAT AWAY FROM ME.
EVEN IF IT HAD WORKED, I'D HAVE RESENTED YOU FOR THE REST OF MY LIFE.
OKAY, BUT WHAT ABOUT MY CHOICE? IT CERTAINLY WASN'T MY DECISION TO END THE ENGAGEMENT.
I KNOW, AND I'M SORRY ABOUT THAT.
UNFORTUNATELY IT TAKES TWO PEOPLE TO CHOOSE TO BE TOGETHER...

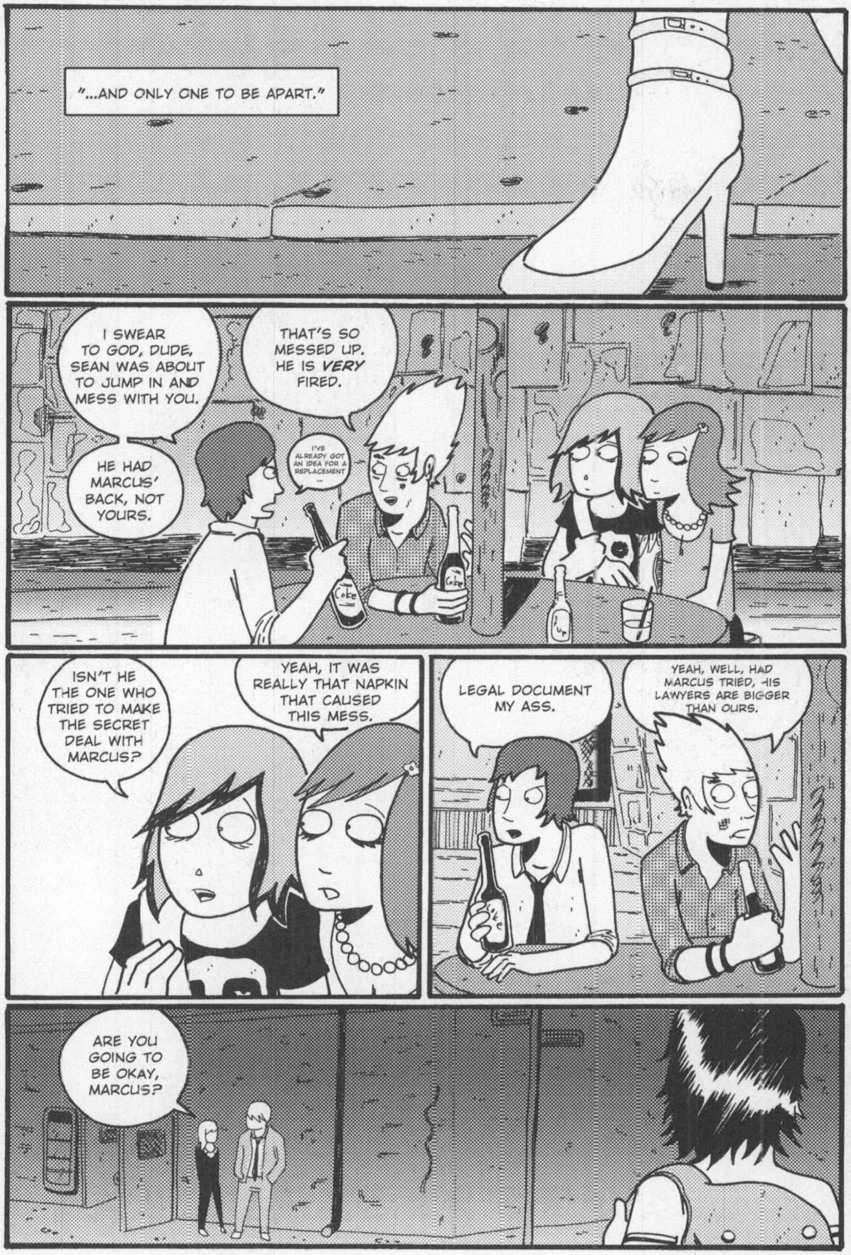
"...AND ONLY ONE TO BE APART."
I SWEAR TO GOD, DUDE, SEAN WAS ABOUT TO JUMP IN AND MESS WITH YOU.
HE HAD MARCUS' BACK, NOT YOURS.
THAT'S SO MESSED UP. HE IS *VERY* FIRED.
I'VE ALREADY GOT AN IDEA FOR A REPLACEMENT...
ISN'T HE THE ONE WHO TRIED TO MAKE THE SECRET DEAL WITH MARCUS?
YEAH, IT WAS REALLY THAT NAPKIN THAT CAUSED THIS MESS.
LEGAL DOCUMENT MY ASS.
YEAH, WELL, HAD MARCUS TRIED, HIS LAWYERS ARE BIGGER THAN OURS.
ARE YOU GOING TO BE OKAY, MARCUS?

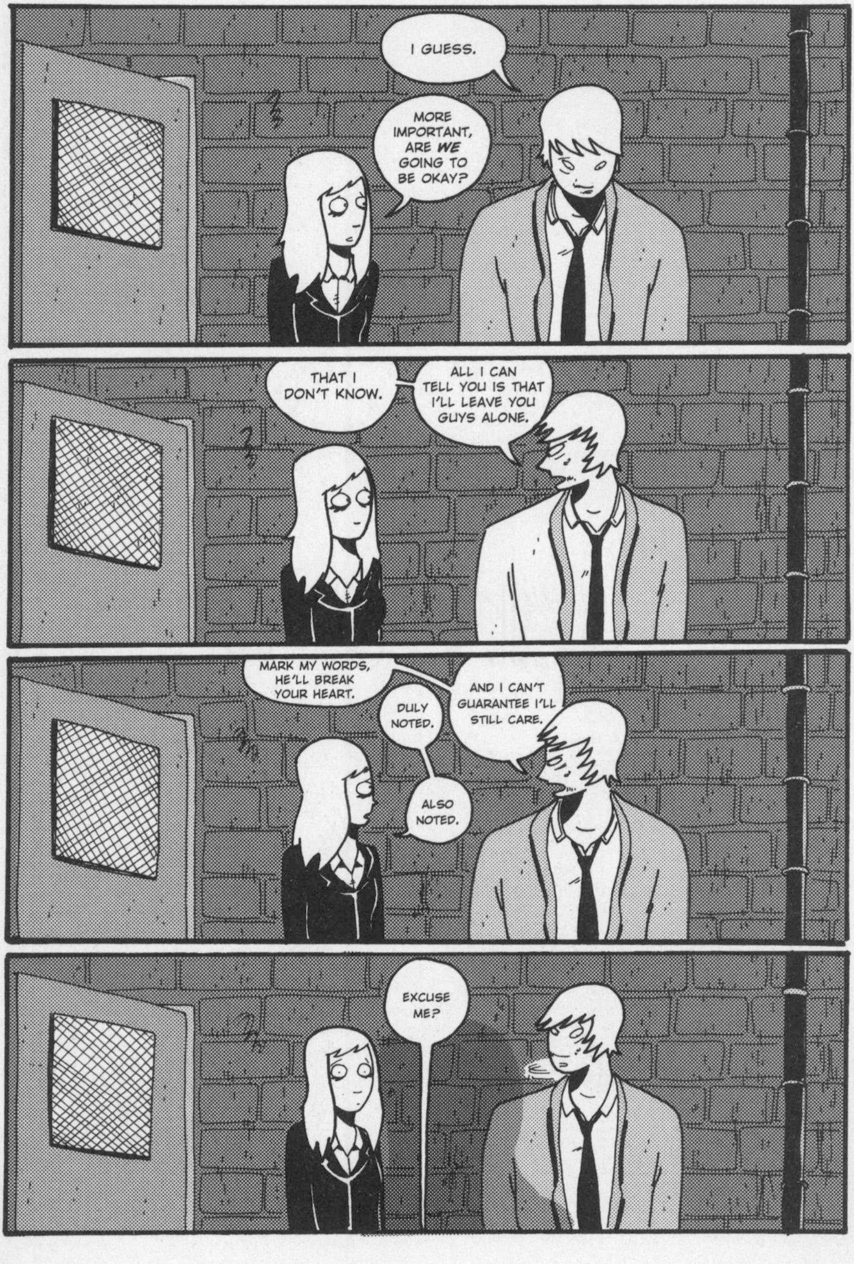
I GUESS.
MORE IMPORTANT, ARE *WE* GOING TO BE OKAY?
THAT I DON'T KNOW.
ALL I CAN TELL YOU IS THAT I'LL LEAVE YOU GUYS ALONE.
MARK MY WORDS, HE'LL BREAK YOUR HEART.
DULY NOTED.
AND I CAN'T GUARANTEE I'LL STILL CARE.
ALSO NOTED.
EXCUSE ME?

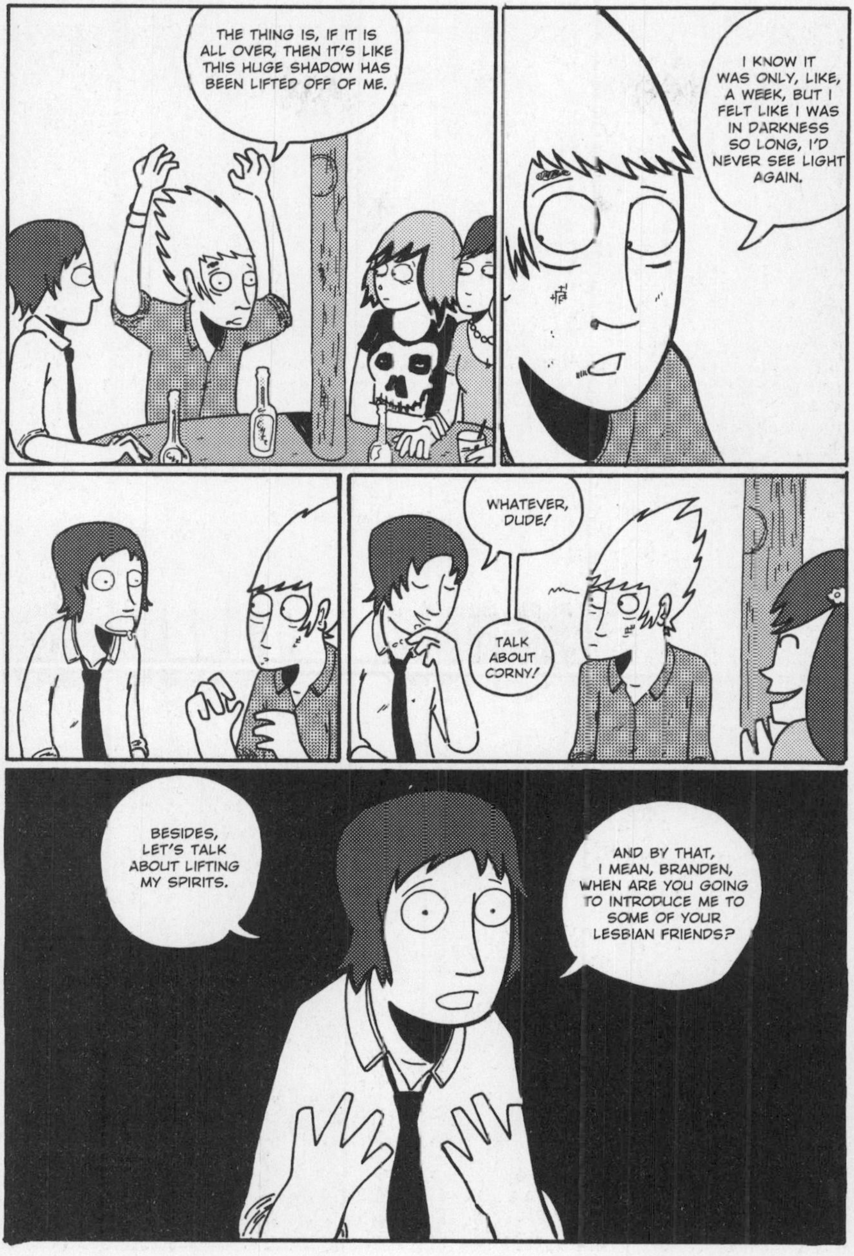
THE THING IS, IF IT IS ALL OVER, THEN IT'S LIKE THIS HUGE SHADOW HAS BEEN LIFTED OFF OF ME.
I KNOW IT WAS ONLY, LIKE, A WEEK, BUT I FELT LIKE I WAS IN DARKNESS SO LONG, I'D NEVER SEE LIGHT AGAIN.
WHATEVER, DUDE!
TALK ABOUT CORNY!
BESIDES, LET'S TALK ABOUT LIFTING MY SPIRITS.
AND BY THAT, I MEAN, BRANDEN, WHEN ARE YOU GOING TO INTRODUCE ME TO SOME OF YOUR LESBIAN FRIENDS?

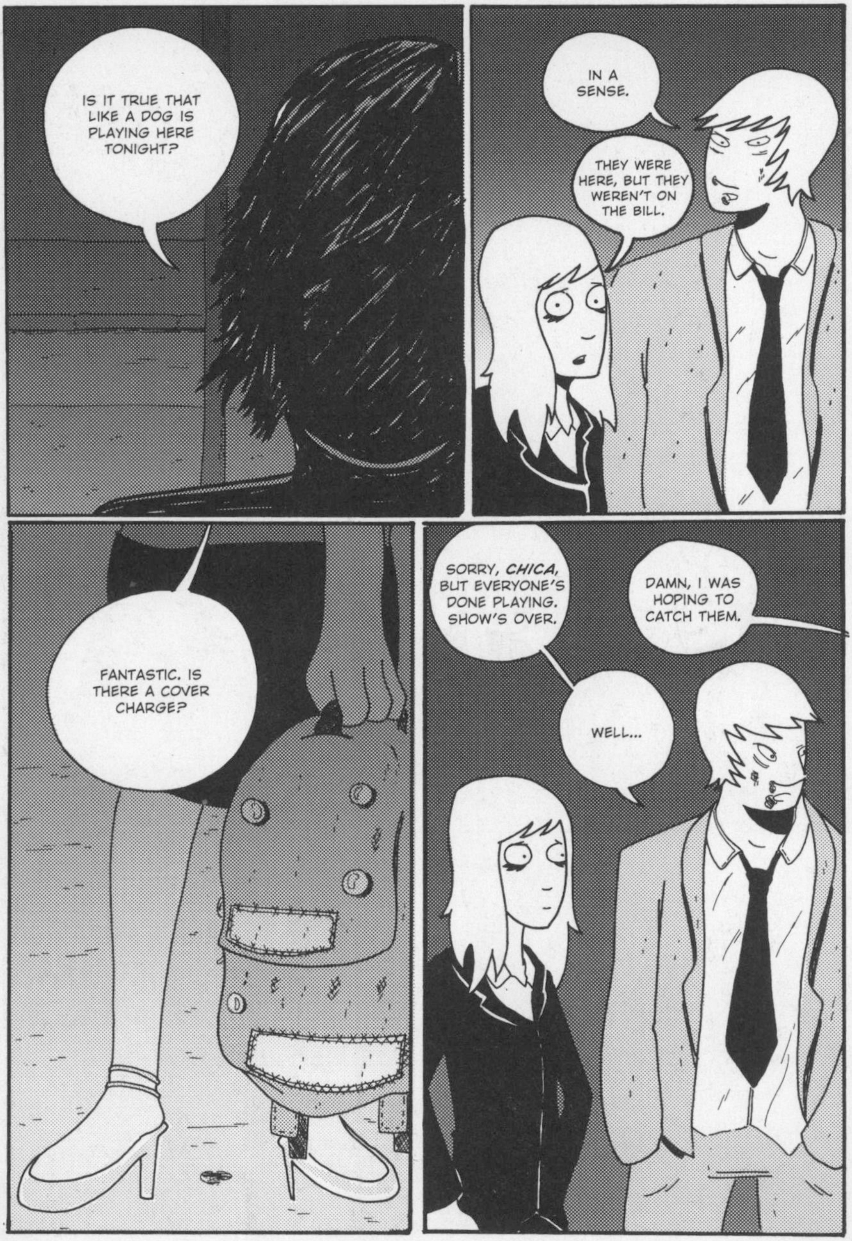
IS IT TRUE THAT LIKE A DOG IS PLAYING HERE TONIGHT?
IN A SENSE.
THEY WERE HERE, BUT THEY WEREN'T ON THE BILL.
FANTASTIC. IS THERE A COVER CHARGE?
SORRY, *CHICA*, BUT EVERYONE'S DONE PLAYING. SHOW'S OVER.
DAMN, I WAS HOPING TO CATCH THEM.
WELL...

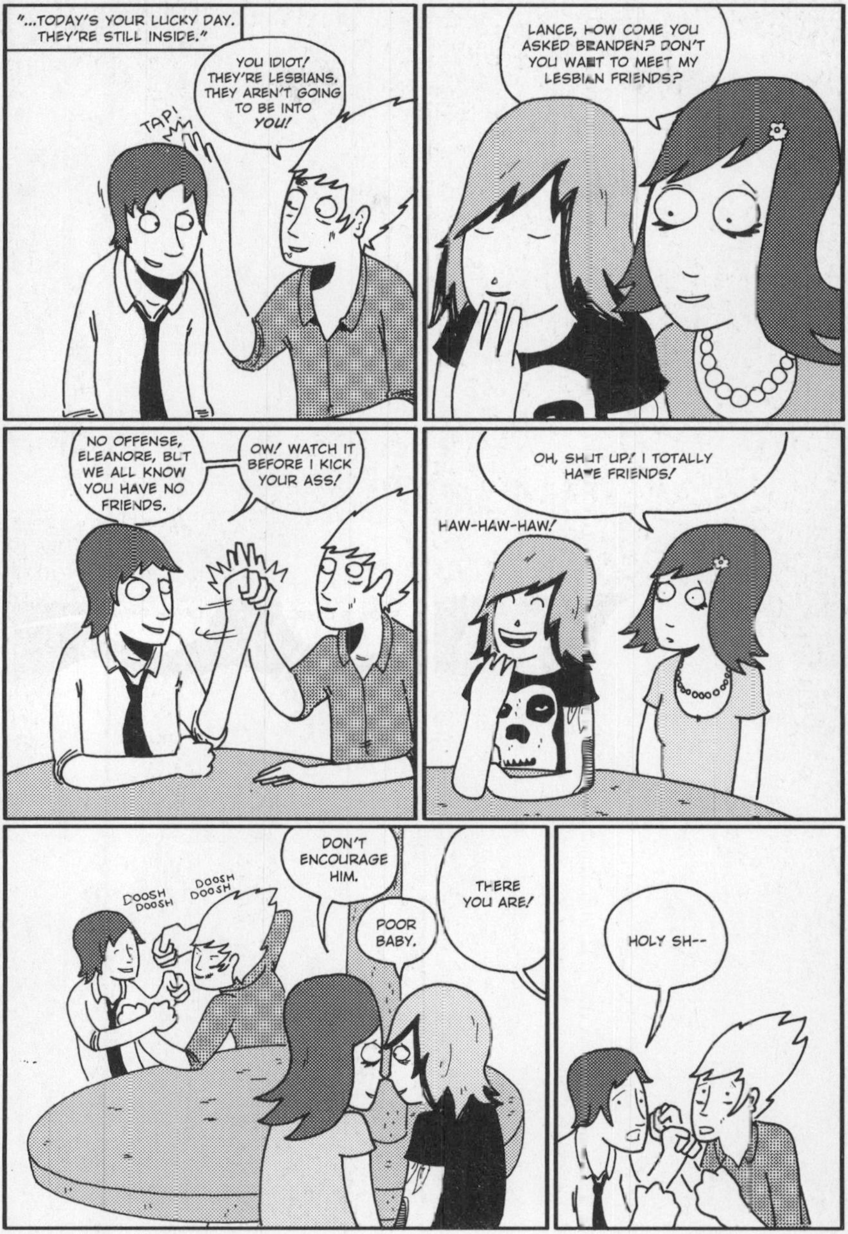
"...TODAY'S YOUR LUCKY DAY. THEY'RE STILL INSIDE."
YOU IDIOT! THEY'RE LESBIANS. THEY AREN'T GOING TO BE INTO *YOU!*
TAP!
LANCE, HOW COME YOU ASKED BRANDEN? DON'T YOU WANT TO MEET MY LESBIAN FRIENDS?
NO OFFENSE, ELEANORE, BUT WE ALL KNOW YOU HAVE NO FRIENDS.
OW! WATCH IT BEFORE I KICK YOUR ASS!
OH, SHUT UP! I TOTALLY HAVE FRIENDS!
HAW-HAW-HAW!
DOOSH DOOSH
DOOSH DOOSH
DON'T ENCOURAGE HIM.
POOR BABY.
THERE YOU ARE!
HOLY SH--

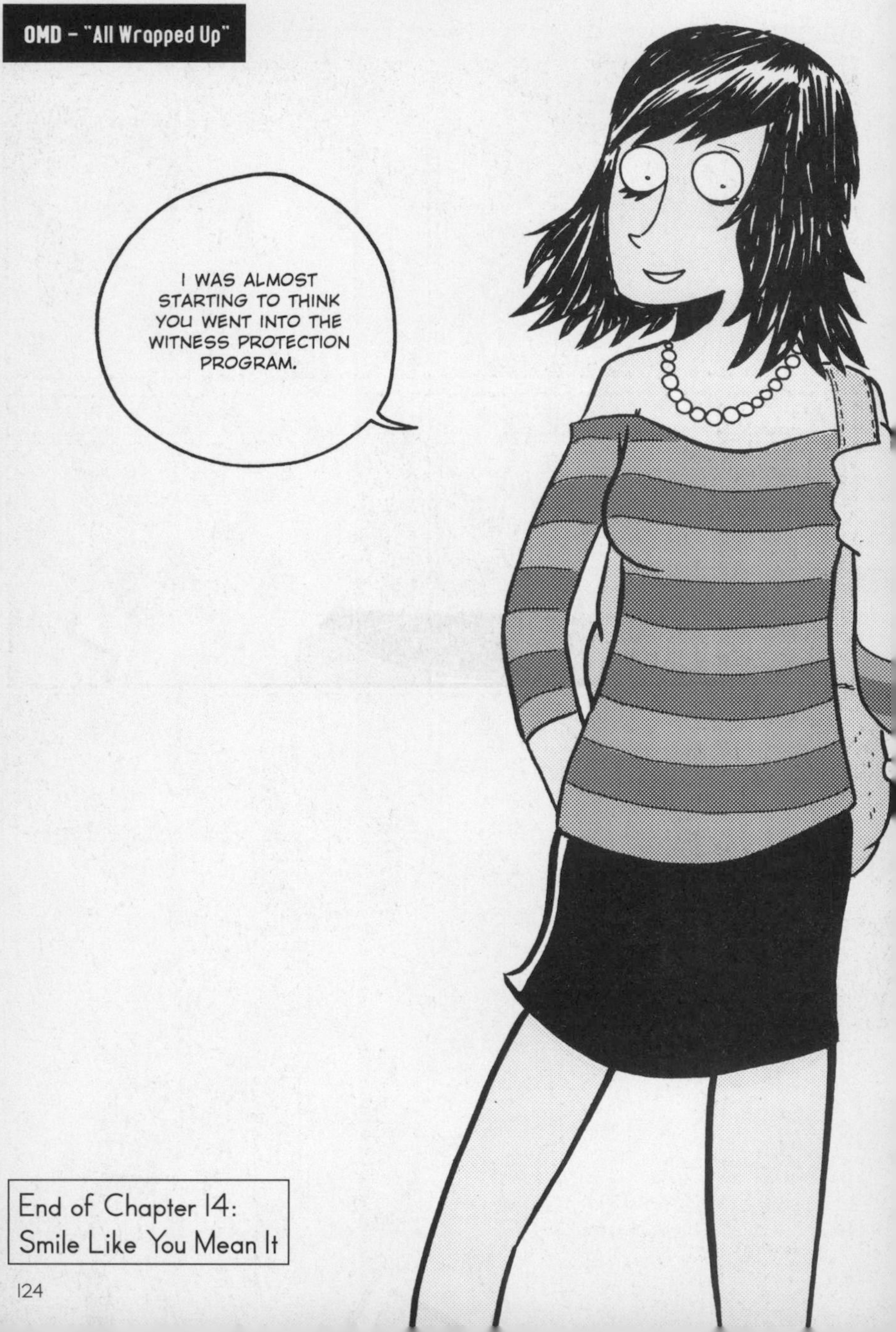
OMD - "All Wrapped Up"
I WAS ALMOST STARTING TO THINK YOU WENT INTO THE WITNESS PROTECTION PROGRAM.

End of Chapter 14:
Smile Like You Mean It

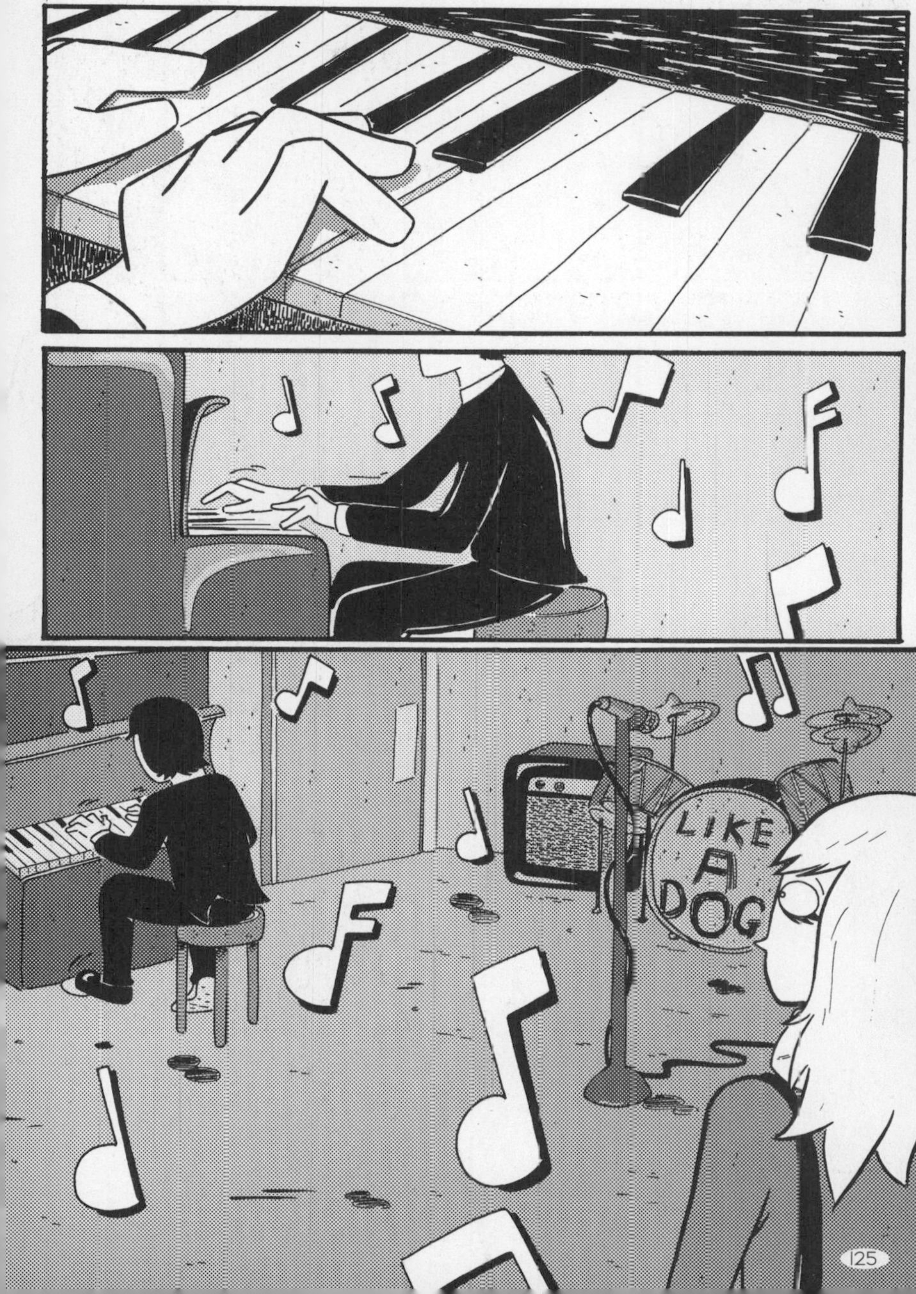
LIKE A DOG

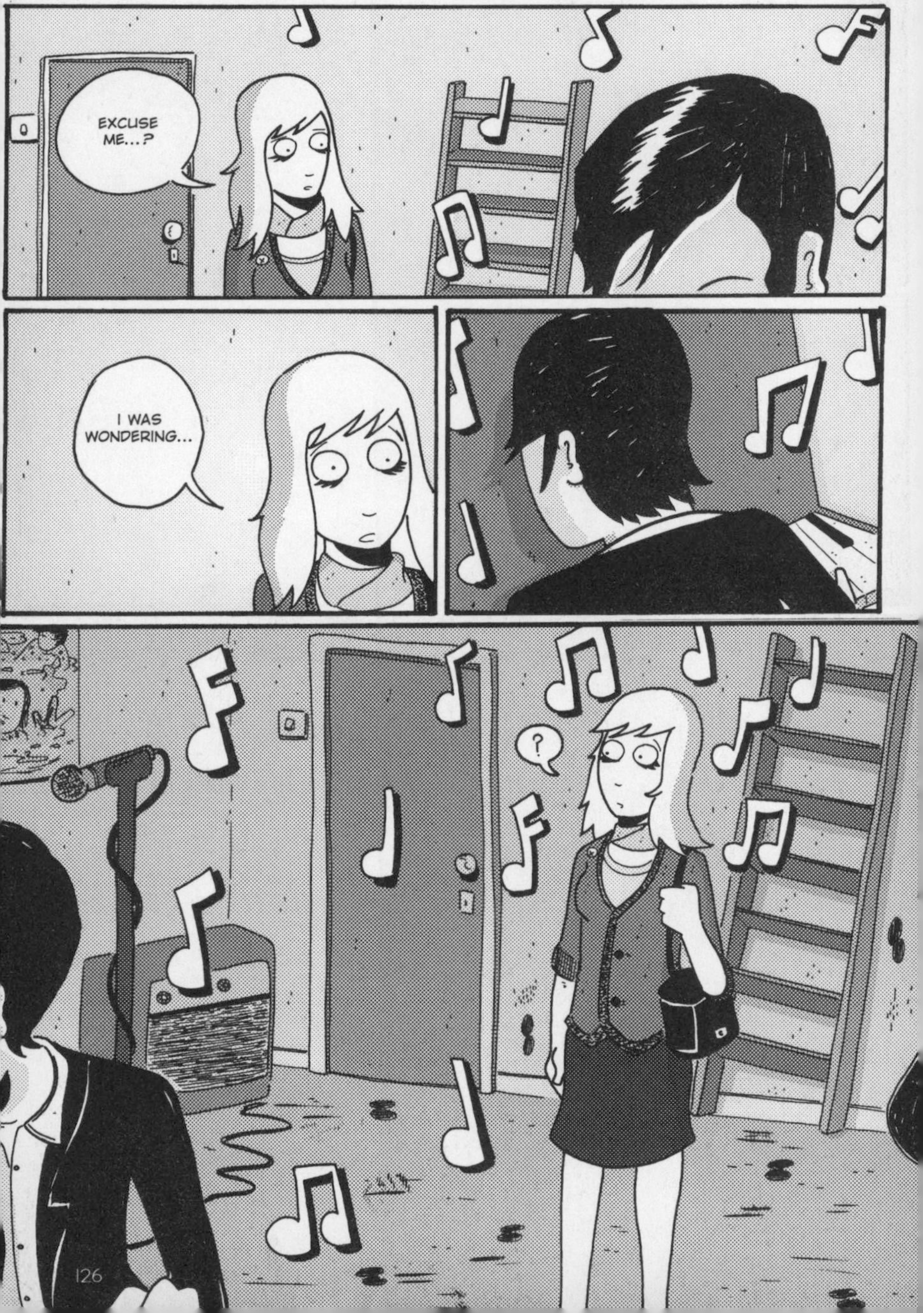
EXCUSE ME...?
I WAS WONDERING...
?

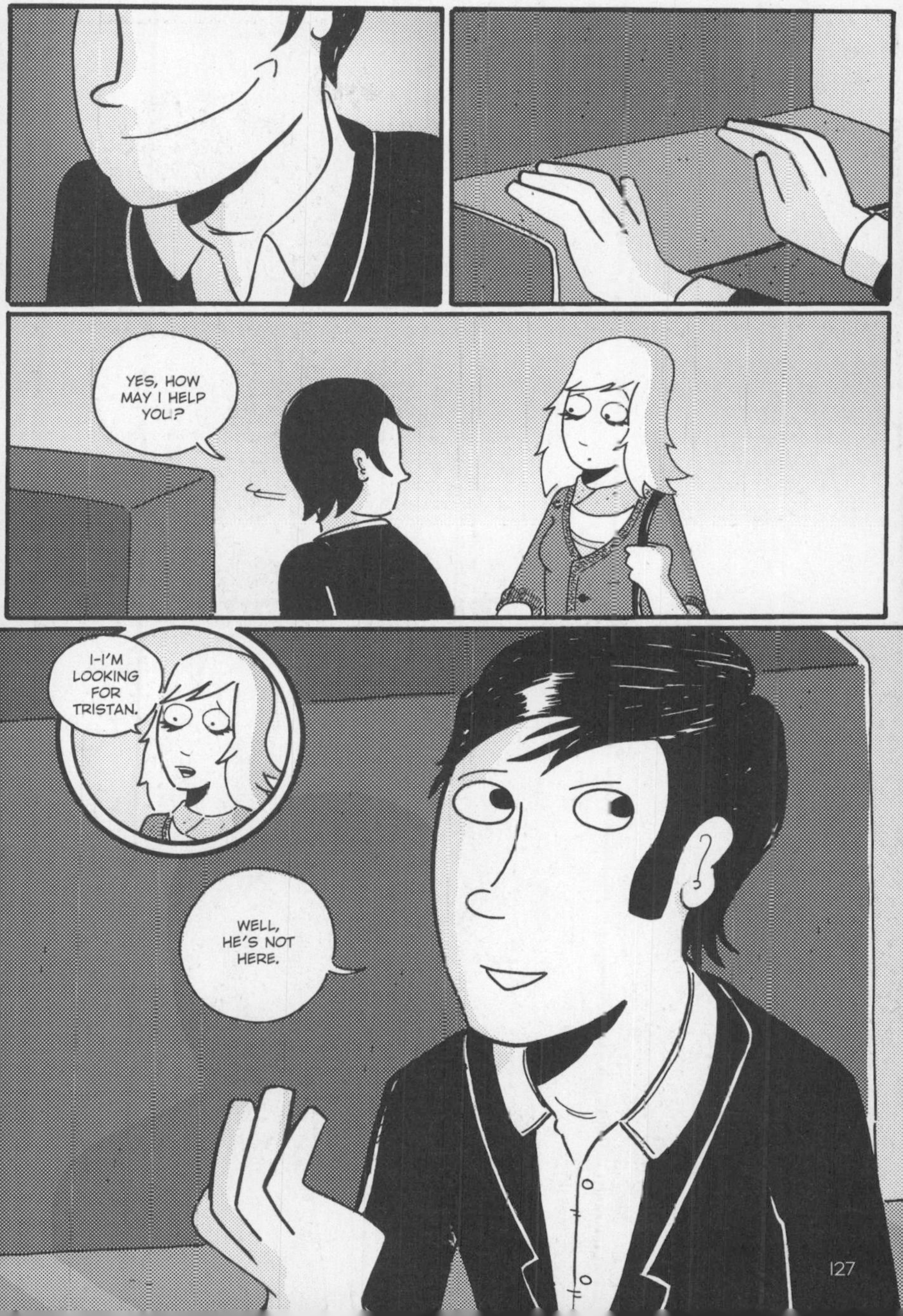
YES, HOW MAY I HELP YOU?
I-I'M LOOKING FOR TRISTAN.
WELL, HE'S NOT HERE.

Chapter 15:
Cheating Judases & Doubting Thomases

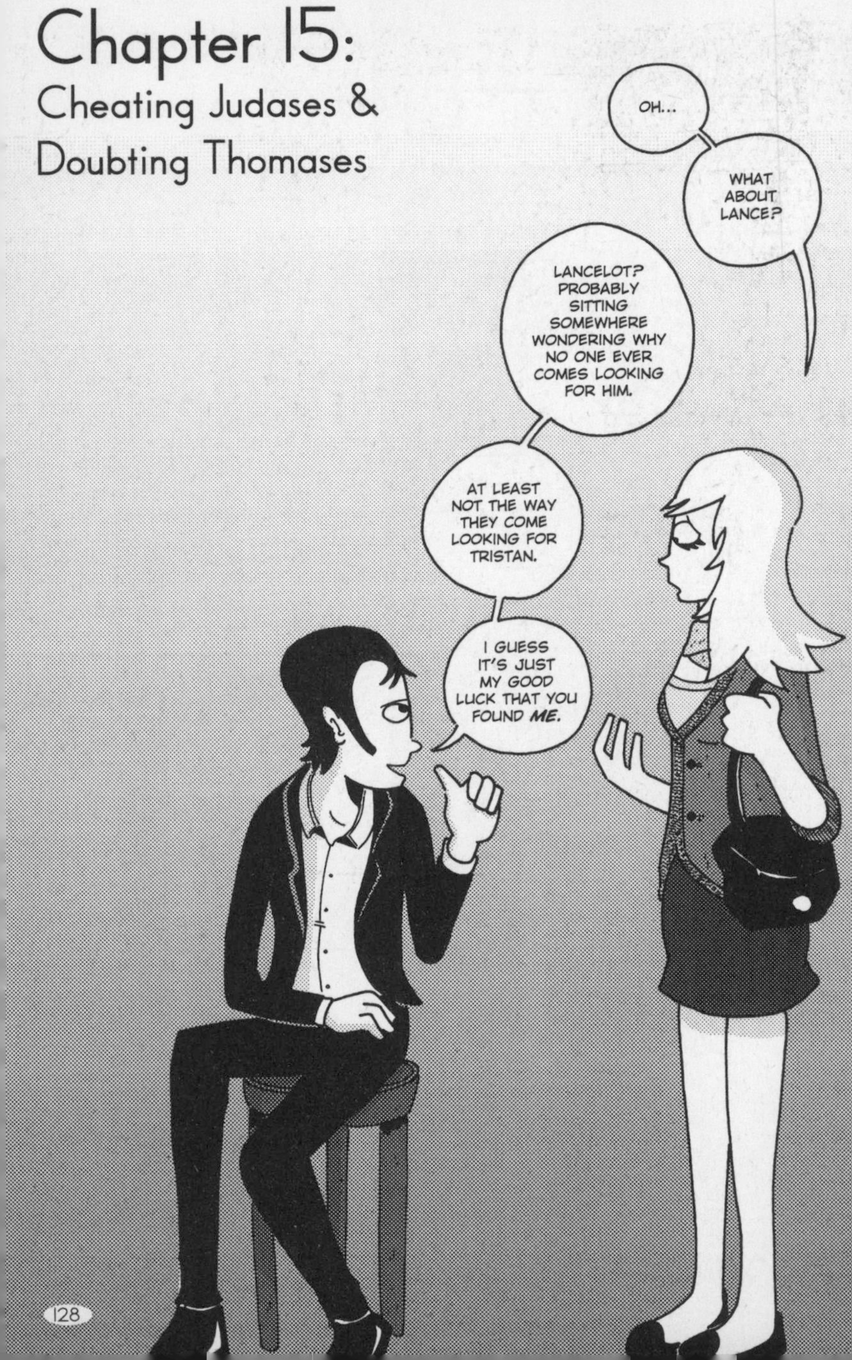
OH...
WHAT ABOUT LANCE?
LANCELOT? PROBABLY SITTING SOMEWHERE WONDERING WHY NO ONE EVER COMES LOOKING FOR HIM.
AT LEAST NOT THE WAY THEY COME LOOKING FOR TRISTAN.
I GUESS IT'S JUST MY GOOD LUCK THAT YOU FOUND ***ME.***

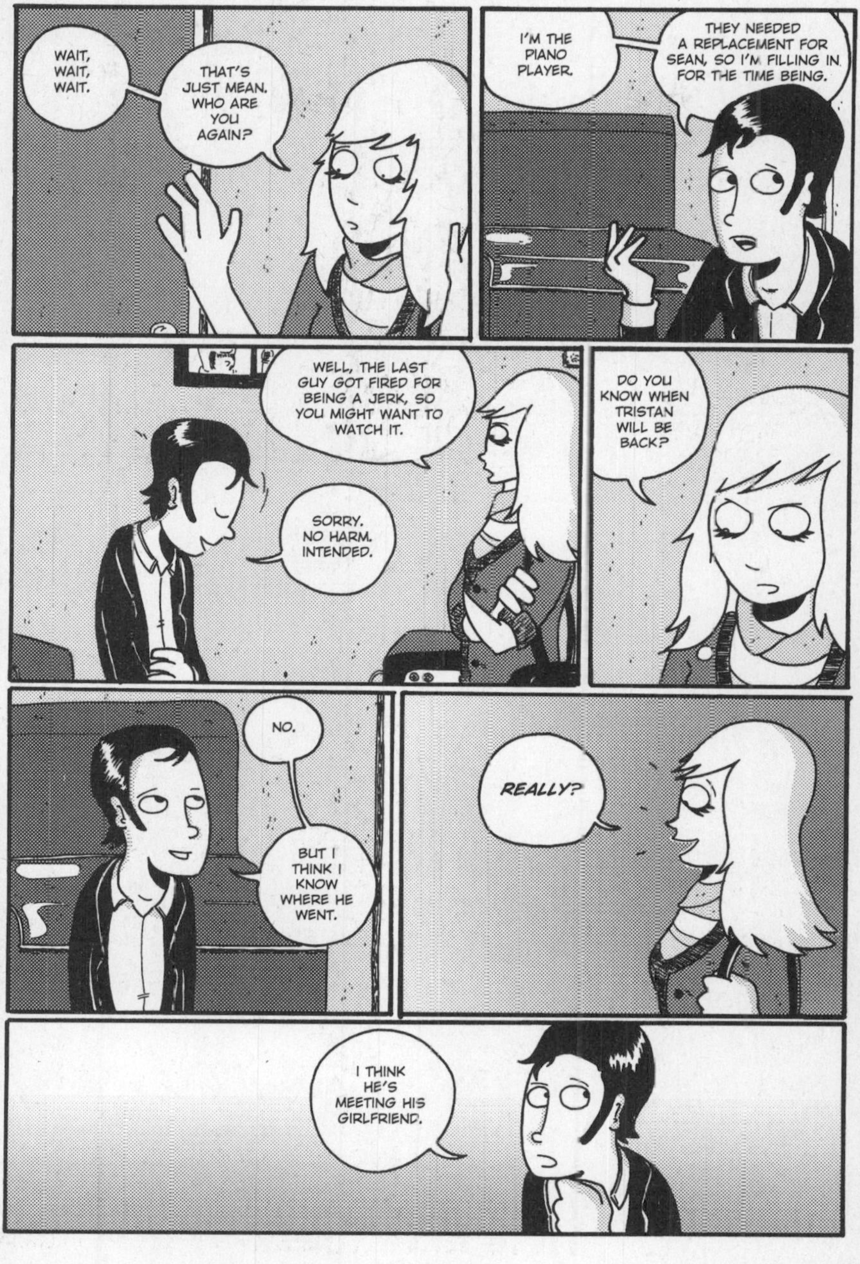
WAIT, WAIT, WAIT.
THAT'S JUST MEAN. WHO ARE YOU AGAIN?
I'M THE PIANO PLAYER.
THEY NEEDED A REPLACEMENT FOR SEAN, SO I'M FILLING IN FOR THE TIME BEING.
WELL, THE LAST GUY GOT FIRED FOR BEING A JERK, SO YOU MIGHT WANT TO WATCH IT.
SORRY. NO HARM. INTENDED.
DO YOU KNOW WHEN TRISTAN WILL BE BACK?
NO.
BUT I THINK I KNOW WHERE HE WENT.
REALLY?
I THINK HE'S MEETING HIS GIRLFRIEND.

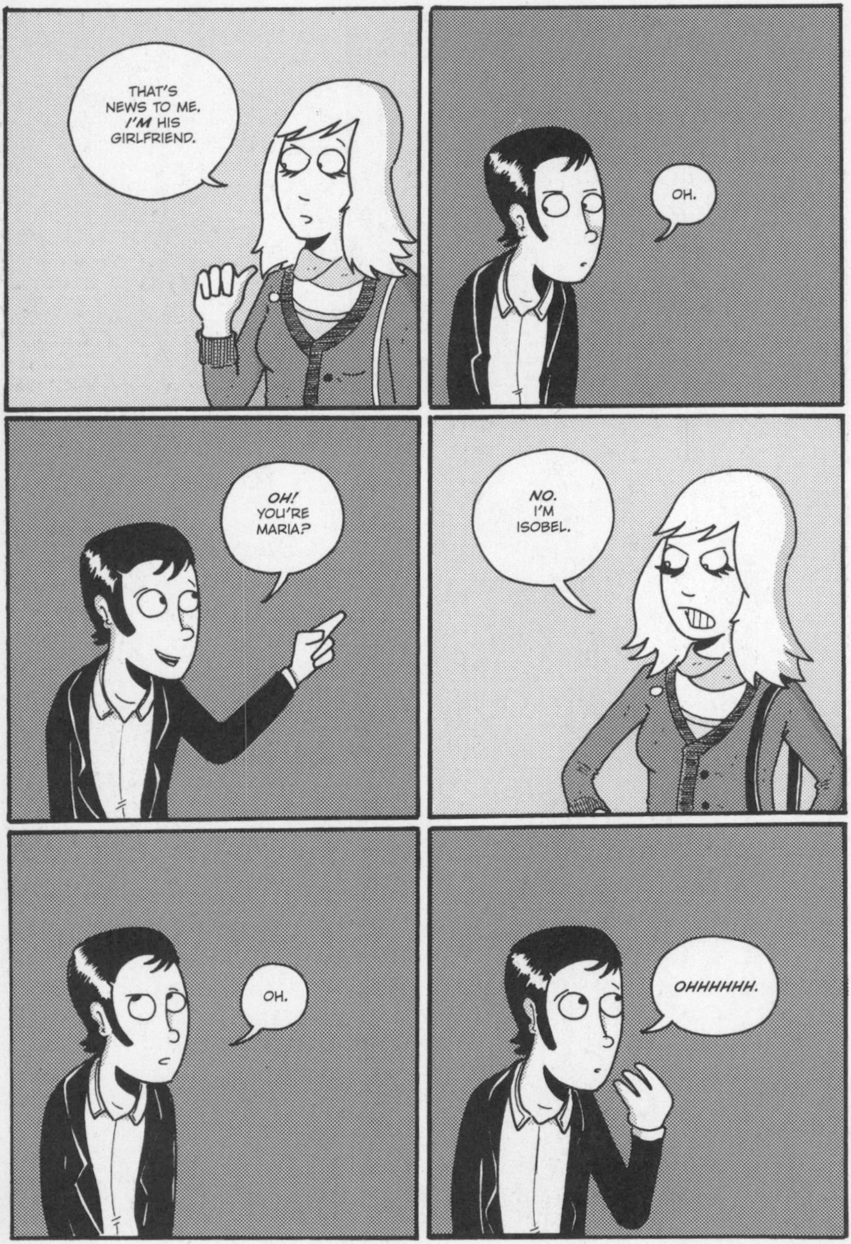
THAT'S NEWS TO ME. *I'M* HIS GIRLFRIEND.
OH.
OH! YOU'RE MARIA?
NO. I'M ISOBEL.
OH.
OHHHHHH.

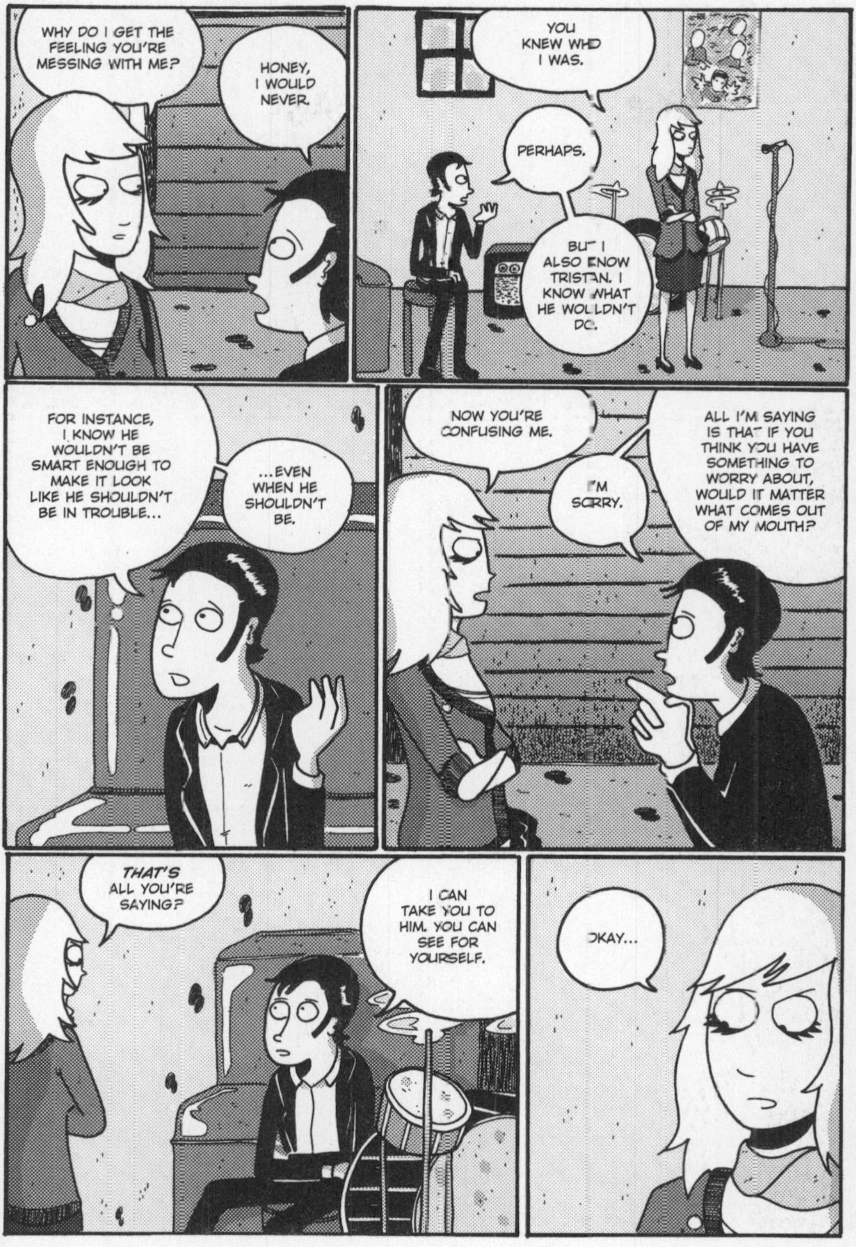
WHY DO I GET THE FEELING YOU'RE MESSING WITH ME?
HONEY, I WOULD NEVER.
YOU KNEW WHO I WAS.
PERHAPS.
BUT I ALSO KNOW TRISTAN. I KNOW WHAT HE WOULDN'T DO.
FOR INSTANCE, I KNOW HE WOULDN'T BE SMART ENOUGH TO MAKE IT LOOK LIKE HE SHOULDN'T BE IN TROUBLE...
...EVEN WHEN HE SHOULDN'T BE.
NOW YOU'RE CONFUSING ME.
I'M SORRY.
ALL I'M SAYING IS THAT IF YOU THINK YOU HAVE SOMETHING TO WORRY ABOUT, WOULD IT MATTER WHAT COMES OUT OF MY MOUTH?
THAT'S ALL YOU'RE SAYING?
I CAN TAKE YOU TO HIM. YOU CAN SEE FOR YOURSELF.
OKAY...

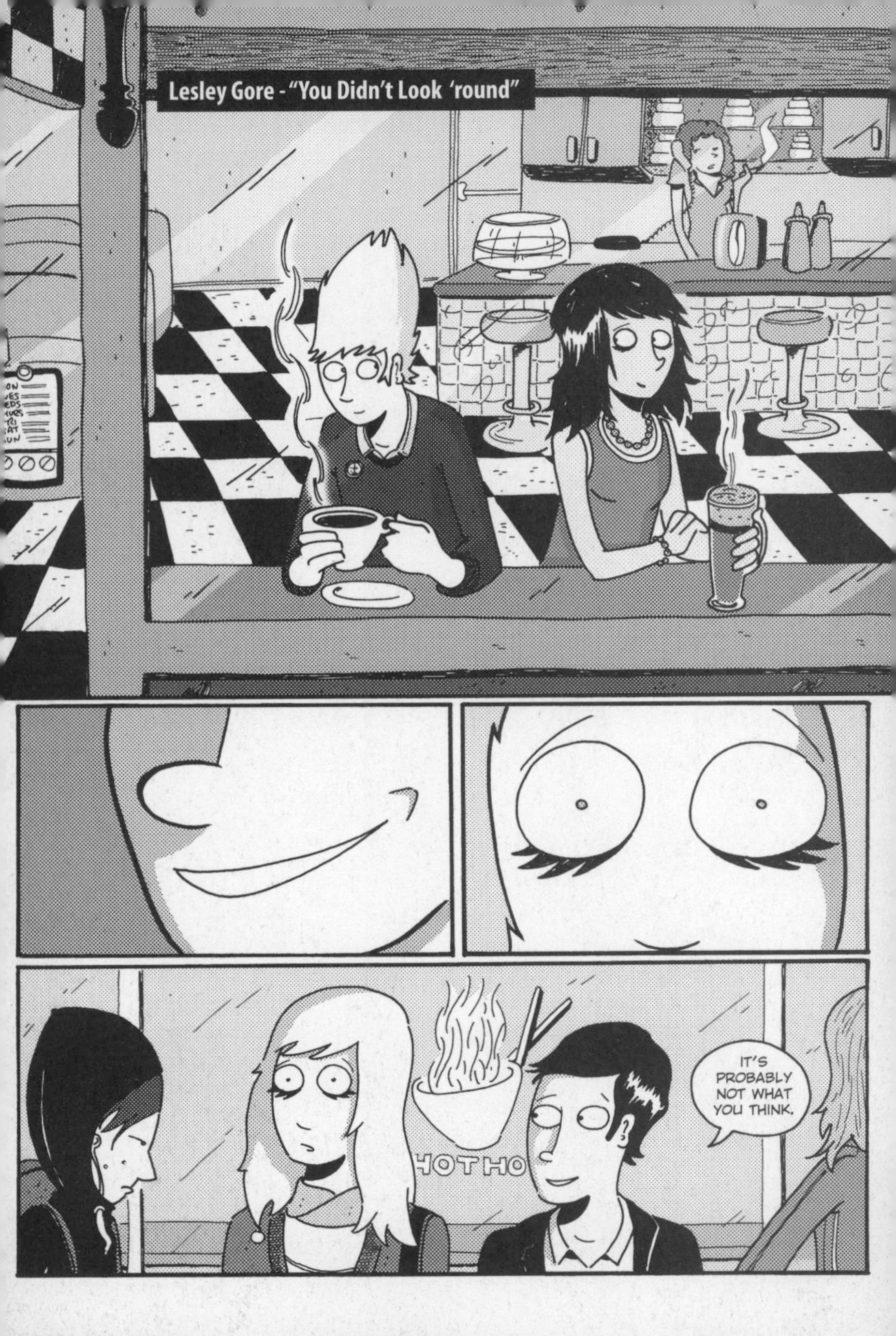
Lesley Gore - “You Didn’t Look ‘round”
IT'S PROBABLY NOT WHAT YOU THINK.

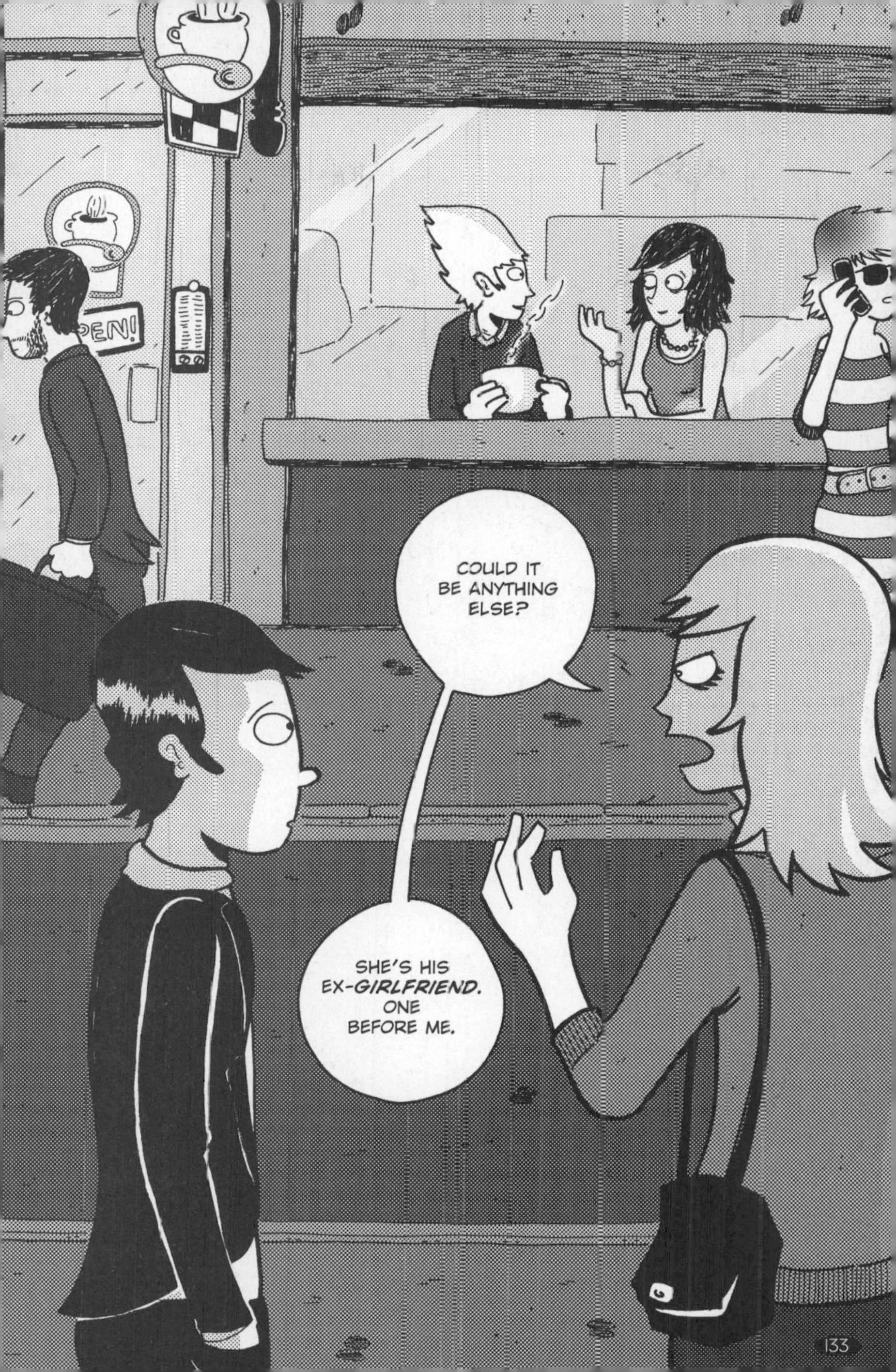

PEN!
COULD IT BE ANYTHING ELSE?
SHE'S HIS EX-*GIRLFRIEND.* ONE BEFORE ME.

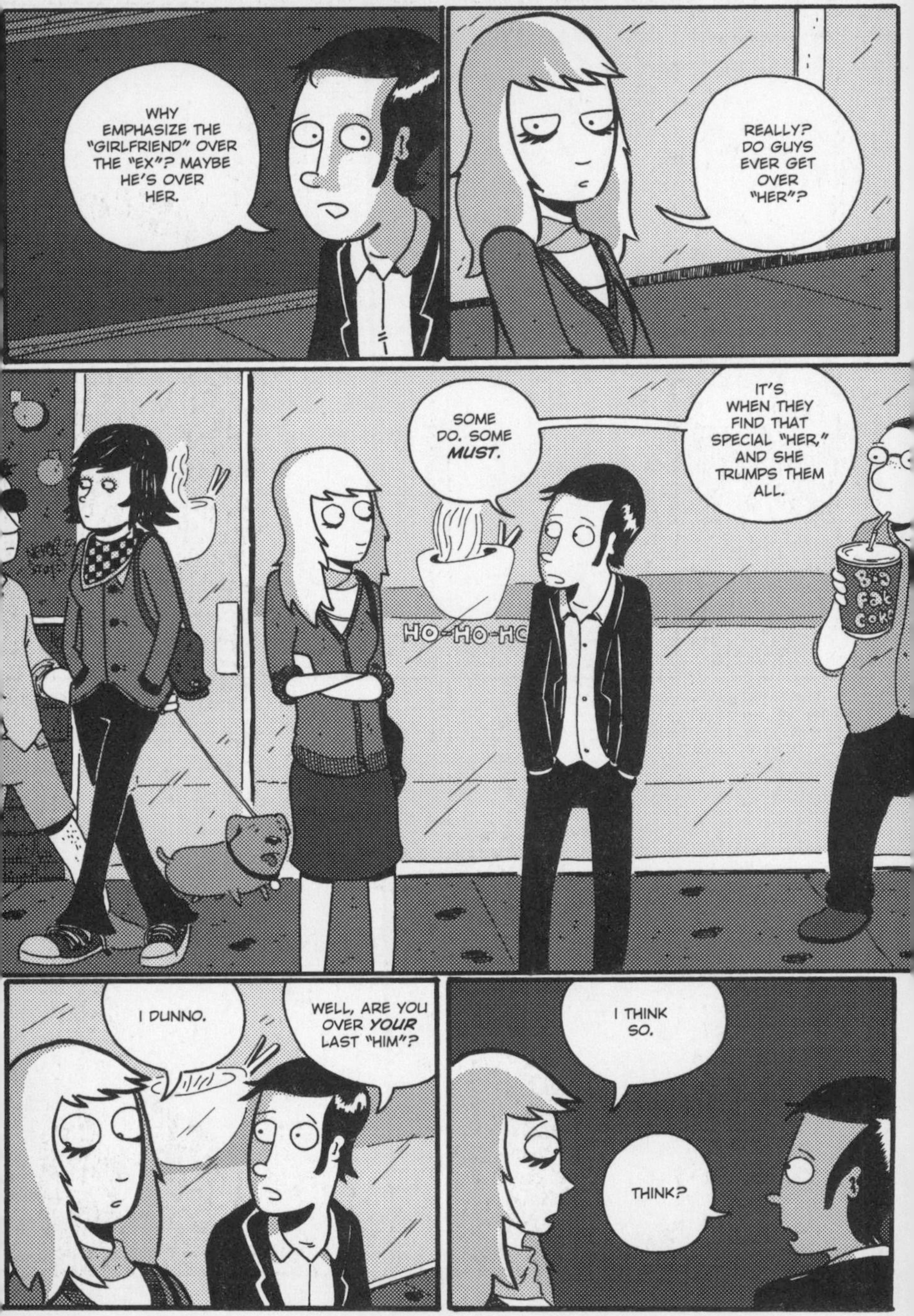

WHY EMPHASIZE THE "GIRLFRIEND" OVER THE "EX"? MAYBE HE'S OVER HER.
REALLY? DO GUYS EVER GET OVER "HER"?
SOME DO. SOME **MUST**.
IT'S WHEN THEY FIND THAT SPECIAL "HER," AND SHE TRUMPS THEM ALL.
HO-HO-HO
BIG FAT COKE
I DUNNO.
WELL, ARE YOU OVER ***YOUR*** LAST "HIM"?
I THINK SO.
THINK?

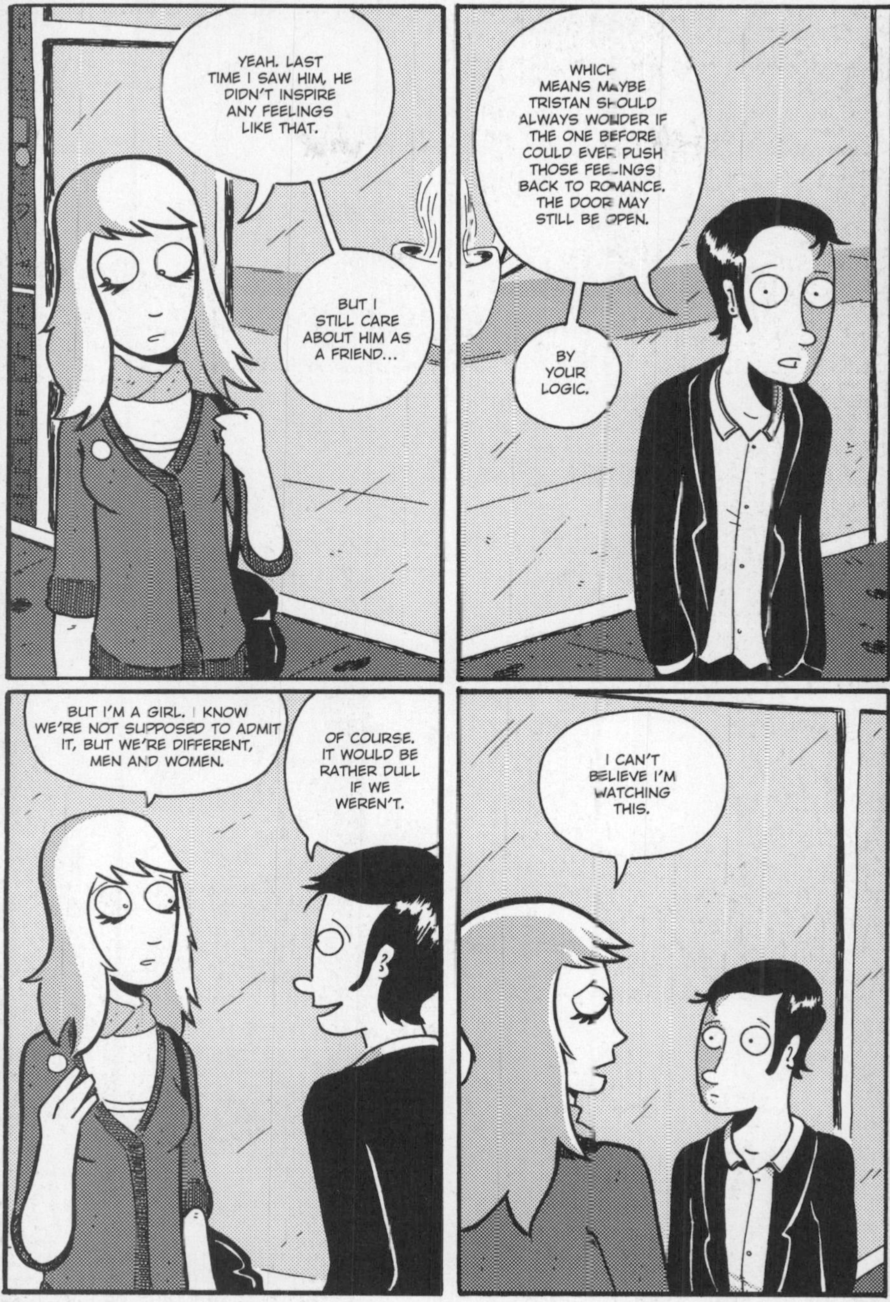
YEAH. LAST TIME I SAW HIM, HE DIDN'T INSPIRE ANY FEELINGS LIKE THAT.
BUT I STILL CARE ABOUT HIM AS A FRIEND...
WHICH MEANS MAYBE TRISTAN SHOULD ALWAYS WONDER IF THE ONE BEFORE COULD EVER PUSH THOSE FEELINGS BACK TO ROMANCE. THE DOOR MAY STILL BE OPEN.
BY YOUR LOGIC.
BUT I'M A GIRL. I KNOW WE'RE NOT SUPPOSED TO ADMIT IT, BUT WE'RE DIFFERENT, MEN AND WOMEN.
OF COURSE. IT WOULD BE RATHER DULL IF WE WEREN'T.
I CAN'T BELIEVE I'M WATCHING THIS.

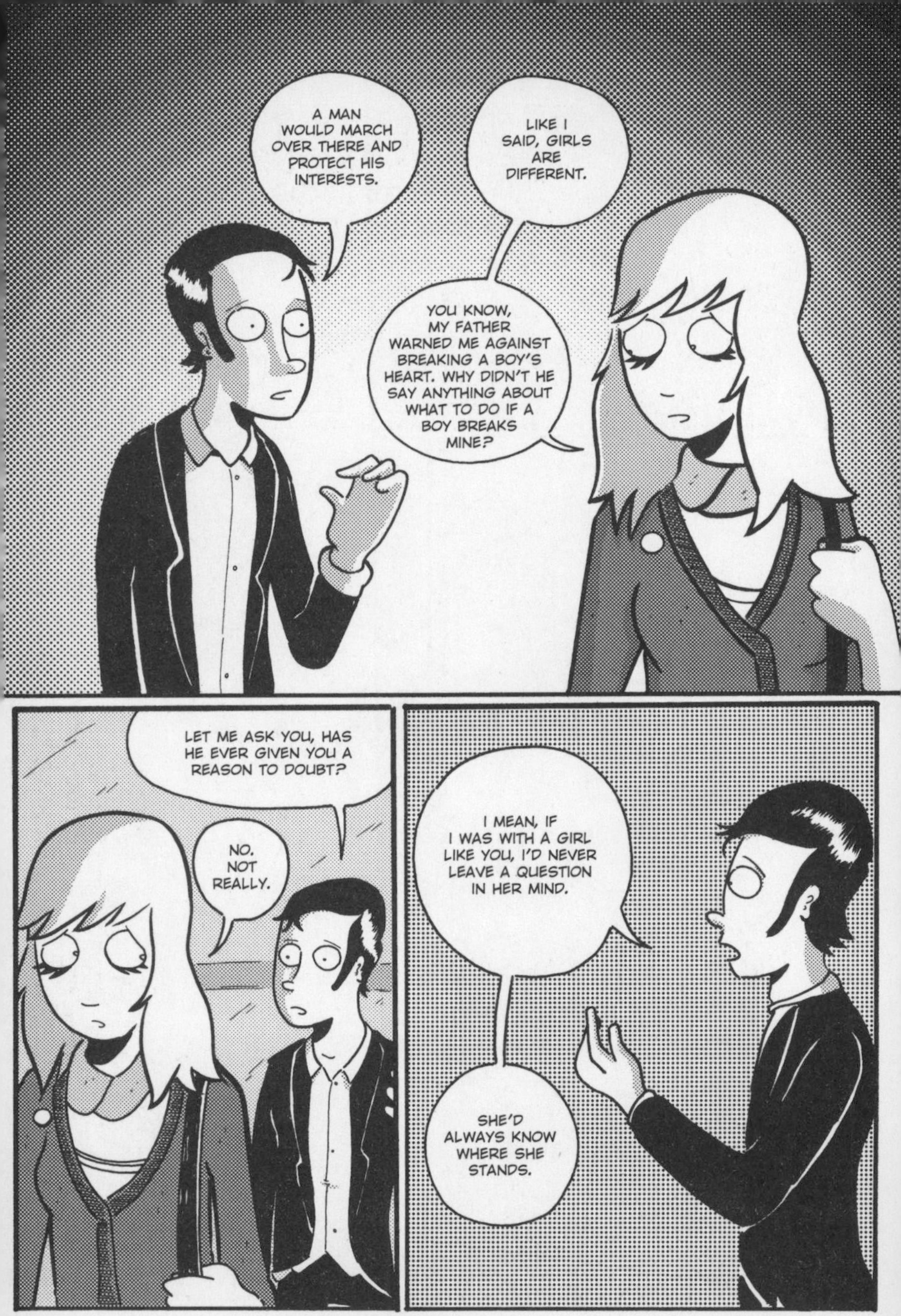
A MAN WOULD MARCH OVER THERE AND PROTECT HIS INTERESTS.
LIKE I SAID, GIRLS ARE DIFFERENT.
YOU KNOW, MY FATHER WARNED ME AGAINST BREAKING A BOY'S HEART. WHY DIDN'T HE SAY ANYTHING ABOUT WHAT TO DO IF A BOY BREAKS MINE?
LET ME ASK YOU, HAS HE EVER GIVEN YOU A REASON TO DOUBT?
NO. NOT REALLY.
I MEAN, IF I WAS WITH A GIRL LIKE YOU, I'D NEVER LEAVE A QUESTION IN HER MIND.
SHE'D ALWAYS KNOW WHERE SHE STANDS.

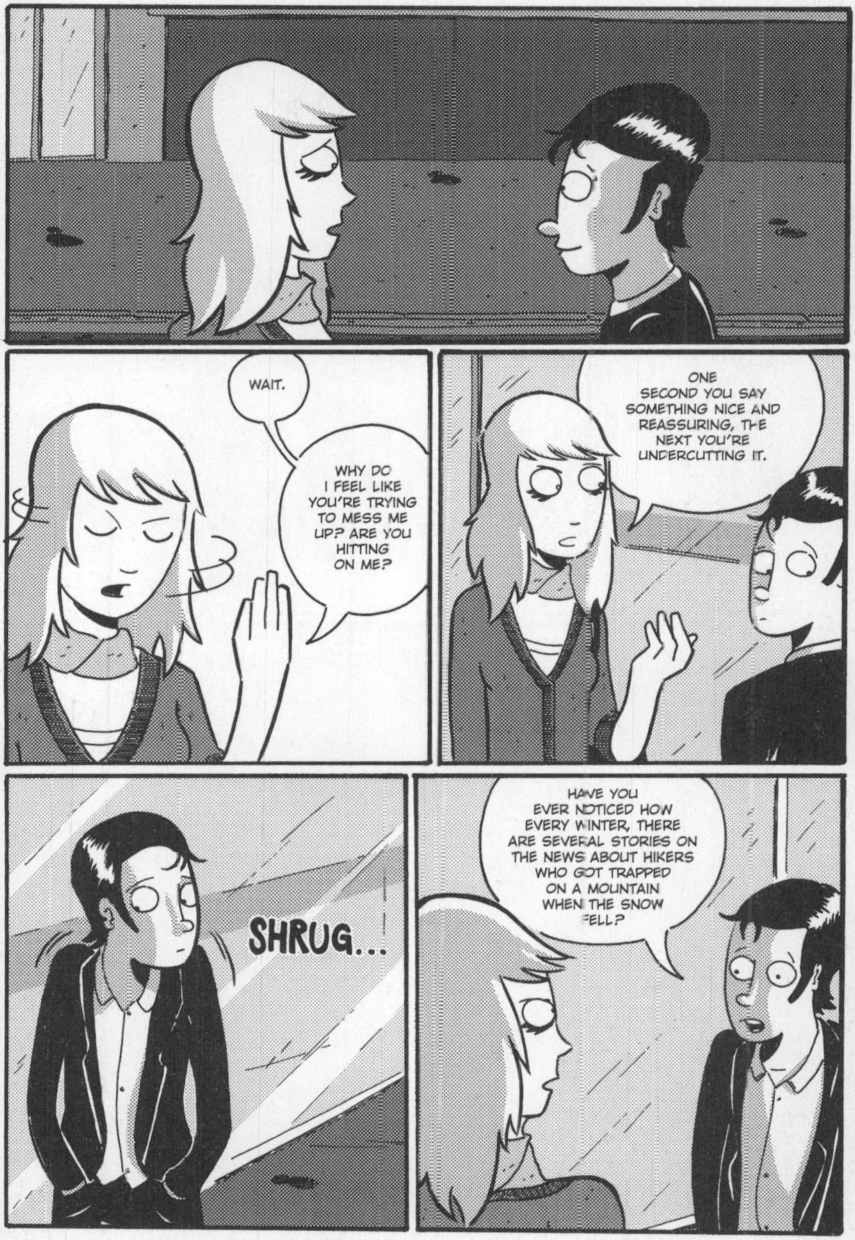
WAIT.
WHY DO I FEEL LIKE YOU'RE TRYING TO MESS ME UP? ARE YOU HITTING ON ME?
ONE SECOND YOU SAY SOMETHING NICE AND REASSURING, THE NEXT YOU'RE UNDERCUTTING IT.
SHRUG...
HAVE YOU EVER NOTICED HOW EVERY WINTER, THERE ARE SEVERAL STORIES ON THE NEWS ABOUT HIKERS WHO GOT TRAPPED ON A MOUNTAIN WHEN THE SNOW FELL?

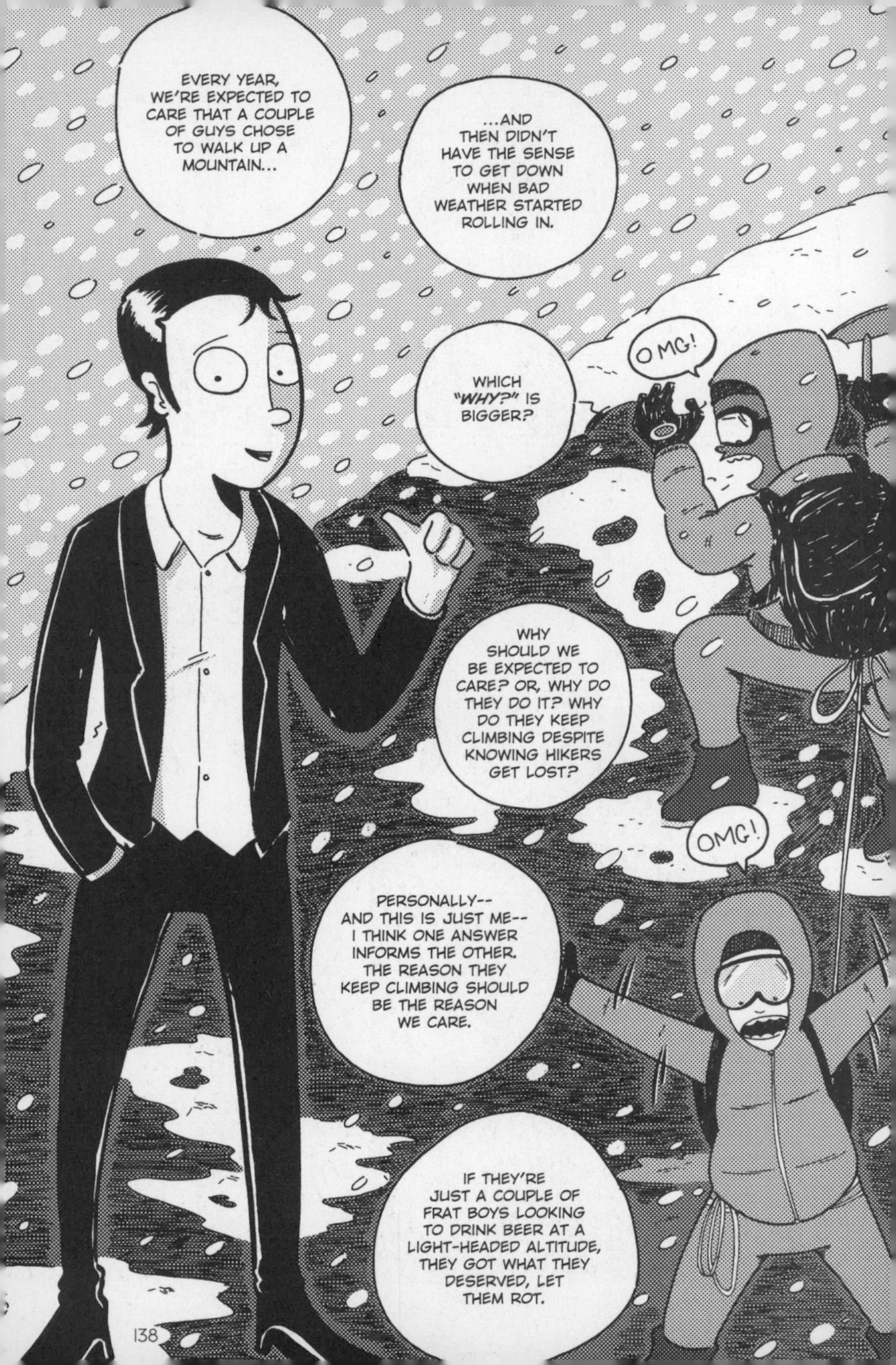
EVERY YEAR, WE'RE EXPECTED TO CARE THAT A COUPLE OF GUYS CHOSE TO WALK UP A MOUNTAIN...
...AND THEN DIDN'T HAVE THE SENSE TO GET DOWN WHEN BAD WEATHER STARTED ROLLING IN.
OMG!
WHICH *"WHY?"* IS BIGGER?
WHY SHOULD WE BE EXPECTED TO CARE? OR, WHY DO THEY DO IT? WHY DO THEY KEEP CLIMBING DESPITE KNOWING HIKERS GET LOST?
OMG!
PERSONALLY-- AND THIS IS JUST ME-- I THINK ONE ANSWER INFORMS THE OTHER. THE REASON THEY KEEP CLIMBING SHOULD BE THE REASON WE CARE.
IF THEY'RE JUST A COUPLE OF FRAT BOYS LOOKING TO DRINK BEER AT A LIGHT-HEADED ALTITUDE, THEY GOT WHAT THEY DESERVED, LET THEM ROT.

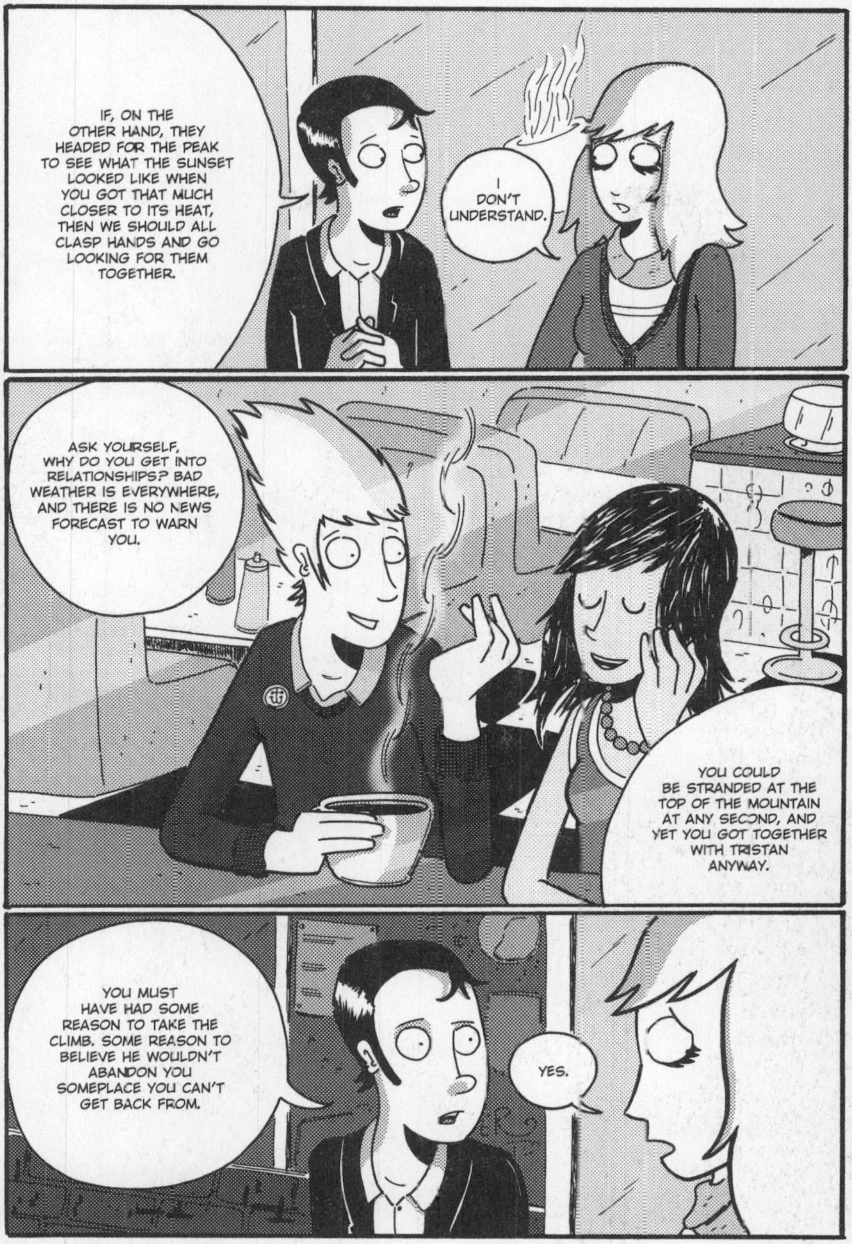
IF, ON THE OTHER HAND, THEY HEADED FOR THE PEAK TO SEE WHAT THE SUNSET LOOKED LIKE WHEN YOU GOT THAT MUCH CLOSER TO ITS HEAT, THEN WE SHOULD ALL CLASP HANDS AND GO LOOKING FOR THEM TOGETHER.
I DON'T UNDERSTAND.
ASK YOURSELF, WHY DO YOU GET INTO RELATIONSHIPS? BAD WEATHER IS EVERYWHERE, AND THERE IS NO NEWS FORECAST TO WARN YOU.
YOU COULD BE STRANDED AT THE TOP OF THE MOUNTAIN AT ANY SECOND, AND YET YOU GOT TOGETHER WITH TRISTAN ANYWAY.
YOU MUST HAVE HAD SOME REASON TO TAKE THE CLIMB. SOME REASON TO BELIEVE HE WOULDN'T ABANDON YOU SOMEPLACE YOU CAN'T GET BACK FROM.
YES.

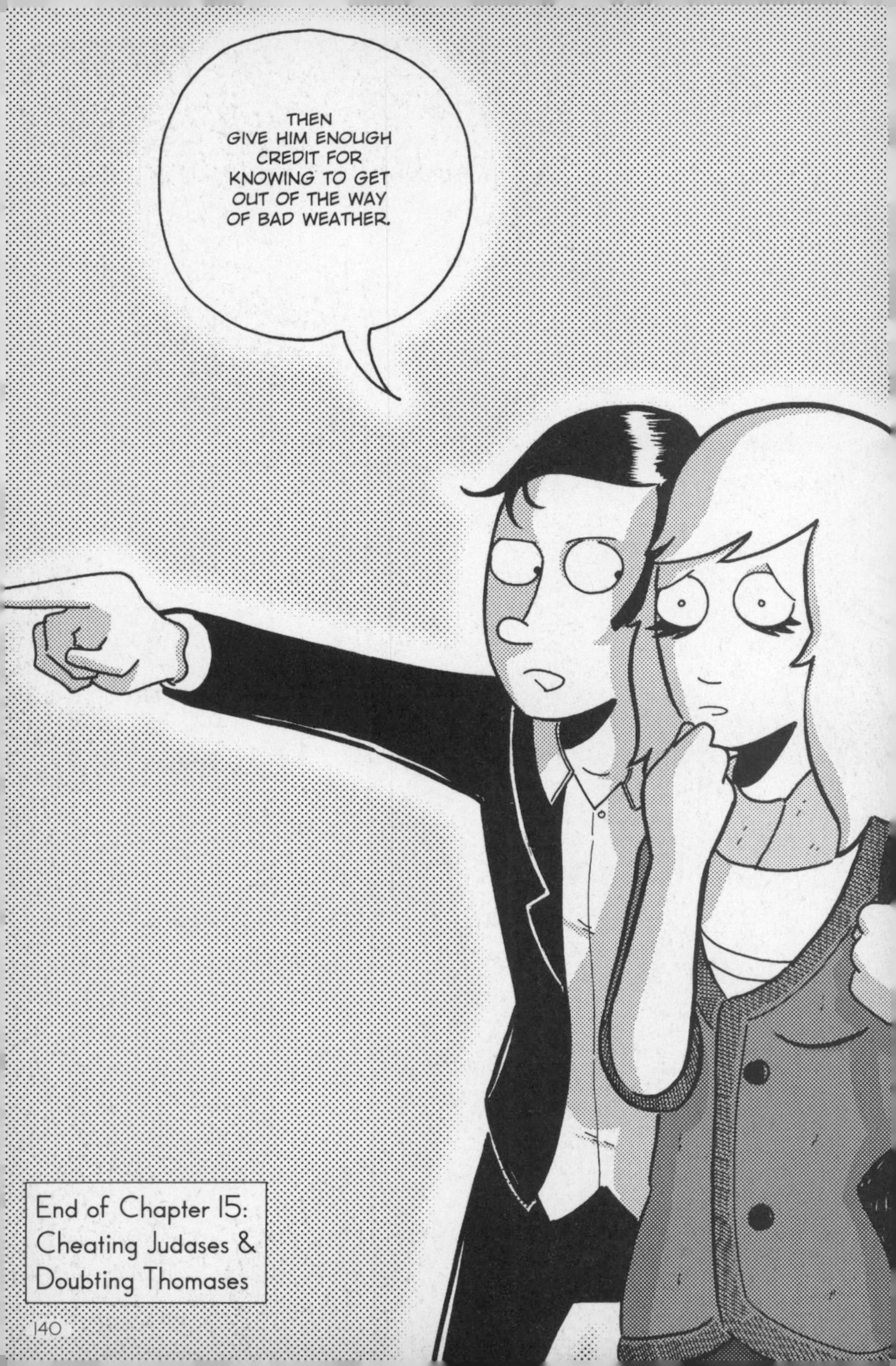
THEN GIVE HIM ENOUGH CREDIT FOR KNOWING TO GET OUT OF THE WAY OF BAD WEATHER.
End of Chapter 15: Cheating Judases & Doubting Thomases

Chapter 16: I Bet You're Mad at Me

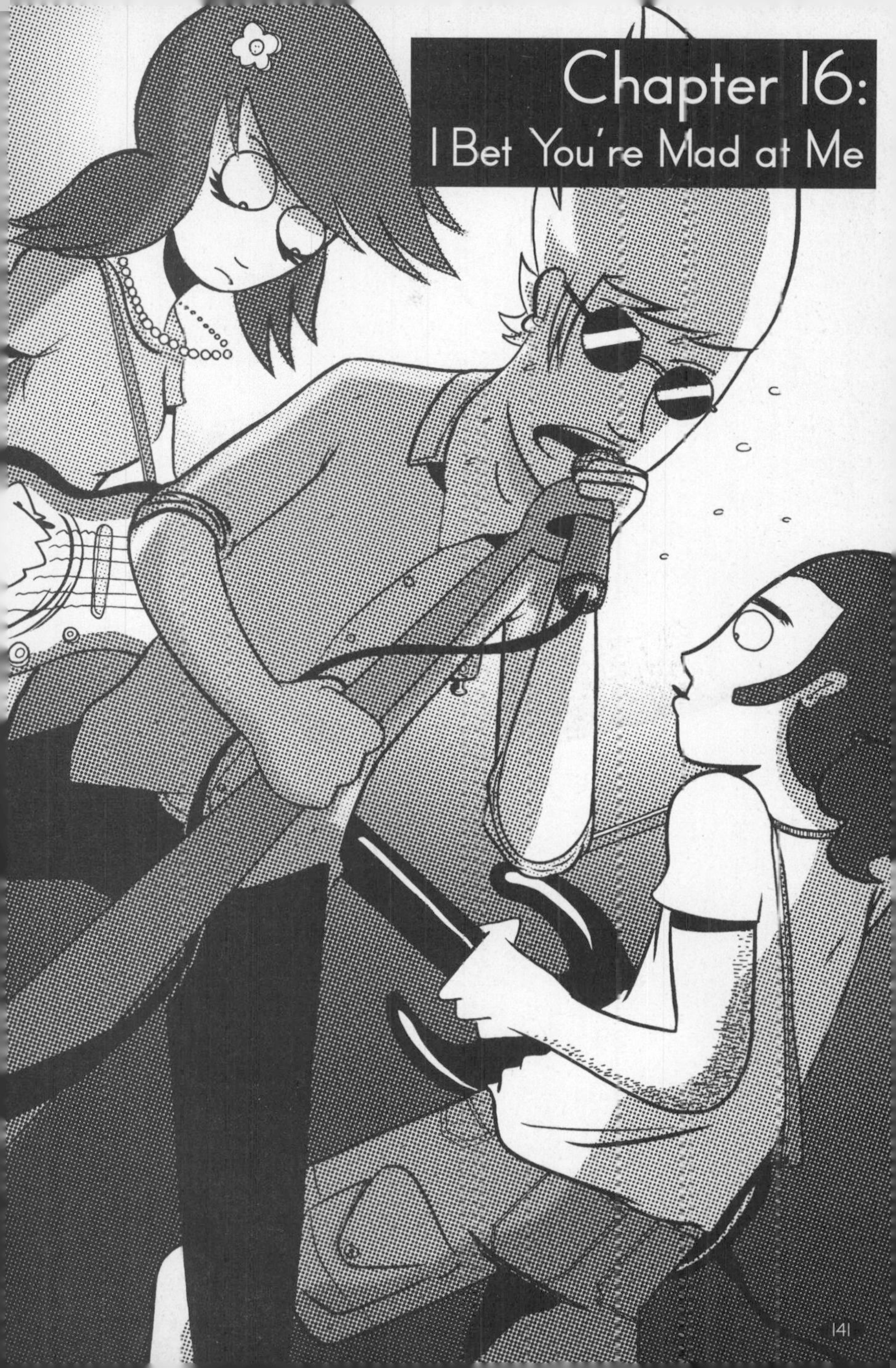

KITTEN STOMP FUTURE DREAM
ISN'T SHE ISOBEL?

Pen Name:
IJA

Full Name:
Isobel J. Anguise ("What's the J stand for? Just keep wondering!" she says)

Vocation:
Fine artist

Birthdate:
February 20 (Pisces)

Hometown:
Los Angeles, CA

Artistic Heroes:
Mucha, Vargas, Shag

Prior Experience:
"Before my internship at *Murmur*, I worked my way through high school as a babysitter."

Favorite Candy:
Chocolate Truffles

Favorite Song:
"Walking in the Rain" by the Ronettes ("After 'Love the Way You Love,' of course!")

Family:
"Anguise is a Scottish name, and believe it or not, the alternate variation of it is 'Anguish.' It actually is a name that denotes strength, not sadness."

Best Thing Ever:
"Having one dream come true, and discovering you have more waiting to keep you going."

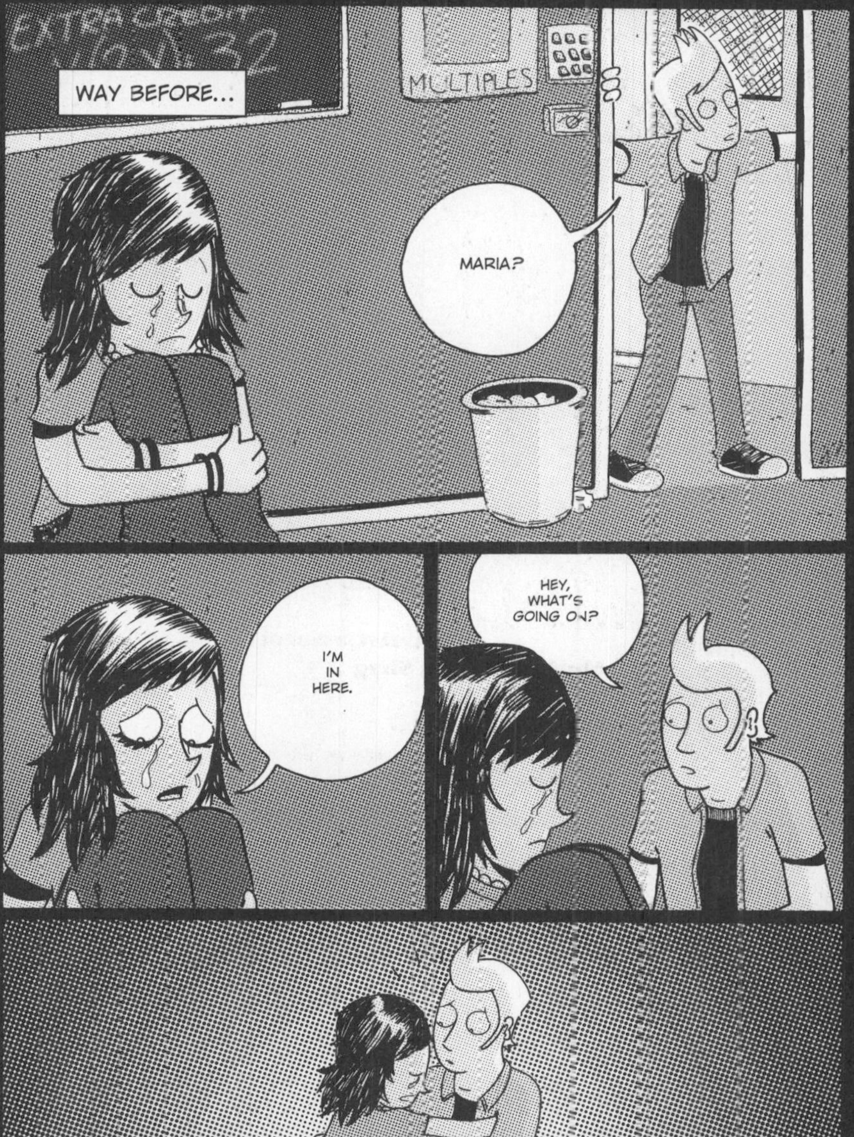
WAY BEFORE...
MULTIPLES
MARIA?
I'M IN HERE.
HEY, WHAT'S GOING ON?

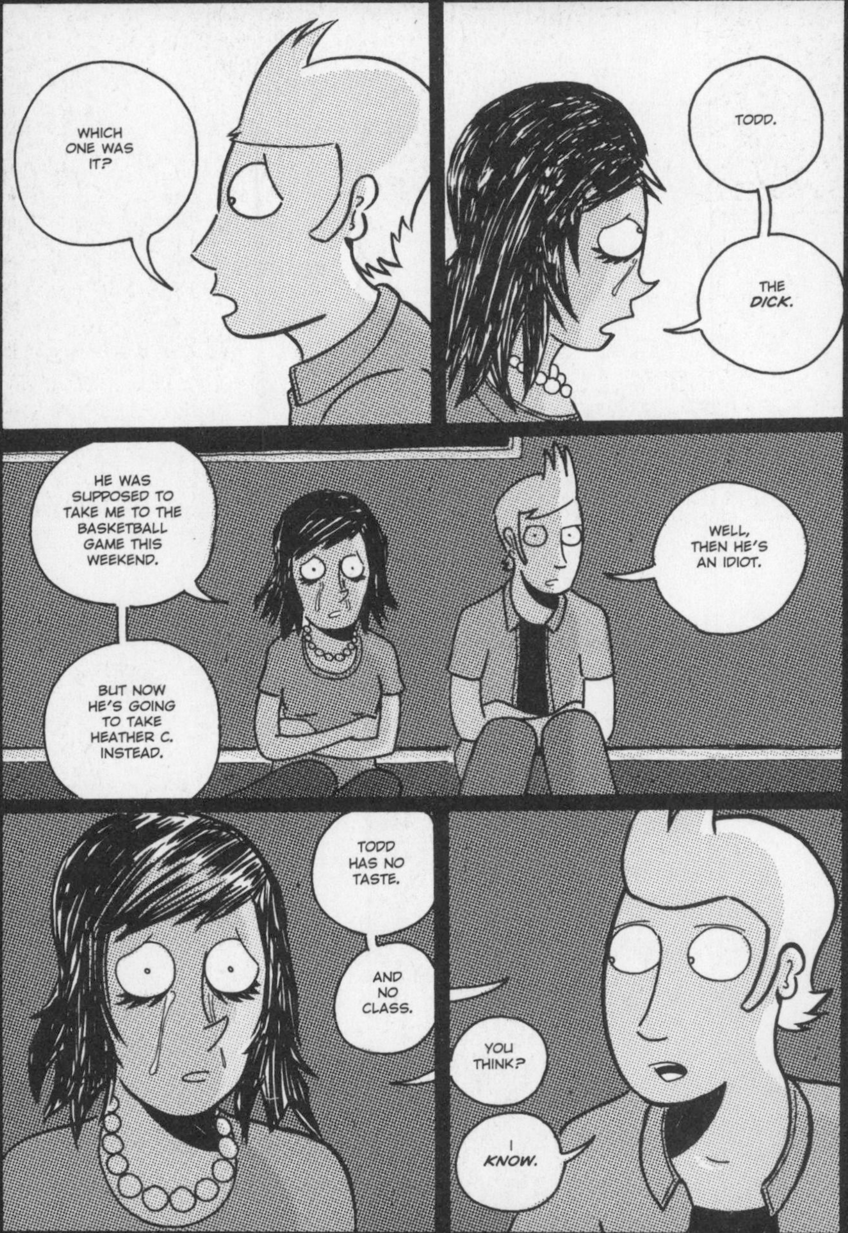
WHICH ONE WAS IT?
TODD.
THE *DICK.*
HE WAS SUPPOSED TO TAKE ME TO THE BASKETBALL GAME THIS WEEKEND.
BUT NOW HE'S GOING TO TAKE HEATHER C. INSTEAD.
WELL, THEN HE'S AN IDIOT.
TODD HAS NO TASTE.
AND NO CLASS.
YOU THINK?
I *KNOW.*

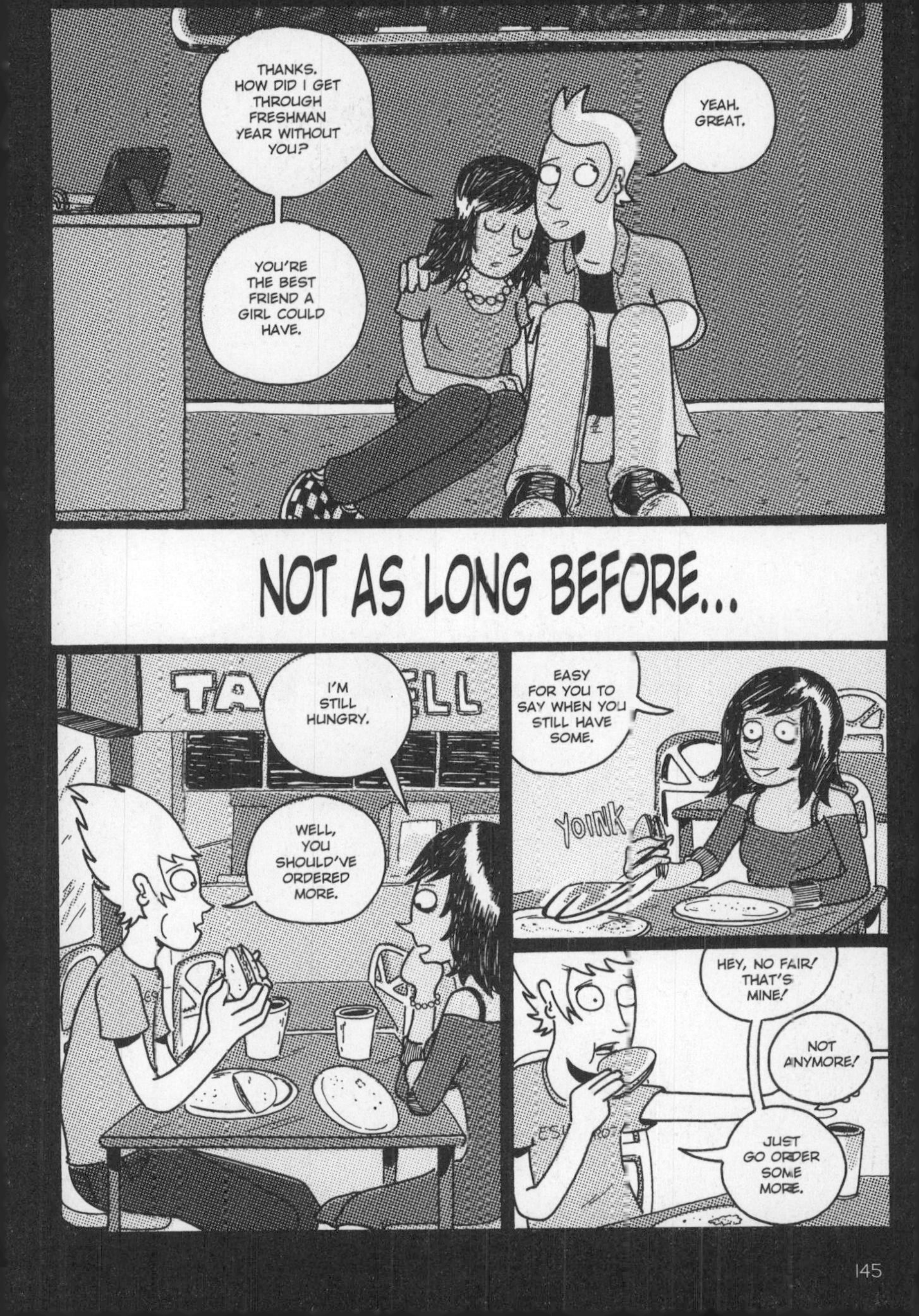
THANKS. HOW DID I GET THROUGH FRESHMAN YEAR WITHOUT YOU?
YOU'RE THE BEST FRIEND A GIRL COULD HAVE.
YEAH. GREAT.
NOT AS LONG BEFORE...
I'M STILL HUNGRY.
WELL, YOU SHOULD'VE ORDERED MORE.
EASY FOR YOU TO SAY WHEN YOU STILL HAVE SOME.
YOINK
HEY, NO FAIR! THAT'S MINE!
NOT ANYMORE!
JUST GO ORDER SOME MORE.

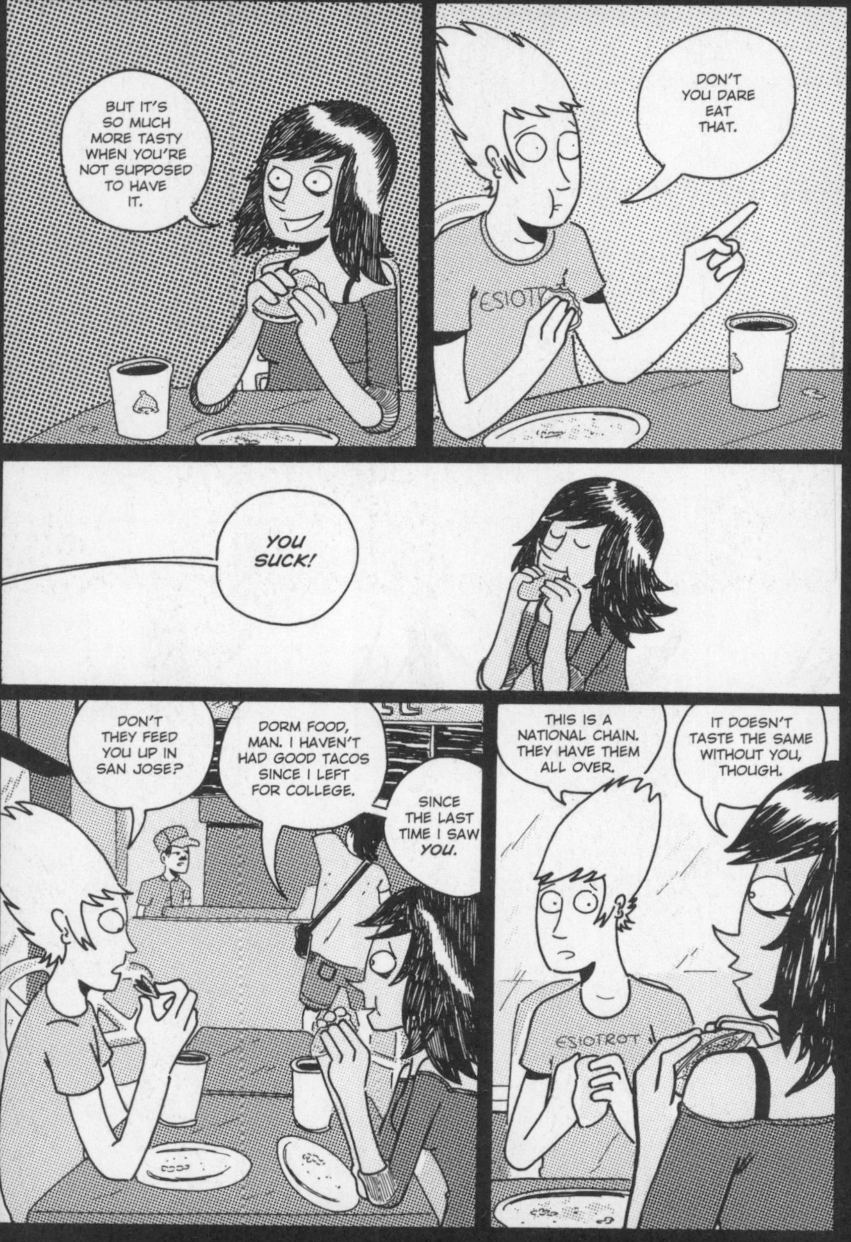
BUT IT'S SO MUCH MORE TASTY WHEN YOU'RE NOT SUPPOSED TO HAVE IT.
DON'T YOU DARE EAT THAT.
ESIOT
YOU SUCK!
DON'T THEY FEED YOU UP IN SAN JOSE?
DORM FOOD, MAN. I HAVEN'T HAD GOOD TACOS SINCE I LEFT FOR COLLEGE.
SINCE THE LAST TIME I SAW *YOU.*
THIS IS A NATIONAL CHAIN. THEY HAVE THEM ALL OVER.
IT DOESN'T TASTE THE SAME WITHOUT YOU, THOUGH.
ESIOTROT

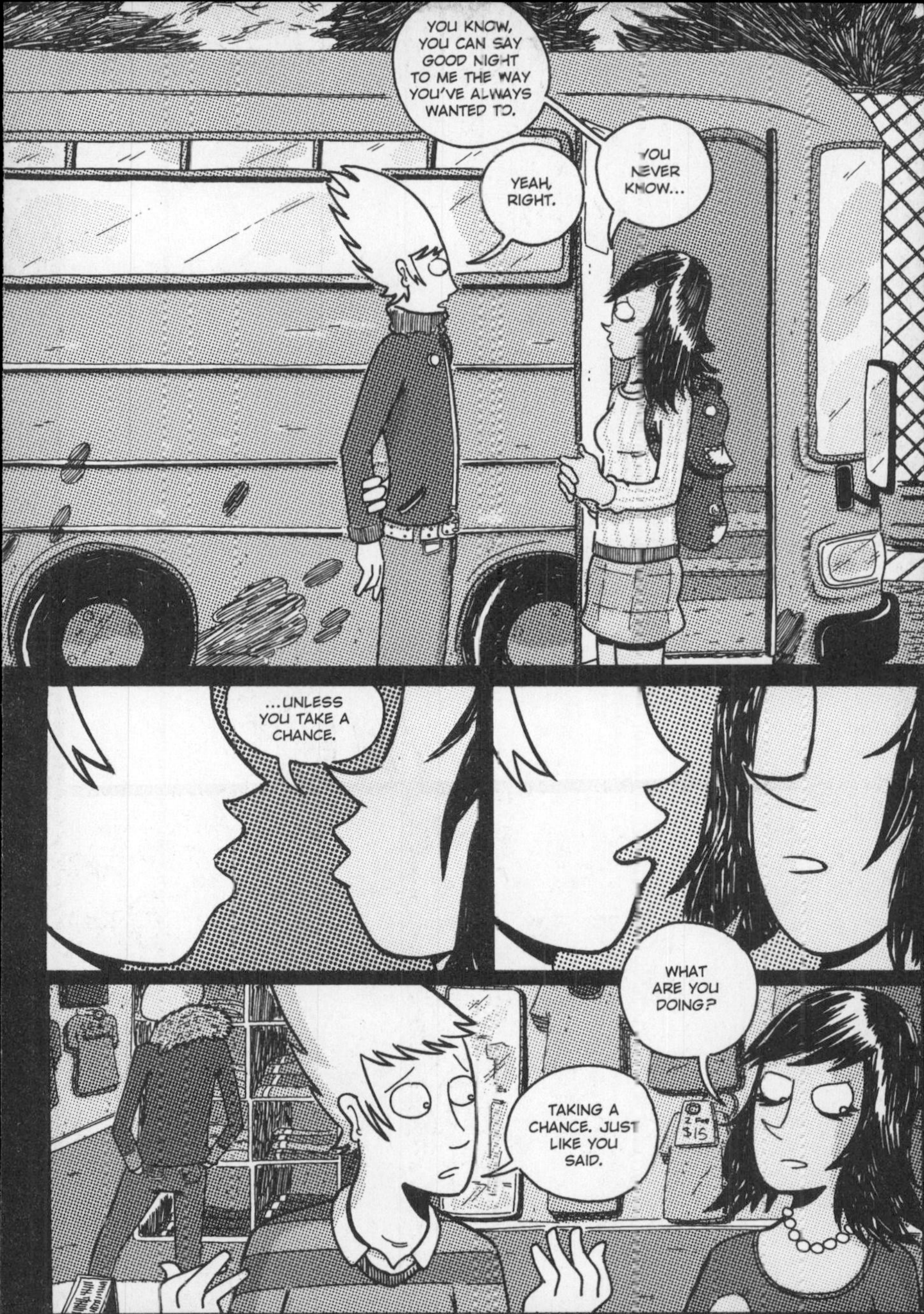
YOU KNOW, YOU CAN SAY GOOD NIGHT TO ME THE WAY YOU'VE ALWAYS WANTED TO.
YEAH, RIGHT.
YOU NEVER KNOW...
...UNLESS YOU TAKE A CHANCE.
WHAT ARE YOU DOING?
TAKING A CHANCE. JUST LIKE YOU SAID.
2 For $15

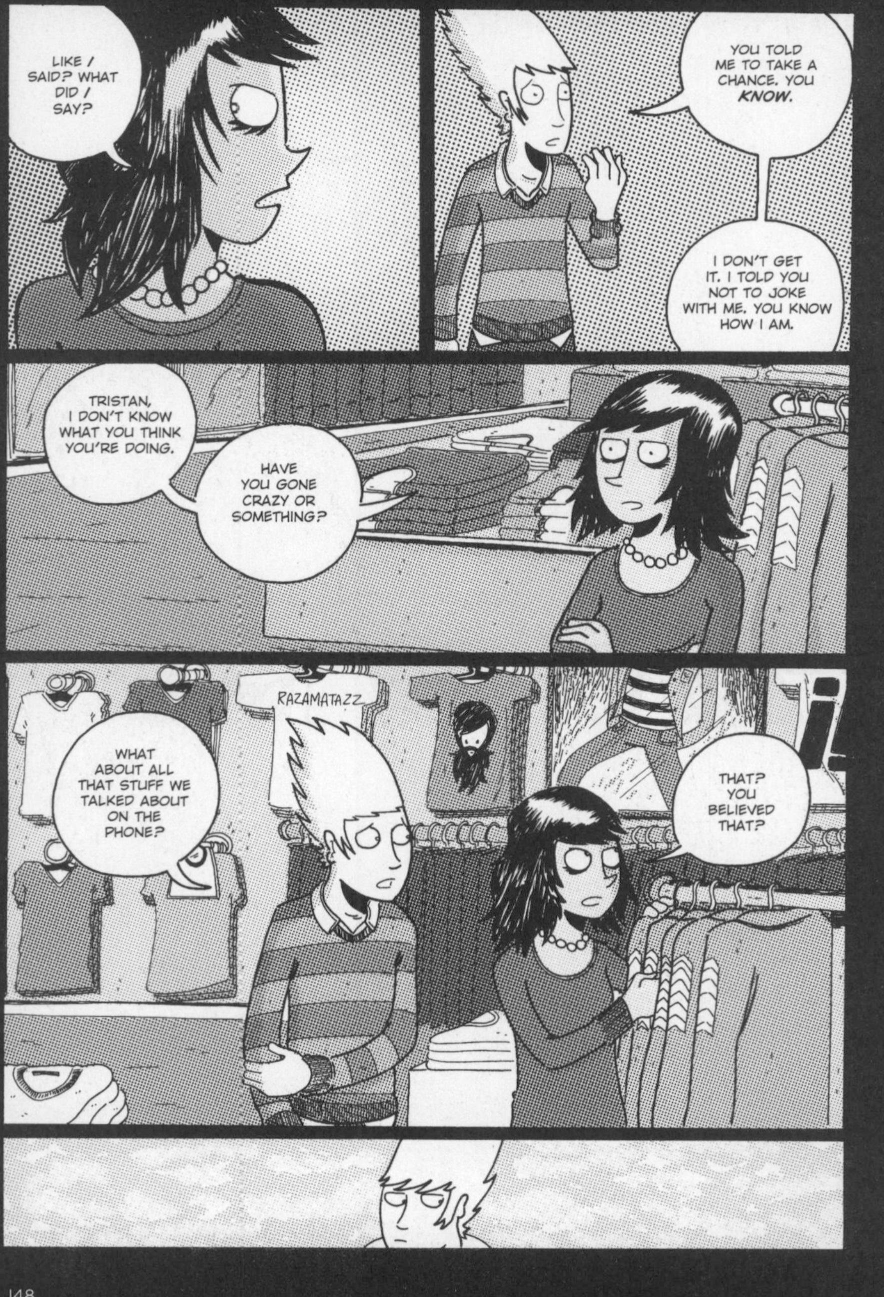
LIKE I SAID? WHAT DID I SAY?
YOU TOLD ME TO TAKE A CHANCE. YOU KNOW.
I DON'T GET IT. I TOLD YOU NOT TO JOKE WITH ME. YOU KNOW HOW I AM.
TRISTAN, I DON'T KNOW WHAT YOU THINK YOU'RE DOING.
HAVE YOU GONE CRAZY OR SOMETHING?
RAZAMATAZZ
WHAT ABOUT ALL THAT STUFF WE TALKED ABOUT ON THE PHONE?
THAT? YOU BELIEVED THAT?

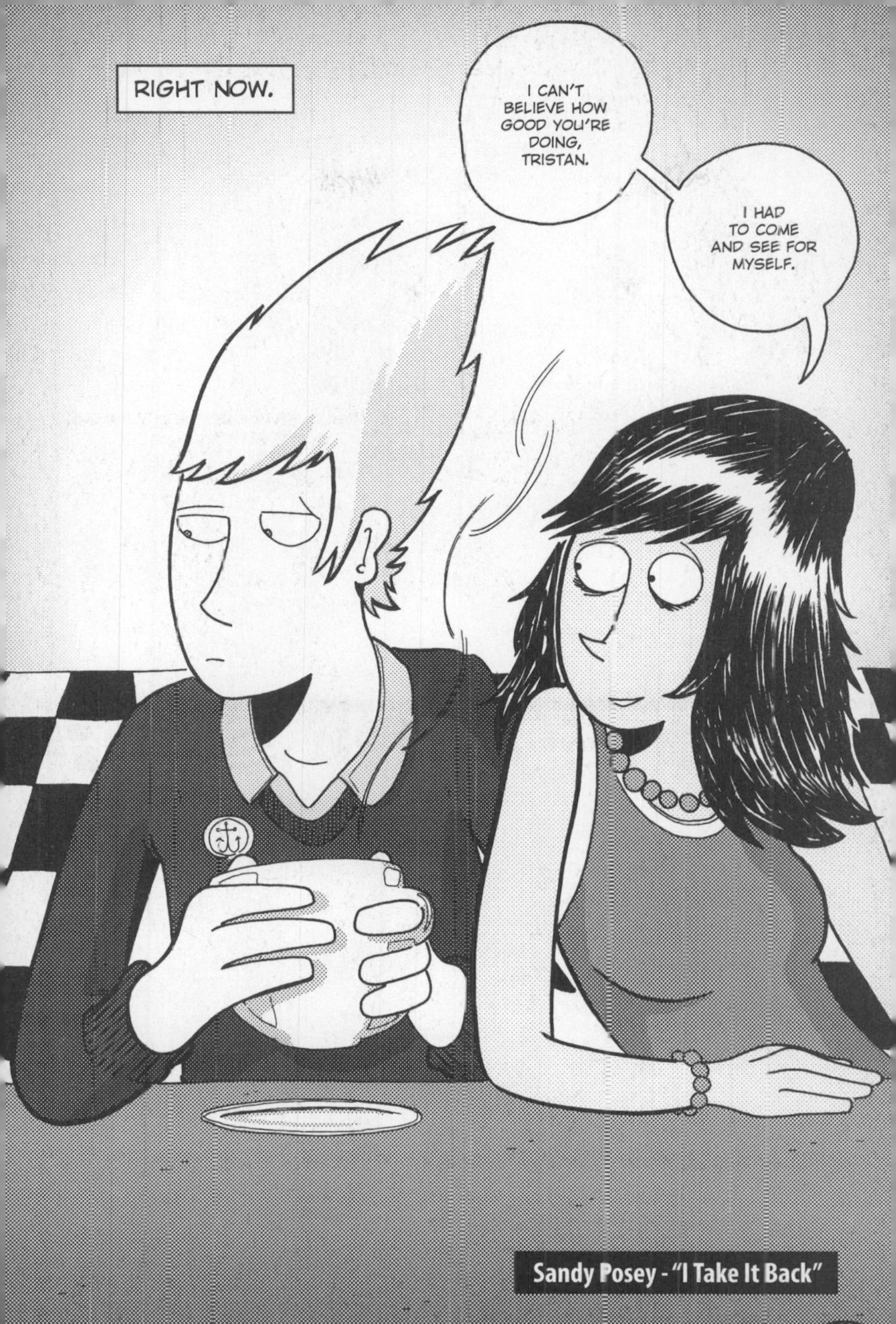
RIGHT NOW.
I CAN'T BELIEVE HOW GOOD YOU'RE DOING, TRISTAN.
I HAD TO COME AND SEE FOR MYSELF.
Sandy Posey - "I Take It Back"

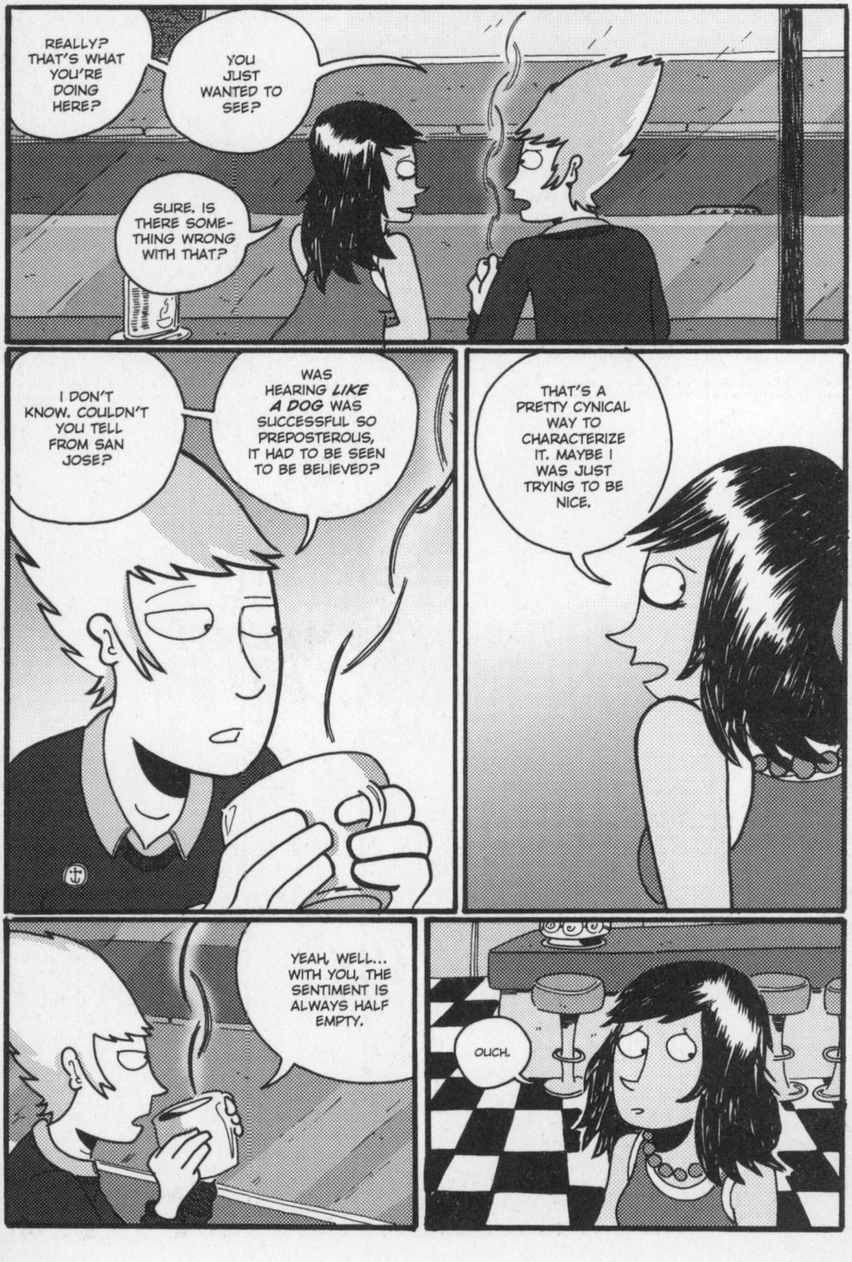
REALLY? THAT'S WHAT YOU'RE DOING HERE?
YOU JUST WANTED TO SEE?
SURE. IS THERE SOMETHING WRONG WITH THAT?
I DON'T KNOW. COULDN'T YOU TELL FROM SAN JOSE?
WAS HEARING *LIKE A DOG* WAS SUCCESSFUL SO PREPOSTEROUS, IT HAD TO BE SEEN TO BE BELIEVED?
THAT'S A PRETTY CYNICAL WAY TO CHARACTERIZE IT. MAYBE I WAS JUST TRYING TO BE NICE.
YEAH, WELL... WITH YOU, THE SENTIMENT IS ALWAYS HALF EMPTY.
OUCH.

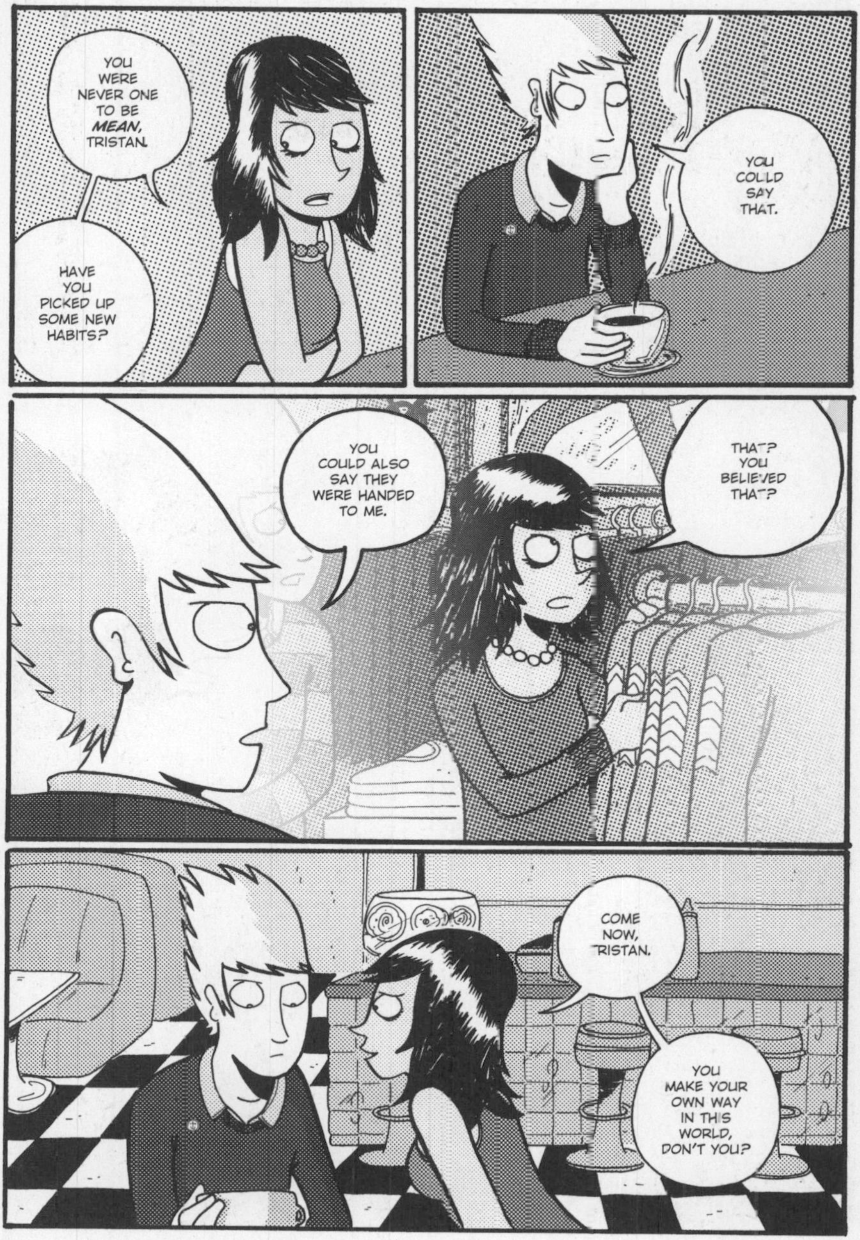
YOU WERE NEVER ONE TO BE ***MEAN,*** TRISTAN.
HAVE YOU PICKED UP SOME NEW HABITS?
YOU COULD SAY THAT.
YOU COULD ALSO SAY THEY WERE HANDED TO ME.
THAT? YOU BELIEVED THAT?
COME NOW, TRISTAN.
YOU MAKE YOUR OWN WAY IN THIS WORLD, DON'T YOU?

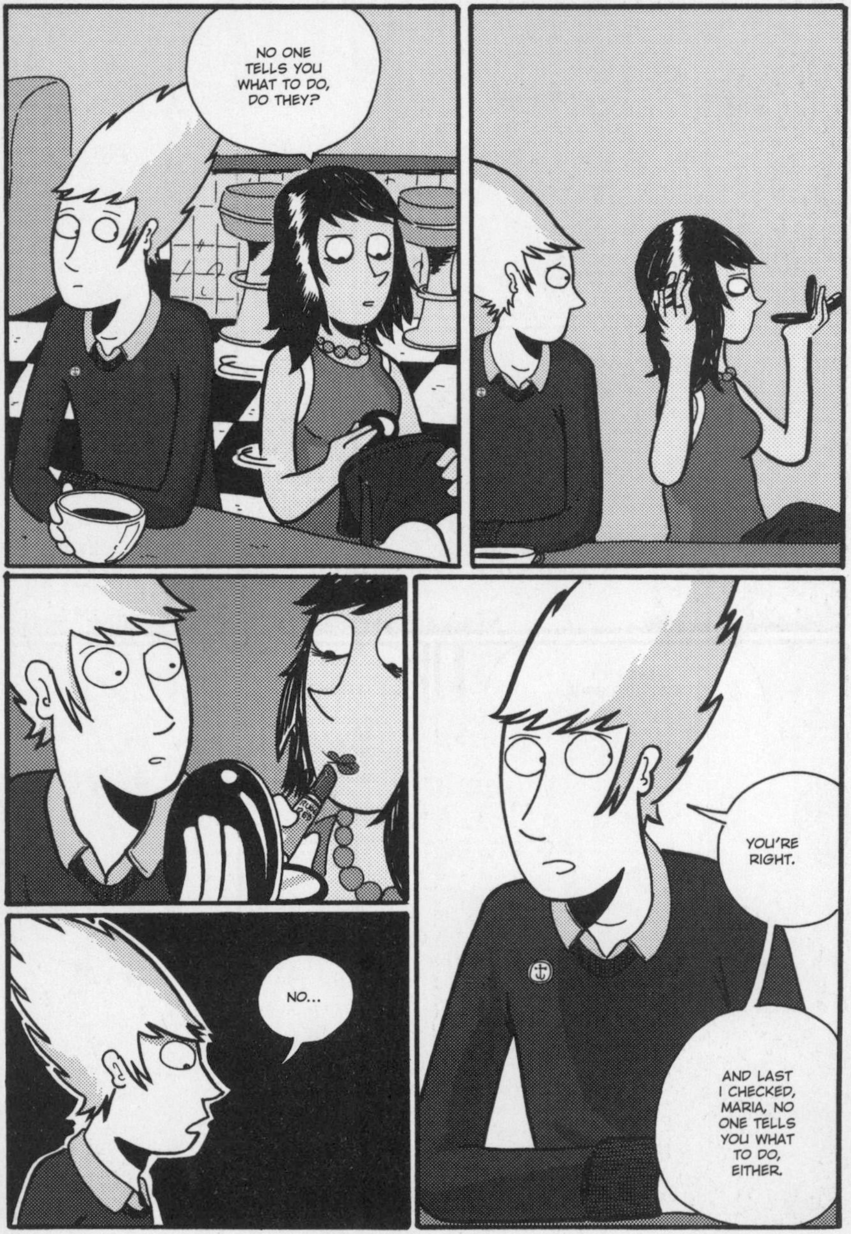
NO ONE TELLS YOU WHAT TO DO, DO THEY?
NO...
YOU'RE RIGHT.
AND LAST I CHECKED, MARIA, NO ONE TELLS YOU WHAT TO DO, EITHER.

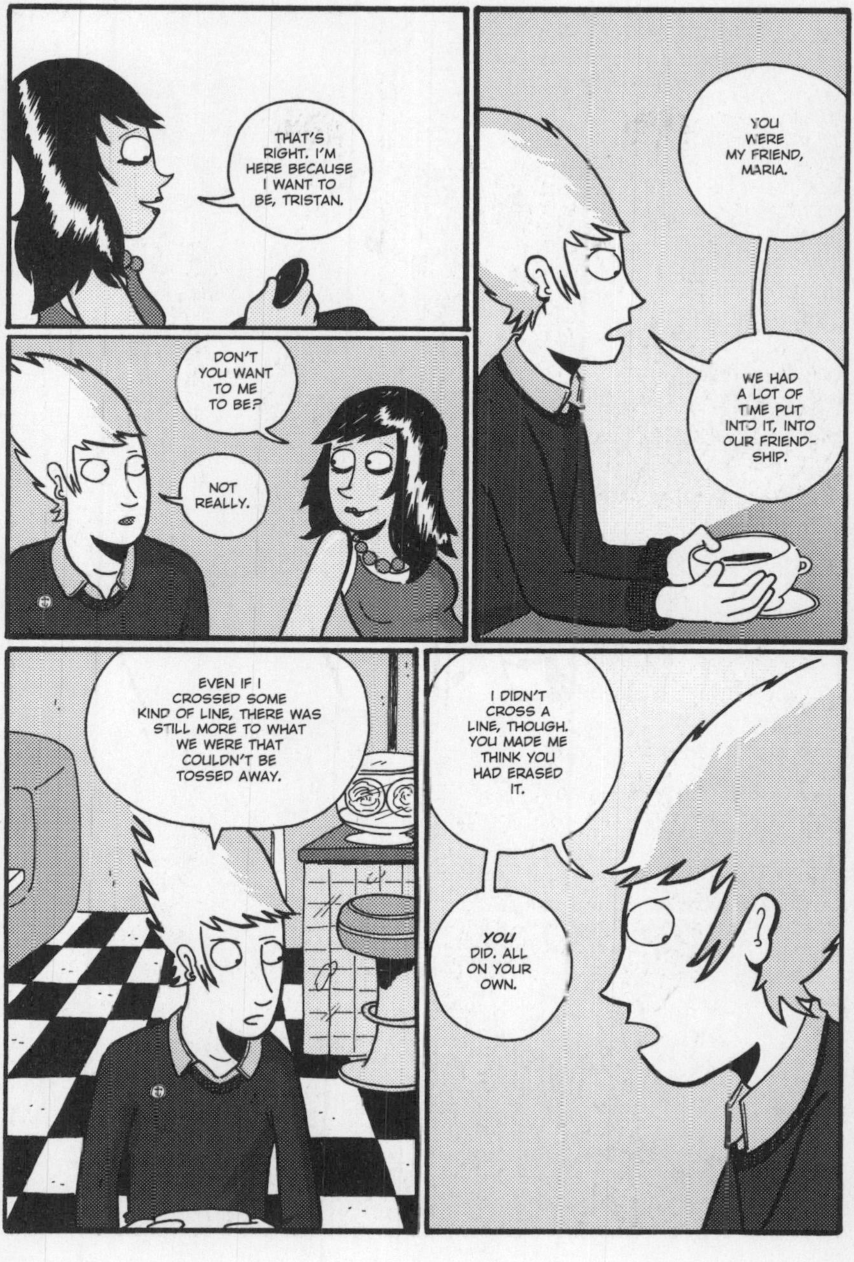
THAT'S RIGHT. I'M HERE BECAUSE I WANT TO BE, TRISTAN.
DON'T YOU WANT TO ME TO BE?
NOT REALLY.
YOU WERE MY FRIEND, MARIA.
WE HAD A LOT OF TIME PUT INTO IT, INTO OUR FRIEND-SHIP.
EVEN IF I CROSSED SOME KIND OF LINE, THERE WAS STILL MORE TO WHAT WE WERE THAT COULDN'T BE TOSSED AWAY.
I DIDN'T CROSS A LINE, THOUGH. YOU MADE ME THINK YOU HAD ERASED IT.
YOU DID. ALL ON YOUR OWN.

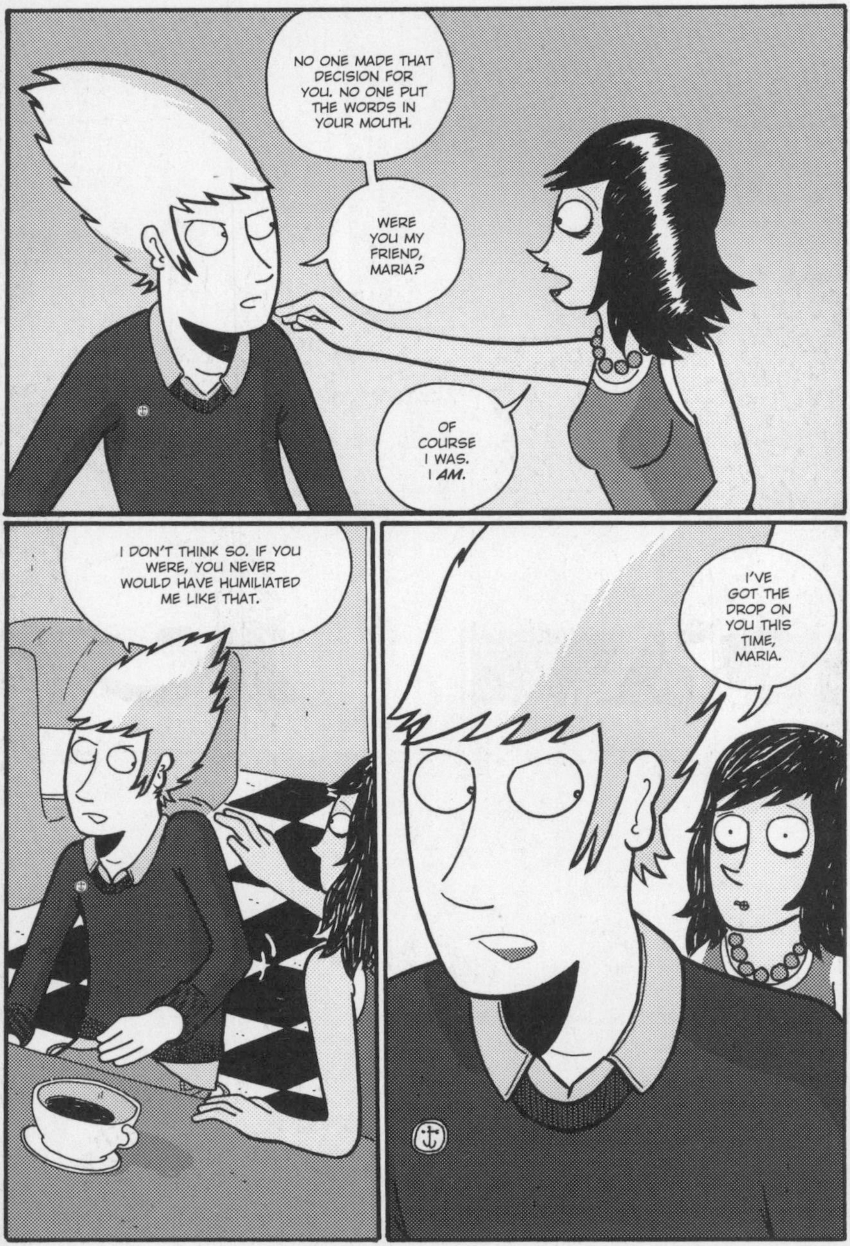
NO ONE MADE THAT DECISION FOR YOU. NO ONE PUT THE WORDS IN YOUR MOUTH.
WERE YOU MY FRIEND, MARIA?
OF COURSE I WAS. I *AM.*
I DON'T THINK SO. IF YOU WERE, YOU NEVER WOULD HAVE HUMILIATED ME LIKE THAT.
I'VE GOT THE DROP ON YOU THIS TIME, MARIA.

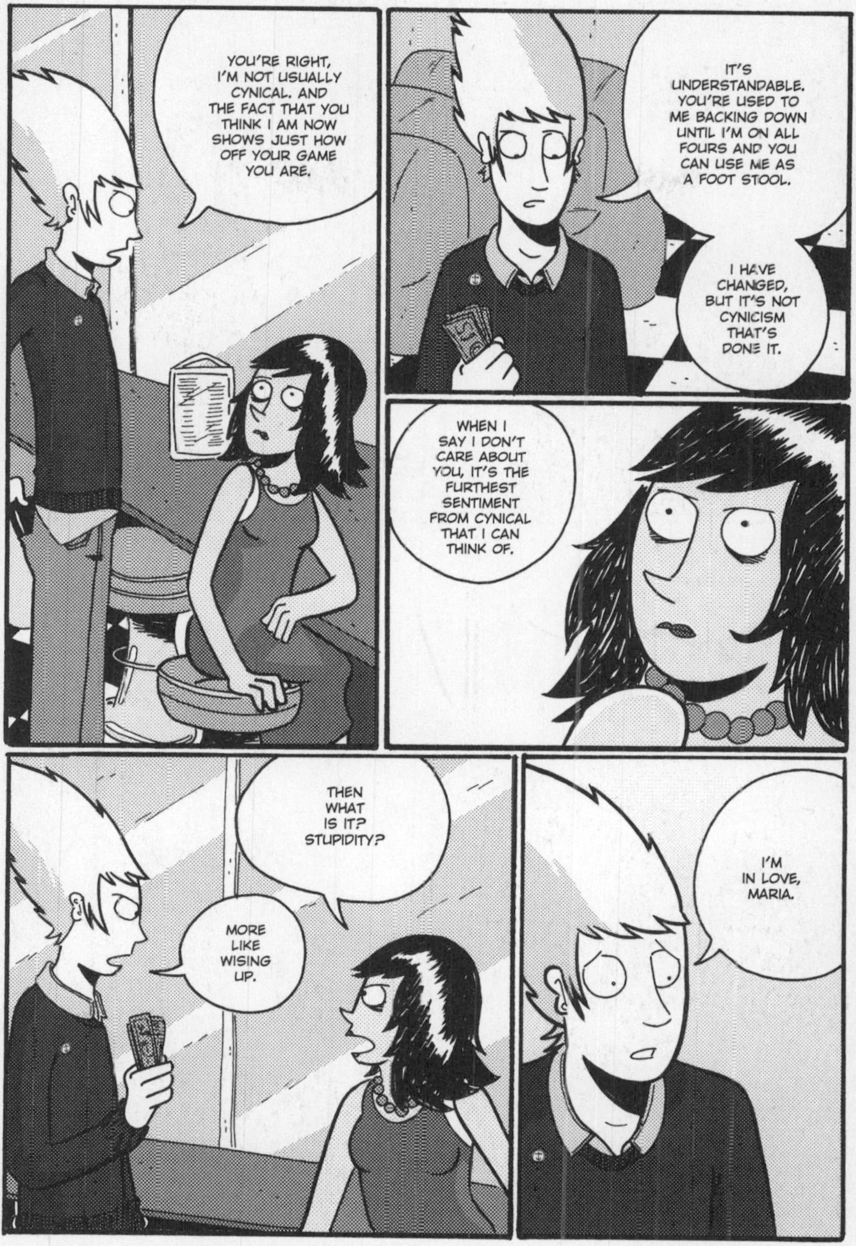
YOU'RE RIGHT, I'M NOT USUALLY CYNICAL. AND THE FACT THAT YOU THINK I AM NOW SHOWS JUST HOW OFF YOUR GAME YOU ARE.
IT'S UNDERSTANDABLE. YOU'RE USED TO ME BACKING DOWN UNTIL I'M ON ALL FOURS AND YOU CAN USE ME AS A FOOT STOOL.
I HAVE CHANGED, BUT IT'S NOT CYNICISM THAT'S DONE IT.
WHEN I SAY I DON'T CARE ABOUT YOU, IT'S THE FURTHEST SENTIMENT FROM CYNICAL THAT I CAN THINK OF.
THEN WHAT IS IT? STUPIDITY?
MORE LIKE WISING UP.
I'M IN LOVE, MARIA.

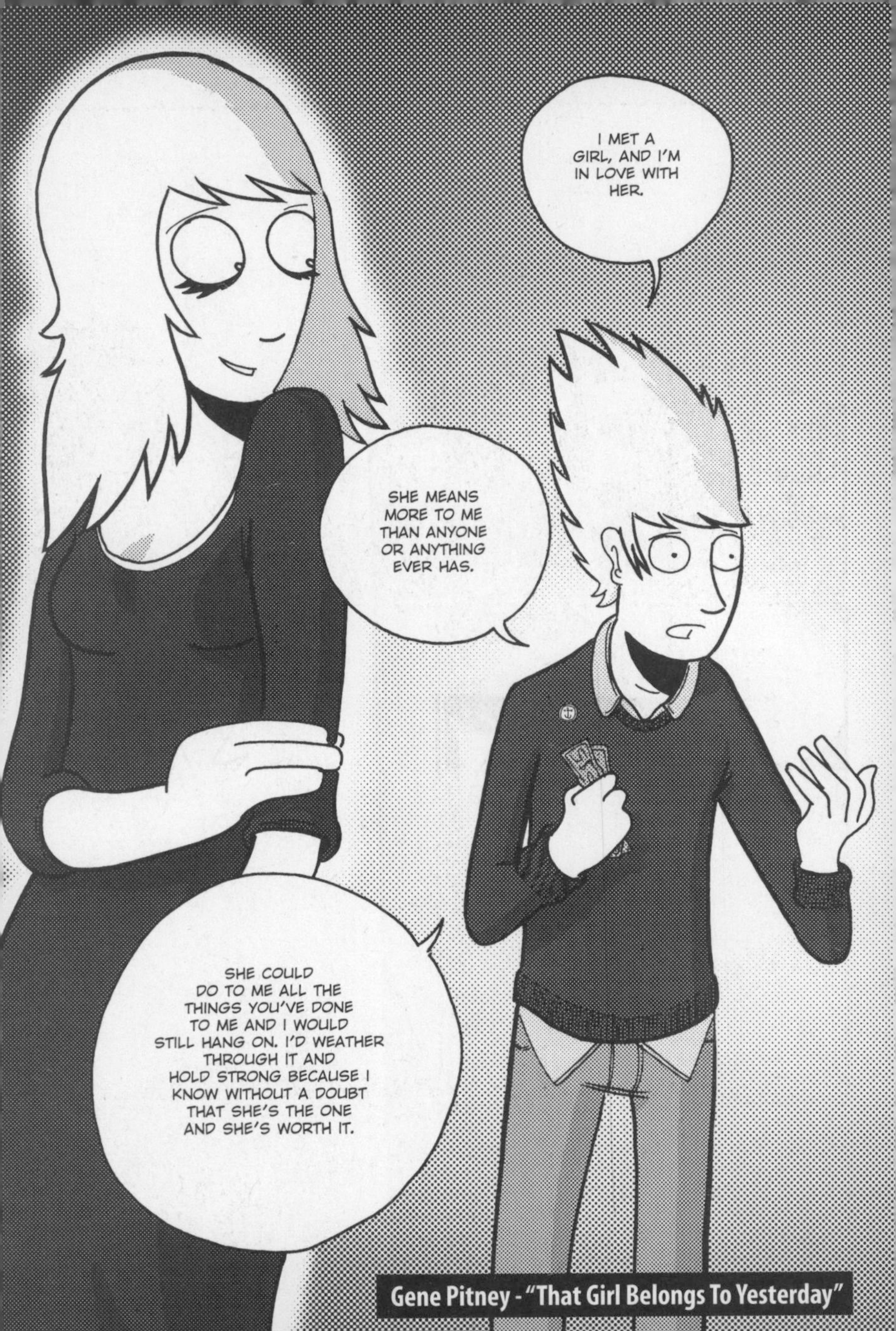
I MET A GIRL, AND I'M IN LOVE WITH HER.
SHE MEANS MORE TO ME THAN ANYONE OR ANYTHING EVER HAS.
SHE COULD DO TO ME ALL THE THINGS YOU'VE DONE TO ME AND I WOULD STILL HANG ON. I'D WEATHER THROUGH IT AND HOLD STRONG BECAUSE I KNOW WITHOUT A DOUBT THAT SHE'S THE ONE AND SHE'S WORTH IT.
Gene Pitney - "That Girl Belongs To Yesterday"

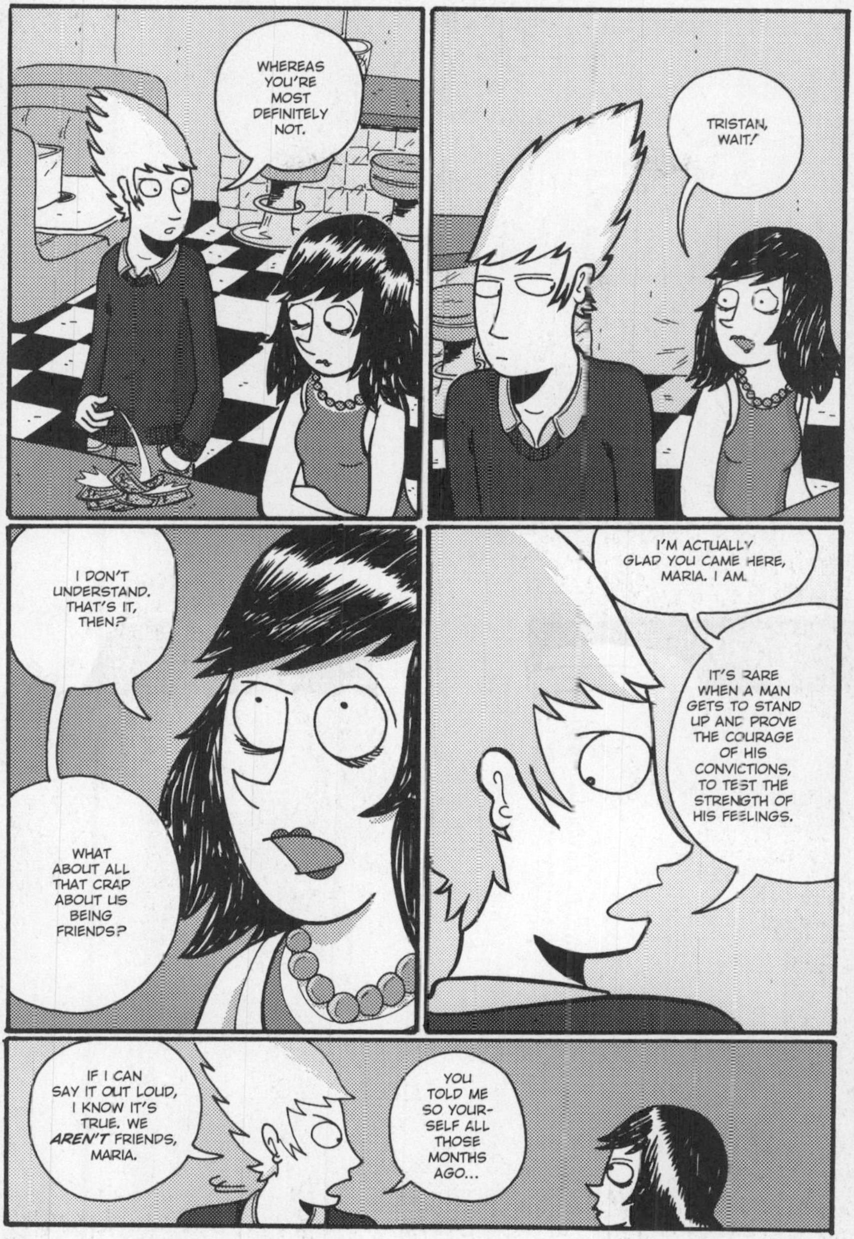
WHEREAS YOU'RE MOST DEFINITELY NOT.
TRISTAN, WAIT!
I DON'T UNDERSTAND. THAT'S IT, THEN?
WHAT ABOUT ALL THAT CRAP ABOUT US BEING FRIENDS?
I'M ACTUALLY GLAD YOU CAME HERE, MARIA. I AM.
IT'S RARE WHEN A MAN GETS TO STAND UP AND PROVE THE COURAGE OF HIS CONVICTIONS, TO TEST THE STRENGTH OF HIS FEELINGS.
IF I CAN SAY IT OUT LOUD, I KNOW IT'S TRUE. WE *AREN'T* FRIENDS, MARIA.
YOU TOLD ME SO YOURSELF ALL THOSE MONTHS AGO...

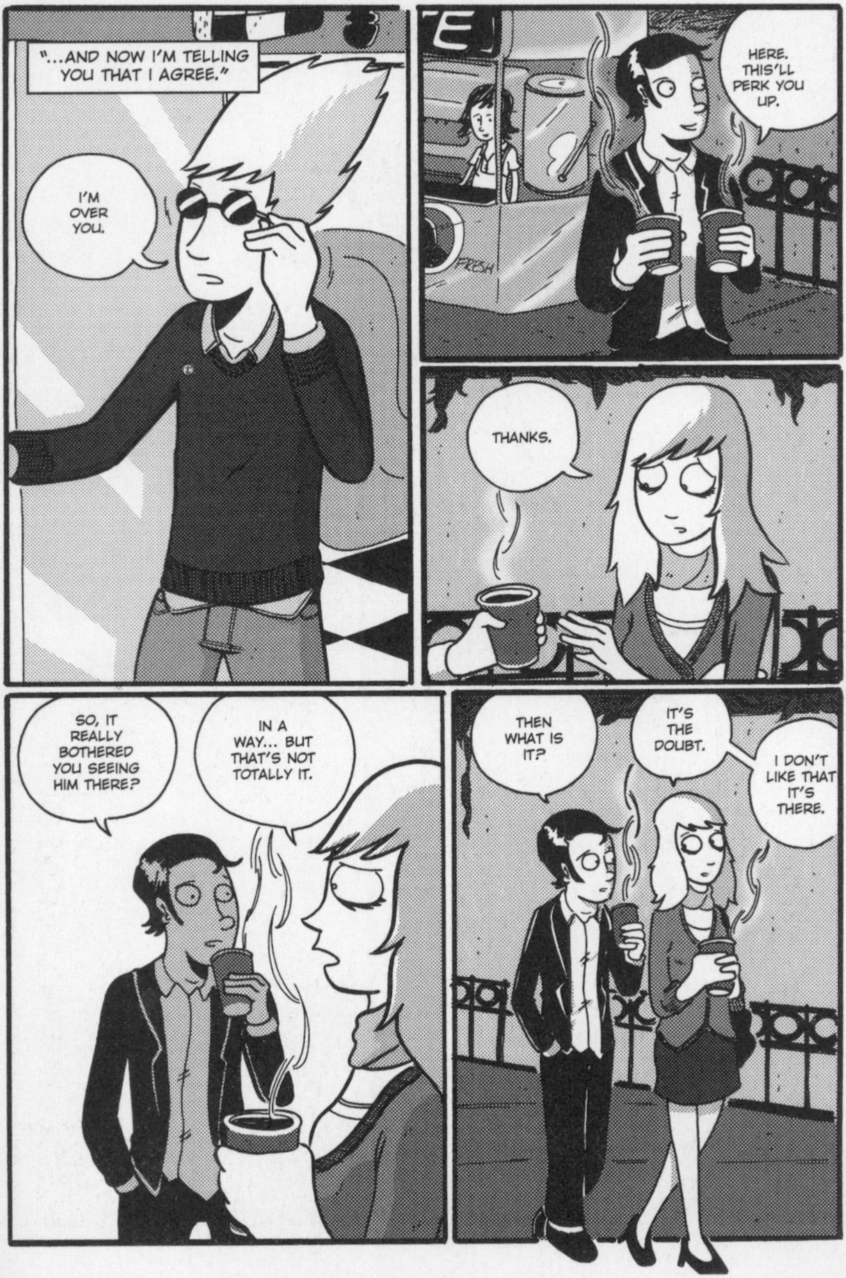
"...AND NOW I'M TELLING YOU THAT I AGREE."
I'M OVER YOU.
HERE. THIS'LL PERK YOU UP.
FRESH
THANKS.
SO, IT REALLY BOTHERED YOU SEEING HIM THERE?
IN A WAY... BUT THAT'S NOT TOTALLY IT.
THEN WHAT IS IT?
IT'S THE DOUBT.
I DON'T LIKE THAT IT'S THERE.

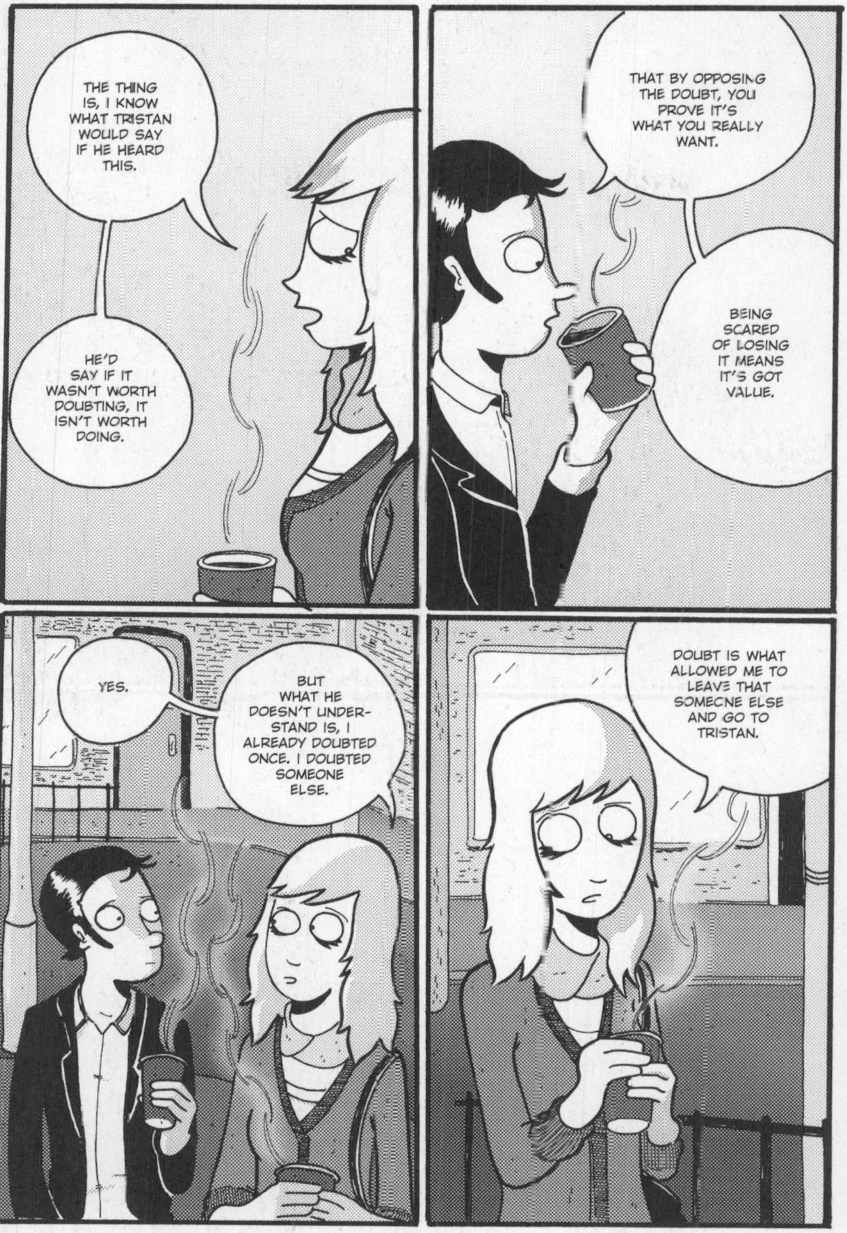
THE THING IS, I KNOW WHAT TRISTAN WOULD SAY IF HE HEARD THIS.
HE'D SAY IF IT WASN'T WORTH DOUBTING, IT ISN'T WORTH DOING.
THAT BY OPPOSING THE DOUBT, YOU PROVE IT'S WHAT YOU REALLY WANT.
BEING SCARED OF LOSING IT MEANS IT'S GOT VALUE.
YES.
BUT WHAT HE DOESN'T UNDERSTAND IS, I ALREADY DOUBTED ONCE. I DOUBTED SOMEONE ELSE.
DOUBT IS WHAT ALLOWED ME TO LEAVE THAT SOMEONE ELSE AND GO TO TRISTAN.

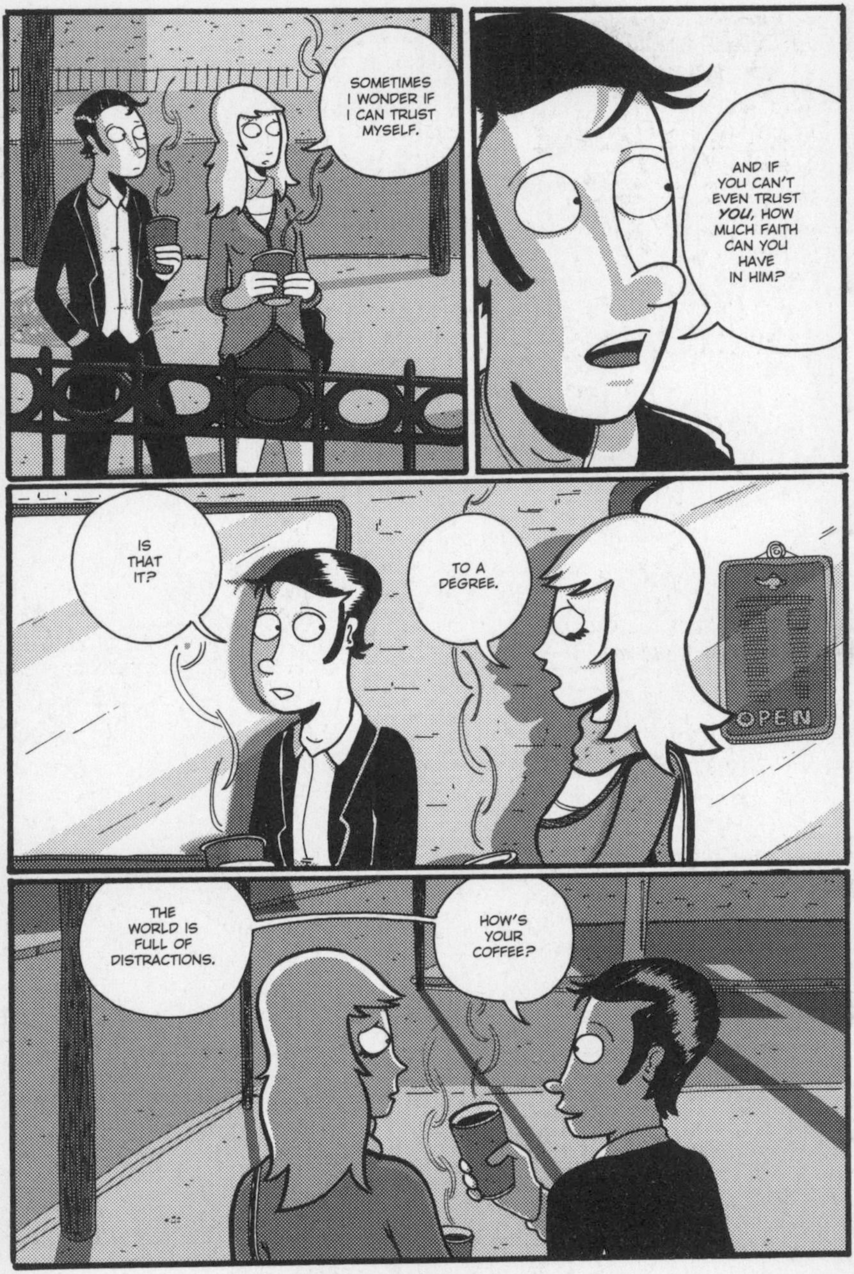
SOMETIMES I WONDER IF I CAN TRUST MYSELF.
AND IF YOU CAN'T EVEN TRUST *YOU*, HOW MUCH FAITH CAN YOU HAVE IN HIM?
IS THAT IT?
TO A DEGREE.
OPEN
THE WORLD IS FULL OF DISTRACTIONS.
HOW'S YOUR COFFEE?

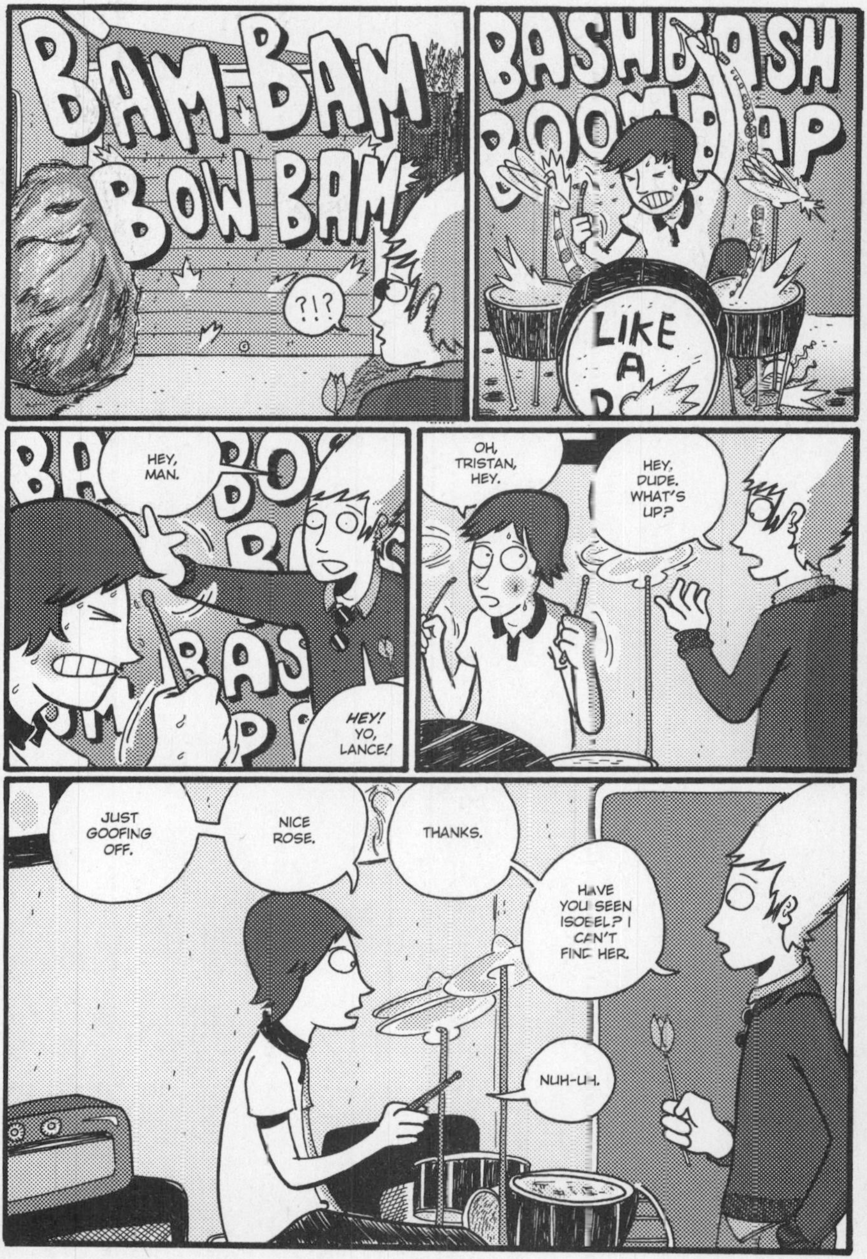

BAM BAM
BOW BAM
?!?
BASH BASH
BOOM BAP
LIKE A
HEY, MAN.
HEY! YO, LANCE!
OH, TRISTAN, HEY.
HEY, DUDE. WHAT'S UP?
JUST GOOFING OFF.
NICE ROSE.
THANKS.
HAVE YOU SEEN ISOBEL? I CAN'T FIND HER.
NUH-UH.

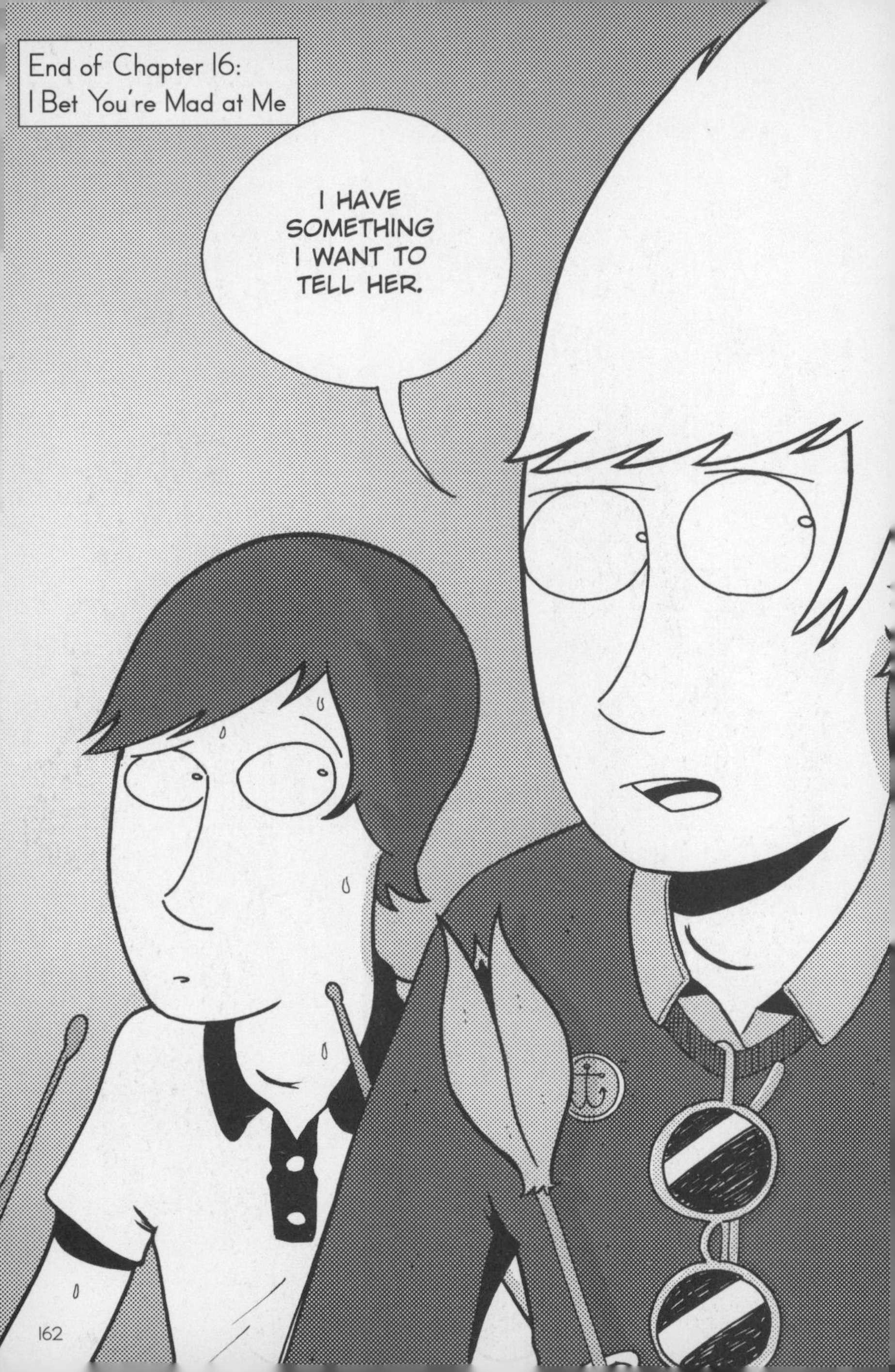
End of Chapter 16:
I Bet You're Mad at Me
I HAVE SOMETHING I WANT TO TELL HER.

Chapter 17:
My Aim is True

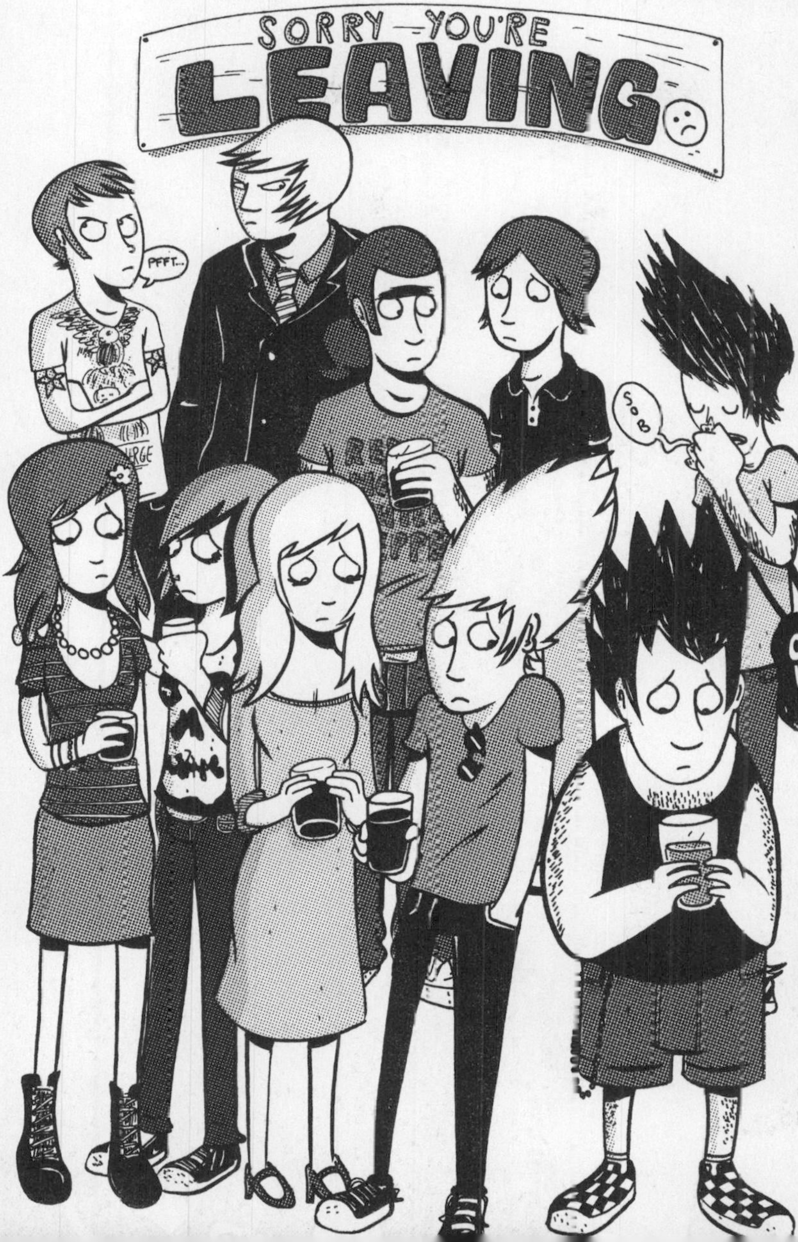
SORRY YOU'RE LEAVING
PFFT...
SOB
ONE LEG

THE *LOVE THE WAY YOU LOVE* DRINKING GAME!

Use your beverage of choice, but remember, drink responsibly, and if you're under 21, stay away from alcohol. It's the devil's drink! (Just look at Marc Ellerby on a hungover Saturday morning if you don't believe me.) Replace it with something highly caffeinated or full of sugar and get yourself amped that way.

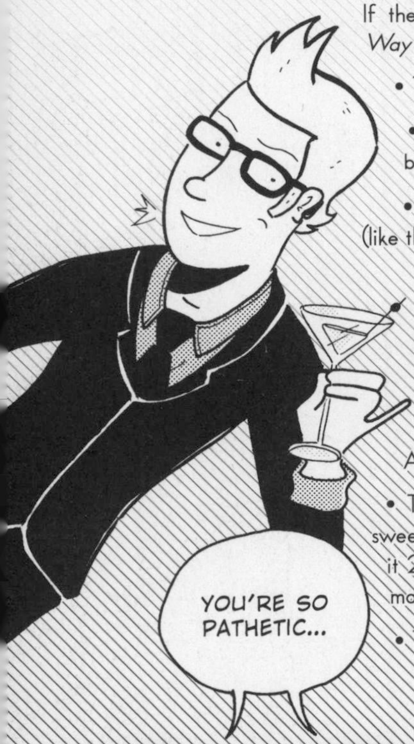
YOU'RE SO PATHETIC...

If the following events occur while reading *Love the Way You Love*, drink as instructed.

- Tristan shouts out, "Isobel!" - 1 shot
- If one character goes looking for another character but is mistaken about where he or she is - 1 shot
- There is a self-referential joke from the creators (like this page) - 1 shot
- If you know a song mentioned in the story - 1 shot for your opponent; however, if you don't know the song, take 2 yourself.
- Lance calls Marcus "Kong" - 1 shot
- Someone makes a crack about the name "Like A Dog" - 2 shots
- Two characters kiss - 1 shot and a kiss from your sweetie. Except if there is no one there to kiss you, make it 2. (It's why Jamie is always drunk.) (Yes, that remark means a shot!)
- There are penguins in the comic - Chug the bottle!

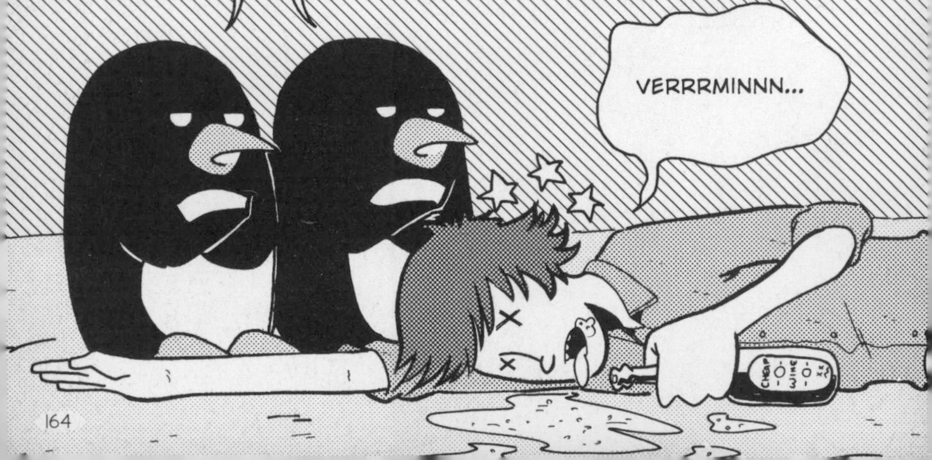
VERRRMINNN...
CHEAP WINE

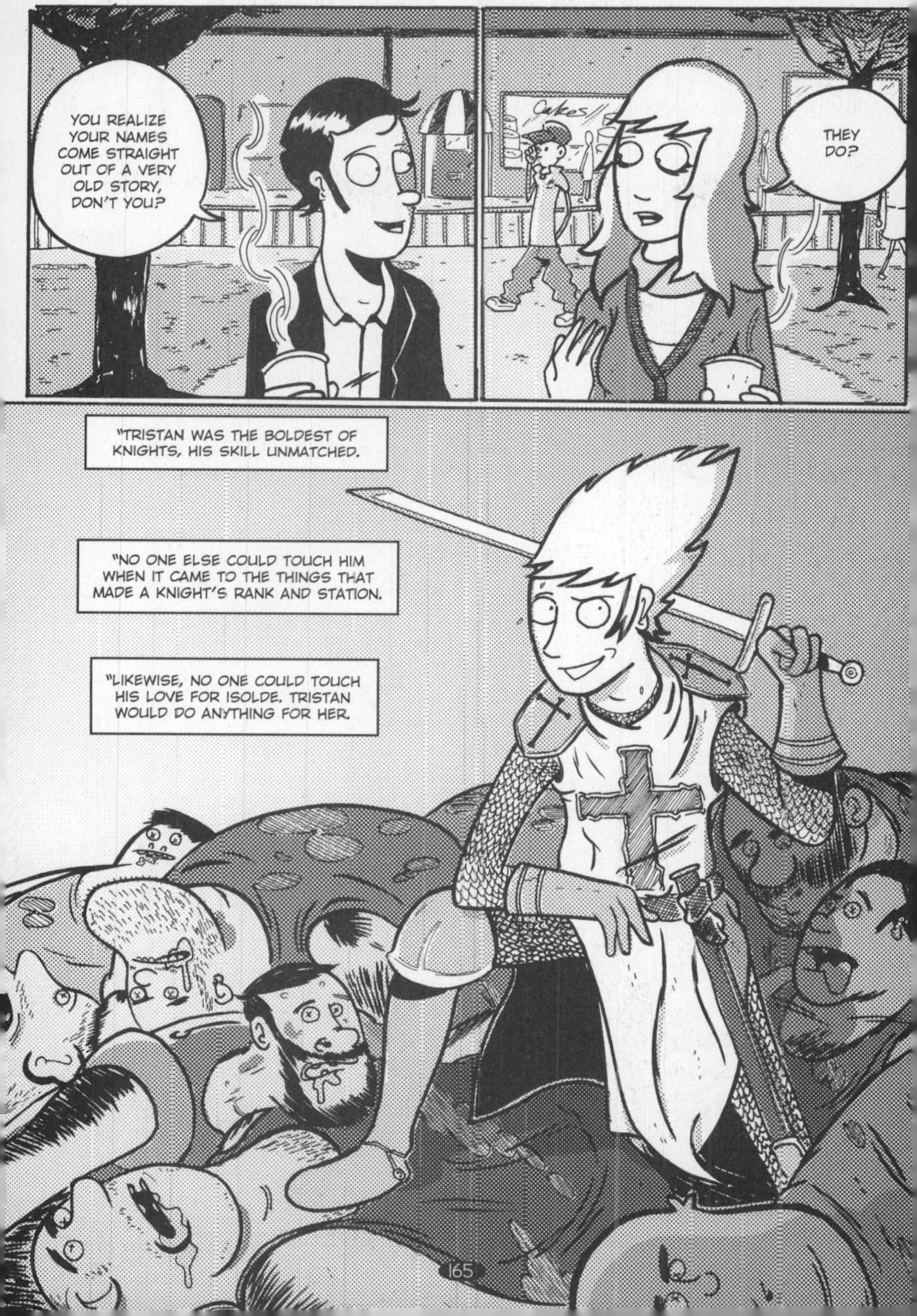
YOU REALIZE YOUR NAMES COME STRAIGHT OUT OF A VERY OLD STORY, DON'T YOU?
Cakes
THEY DO?
"TRISTAN WAS THE BOLDEST OF KNIGHTS, HIS SKILL UNMATCHED.
"NO ONE ELSE COULD TOUCH HIM WHEN IT CAME TO THE THINGS THAT MADE A KNIGHT'S RANK AND STATION.
"LIKEWISE, NO ONE COULD TOUCH HIS LOVE FOR ISOLDE. TRISTAN WOULD DO ANYTHING FOR HER.

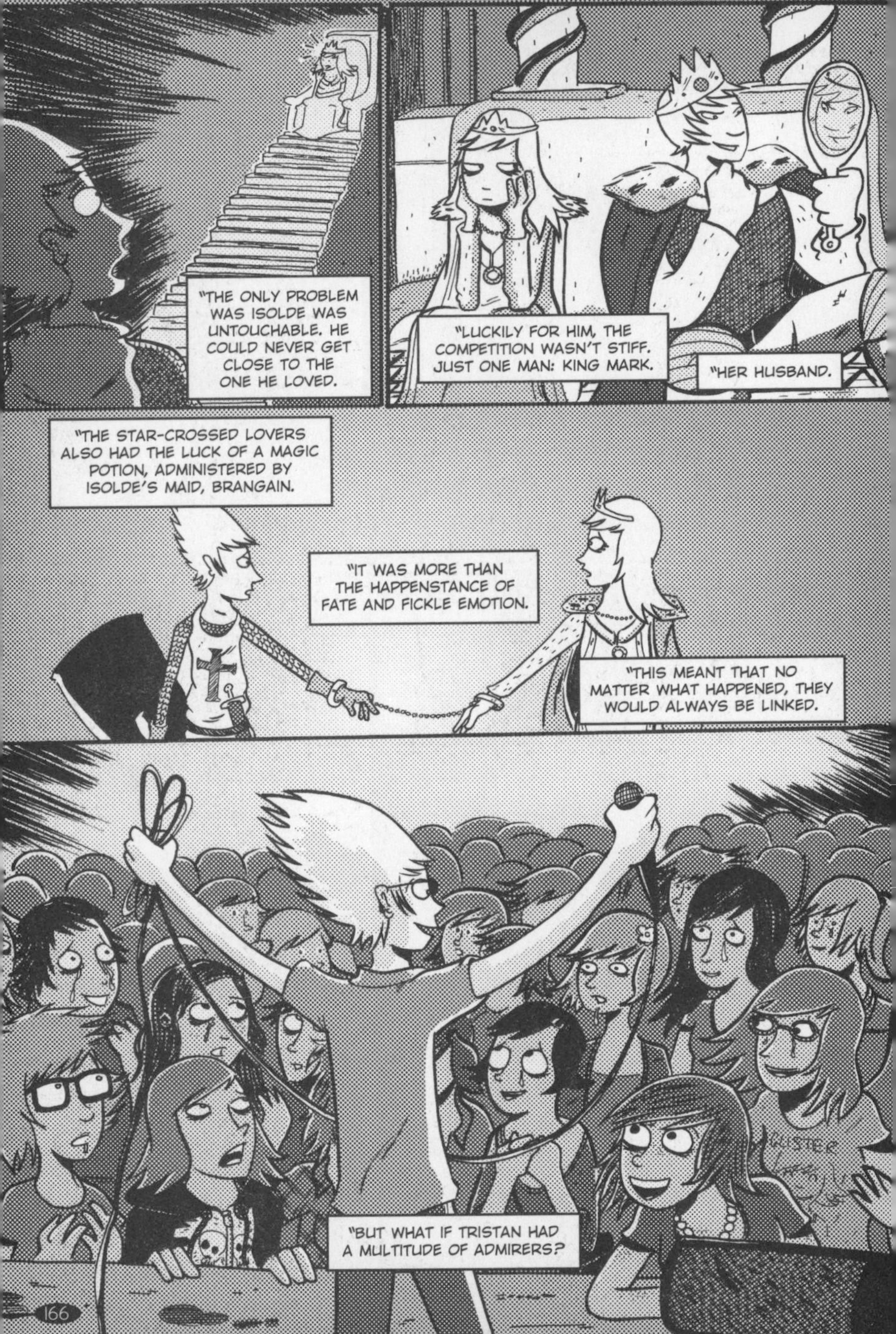
"THE ONLY PROBLEM WAS ISOLDE WAS UNTOUCHABLE. HE COULD NEVER GET CLOSE TO THE ONE HE LOVED.
"LUCKILY FOR HIM, THE COMPETITION WASN'T STIFF. JUST ONE MAN: KING MARK.
"HER HUSBAND.
"THE STAR-CROSSED LOVERS ALSO HAD THE LUCK OF A MAGIC POTION, ADMINISTERED BY ISOLDE'S MAID, BRANGAIN.
"IT WAS MORE THAN THE HAPPENSTANCE OF FATE AND FICKLE EMOTION.
"THIS MEANT THAT NO MATTER WHAT HAPPENED, THEY WOULD ALWAYS BE LINKED.
"BUT WHAT IF TRISTAN HAD A MULTITUDE OF ADMIRERS?

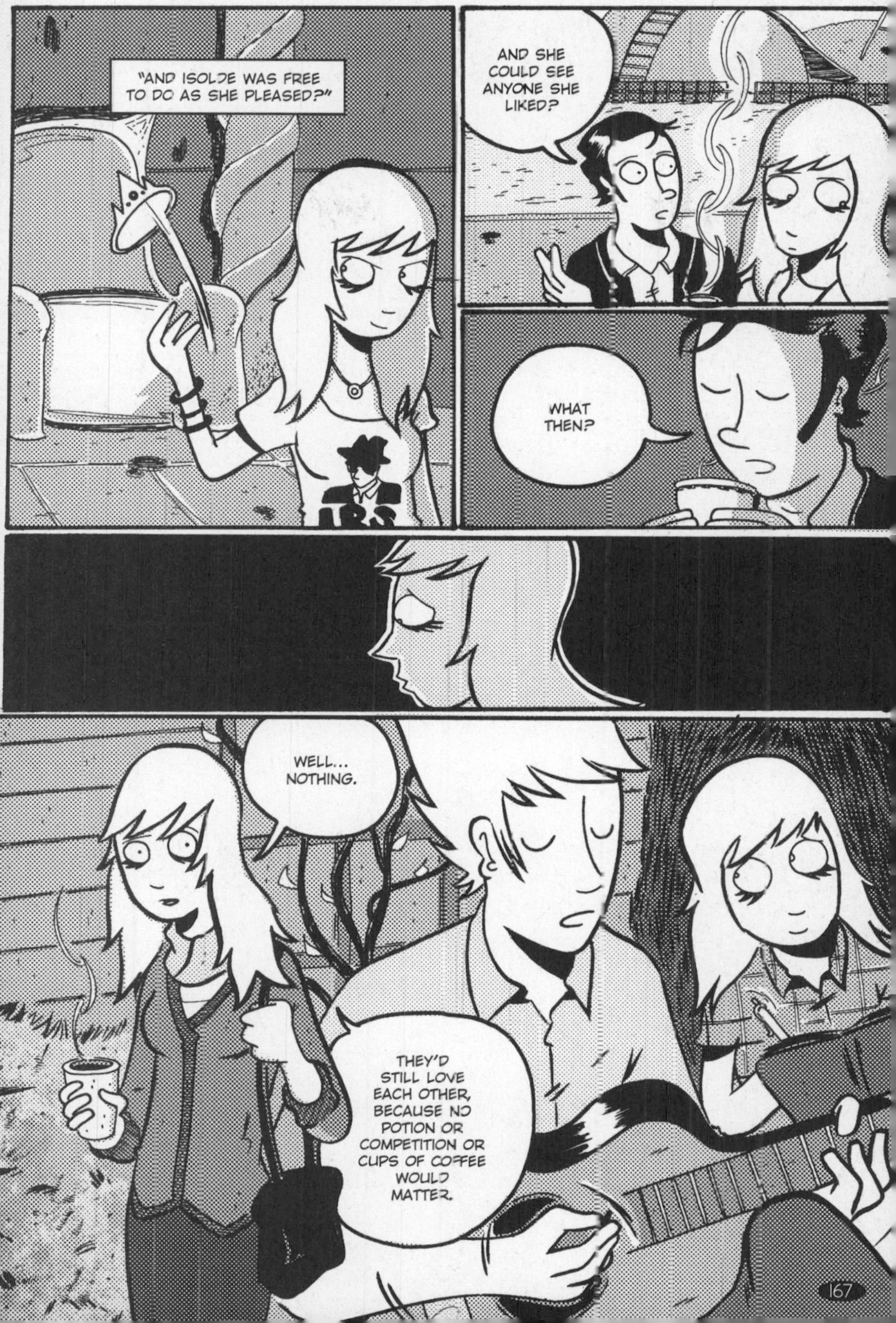
"AND ISOLDE WAS FREE TO DO AS SHE PLEASED?"
AND SHE COULD SEE ANYONE SHE LIKED?
WHAT THEN?
WELL... NOTHING.
THEY'D STILL LOVE EACH OTHER, BECAUSE NO POTION OR COMPETITION OR CUPS OF COFFEE WOULD MATTER.

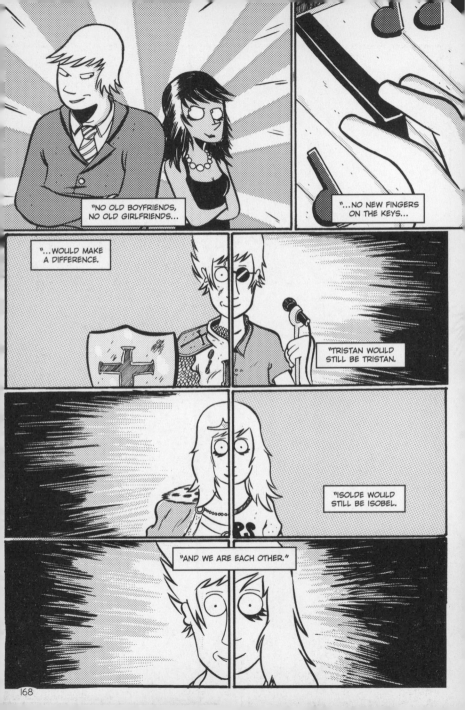

"NO OLD BOYFRIENDS,
NO OLD GIRLFRIENDS...

"...NO NEW FINGERS
ON THE KEYS...

"...WOULD MAKE
A DIFFERENCE.

"TRISTAN WOULD
STILL BE TRISTAN.

"ISOLDE WOULD
STILL BE ISOBEL.

"AND WE ARE EACH OTHER."

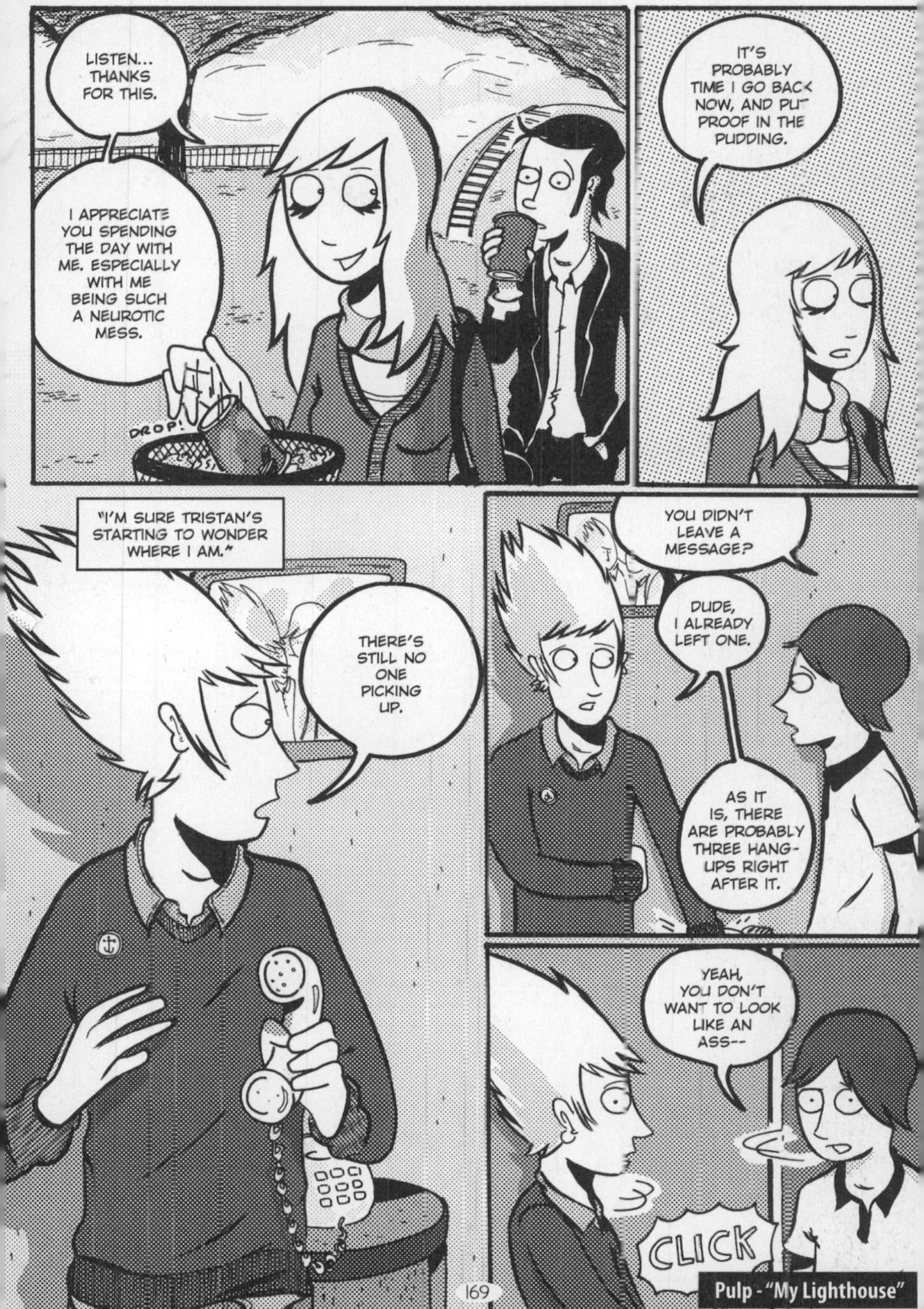
LISTEN... THANKS FOR THIS.
I APPRECIATE YOU SPENDING THE DAY WITH ME. ESPECIALLY WITH ME BEING SUCH A NEUROTIC MESS.
DROP!
IT'S PROBABLY TIME I GO BACK NOW, AND PUT PROOF IN THE PUDDING.
"I'M SURE TRISTAN'S STARTING TO WONDER WHERE I AM."
THERE'S STILL NO ONE PICKING UP.
YOU DIDN'T LEAVE A MESSAGE?
DUDE, I ALREADY LEFT ONE.
AS IT IS, THERE ARE PROBABLY THREE HANG-UPS RIGHT AFTER IT.
YEAH, YOU DON'T WANT TO LOOK LIKE AN ASS--
CLICK
Pulp - "My Lighthouse"

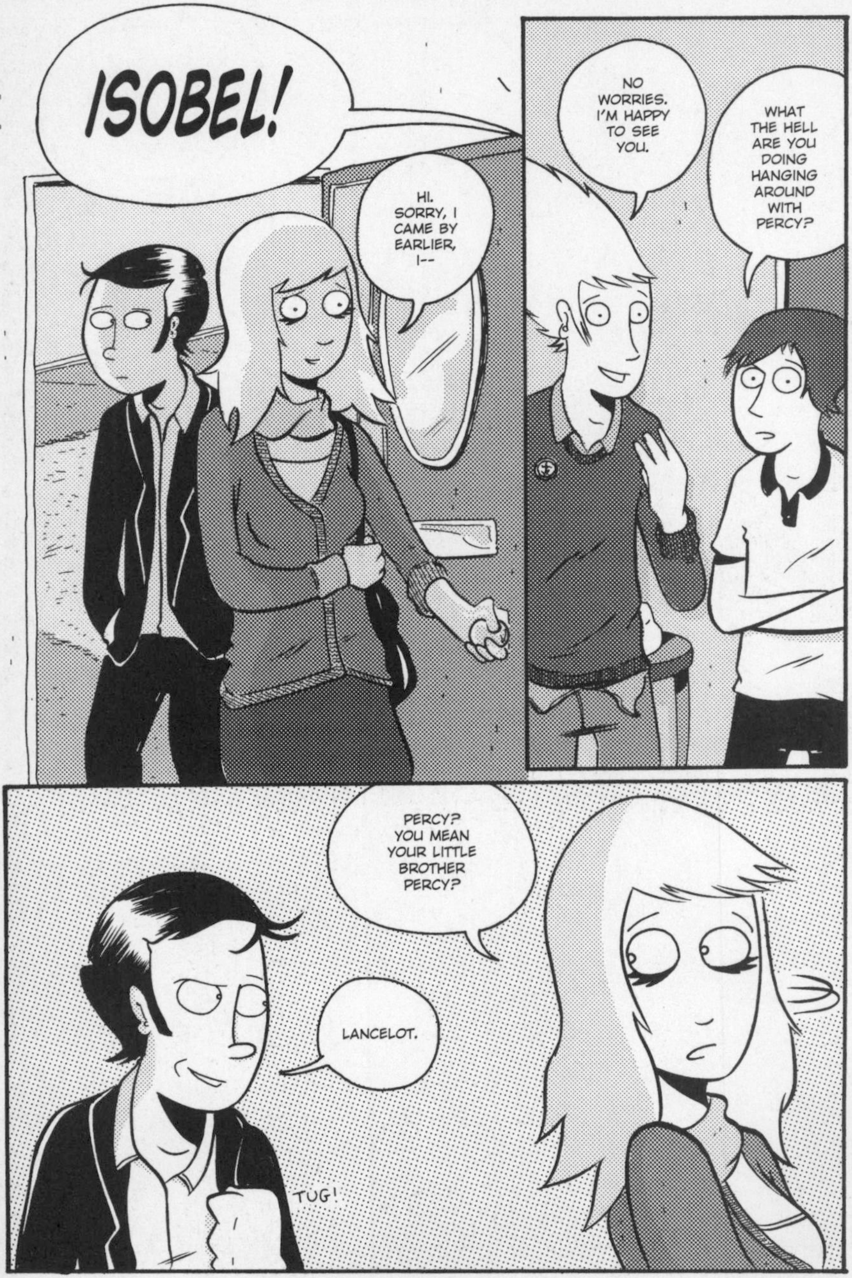
ISOBEL!
HI. SORRY, I CAME BY EARLIER, I--
NO WORRIES. I'M HAPPY TO SEE YOU.
WHAT THE HELL ARE YOU DOING HANGING AROUND WITH PERCY?
PERCY? YOU MEAN YOUR LITTLE BROTHER PERCY?
LANCELOT.
TUG!

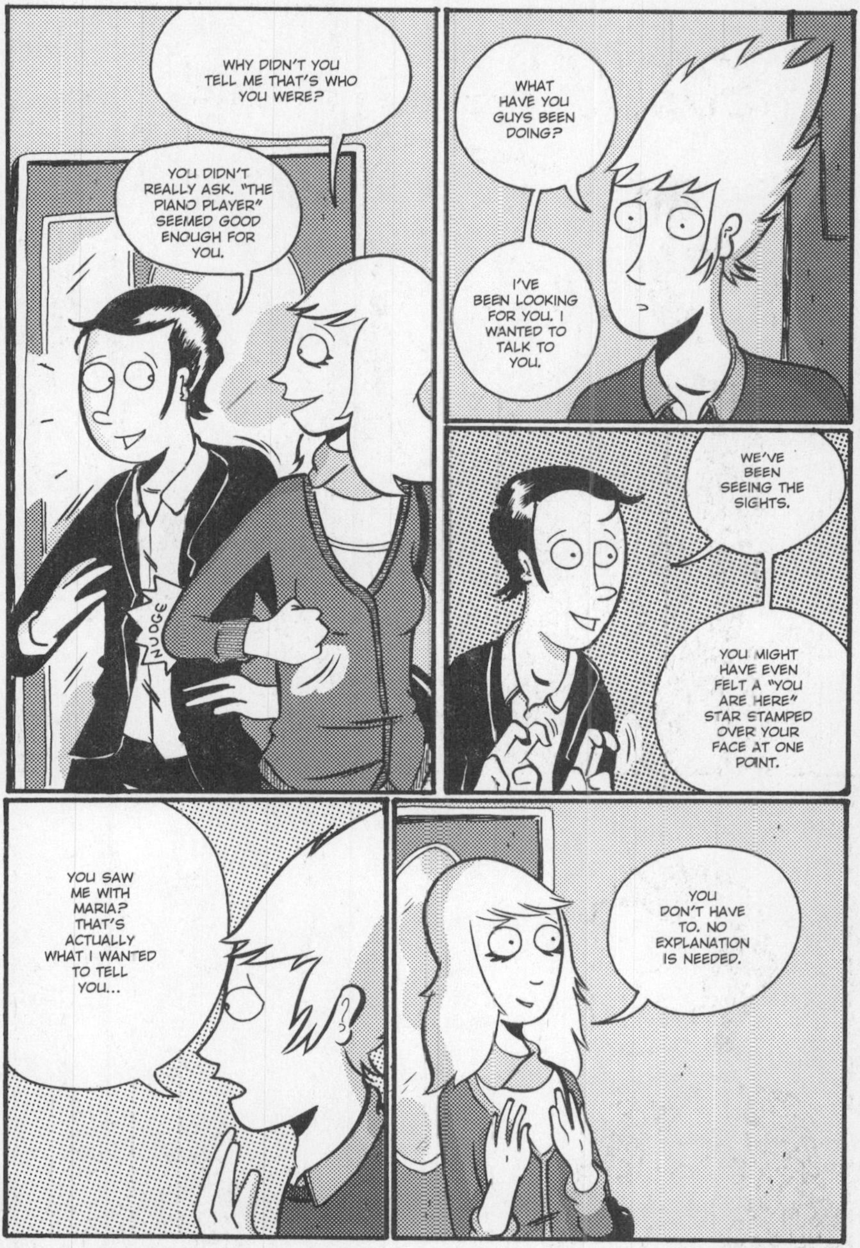
WHY DIDN'T YOU TELL ME THAT'S WHO YOU WERE?
YOU DIDN'T REALLY ASK. "THE PIANO PLAYER" SEEMED GOOD ENOUGH FOR YOU.
NUDGE
WHAT HAVE YOU GUYS BEEN DOING?
I'VE BEEN LOOKING FOR YOU. I WANTED TO TALK TO YOU.
WE'VE BEEN SEEING THE SIGHTS.
YOU MIGHT HAVE EVEN FELT A "YOU ARE HERE" STAR STAMPED OVER YOUR FACE AT ONE POINT.
YOU SAW ME WITH MARIA? THAT'S ACTUALLY WHAT I WANTED TO TELL YOU...
YOU DON'T HAVE TO. NO EXPLANATION IS NEEDED.

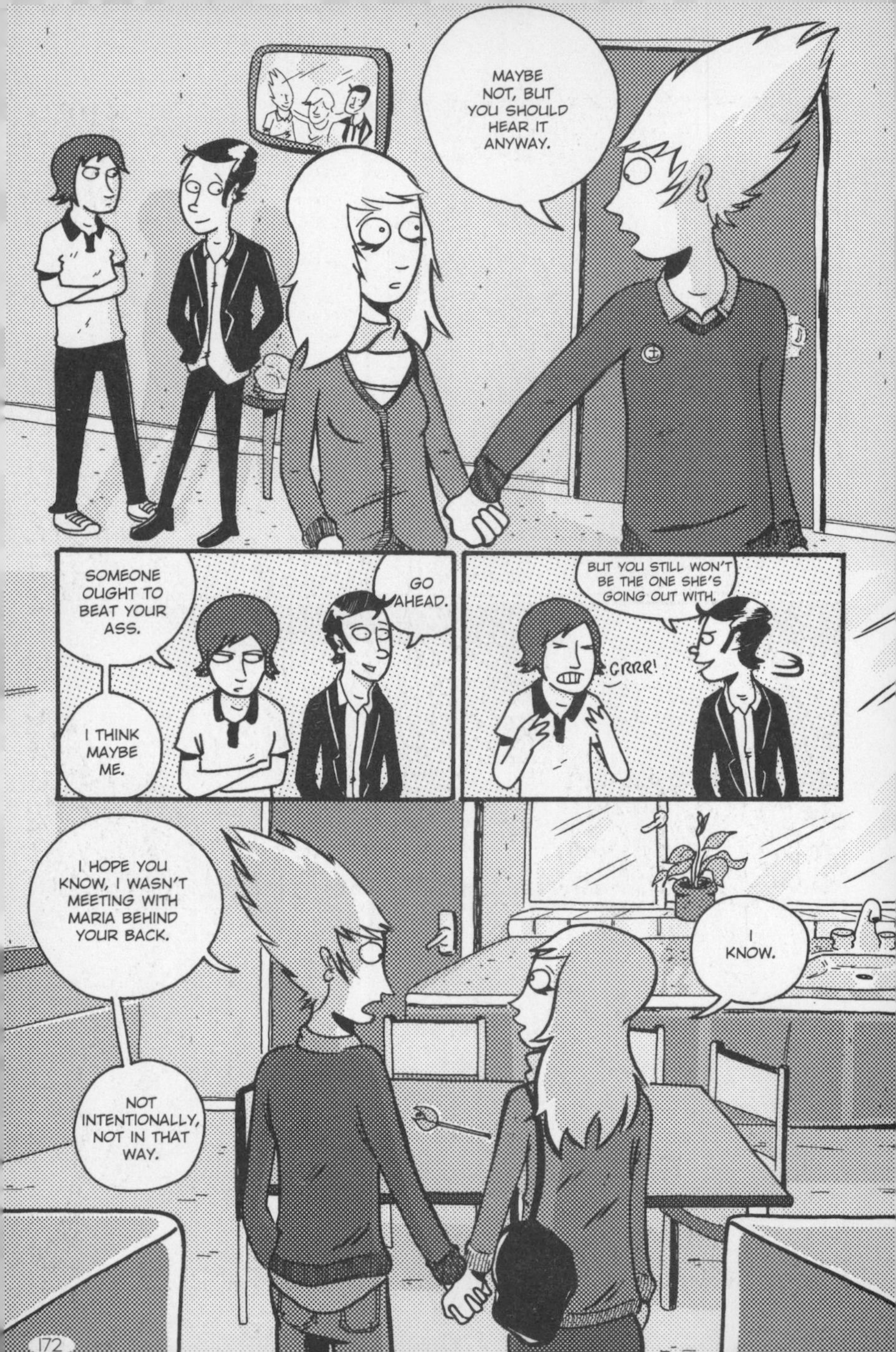
MAYBE NOT, BUT YOU SHOULD HEAR IT ANYWAY.
SOMEONE OUGHT TO BEAT YOUR ASS.
I THINK MAYBE ME.
GO AHEAD.
BUT YOU STILL WON'T BE THE ONE SHE'S GOING OUT WITH.
GRRR!
I HOPE YOU KNOW, I WASN'T MEETING WITH MARIA BEHIND YOUR BACK.
NOT INTENTIONALLY, NOT IN THAT WAY.
I KNOW.

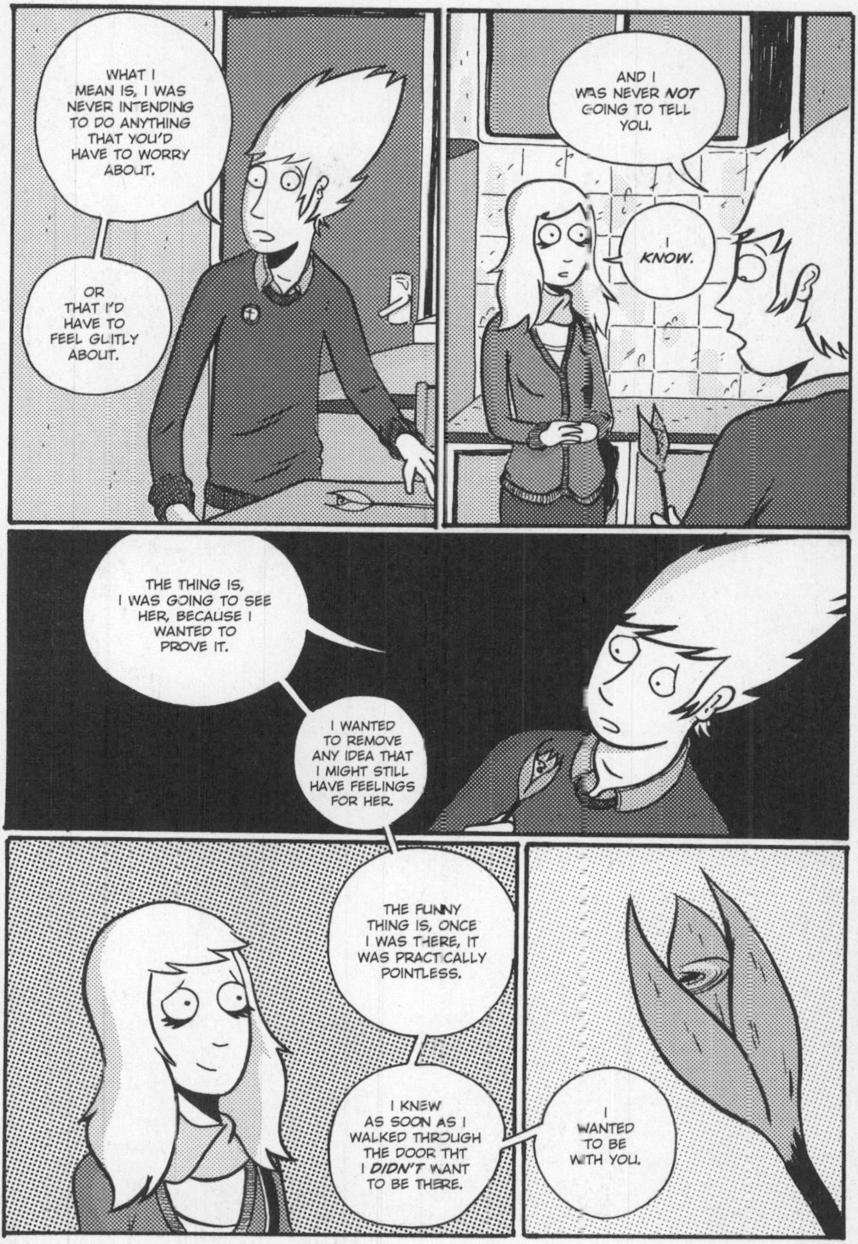
WHAT I MEAN IS, I WAS NEVER INTENDING TO DO ANYTHING THAT YOU'D HAVE TO WORRY ABOUT.
OR THAT I'D HAVE TO FEEL GLITLY ABOUT.
AND I WAS NEVER *NOT* GOING TO TELL YOU.
I *KNOW.*
THE THING IS, I WAS *GOING* TO SEE HER, BECAUSE I WANTED TO PROVE IT.
I WANTED TO REMOVE ANY IDEA THAT I MIGHT STILL HAVE FEELINGS FOR HER.
THE FUNNY THING IS, ONCE I WAS THERE, IT WAS PRACTICALLY POINTLESS.
I KNEW AS SOON AS I WALKED THROUGH THE DOOR THT I ***DIDN'T*** WANT TO BE THERE.
I WANTED TO BE WITH YOU.

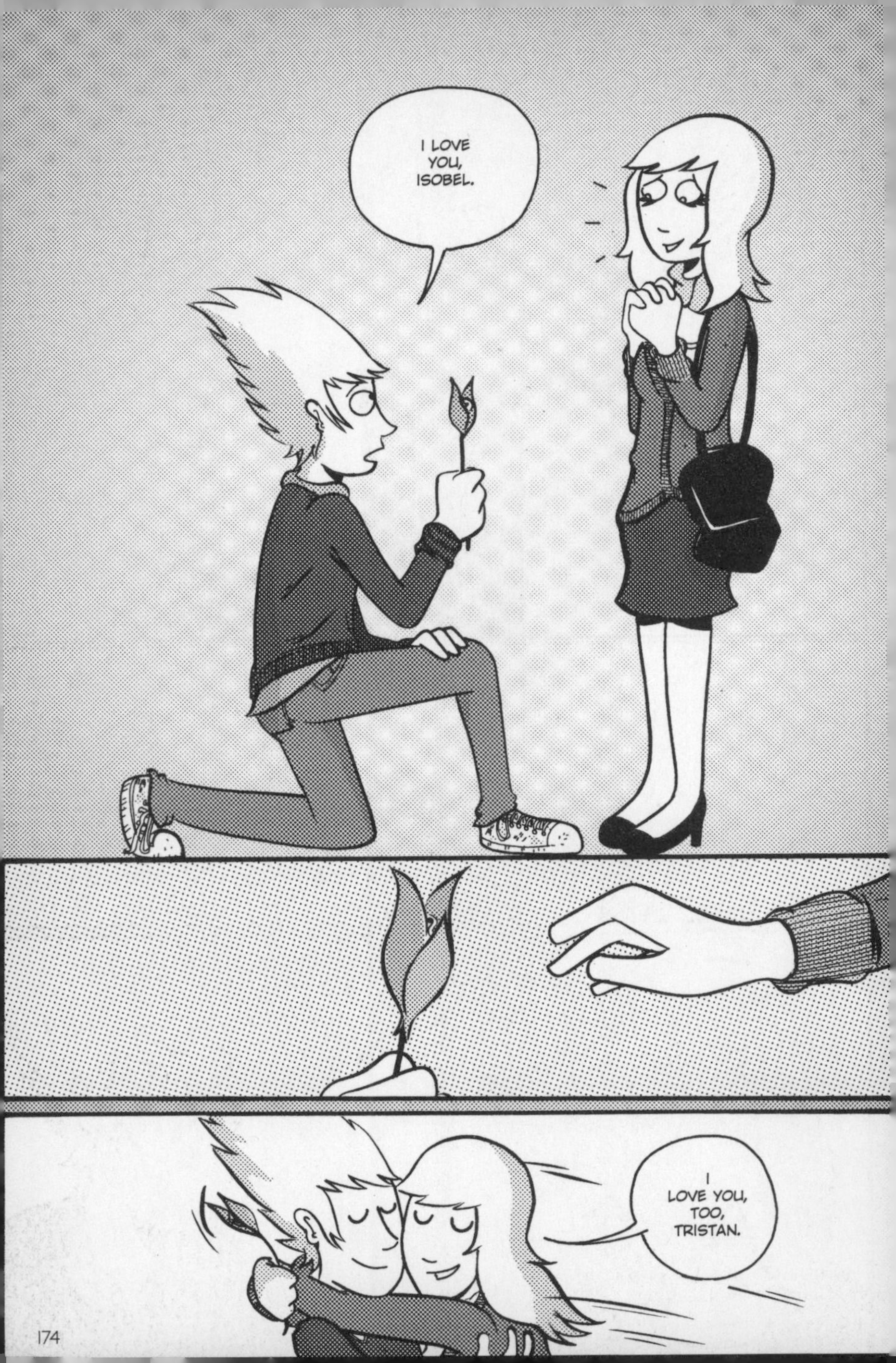
I LOVE YOU, ISOBEL.
I LOVE YOU, TOO, TRISTAN.

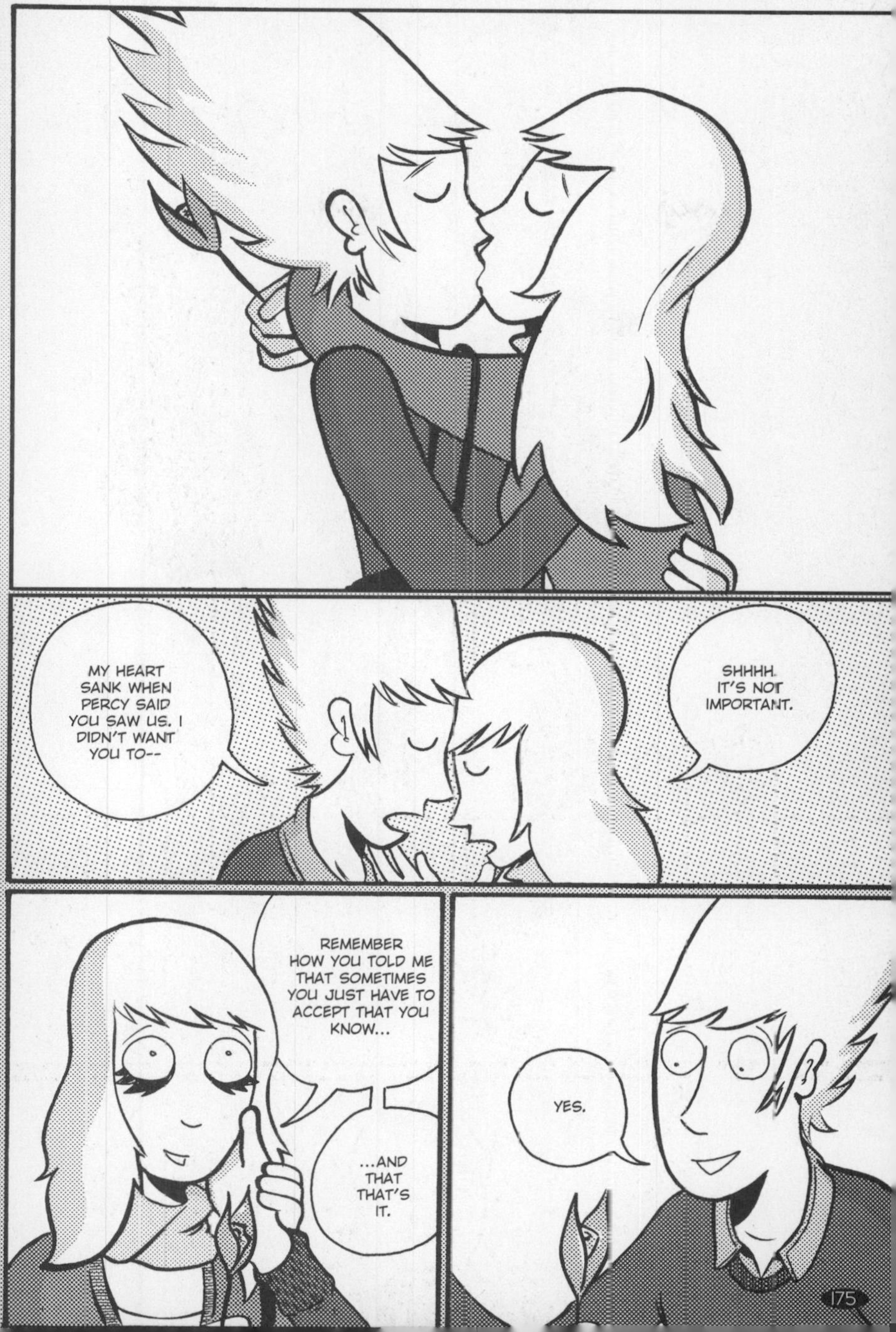
MY HEART SANK WHEN PERCY SAID YOU SAW US. I DIDN'T WANT YOU TO--
SHHHH. IT'S NOT IMPORTANT.
REMEMBER HOW YOU TOLD ME THAT SOMETIMES YOU JUST HAVE TO ACCEPT THAT YOU KNOW...
...AND THAT THAT'S IT.
YES.

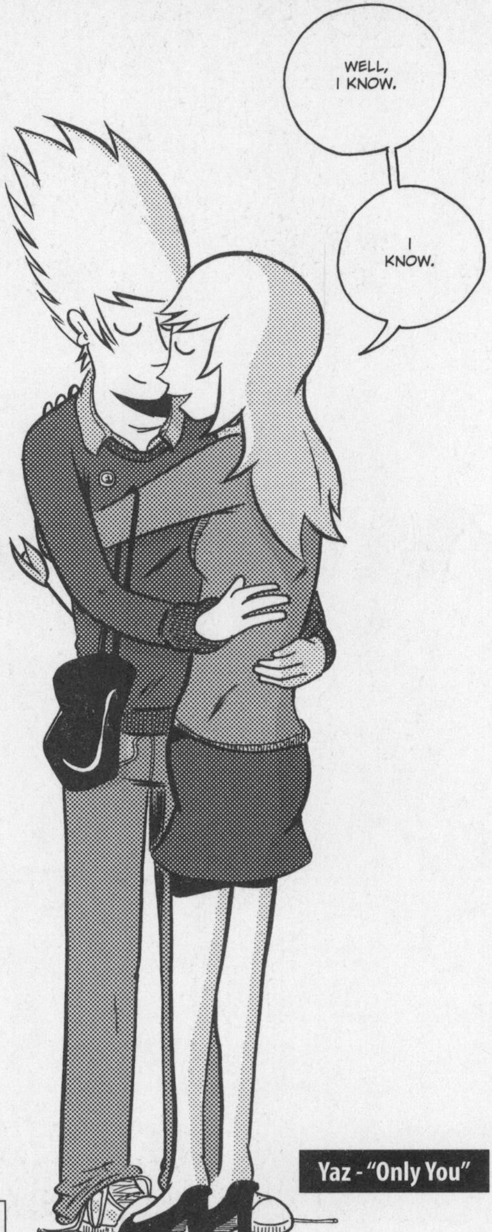
WELL,
I KNOW.
I
KNOW.
Yaz - "Only You"

End of Chapter 17:
My Aim is True

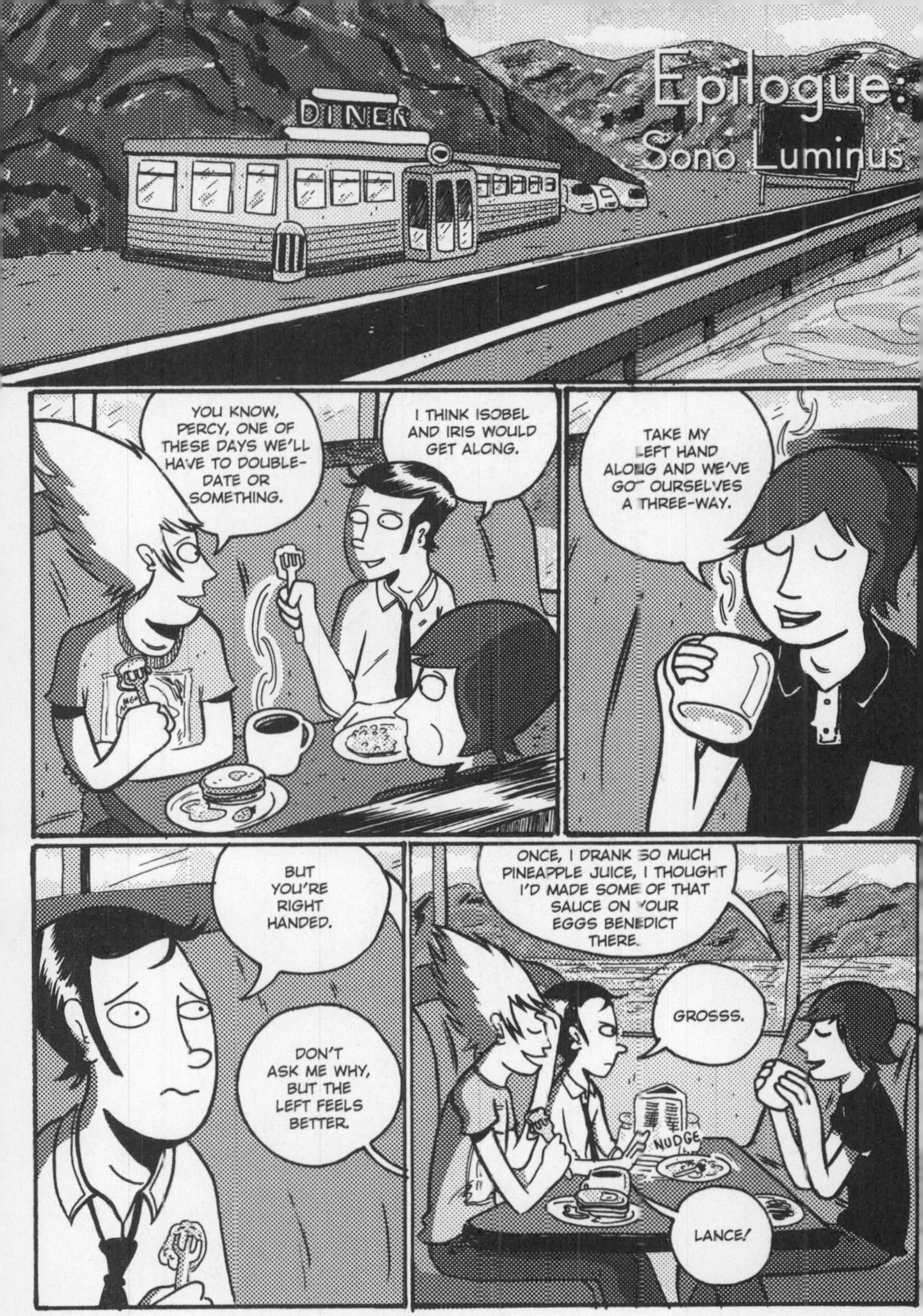
Epilogue:
Sono Luminus
DINER
YOU KNOW, PERCY, ONE OF THESE DAYS WE'LL HAVE TO DOUBLE-DATE OR SOMETHING.
I THINK ISOBEL AND IRIS WOULD GET ALONG.
TAKE MY LEFT HAND ALONG AND WE'VE GOT OURSELVES A THREE-WAY.
BUT YOU'RE RIGHT HANDED.
DON'T ASK ME WHY, BUT THE LEFT FEELS BETTER.
ONCE, I DRANK SO MUCH PINEAPPLE JUICE, I THOUGHT I'D MADE SOME OF THAT SAUCE ON YOUR EGGS BENEDICT THERE.
GROSSS.
NUDGE
LANCE!

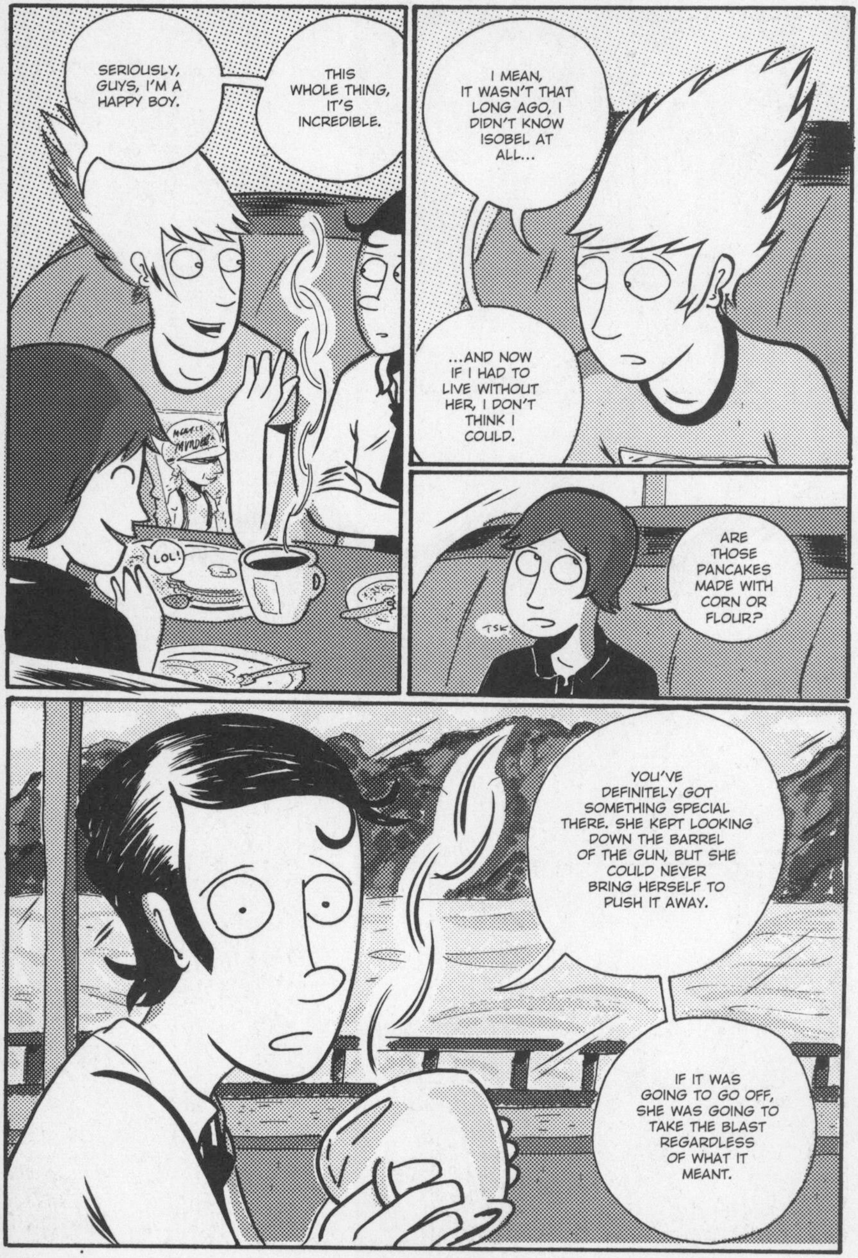
SERIOUSLY, GUYS, I'M A HAPPY BOY.
THIS WHOLE THING, IT'S INCREDIBLE.
LOL!
I MEAN, IT WASN'T THAT LONG AGO, I DIDN'T KNOW ISOBEL AT ALL...
...AND NOW IF I HAD TO LIVE WITHOUT HER, I DON'T THINK I COULD.
TSK
ARE THOSE PANCAKES MADE WITH CORN OR FLOUR?
YOU'VE DEFINITELY GOT SOMETHING SPECIAL THERE. SHE KEPT LOOKING DOWN THE BARREL OF THE GUN, BUT SHE COULD NEVER BRING HERSELF TO PUSH IT AWAY.
IF IT WAS GOING TO GO OFF, SHE WAS GOING TO TAKE THE BLAST REGARDLESS OF WHAT IT MEANT.

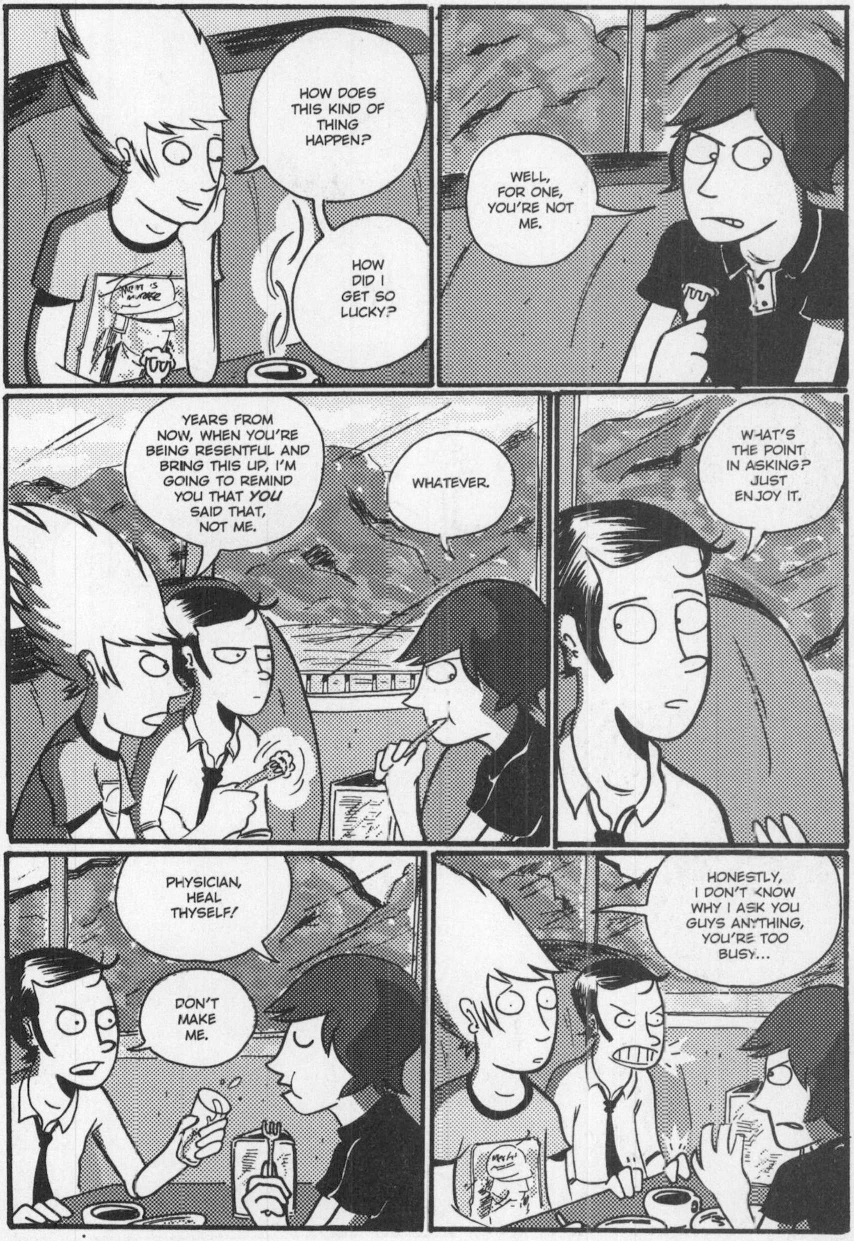
HOW DOES THIS KIND OF THING HAPPEN?
HOW DID I GET SO LUCKY?
WELL, FOR ONE, YOU'RE NOT ME.
YEARS FROM NOW, WHEN YOU'RE BEING RESENTFUL AND BRING THIS UP, I'M GOING TO REMIND YOU THAT *YOU* SAID THAT, NOT ME.
WHATEVER.
WHAT'S THE POINT IN ASKING? JUST ENJOY IT.
PHYSICIAN, HEAL THYSELF!
DON'T MAKE ME.
HONESTLY, I DON'T KNOW WHY I ASK YOU GUYS ANYTHING, YOU'RE TOO BUSY...

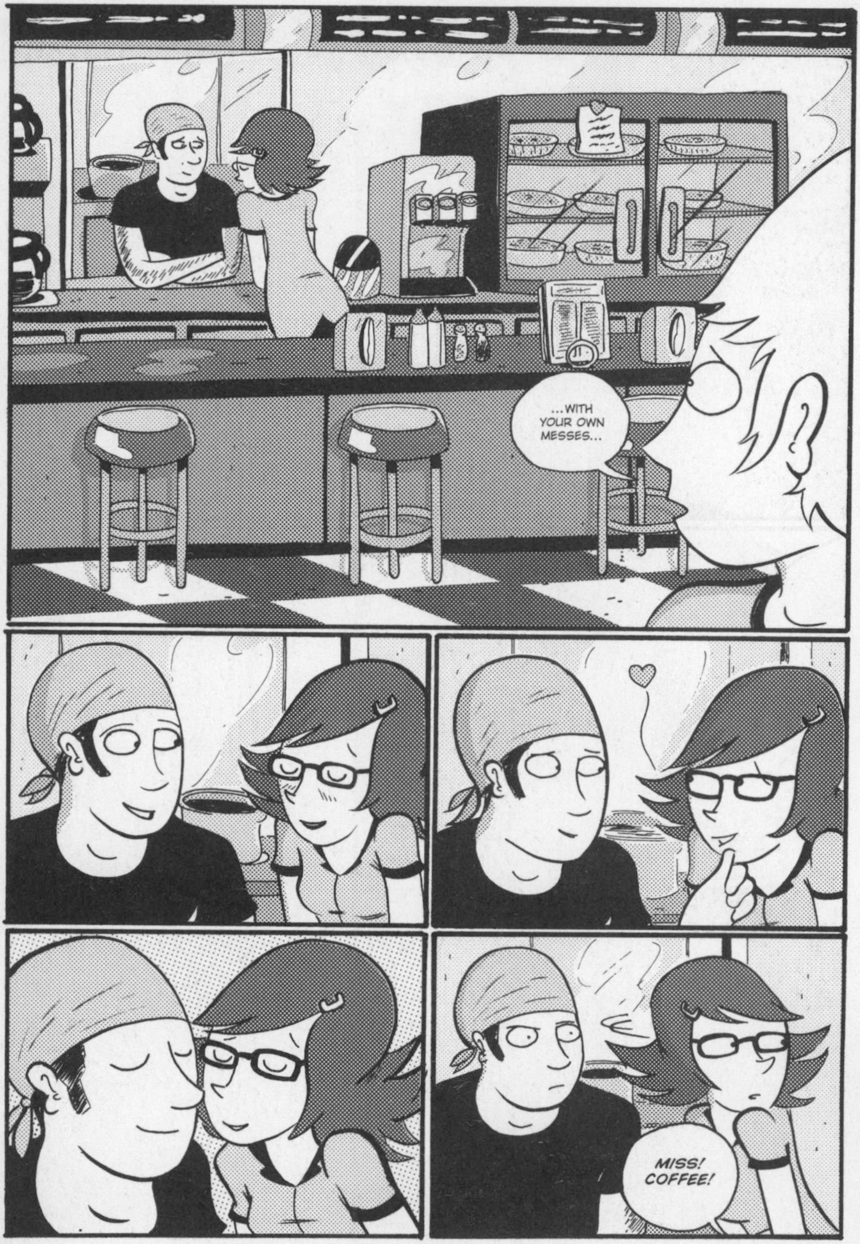
...WITH YOUR OWN MESSES...
MISS! COFFEE!

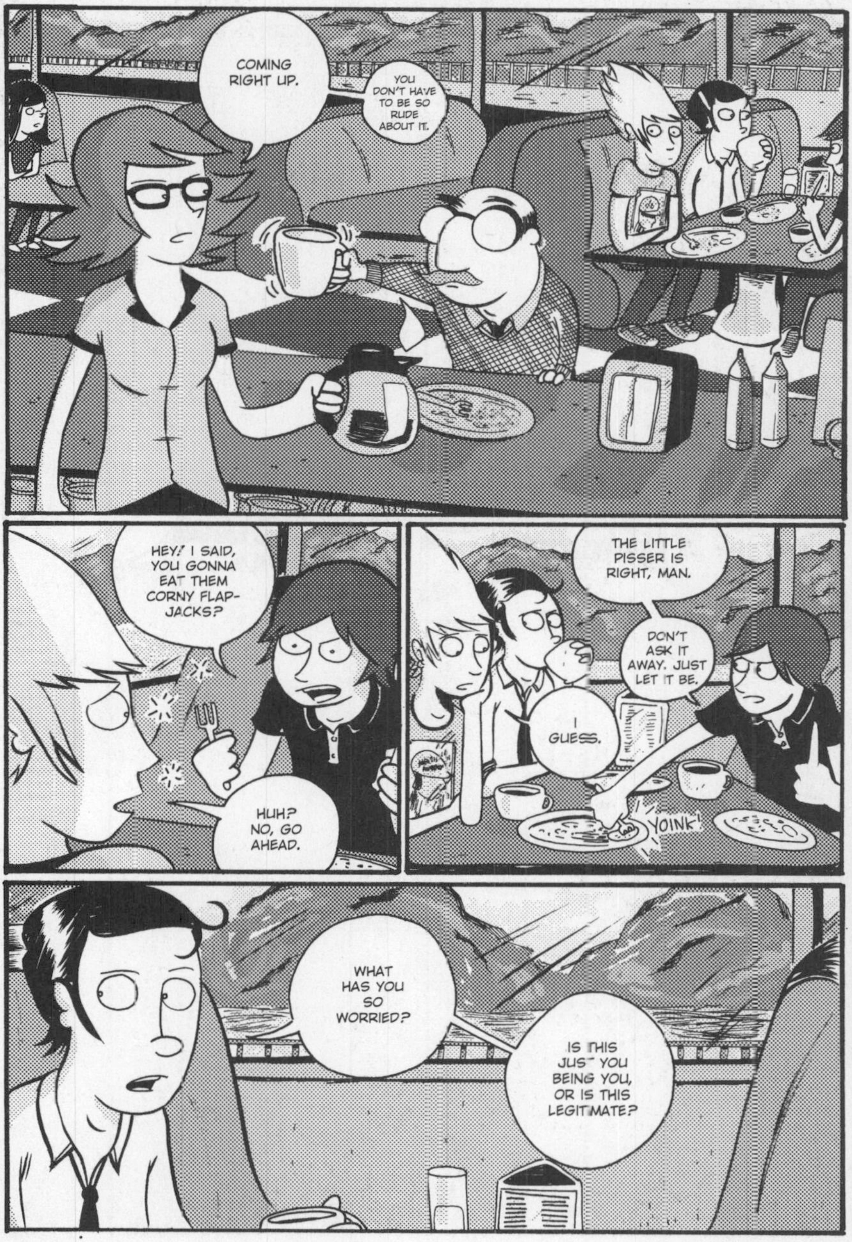
COMING RIGHT UP.
YOU DON'T HAVE TO BE SO RUDE ABOUT IT.
HEY! I SAID, YOU GONNA EAT THEM CORNY FLAP-JACKS?
HUH? NO, GO AHEAD.
THE LITTLE PISSER IS RIGHT, MAN.
DON'T ASK IT AWAY. JUST LET IT BE.
I GUESS.
YOINK!
WHAT HAS YOU SO WORRIED?
IS THIS JUST YOU BEING YOU, OR IS THIS LEGITIMATE?

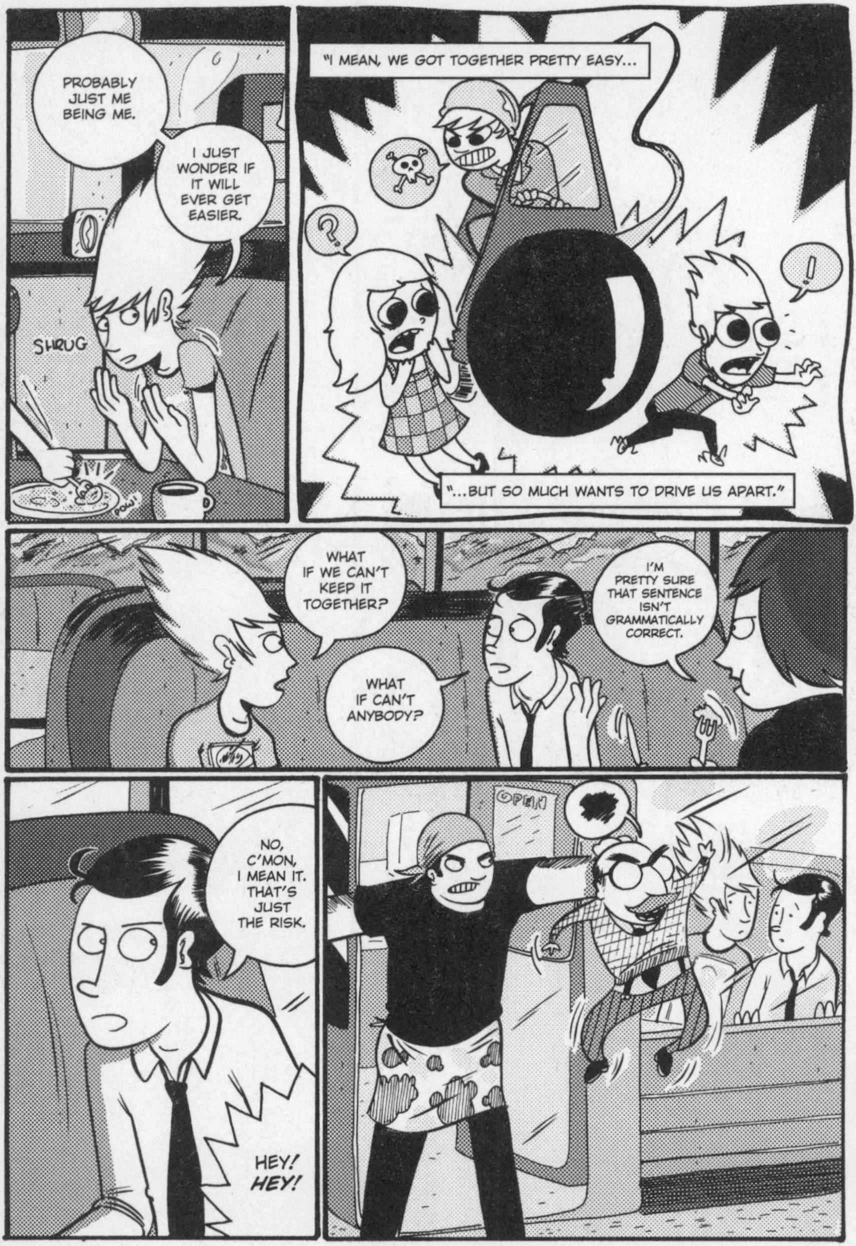
PROBABLY JUST ME BEING ME.
I JUST WONDER IF IT WILL EVER GET EASIER.
SHRUG
POW!
"I MEAN, WE GOT TOGETHER PRETTY EASY...
"...BUT SO MUCH WANTS TO DRIVE US APART."
WHAT IF WE CAN'T KEEP IT TOGETHER?
WHAT IF CAN'T ANYBODY?
I'M PRETTY SURE THAT SENTENCE ISN'T GRAMMATICALLY CORRECT.
NO, C'MON, I MEAN IT. THAT'S JUST THE RISK.
HEY! *HEY!*
OPEN

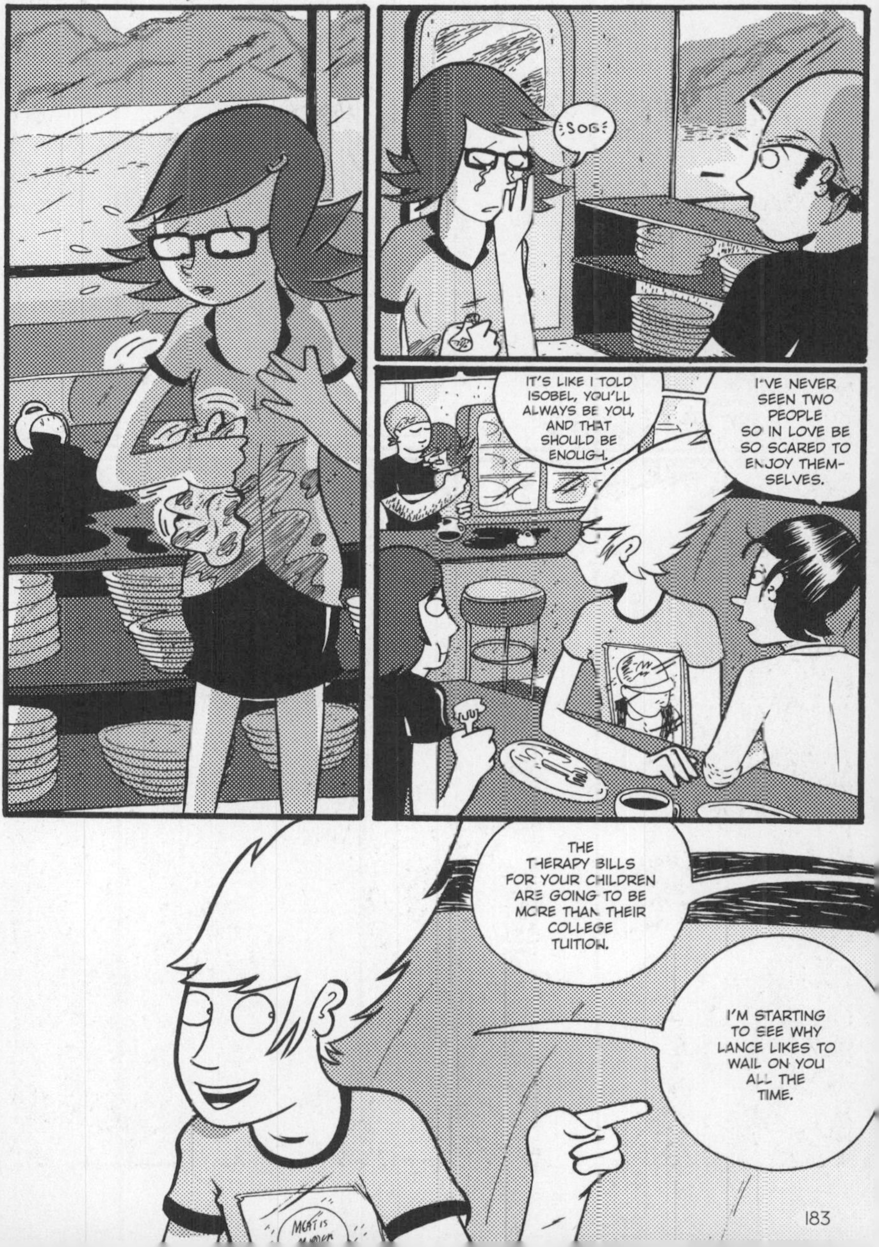
SOB
IT'S LIKE I TOLD ISOBEL, YOU'LL ALWAYS BE YOU, AND THAT SHOULD BE ENOUGH.
I'VE NEVER SEEN TWO PEOPLE SO IN LOVE BE SO SCARED TO ENJOY THEMSELVES.
THE THERAPY BILLS FOR YOUR CHILDREN ARE GOING TO BE MORE THAN THEIR COLLEGE TUITION.
I'M STARTING TO SEE WHY LANCE LIKES TO WAIL ON YOU ALL THE TIME.

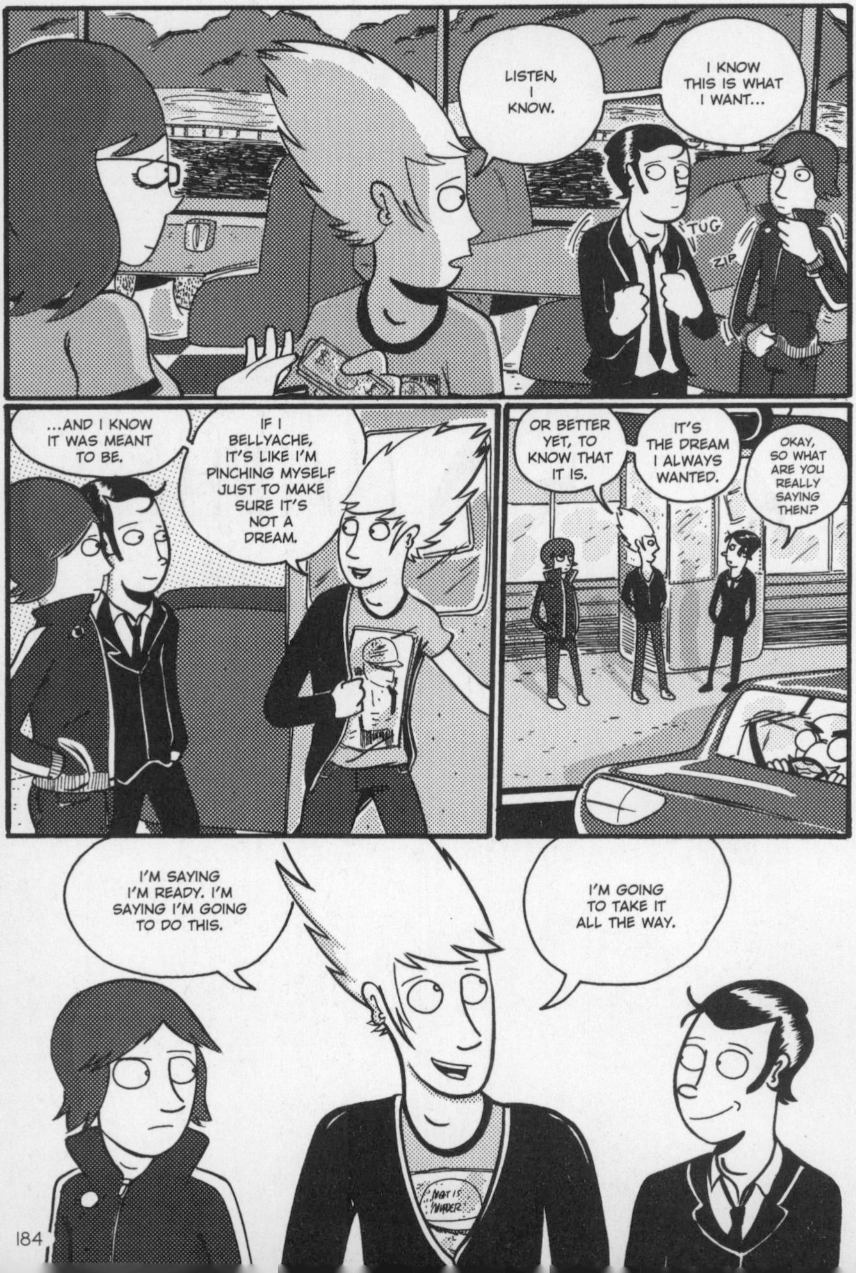
LISTEN, I KNOW.
I KNOW THIS IS WHAT I WANT...
TUG
ZIP
...AND I KNOW IT WAS MEANT TO BE.
IF I BELLYACHE, IT'S LIKE I'M PINCHING MYSELF JUST TO MAKE SURE IT'S NOT A DREAM.
OR BETTER YET, TO KNOW THAT IT IS.
IT'S THE DREAM I ALWAYS WANTED.
OKAY, SO WHAT ARE YOU REALLY SAYING THEN?
I'M SAYING I'M READY. I'M SAYING I'M GOING TO DO THIS.
I'M GOING TO TAKE IT ALL THE WAY.

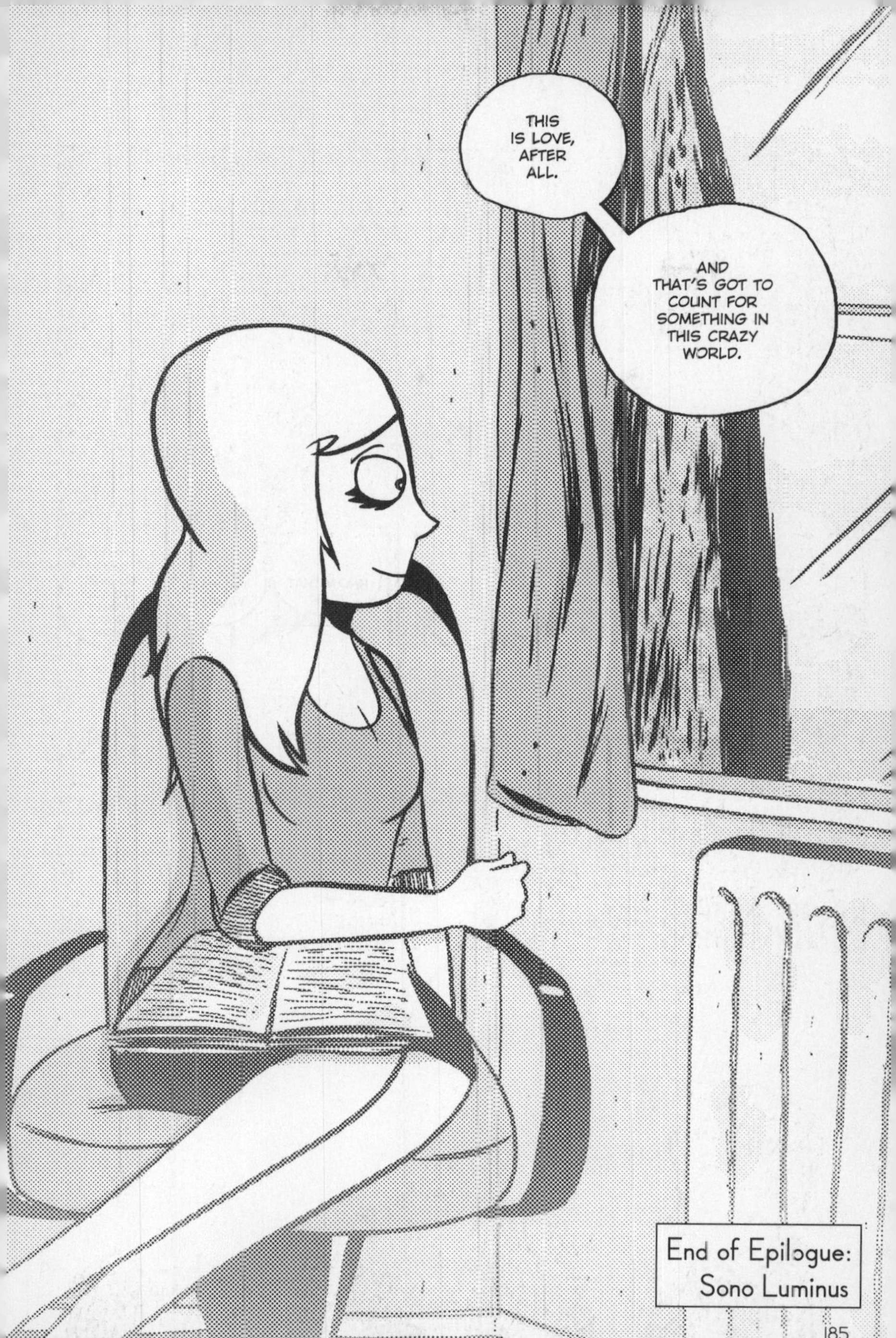
THIS IS LOVE, AFTER ALL.
AND THAT'S GOT TO COUNT FOR SOMETHING IN THIS CRAZY WORLD.
End of Epilogue: Sono Luminus

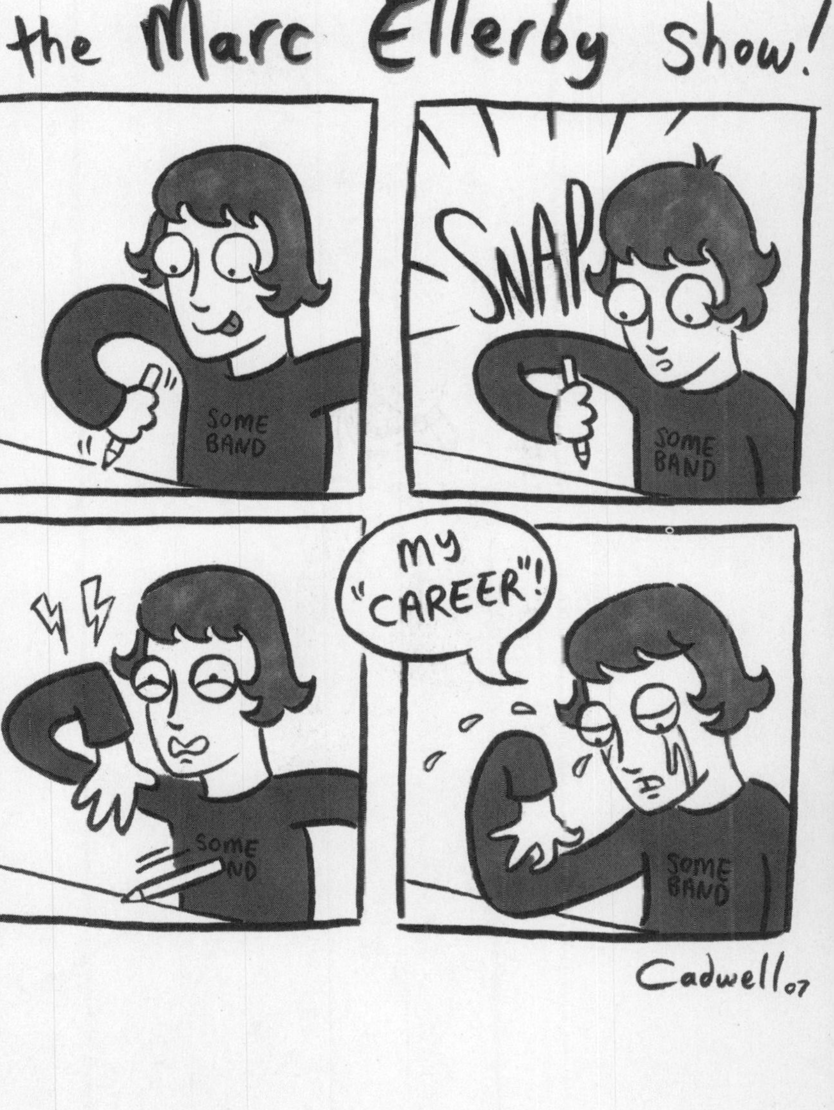
the Marc Ellerby Show!
SOME BAND
SNAP
SOME BAND
SOME
ND
MY "CAREER"!
SOME BAND
Cadwell 07

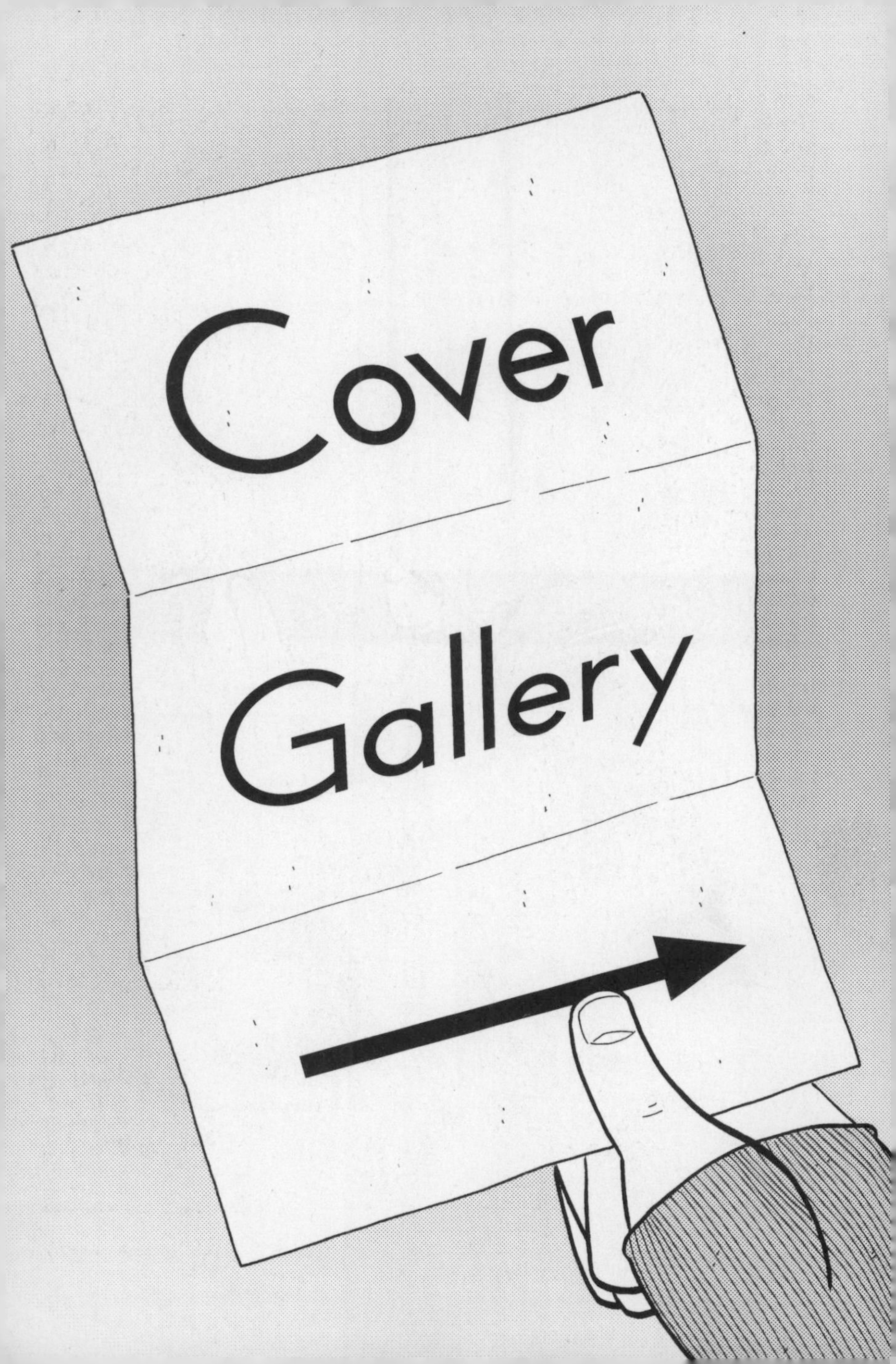
Cover
Gallery

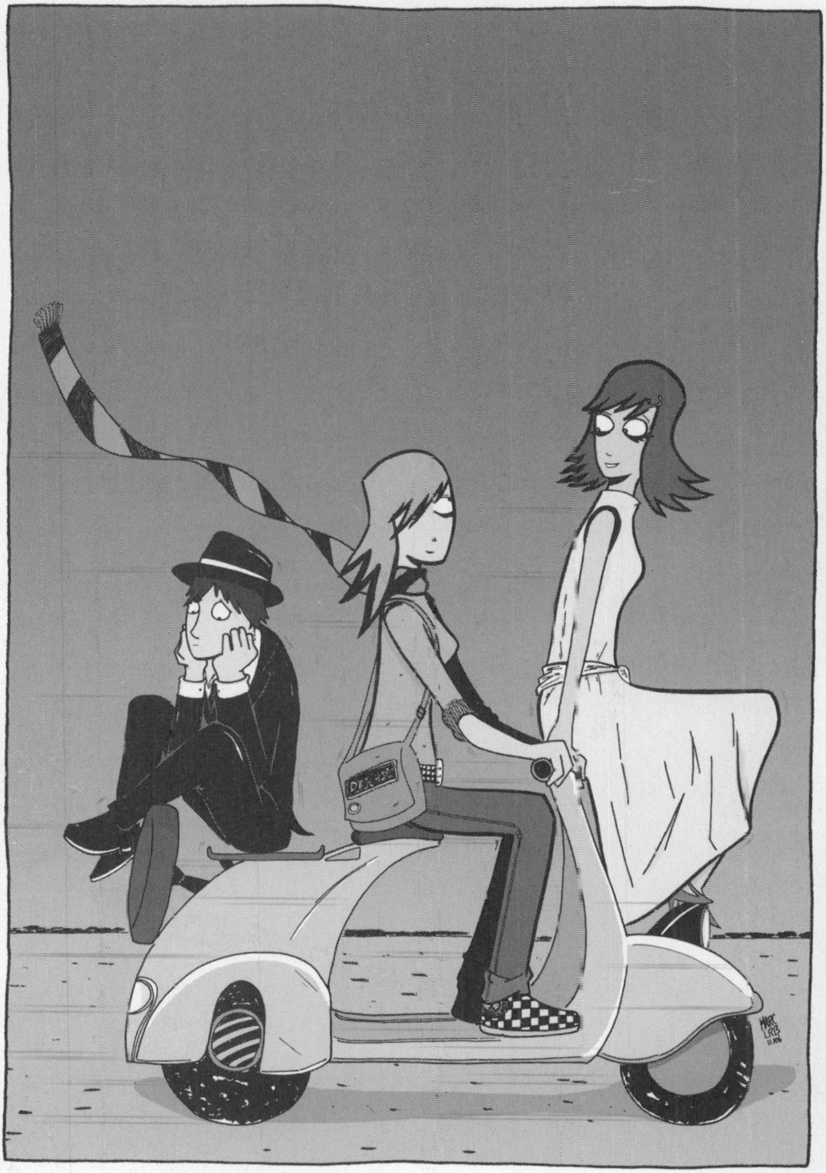

Original cover for *Love the Way You Love* #4 by Marc Ellerby

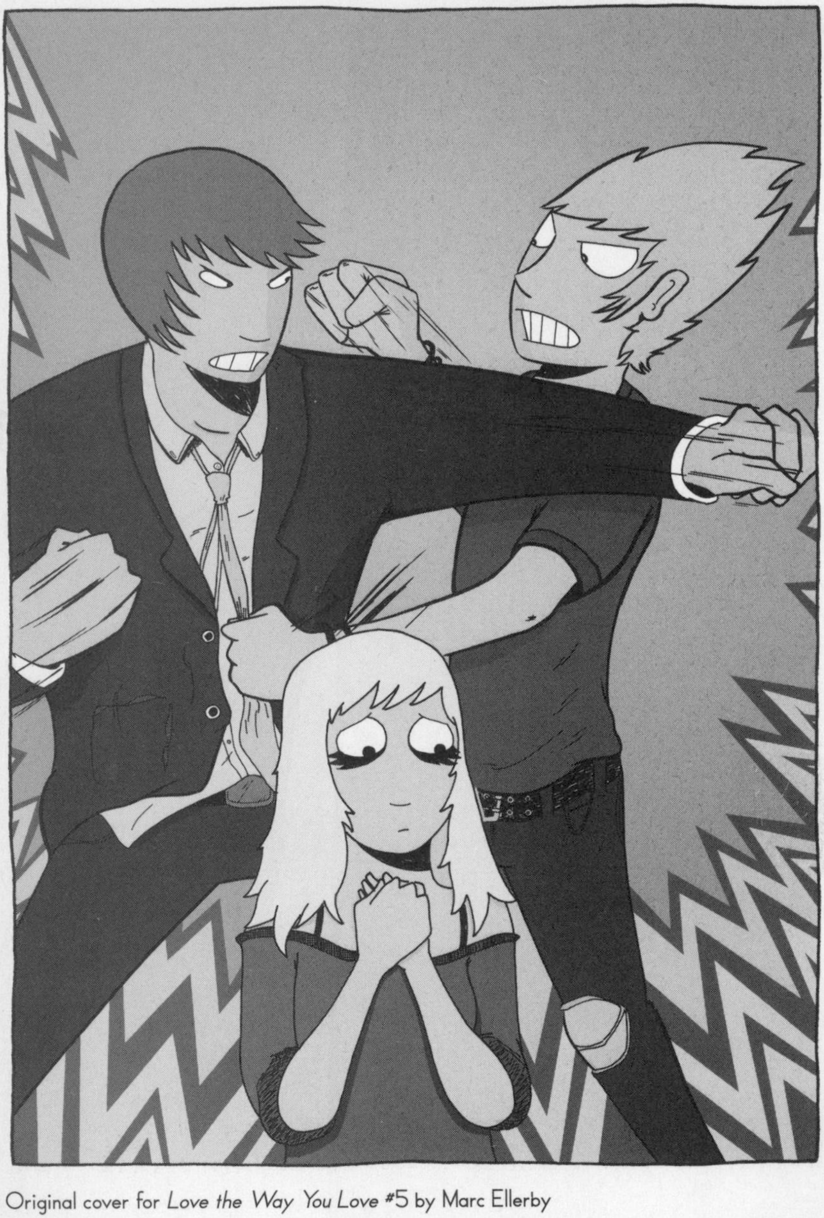

Original cover for *Love the Way You Love* #5 by Marc Ellerby